COME TO JUDGMENT

ALDEN WHITMAN

COME TO JUDGMENT

THE VIKING PRESS · NEW YORK

First published in 1980 by The Viking Press
625 Madison Avenue, New York, N.Y. 10022
Published simultaneously in Canada by
Penguin Books Canada Limited

Library of Congress Cataloging in Publication Data
Whitman, Alden.
Come to judgment.
Includes index.
1. Biography—20th century.   2. Obituaries.
I. Title.
CT120.W475   920'.009'04   79-22876
ISBN 0-670-23169-X

Printed in the United States of America
Set in CRT Caslon

Page 373 constitutes an extension of the copyright page.

CONTENTS

He hath not lived that lives not after death.

George Herbert
Outlandish Proverbs (1640)

INTRODUCTION

The men and women whose lives are briefly chronicled here share several attributes. They all achieved fame in the first half of our century. They all died between 1965 and 1979, mostly at quite advanced years, having lived long enough to savor the rewards of their accomplishments. Their obituaries (after which these lives are fashioned) were all the product of my typewriter and appeared in the pages of *The New York Times*. I selected them for this book not only because I fancied their obits, but also because these men and women all led lives of extraordinary vitality. In this respect, as in a truly remarkable range of occupation, they are symbolic of the much larger roster from which they were drawn.

Although the evidence of a few hundred obituaries does not

constitute proof, there does seem to be some connection between longevity and the creative energy that leads to accomplishment. None of the men and women in this book was born famous, nor are there many Mozarts among them. The road to accomplishment was uphill all the way, and it required more than mere ability to negotiate: it took curiosity, persistence, alertness, and sparkle—all ingredients of vitality, or creative energy. These characteristics are common to the subjects of the book, who, with one or two exceptions, continued to be involved with life until they died.

And they lived a long time. Picasso, Casals, Schweitzer, and Bertrand Russell lived into their nineties. Many were active well into their eighties: Norman Thomas, Mies van der Rohe, Maurice Chevalier, Samuel Eliot Morison, Sol Hurok, to mention some of them. Others were in their seventies: André Malraux, Bennett Cerf, Ho Chi Minh. The youngest person in the book is J. Robert Oppenheimer, who died at sixty-three, from lung cancer.

Everyone in this book had a strong character. That is to say that they all had ambition and the drive, or persistence, necessary to sustain it. Albert Schweitzer's ambition was to be a medical missionary in Africa; Elizabeth Arden's was to be a cosmetics queen; Joseph Kennedy's was to be rich and to found a political dynasty; Paul Strand wanted to capture social reality on film; and Ho Chi Minh sought a Vietnam free of foreign domination. So it went. The striving to fulfill an aim, and the notion that life has a nonmaterial purpose, are ideas that trace back to the nineteenth century; but this is not astonishing, for the men and women I have written about all bear the impress of that century. They were born toward its close or near the start of the twentieth century, so it is not surprising that their value systems are in part those of the Victorian years, as explicated by their parents.

The parameters of fame were liberalized for Americans of this century. Consider the range in this book as an indication of hospitality to a larger world. In life and in death Americans paid attention to a secular saint, an atomic physicist, a vendor of feminine pulchritude, a prince of the Catholic church, a successful Communist nationalist, an African emperor, a mighty trade union leader, a seminal artist, a heretic in philosophy, a superman of films, writers, playwrights, an architect of spareness.

It was no intention of mine ever to be their obituarian, but that was what I became by an act of transfiguration that only *The New York Times* can perform. The act, occurring in late 1964, transformed me from a copy editor to an obituary writer; it put me into a job that filled the rest of my newspaper life, quite pleasantly on the whole, until I retired in early 1976. Over this span I wrote about four hundred obits, most of them in advance of their subjects' deaths. I traveled to Europe and Asia on obit business, and met and interviewed scores of men and women of attainment. I talked with persons as disparate as Anthony Eden and Juan Perón, Earl Warren and Charlie Chaplin, Jean Monnet and Mme. Chiang Kai-shek, Charles A. Lindbergh and Graham Greene, Earl Browder and Henry Miller, Vladimir Nabokov and Harry Bridges, Harry Truman and André Maurois. The list seems endless, but of course it isn't; I interviewed no more than ten percent of the total number of people I wrote about.

In revising and editing the thirty-four obituaries that make up this book I have added material here and there, but I have not tampered with the substance or the basic newspaper format of any. As for the choice of the thirty-four, I picked those obits that I felt best exhibited the suppleness of my craft as well as its range. I also tried to choose men and women I felt I had come to understand, without necessarily liking or admiring them. Obituaries do express judgments, of course, but these are best implied, often by the length assigned to them.

In its simplest form, an obit is a news story, long or short, reporting a death and reciting the deceased's attainments, his claims to fame. Many obits consist of one or two short paragraphs, which may be a just measure of their interest for the general reader. The majority of obits, even in such a conscientious paper as *The Times*, run five hundred words or less. A major obit, one of several thousand words and running one or more newspaper pages, is obviously something special, a treatment reserved for a man or woman whose accomplishments have caught the public eye or whose station in life has made him or her an object of general curiosity. It is, alas, not accomplishment alone that determines one's reward in print. Casimir Funk, the Polish-American biochemist and vitamin pioneer who formulated the vitamin-deficiency theory of some diseases, was an undoubted benefactor of mankind, yet he died in virtual obituary obscurity in the late 1960's. By contrast, Elvis Presley, whose accomplishments were not nearly so grand, received handsome space.

Given public prominence or station in life, many persons are written about in death under the *nihil nisi bonum* rule, which is to say that their obits fulsomely accent only the positive. This was the case with John D. Rockefeller 3d, whose darker hues and shadows were either glossed over or omitted, so that his philanthropic figure emerged as an object of unalloyed eulogy. But it should not be an obit's function to eulogize; that is best left to the clergy and others who beseech a happy afterlife for the dead. Saints we are not in life, nor should we be in death.

Many major obits suffer from dullness; they are little more than laundry lists of positions occupied, jobs held, books published, honors bestowed, a curriculum vitae wrestled into print. Often scrupulously accurate and detailed, they nonetheless lack the breath of life. Except for an occasional high-minded quote, the subject never speaks for himself in his normal voice; and others do not speak of him, save in conventionalities. A living, spirited, sentient person is seldom apparent as the author of the many deeds attributed to him.

A good obit, by comparison, is a lively expression of personality and character as well as a conscientious exposition of the main facts of a person's life. It is not a comprehensive biography, not a scholarly essay, not a tribute, not totally a personality sketch. A good obit has all the characteristics of a well-focused snapshot, the fuller the length the better. It does not disclose everything, yet it conveys a vivid and accurate impression. If the snapshot is clear, the viewer gets a quick fix on the subject, his attainments, his shortcomings, and his times. Composing the snapshot is much easier said than done; it takes time, patience, digging, and, finally, a certain skill with words.

My primary research resource as an obit writer was *The Times*'s morgue, its incomparable collection of clippings, mostly from *The Times* itself, filed by subject and name. If I were venturing on, say, John L. Lewis, I would betake myself to the morgue and comb Lewis's file, which would contain a clipping of every article ever published by *The Times* in which his name was printed. If I were lucky, the file would also include stray articles from other publications, references to books about him or about the labor movement in which he played such a puissant role. Riffling through the voluminous clippings and taking notes, I would begin to organize a skeleton of Lewis's life and to pick up impressions of his personality and character.

In Lewis's case, the file was copious because he had been a headline figure for so many years, a man in the very cockpit of the trade unions' struggle for basic rights. By contrast, the file on Marianne Moore was slim, hardly meaty enough for even a brief obit; but there was enough to direct me to other sources. With Lewis, I also felt the need for additional backgrounding, a decision that took me to *The Times*'s library, a large and expertly manned collection of topical books and reference works, in which I found useful material about the United Mine Workers and the temper of America in the thirties and forties. I also consulted *The Readers' Guide to Periodical Literature* for other references to Lewis or to the industrial turmoil of his era. Having lived through the period myself, I consulted my own recollections, my memories of newsreels and conversations when Lewis and the CIO were the center of discussion. Finally, to get a more intimate picture of the man, I talked with A. H. Raskin, then *The Times*'s reigning labor reporter, who had covered Lewis in some of his later manifestations and who was generous enough to share his insights with me.

At that point I had an embarrassment of riches, and the prob lem was organization and concision. Obits are written to space—so many words, so many columns—and this inflexibility puts a premium on selection. Out of the sizable pile of Lewisiana, I selected what seemed representative and right, what added up to a veritable (and verifiable) snapshot. Putting it all down on paper was a slow process; not only was choice painful—one parts reluctantly with his research—but also I tended to agonize over the typewriter.

Sometimes, to be sure, I was obliged to write speedily at considerable length. When Adlai E. Stevenson died unexpectedly in London in 1965, there was no advance obit; and, may John Bartlow Martin forgive me, I wrote about four columns on the man based on a frantic hunt through the clips and my own recollections of his two presidential campaigns and his chore at the United Nations. Again, when Robert F. Kennedy was shot in 1968, I turned out a full newspaper page from a standing start. Fortunately, I turned up some good clips early in the day and, equally fortunately, I had only recently been up front in an audience that he had addressed. In writing, I also drew on accumulated knowledge of the Kennedy family and all the general reading I had done over the years on RFK. These forced drafts (neither of them included in this volume) demonstrate that it is indeed possible to turn out acceptable obits with rather little preparation; but it would be madness to count on luck every time.

Paucity of clips, as with Miss Moore, or clips that were unrevealing though fairly numerous, created problems that could best be solved by going outside *The Times*—to books, magazines, and people who could inform me. In this respect, the writer's most useful starting point is himself and those nuggets of miscellaneous information that he has stored away in a lifetime of reading and observing. I remembered, for example, having read Miss Moore's enchantingly wry correspondence with the Ford Motor Company over the naming of the Edsel. I reread it in *The New Yorker*. I remembered, too, having met and talked with her when she was old and quite frail and the wisps of her gray hair fluttered from beneath her tricorn.

The notion of interviewing for specifically obituary purposes was the brainchild of Clifton Daniel, *The Times*'s managing editor in my early years on the job, who was always a source of generous encouragement. "We interview people about everything else, why shouldn't we interview them for their obituaries?" he asked quite reasonably one day. He proposed that I start with his father-in-law, Harry Truman, whose door he just might be able to open.

After several false starts, I wrote to Independence, Missouri, seeking an appointment. My letter said that I was working on a biographical profile and felt that it would be helpful if he would comment on various aspects of his career for future publication. In this and in dozens of subsequent letters I never used the words "death" or "obituary" on the ground that no one likes to be reminded explicitly of his mortality, although he might be flattered that an oblique reference to it implied that *The Times* thought him special. The power of *The Times* is awesome. Harry Truman startled me with his directness. "I know why you're here," he announced, "and I want to help you all I can." Among other things, he put me in touch with the man who was planning his funeral. Graham Greene greeted me at the door to his apartment with, "Oh, so you're the young man who's come to write my obituary, are you?" Anthony Eden, sipping China tea, remarked, "This is all for after I'm dead, isn't it?" Harry Bridges, the labor leader, leaked the fact of my interview to a friendly newspaper columnist; and Jules Romains, the French novelist, reported my visit with him in a Paris newspaper piece.

None of those with whom I talked over the years appeared to have been taken in by the thinness of my disguise, nor to have resented talking about themselves in the past tense. I realized after a short while that only youth is immortal, only the young are certain they will live forever. When men and women get beyond sixty-five and into their seventies, they have begun to accept the finitude of life, they have learned how to count and to accept the likelihood of death as an everyday companion. This is not to suggest that the elderly are lugubrious or melancholic; rather, they have acceded to reality with equanimity.

Contemplating my first interview, I thought it would be foolish to retrace simple biographical data available from standard sources and that it would be equally time-wasting to come in with a list of twenty questions, record the answers, and depart. Serendipitously, I hit upon the idea of conducting interviews as informal conversations, into which I could poke my questions unobtrusively. I decided that what would serve me best from an interview was a series of impressions of the subject. Having done as much homework as possible, I could concentrate on observing and recording manner, attitude, point of view, personality, and at appropriate moments I could then bring up matters on which I wanted elucidation. A "Tell me more about so-and-so" ordinarily elicited an answer. This method of interviewing was indirect, allusive, and remarkably productive for my purposes. And sometimes the quotes were memorable and fresh. I have always been impressed by how much a person reveals himself in a semistructured conversation without realizing it.

I did not interview everyone. Relative lack of prominence and brevity of obit space excluded many persons. There were some few—Picasso and Casals, among others—to whom I was never able to get through. Some interviews were never used: John O'Hara and Abel Green of *Variety* died too soon—both on my days off. Others were random over a period of time; I talked to Bennett Cerf and Charles Lindbergh at odd moments over several years. Only one interview was stilted and uncomfortable, that with Mme. Chiang. I had been charged to see her and, after much waiting around in Taipei, I was given an audience in her palace in the hills outside the city. Shepherded by two officials of the Ministry of Information, I was ushered into an opulently furnished room, full of fresh-cut flowers and teak tables inlaid with mother of pearl. Two elegant sofas had been drawn up facing each other across another teak table, at the head of which, on a slightly elevated dais, was an empty chair.

After several minutes, the Madame swept in, escorted by an armed guard, which promptly melted away. She extended her hand to be shaken and sat in the raised chair. Cups of tea appeared as I tried to exclaim over the splendors of the room and her graciousness in seeing me. In a few moments, the seventy-one-year-old but still beautiful Madame reached into a pocket of her close-fitting, impeccably tailored gown and drew out several sheets of paper. Fixing me with flashing dark eyes, she said, "I did not know at first if I should receive you, but I finally decided to as a gesture." Whereupon she proceeded to read for fifteen minutes her prepared statement, a woeful account of how a Communist conspiracy in America that reached down to Bella Dodd of the New York teachers' union of many years ago had lost China for her husband and herself. The American people, she concluded, would surely live to regret their complacency in the conspiracy. The reading of her rescript was an altogether remarkable performance. Afterward, she let me look at it, and it bore her penciled interlineations. After a minute or two of chat, the Madame's guard reappeared and she vanished. When I turned to pick up my tape recorder, which had been lying on the sofa unused at the command of the ministry aide, I discovered that the microphone had also been unplugged.

Most interviews were more productive, however. Their chief benefit was to provide an ear- and eyewitness likeness that I could flash in mind as I wrote. Without that, one falls back on the accounts of friends and enemies, on the oral tradition, on what is presumptively reliable from what has already appeared in print, and, of course, on one's storehouse of general knowledge.

In paying my respects to those who have influenced me, I recall with delight a generative luncheon many years ago with E. L. Doctorow, who was kind enough to suggest that obits might well have second lives.

I acknowledge with gratitude *The New York Times*'s permission to use copyrighted material. At *The Times* I am indebted, for their many kindnesses, to Turner Catledge, Clifton Daniel, A. M. Rosenthal, Arthur Gelb, Sydney Gruson, Linda Amster, Bob Medina, Paul Greenfeder, Samuel L. Solovitz, and scores of other colleagues with whom I have shared twenty-five good years.

For wise counsel in editing and for a friendship I prize, I have amassed unpayable obligations to Malcolm Cowley. Few writers have such a felicitous friend.

Alan D. Williams of Viking thought this book a good idea, and blessed it with its title. I am not one to question his judgment, which is that of a friend.

Jane Alpert read copy on the manuscript, much to its betterment.

For many happy years, Joan McCracken Whitman has abided my idiosyncrasies. She holds my life together in uncountable ways; so to her truly belongs this book.

Southampton, N.Y.
June 1979

ALBERT SCHWEITZER

The concept of man's redemption through beneficent activity—
the theme of Part II of Goethe's *Faust,* a metaphysical poem much
admired by Albert Schweitzer—threaded through his long, complex, and sometimes curious life. With Faust himself he could join
in saying:

> This sphere of earthly soil
> Still gives us room for lofty doing.
> Astounding plans e'en now are brewing:
> I feel new strength for bolder toil. . . .
> The Deed is everything, the Glory naught.

"You must give some time to your fellow man," Schweitzer counseled in paraphrase. "Even if it's a little thing, do something for those who have need of a man's help, something for which you get no pay but the privilege of doing it." This was an essential of his ethical system, more formally known as Reverence for Life, which he elaborated before his death at the age of ninety. Fittingly, he died in Gabon—formerly part of French Equatorial Africa—at the jungle-compound hospital that he had established and maintained against great odds.

Like Goethe, on whose life and works he was an authority, Schweitzer came near to being a comprehensive man. Theologian, musicologist, virtuoso on the organ, physician and surgeon, missionary, lecturer, writer, and philosopher with his own system of ethics: he was all these things besides being the builder and animating force of the famous hospital complex at Lambaréné. He was eclectic, and to a marked degree. Franco-German in culture, yet cosmopolitan, he drew deeply from eighteenth-century sources, especially Bach in music and Kant in philosophy. At the same time he was a child of the late nineteenth century; he accepted its creature comforts, but rejected its complacent attitudes toward progress. In line with the twentieth century, he sought to put religion on a rational footing and comprehend the advances of science; yet he was a foe to materialism and to twentieth-century standards of material success.

As a person, Schweitzer was an equally curious mixture. Widely honored with degrees, citations, scrolls, medals, special stamps, even the Nobel Prize for Peace in 1952, he seemed oblivious to panoply. He did not preen himself or utter cosmic statements at the drop of a cause. Instead, he seemed to many observers a simple, almost rustic man who dressed in rumpled clothing, suffered fools gladly, stated fundamental verities patiently and paternally, and worked unobtrusively. In this respect, he was undoubtedly made more of by cultists than he was willing to make of himself, although he was by no means a man with a weak ego. Some of his more ardent admirers insisted that he was a jungle saint, even a modern Christ. But Schweitzer would have none of this adulation; he was quite satisfied that his spiritual life was its own reward, that he was redeemed by works. For him the search for the good life had profound religious implications. "Anyone can rescue his human life," he once said, "who seizes every opportunity of being a man by means of personal action, however unpretending, for the good of fellow men who need the help of a fellow man." He sought to exemplify the idea that man, through good works, can be in the world and in God at one and the same time.

For all his self-abnegation, Schweitzer had a bristly character, at least in his later years, a formidable sense of his own importance to Lambaréné, and a do-good paternalism toward Africans that smacked more of the nineteenth than of the twentieth century. For example, John Gunther, the American journalist, got a dressing-down from Schweitzer for writing that he resembled Buffalo Bill and also, perhaps, for implying that he did not know what was going on in nationalist Africa. If Schweitzer was thin-skinned to criticism from irreverent journalists, he heard little of it at Lambaréné, where his proprietorship was unquestioned. Not only did he design the station, but he helped build it with his own hands. His coworkers were quite familiar with the businesslike and sometimes grumpy and brusque Schweitzer in a solar hat, who hurried along the construction of a building by gingering up the native craftsmen with a sharp: "Allez-vous OPP! Allez-vous OPP-opp. Hupp, upp, OPP!"

When Schweitzer was in residence at Lambaréné, virtually nothing was done without consulting him. Once, for instance, he all but halted the station's work when he received a letter from a Norwegian child seeking a feather from Parsifal, his pet pelican. He insisted on seeing to it personally that the youngster got a prompt and touching reply from his pen before work was permitted to resume. His autocracy, however, was more noticeable as his years advanced and as his medical assistants grew less awed by him. He regarded most Africans as children or primitives. It was said that he had scarcely ever talked with an adult African on adult terms. He had little but contempt for the nationalist movement, for his attitudes were firmly grounded in nineteenth-century benevolence. Although thousands of Africans called him "le grand docteur," others plastered his village with signs, "Schweitzer, go home!"

"At this stage," Schweitzer said in 1963, "Africans have little need for advanced training. They need very elementary schools run along the old missionary plan with the Africans going to school for a few hours every day and then going back to the fields. Agriculture, not science or industrialization, is their greatest need." His attitude was sharply expressed in a story he liked to tell of his orange trees. "I let the Africans pick all the fruit they want," he said. "You see, the good Lord has protected the trees. He made the Africans too lazy to pick them bare." Although his views on Africa were sadly out of date, he did what no man had done before him—healed thousands and welded world attention to Africa's many plights. A jungle saint he may not have been; a jungle pioneer he surely was.

Whatever Schweitzer's personal idiosyncrasies, he constructed a profound and enduring ethical system expressed in the principle *Ehrfurcht vor dem Leben,* or Reverence for Life. It is conceivably the only philosophical concept ever to spring to life amid a herd of hippopotamuses. According to Schweitzer's account, he had been baffled in getting an answer to the question: Is it at all possible to find a real and permanent foundation in thought for a theory of the universe that shall be both ethical and affirmative of the world and life? The answer came in a flash of mystic illumination in September 1915, as he was steaming up the Ogoué River in Africa. Late in the third day of his journey he was on deck thinking and writing. "At the very moment when, at sunset, we were making our way through a herd of hippopotamuses, there flashed upon my mind, unforeseen and unsought, the phrase 'Reverence for Life.'

"The iron door had yielded," he went on, "the path in the thicket had become visible. Now I had my way to the idea in which world- and life-affirmation and ethics are contained side by side! Now I knew that the world-view of ethical world- and life-affirmation, together with its ideal of civilization, is founded in thought."

Schweitzer's ethical system, elucidated at length in *The Philosophy of Civilization,* is boundless in its domain and in its demands. He summarized it once by saying, "A man is ethical only when life, as such, is sacred to him, that of plants and animals as that of his fellow men, and when he devotes himself helpfully to all life that is in need of help." "Let me give you a definition of ethics," he wrote on another occasion. "It is good to maintain and further life; it is bad to damage and destroy life. And this ethic, profound, universal, has the significance of a religion. It *is* religion."

Called upon to be specific about Reverence for Life, he explained that the concept "does not allow the scholar to live for science alone, even if he is very useful to the community in so doing. It does not permit the artist to exist only for his art, even if it gives the inspiration to many by its means. It refuses to let the businessman imagine that he fulfills all legitimate demands in the course of his business activity. It demands from all that they should sacrifice a portion of their own lives for others."

Schweitzer earnestly sought to live his philosophy. He was genuinely proud of his medical and missionary station at Lambaréné. He had scratched it out of the jungle beginning in 1913; and, although the station was many times beset by adversities that would have discouraged a less dedicated man, it had grown at his death to more than 70 buildings, 350 beds, and a leper village of 200 persons.

The compound was staffed by five unpaid physicians, seven nurses, and thirteen volunteer helpers. Visitors who equated cleanliness and tidiness with medicine were horrified by the station, for every patient was encouraged to bring one or two members of his family to cook for him in the ditches beside the wards. Babies, even in the leper enclave, dropped toys into the dust of unpaved streets, then popped the playthings into their mouths.

Animals wandered freely in and out of the compound, including Schweitzer's pet parrot (which was not taught to talk because that would lower its dignity) and a hippopotamus that once invaded the vegetable garden. Lambaréné resembled not so much a hospital as a native village where physicians cared for the sick. Actually, Schweitzer preferred (and planned) it in this fashion on the ground that the natives would shun an elaborate, shiny, and impersonal institution. The compound even lacked electricity, except for the operating and dental rooms, and members of the staff read by kerosene lamp. Of course it had no telephone or radio or airstrip.

His view that "simple people need simple healing methods," however it might have outraged medical sophisticates, won for Lambaréné a tremendous measure of native confidence. Thousands flocked there; thousands responded to Schweitzer's sermons as well as to his scalpel; for he believed that the good shepherd saves not only the animal but also his soul. Lambaréné was suffused with Reverence for Life to what some critics thought was an exaggerated degree. Mosquitoes were not swatted, nor pests and insects doused with chemicals; they were let alone, and humans put up with them. Indeed, building was often brought to a halt lest nests of ants be killed or disturbed. On the other hand, patients received splendid medical care; and few seemed to suffer greatly from the compound's lack of spit and polish.

Schweitzer's accomplishments are recognized even by his most caustic critics. One of them, Gerald McKnight, wrote in his book *Verdict on Schweitzer:* "The temptation for Schweitzer to see Lambaréné as a place cut off from the world, in which he can preserve its original forms and so reject any theory of treatment or life other than his own, is understandable when one considers the enormous achievement he has attained in his own lifetime. He came to the Ogoué in 1913 when horses drew the buses of London and leprosy was considered an incurable scourge. Housed originally in the grounds of a mission, he chose to leave this comparative sanctuary for the unknown and forbidding regions of the jungle nearby.

"No doubt a wish to have absolute dominion over his hospital drove him to this course, linked with the inner purpose which had brought him to Africa, but it was none the less heroic. Today, the hospital has grown, entirely under his hand and direction, into a sizable colony where between 500 and 600 people live in reasonable comfort. No greater tribute to his abilities as a conqueror of the jungle need be cited than the fact—regarded locally as something of a miracle—of his own survival."

Schweitzer came to French Equatorial Africa as a tall, handsome, broadly powerful young man with a shock of rich black hair, enormous mustaches, and a look of piercing determination in his bold eyes. The years thinned and grayed his hair (without making it less unruly); age seamed his face, shrank his frame, made him appear bandy-legged; time softened his eyes, made them less severe; but determination to make his life an "argument" for his ethical creed was as firm at ninety as it was on his thirtieth birthday, the day he decided to devote the rest of his life as a physician to the natives of Africa. Schweitzer's arrival at this decision was calculated, a step in a quest for a faith to live by. It was a search that had haunted him, driven him, since childhood.

Albert Schweitzer was born at Kayserberg, Haute Alsace (now Haut-Rhin), on January 14, 1875, not long after Germany had annexed the province from war-prostrate France. During that year his father, a Lutheran pastor, moved with his wife and eldest son to the neighboring village of Günsbach among the foothills of the Vosges. It was to this picture-book Franco-German village and its vineyards that Schweitzer would always return between periods of self-imposed exile in Africa. As a child he was frail and an indifferent student in everything but music, for which he showed the interest of a prodigy. He began to play the church organ at eight, when his feet barely reached the pedals. At eighteen he entered the University of Strasbourg as a student in theology, philosophy, and musical theory. By this time he had also studied the organ briefly in Paris under the legendary Charles-Marie Widor, who was so impressed with his pupil's talents that he taught him then and later without fee. He became a notable organist, especially in the works of Bach, and his recitals in Europe helped to finance his medical work in Africa.

Schweitzer's university life was interrupted by a year of compulsory military service in 1894, a period that proved crucial to his religious thinking and to his life's vocation. The moment of awakening came as he was reading Matthew 10 and 11 in Greek, chapters that contain Jesus' injunctions to his apostles, among them the one that commands, "Heal the sick, cleanse the lepers, raise the dead, cast out devils: freely ye have received, freely give," and the verse that urges men, "Take my yoke upon you, and learn from me; for I am meek and lowly in heart: and ye shall find rest unto your souls."

Schweitzer was struck not only by the application of these verses to himself, but even more by the overall content of the two chapters as expressed in Jesus' assertion that "the kingdom of heaven is at hand." These chapters started a chain of thought that resulted in *The Quest for the Historical Jesus.* Published in 1910, it at once established its author as an eminent, if controversial, theologian whose explosive ideas had a profound influence on contemporary religious thinking. He depicted Jesus as a man of his times who shared the eschatological ideas of late Judaism and who looked for an immediate end of the world. Jesus, Schweitzer contended, believed himself the Messiah who would rule in a new kingdom of God when the end came; at first Jesus believed that his Messianic reign would begin before his disciples returned from the teaching mission commanded of them in Matthew 10. When the world's end did not occur, according to Schweitzer's view, Jesus concluded that he must undergo an atoning sacrifice, and that the great transformation would take place on the cross. This, too, failed; hence, Schweitzer argued, the despairing cry, "My God, my God, why hast thou forsaken me?"

"The Jesus of Nazareth ... who founded the kingdom of Heaven upon earth, and died to give his work the final consecration, never had any existence," he wrote. "He is a figure designed by rationalism, endowed with life by liberalism and clothed by modern theology in an historical garb." Schweitzer maintained, nonetheless, that Jesus' concepts are eternal. "In reality, that which is eternal in the words of Jesus is due to the very fact that they are based on an eschatological world-view, and contain the expression of a mind for which the contemporary world with its historical and social circumstances no longer had any existence. They are appropriate, therefore, to any world, for in every world they raise the man who dares to meet their challenge, and does not turn them and twist them into meaninglessness, above his world and time, making him inwardly free, so that he is fitted to be, in his own world and in his own time, a simple channel of the power of Jesus."

While these beliefs were maturing in Schweitzer's mind, he continued his student life at Strasbourg and fixed with great precision the course of his future. In 1896, at the age of twenty-one, he pledged himself that he would give the following nine years to science and art and then devote himself to the service of suffering humanity. In those nine years he completed his doctoral thesis in philosophy, a study of Immanuel Kant's views on religion; studied the organ, again with Widor in Paris; won another doctorate in theology; was ordained a curate; taught theology and became principal of the faculty at Strasbourg; wrote *The Mystery of the Kingdom of God*; and, at Widor's urging, completed a study of the life and art of Johann Sebastian Bach. The English version, *J. S. Bach*, is a two-volume translation of the German text, itself an entire reworking of the first version written in French. It approaches Bach as a musician-poet and concentrates on his chorales, cantatas, and Passion music. Schweitzer presents Bach as a religious mystic, as cosmic as the forces of nature. Bach, he said, was chiefly a church composer. As such, and as a Lutheran, "it is precisely to the chorale that the work of Bach owes its greatness."

"The chorale not only puts in his possession the treasury of Protestant music," Schweitzer wrote, "but also opens to him the riches of the Middle Ages and of the sacred Latin music from which the chorale itself came. From whatever direction he is considered Bach is, then, the last word in an artistic evolution which was prepared in the Middle Ages, freed and activated by the Reformation, and arrives at its full expression in the eighteenth century."

Turning to Bach's nonchurch music, Schweitzer said: "The Brandenburg concertos are the purest product of Bach's polyphonic style. We really seem to see before us what the philosophy of all ages conceives as the fundamental mystery of things—that self-unfolding of the idea in which it creates its own opposite in order to overcome it, and so on and on until it finally returns to itself, having meanwhile traversed the whole of existence." Schweitzer's probing conception of Bach created a sensation in its time. It still remains a classic study, not only for the detailed instructions it provides for the playing of Bach, but also for its challenging esthetic. As a virtuoso of the organ, Schweitzer brought to his playing a scholarship that was infused with romanticism, in which the printed note was sometimes ignored while the composer's pictorial poetry and symbolism were accentuated.

True to his pledge, Schweitzer turned from music and theology to service to others. On October 13, 1905, he posted letters from Paris to his parents and friends saying that at the start of the winter term he would become a medical student to prepare himself for the life of a physician in French Equatorial Africa. His friends objected vigorously, but he did not listen. This decision, like so many others in his life, was the product of religious meditation. He had pondered the meaning of the parable of Dives and Lazarus and its application to his times, and he had concluded that Dives represented opulent Europe, and Lazarus, with his open sores, the sick and helpless of Africa. Explaining his decision later in more mundane terms, Schweitzer said: "I wanted to be a doctor that I might be able to work without having to talk. For years I had been giving myself out in words. This new form of activity I could not represent to myself as talking about the religion of love, but only as an actual putting it into practice."

For seven years, from 1906 until he received his M.D. degree in February 1913, Schweitzer studied medicine, but he did not entirely cut himself off from his other worlds. Attending the University of Strasbourg, he still served as curate at St. Nicholas, played concerts on the organ, conducted a heavy correspondence, and examined Pauline ideas, especially that of dying and being born again "in Jesus Christ." This last resulted in a book, *Paul and His Interpreters,* published in English in 1912. That same year he resigned his curateship and his posts at the university and married Hélène Bresslau, the daughter of a well-known Strasbourg historian. A scholar herself, she became a trained nurse in order to share her husband's life in Africa.

On Good Friday 1913, the couple set sail from Bordeaux for Africa, where Schweitzer established a hospital on the grounds of the Lambaréné station of the Paris Missionary Society. The society, wary of Schweitzer's unorthodox religious views, had barred him from preaching at the station, but agreed to accept his medical skills. Lambaréné, on the Ogoué River a few miles from the Equator, is in the steaming jungle. Its climate is among the world's worst, with fiercely hot days, clammy nights, and seasonal torrents of rain. The natives had all the usual diseases, plus Hansen's disease (leprosy), dysentery, elephantiasis, sleeping sickness, malaria, yellow fever, and animal wounds. From the first, when the hospital was a broken-down hen coop, natives flocked to it on foot, by improvised stretcher, or by dugout canoe for medical attention.

Schweitzer had barely started to clear the jungle when World War I broke out. He and his wife, both German citizens, were interned as prisoners of war for four months, then released to continue the work of the hospital. In this time and the succeeding months he started to write the two-volume *The Philosophy of Civilization,* his masterwork in ethics, which was published in 1923. It is a historical review of ethical thought leading to his own original contribution of Reverence for Life as an effective basis for a civilized world. The book (and other of his writings) disputed the theory that human progress toward civilization was inevitable. He disagreed sharply with Aristotle that man's knowledge of right and wrong would surely lead him to make the right choices; he maintained, instead, that man must rationally formulate an ethical creed and then strive to put it into practice. In Reverence for Life, he concluded, "knowledge passes over into experience."

In 1917 the Schweitzers were returned to France and later to Alsace. To support himself and to carry on the work at Lambaréné, he joined the medical staff of the Strasbourg Hospital, preached, gave lectures and organ recitals, traveled, and wrote. He returned to Africa alone in 1925, while his wife and his daughter, Rhena, who was born in 1919, remained in Europe. In the almost eight years of his absence, the jungle had reclaimed the hospital grounds, and the buildings had to be rebuilt. This was no sooner under way than Schweitzer fell ill, an epidemic of dysentery broke out, and a famine set in. The epidemic prompted him to move his hospital to a larger site two miles up the Ogoué, where expansion was possible and where gardens and orchards could be planted. Two physicians had arrived from Europe, and he turned over all medical responsibilities to them and to two nurses for a year and a half while he supervised and helped to fell trees, clear ground, and construct buildings. The main hospital room and the dispensary were complete when he departed for Europe in midsummer, 1927. He returned to Lambaréné in 1929 and remained for two years, establishing a pattern of work in Africa and sojourns in Europe during which he lectured, wrote, and gave concerts to raise funds for his hospital. On one of these occasions, in 1949, he visited the United States and lectured on Goethe at a conference in Aspen, Colorado.

Hundreds flocked to hear him and to importune him. On one occasion a group of tourists pulled him away from the dinner table to get an explanation of his ethics. He responded with remarkable courtesy for about twenty minutes until one questioner prodded him for a specific application of Reverence for Life. "Reverence for Life," he replied, "means my answering your kind inquiries; it also means your reverence for my dinner hour." The tourists got the point and he returned to his meal. On his trips to Europe, he invariably made his headquarters at his home in Günsbach, which was expanded into a leave and rest center for the hospital staff. Of an afternoon he could often be glimpsed leaving his house to slip over to the church to play the organ; and sometimes he ventured afield to repair old church instruments.

In the closing years of his life he received many honorary degrees and other tokens of the esteem in which he was held, including honorary membership in the British Order of Merit. His choice as a Nobelist was popular, for Schweitzer was widely perceived in Europe and the United States as a person who had done much good without having wrought much harm. This perception was certainly prevalent when he celebrated his ninetieth birthday at Lambaréné in 1965 (he had lived there almost continuously since his wife's death in 1957), when hundreds of Africans, Europeans, and Americans gathered to wish him well. By this time he was virtually a secular saint, and criticisms were not welcomed. The overwhelming view was summed up in a message from the president of the United States; "In your commitment to truth and service," the cable read, "you have touched and deepened the lives of millions you have never met."

As an epitaph, it serves Schweitzer well. He could easily be diminished for his faults, but his accomplishments, on balance, were testimony to a singular devotion to the ideals of his youth, ideals of service that Goethean men of good will have always found ennobling.

✥

ELIZABETH ARDEN

Elizabeth Arden, the queen of the beauty industry who built a multimillion-dollar business in salons, cosmetics, and clothes from a stake of less than one thousand dollars, died in New York at a never-specified age. Over fifty years the chairman of the board and president of Elizabeth Arden, Inc., she managed her company with the same assiduity with which, under the name of Elizabeth N. Graham, she operated her race-horse affairs. In achieving success she treated women like horses and horses like women; both gave every appearance of loving her pampering.

What the horses wanted they did not divulge. Her women, on the other hand, made it evident that they craved that mystical state called beauty; and Miss Arden convinced them they could attain it if they permitted themselves to be steamed, rolled, bathed in wax, massaged, and showered in one of her more than fifty sumptuous salons. The many-billion-dollar beauty business, which Elizabeth Arden helped to create, gave her an annual income in the millions. "Arden made the cosmetic industry," an analyst said. "She is the mother of the treatment business."

Also adding to her income were Maine Chance Farm horses that she raced under the self-conceived name of Mrs. Elizabeth N. Graham. Her thoroughbreds included Jet Pilot, which won the Kentucky Derby in 1947. Mrs. Graham encouraged her horses by addressing them in baby talk—she called them "my darlings"—feeding them special clover ("It's their spinach"), piping music into their fly-free stalls, seeing to it that they were massaged and conditioned with Elizabeth Arden creams and lotions, and keeping them in clean, tastefully decorated stables. She liked only handsome horses (those flunking her beauty test were quickly sold off), and she insisted that her jockeys spare the whip and that her trainers not overexert the animals. Nonetheless, she was serious about horses and she seemed to enjoy the confidence of many of them.

Elizabeth Arden was also serious about women, and she enjoyed the friendship of hundreds who were wealthy and highly placed socially. They constituted the bulk of the trade at her major temples of glamour and at her two beauty-restorative resorts, both called Maine Chance Farm.

The fifty big salons were in the principal cities and resorts of the United States, Canada, Mexico, Peru, Europe, and Australia. The New York salon occupied eleven of twelve floors at 691 Fifth Avenue, near Fifty-fourth Street. Like every other major Arden salon, it was entered through a bright red door. In Paris, the Arden salon was in the Place Vendôme, a few steps from the Ritz. It was managed by Miss Arden's sister, a vicomtesse, and it employed a countess to handle its press relations. The salon's socially distinguished clients included the Duchess of Windsor, Princess Peggy d'Arenberg, Olivia de Havilland, and the Begum Aga Khan.

In addition to these salons, Elizabeth Arden operated about

fifty establishments throughout the world for facials and hair-dressing. These are elegant but less elaborate than the full-treatment salons. Moreover, Elizabeth Arden manufactured about three hundred scented cosmetics products sold in department stores and pharmacies around the globe. The best seller over the years was Velva Moisture Film, a lotion available in a number of shades to be applied before makeup.

Through her clients in the beauty business and her friendships in the horse world, Mrs. Graham became prominent in society. She gave many parties, some at her duplex apartment on Fifth Avenue. For many years she was a patron of the annual luncheon and fashion show for the benefit of the American Women's Voluntary Services; she sponsored the annual Blue Grass Ball (named for one of her perfumes) for the New York Travelers Aid Society; she was active in the Friends of the Philharmonic and in obtaining financial support for the now-defunct American Symphony Orchestra, which was directed by Leopold Stokowski. In whichever of her worlds Mrs. Graham was present, she appeared comely, fragile, fluttery, and ageless. But although she stood only a little over five feet tall and was slender, she was about as fragile as a football tackle; and anyone who mistook her wispiness for indecision quickly discovered that she had a will of steel and the power to execute it.

She was, however, undeniably ageless, a circumstance that she accentuated by concealing her birth date. A company spokesman said it was December 31, 1884, but others were certain it was 1880. Whatever it may have been, Mrs. Graham, in her sixties and seventies, looked twenty years younger, even on close inspection of her face. Moreover, her hair never grayed publicly, but remained mostly a beige-blond. "I can't see any reason why any woman should ever have to have gray hair," she told a gray-haired reporter in 1965. This was just one reflection of her vanity and her uncompromising belief that youthfulness was an important ingredient of beauty.

Mrs. Graham suffused herself in pink. Early in her business

career she came to the conclusion that it was the most flattering color in the spectrum, and she never changed her mind about its power to make drab subjects glow in its reflected warmth. She dressed mostly in pink or its variations (once in a great while she wore blue or beige), and she once doused her hair in a pink rinse. The intensity of her pink changed with the fashions. Some seasons it was bright cherry and some seasons it might have undertones of lavender. When ethereal complexions were fancied, Elizabeth Arden pink was as pale as the dawn's early light.

Pink also dominated the decor of Mrs. Graham's Manhattan residence, her apartment adjoining the Surf Club at Miami Beach, her cottages at the Belmont and Saratoga race tracks, and her living quarters at Maine Chance Farm, Lexington, Kentucky. Pink was in evidence, too, in her twelfth-century gothic castle in Ballymore Eustace, twenty miles outside Dublin. The castle is part of a 507-acre estate for horses and cattle. Pink was the signature color of the jars and covers for Elizabeth Arden products. She once halted production on a jar because the color was not exactly right. The step cost $100,000, but she regarded that as a trifle. Even Elizabeth Arden press releases were mimeographed on pink paper. Unaccountably, they arrived at newspaper offices in plain brown envelopes.

Although Elizabeth Arden subscribed to the notion that cosmetics made the woman, she did not neglect the role of smart clothes. Negligees, lingerie, and day and evening costumes were offered for sale in her salons. She employed several designers over the years, including Antonio del Castillo, Oscar de la Renta, and Ferdinando Sarmi. The custom and ready-made collections were considered elegant for women verging on middle age. Miss Arden herself was always well dressed, in either a trim suit or a gently flowing gown. She invariably wore diamonds, a pearl necklace, and earrings. The scent of Mémoire Chérie, an Arden perfume, was rarely absent; nor was a small alligator handbag, which she carried even in her own living room.

The chief ingredients of beauty, in her view, were clean skin, natural makeup, a slim waistline, and a simple hairdo. In her later years she condoned rather flamboyant eye makeup, but she was adamantly against close-cropped hairdos. "If you read the papers, you will notice that no girl with short hair has made an advantageous marriage lately," she remarked in 1950. "So what's the sense of looking like a shaved bulldog?"

Born near Toronto of Scotch-English parents, Florence Nightingale Graham grew into a young woman of ambition who migrated to New York in 1908 in search of a more active life than Toronto provided. She got a job with Eleanor Adair, a beauty specialist, learned massage, and looked into the elementary formulas for cosmetics. Miss Graham, as she was then, entered the beauty business at an opportune moment. Only hoydens used rouge and lipstick. Respectable women employed, in moderation, talcum powder and some rose water and glycerin; but in the new freedom that was then beginning, they yearned for ladylike beauty aids. Miss Graham capitalized on that desire by helping to create and popularize creams, lotions, and oils—and salons at fashionable addresses in which they could be professionally applied.

Leaving Adair's by 1910, Flo Graham went into business with Elizabeth Hubbard in a salon in a brownstone at 509 Fifth Avenue, near Forty-second Street. The partners, both strong-minded, drifted apart, and Miss Graham carried on alone. At first she decided to change her corporate name to Florence Nightingale and then she hit upon Elizabeth Arden. The "Elizabeth" derived from Miss Hubbard and the "Arden" from Tennyson's *Enoch Arden,* her favorite poem at the moment. Shortly afterward, Miss Graham became Mrs. Graham in the belief that a married woman inspired more confidence in her customers. (Over the years she answered both to "Miss Arden" and to "Mrs. Graham," although she generally reserved the latter name for her racing activities.)

From the outset Elizabeth Arden prospered. The owner, then as later, was certain that her point of view in any situation was the right one. When chemists told her that a fluffy face cream—"like whipped cream"—was an impossibility, she autocratically disagreed. And, of course, she was right. A. F. Swanson, a chemist with Stillwell and Gladdings, was the man who produced the light cream, called Cream Amoretta, in 1914. Ardena Skin Tonic, an astringent lotion, was devised next. These two products were the basis of the Arden fortune, which was also, in the early days, augmented by the addition of rouge and eye shadow.

In 1915 Miss Arden moved up Fifth Avenue and opened a wholesale department to produce and sell her expanding line to department and drugstores around the world. She moved into 691 Fifth Avenue in 1930. From 1915 to 1934 the Arden wholesale division was managed by Thomas Jenkins Lewis, Miss Graham's first husband and a man with a flair for advertising and salesmanship. When they were divorced, Mr. Lewis, who had not been permitted to own stock in Arden, went to work for Helena Rubinstein, Elizabeth Arden's archrival in the beauty field. (There was a second marriage in 1942, to Prince Michael Evlanoff; it ended in divorce thirteen months later.)

Miss Arden was a hard taskmaster. She demanded perfection from her employees, not all of whom were capable of rendering it. But those who did remained on the payroll for decades. Those who did not meet her standards were dismissed out of hand. Creating cosmetics was her specialty. She tried them all on herself and on her employees; but the final decisions were made by Miss Arden, whose passion for detail was legendary. This extended to every phase of her business—the color of the package, the wording or mood of an advertisement, the naming of a perfume.

By and large Elizabeth Arden's salons catered to women forty years of age and older. For them a basic day at her New York salon included exercise, steam cabinet and massage, shampoo, set, and restyling, manicure, pedicure, facial, makeup, and lunch. All this, done in a setting of eighteenth-century French and Regency decor, cost about fifty dollars—without tips, which might readily run twenty percent. The Maine Chance Farm in Mount Vernon, Maine, was open from June to September; the other, near Phoenix, was open in the winter only. A week's restorative course cost about $750, exclusive of tips. For this sum a client lived in a combination of Byzantine luxury and Spartan spareness. A number of distinguished women were guests at a Maine Chance Farm, including Mrs. Dwight D. Eisenhower, Mrs. Barry Goldwater, Clare Boothe Luce, Perle Mesta, Beatrice Lillie, and Gwen Cafritz, a Washington society leader.

Mrs. Graham became acquainted with race horses through her devotion to society. Her stable did very well into the early 1960s; but the sale of Gun Bow in December 1963 marked the beginning of the decline of Maine Chance Farm; its name did not figure in big races thereafter. The stable's total earnings from 1943 through September 1966, were $4,711,437, according to *The Daily Telegraph,* the racing newspaper. When her horses won (which was perfection), she was openhanded with the jockeys. For example, Eric Guerin, Jet Pilot's rider in the Derby, was rewarded with twenty percent of the $92,160 purse, twice the usual fee. Presenting a double fee gave Mrs. Graham pleasure.

Elizabeth Arden was a delightful anachronism. She made her fame and fortune from rich women and fast horses, a rare personal parlay in an era when business and sport were more and more conducted by corporate committees.

FEBRUARY 18, 1967

J. ROBERT OPPENHEIMER

Starting at precisely 5:30 A.M., Mountain War Time, July 16, 1945, J. (for nothing) Robert Oppenheimer lived the remaining twenty-two years of his life in the blinding light and the crepuscu-line shadow of the world's first man-made atomic explosion, an event for which he was largely responsible. That sunlike flash illu-minated him as a scientific genius, the technocrat of a new and awesome age for mankind. At the same time, it led to his public disgrace when, in 1954, he was officially described as a security risk to his country and a person with "fundamental defects in his character." Rehabilitated in 1963 by a singular government honor, this bafflingly complex physicist nonetheless never fully succeeded in dispelling doubts about his conduct during a crucial

21

period of his life. These perplexities centered on a bizarre story of attempted atomic espionage that he told Army counterintelligence officers in 1943 and that he later repudiated as a fabrication. Misgivings also sprang from the manner in which he implicated a close friend in the incident.

An astonishingly brilliant nuclear physicist, with a comprehensive grasp of his discipline, Oppenheimer was also a cultivated scholar, a humanist, a linguist of eight tongues, and a solitary, brooding searcher for ultimate spiritual values. From the moment that the test bomb exploded at Alamogordo, New Mexico, he was haunted by the implications for man in the unleashing of the basic forces of the universe. As he clung to one of the uprights in the desert control room that July morning and saw the mushroom cloud rising in the explosion, a passage from the *Bhagavad Gita,* the Hindu sacred epic, flashed through his mind: "If the radiance of a thousand suns were to burst into the sky, that would be like the splendor of the Mighty One." And as the black, then gray atomic cloud pushed higher above Point Zero, another line—"I am become Death, the shatterer of worlds"—came to him from the same scripture.

Two years later, he was still beset by the moral consequences of the bomb, which, he told fellow physicists, had "dramatized so mercilessly the inhumanity and evil of modern war. . . . In some sort of crude sense which no vulgarity, no humor, no overstatements can quite extinguish," he said, "the physicists have known sin; and this is a knowledge which they cannot lose." In later years, he seemed to indicate that "sin" was not to be taken personally. "I carry no weight on my conscience," he said in 1961 in reference to the atomic bombing of Hiroshima and Nagasaki. "Scientists are not delinquents," he added. "Our work has changed the conditions in which men live, but the use made of those changes is the problem of governments, not of scientists."

With the detonation of the first three atomic bombs (actually, the uranium Hiroshima bomb exploded and the plutonium-test and Nagasaki bombs imploded) and the immediate Allied victory in World War II, Oppenheimer, at the age of forty-one, reached the apogee of his career. Acclaimed as "the father of the atomic bomb," he was officially credited by the War Department "with achieving the implementation of atomic energy for military purposes." Secretary of War Henry L. Stimson led a chorus of national praise when he said of the scientist: "The development of the bomb itself has been largely due to his genius and the inspiration and leadership he has given to his colleagues." Shortly thereafter, in 1946, Oppenheimer received a Presidential Citation and a Medal of Merit for his direction of the Los Alamos laboratory where the bomb had been developed.

His prestige among physicists, especially the younger ones, and in the scientific community at large, rose to spectacular heights. He was looked to as a spokesman, a senior statesman, and something of a wizard for having developed in only two years what many thought would take much longer—if indeed it could be put together at all.

In the years from 1945 to 1952, Oppenheimer was one of the foremost government advisers on key phases of United States atomic policy. He was the dominant author of the Acheson-Lilienthal Report (named for Secretary of State Dean Acheson and David Lilienthal, first chairman of the Atomic Energy Commission), which offered a plan for international control of atomic energy. He was also the virtual author of the Baruch Plan, which was based on the Acheson-Lilienthal Report, calling for United Nations supervision of nuclear power. He was consultant to Bernard Baruch and to Frederick H. Osborn, his successor, in futile United Nations negotiations over the plan, which was rejected by the Soviet Union. From 1947 to 1952, Oppenheimer headed the Atomic Energy Commission's general advisory committee of top nuclear scientists, and for the following two years he was its consultant. He also served on the atomic committee of the Research and Development Board to advise the military, the science advisory committee of the Office of Defense Mobilization, and study groups by the dozen. He had a desk in the president's Executive Offices, across the street from the White House.

This eminence ended with shocking abruptness in December

1953, when President Dwight D. Eisenhower ordered that a "blank wall be placed between Dr. Oppenheimer and any secret data" pending a security hearing. The following June he was stripped of his security clearance by the Atomic Energy Commission. It was never restored to him.

Up to 1954 Oppenheimer's big-brimmed brown porkpie hat, size 6⅞, was a frequent (and telltale) sight in Washington and the capitals of Western Europe, where he traveled to lecture or consult. (The trademark hat was also in evidence at Princeton, New Jersey, where he headed the Institute for Advanced Study from 1947 to 1966.) He was Oppy, Oppie, or Opje to hundreds of persons who were captivated by his charm, his eloquence, his sharp, subtle humor, and his easy smile, or who were awed by the scope of his erudition, the incisiveness of his mind, the chill of his sarcasm, and his impatience with those he thought were slow or shoddy thinkers.

He was six feet tall, a bit stooped, and as thin as the wisps from his chain-smoked cigarettes or pipes. Blue-eyed, with close-cropped hair (it was dark in 1943, gray by 1954, and white a few years later), he had a mobile, expressive face that, once young and ageless and poetic, became lined and worn and haggard after his security hearings. He was extremely fidgety when he sat, and he constantly shifted in his chair, bit his knuckles, scratched his head, hooked and unhooked his legs. When he spoke on his feet, he paced and stalked, smoking incessantly and jerking a cigarette or pipe out of his mouth almost violently when he wanted to emphasize a word or phrase with a gesture of his nicotine-stained fingers. He was an energetic man at parties, where he was usually the center of attention. He was gracious as a host and the maker of fine and potent martinis. He was full of droll stories, but he could switch in a flash from frivolity to gravity.

What bedazzled people first about Oppenheimer was his da Vinci intellect. "Robert is the only authentic genius I know," Lilienthal said of him. Echoing this appraisal, Charles Lauritsen, a former colleague at the California Institute of Technology, once remarked: "The man was unbelievable. He always gave you the right answer before you formulated the question." Knowledge came effortlessly. As a young man he learned enough Dutch in six weeks to deliver a technical lecture while on a visit to the Netherlands. At the age of thirty he learned Sanskrit, and he used to enjoy passing notes to other savants in that language. On a train trip from San Francisco to the East Coast he read Edward Gibbon's seven-volume *The Decline and Fall of the Roman Empire.* On another such trip he read the four volumes of Karl Marx's *Das Kapital* in German. On a short summer holiday in Corsica he read in French Marcel Proust's *A la Recherche du temps perdu,* which he later said was one of the great experiences of his life. This almost compulsive avidity for learning was not sterile, for he invariably made some use of what he read. He was, moreover, an authority, if not an expert, in baroque and classical music, to which he liked to listen. In the words of a friend, Oppenheimer was "a culture hound."

Even as a child he was made much of for his formidable ability to absorb knowledge. He was born in New York on April 22, 1904, the son of Julius and Ella Freedman (or Friedman) Oppenheimer. Julius Oppenheimer was a prosperous textile importer who had immigrated from Germany, and his wife was a Baltimore artist who died when her elder son was ten. (The younger son, Frank Friedman Oppenheimer, also became a physicist.) The family lived in comfort, with a private art collection that included three Van Goghs. Robert was encouraged to delve into rocks after he started a collection at the age of five, and he was admitted to the Mineralogical Club of New York when he was eleven.

He was a shy, delicate boy (he was once thought to have tuberculosis), concerned more with his homework and with poetry and architecture than with mixing with other youngsters. After attending the Ethical Culture School ("It is characteristic that I don't remember any of my classmates," he said), he entered Harvard College in 1922, intending to become a chemist. He was a solitary student with an astonishing appetite for work. "I had a real chance to learn," he said later. "I loved it. I almost came alive. I took more courses than I was supposed to, lived in the [library] stacks, just raided the place intellectually." Typical of his absorption was this note that he wrote about himself: "It was so hot today the only thing I could do was lie on my bed and read Jeans's 'Dynamical Theory of Gases.'" In addition to studying physics and other sciences, he learned Latin and Greek and was graduated summa cum laude in 1925, having completed four years' work in three.

From Harvard, Robert Oppenheimer went to Cambridge University, where he worked in atomics under Lord Rutherford, the eminent physicist. From there he went to the Georgia Augusta University at Göttingen, Germany, at the invitation of Max Born, also a celebrated scientist interested in the quantum theory of atomic systems. He received his doctorate there in 1927, along with a reputation for being pushy. In 1927–28 he was a National Research Fellow at Harvard and Cal Tech, and the following year he was an International Education Board Fellow at the University of Leyden, in the Netherlands, and the Technische Hochschule in Zurich, Switzerland.

Returning to the United States in 1929, Oppenheimer joined the faculties of Cal Tech at Pasadena, California, and the University of California at Berkeley. He was attached to both schools until 1947 and rose to the rank of professor. He proved an outstanding teacher. Magnetic, lucid, always accessible, he developed hundreds of young physicists, some of whom were so devoted to him that they migrated with him back and forth from Berkeley to Pasadena and even copied his mannerisms. Describing to his security hearings his ivory-tower life up to late 1936, he said: "I was not interested in and did not read about economics or politics. I was almost wholly divorced from the contemporary scene in this country. I never read a newspaper or a current magazine like *Time* or *Harper's;* I had no radio, no telephone; I learned of the stock market crash in the fall of 1929 only long after the event; the first time I ever voted was in the presidential election of 1936."

In the 1930's, however, Oppenheimer greatly influenced American physics as a leader of a dynamic school of theoreticians in California. His influence continued in his later years at the Institute for Advanced Study. In the words of one Nobel laureate in physics: "No one in his age group has been as familiar with all aspects of current developments in theoretical physics." One of his earliest contributions was in 1926–27 while he was working with Born, then at Göttingen. Together they helped lay the foundations of modern theory of the quantum behavior of molecules. In 1935, he and Melba Phillips made another basic contribution to quantum theory, discovering what is known as the Oppenheimer-Phillips process. It involves the breakup of deuterons in collisions that had been thought far too weak for such an effect. The deuteron consists of a proton and neutron bound into a single particle. The two physicists found that when a deuteron is fired into an atom, even weakly, the neutron can be stripped off the proton and penetrate the nucleus of the atom. It had been assumed that since the deuteron and nucleus are both positively charged, each would repel the other except in high-energy collisions.

Another theoretical study by Oppenheimer figured prominently in recent efforts to explain the astronomical objects, known as quasars, that radiate light and radio waves of extraordinary intensity. One possibility is that the quasar is a cloud of material being drawn together by its own gravity. In 1938–39, Oppenheimer with Dr. George M. Volkoff and others had analyzed such a "gravitational collapse" in terms of the general theory of relativity. Their calculations are now cited in efforts to explain quasars.

Beginning in late 1936, Oppenheimer's life underwent a dramatic change of direction that involved him in numerous Communist, trade-union, and liberal causes to which he devoted time and money and which added to his circle of acquaintances many Communists and liberals, some of whom became intimate friends. These commitments and associations, which were to be recalled with sinister overtones at his security hearings, ended around 1940, according to the scientist; or, in the version of some others, they persisted until the end of 1942, when he was about to go to Los Alamos.

One precipitating factor in his awakening to the world about him was a love affair, starting in 1936, with a woman Communist who died years later. (In 1940 he married Katherine Puening, a onetime Communist whose second husband had been Joseph Dallet, a Communist who died fighting for the Spanish Republican government.) Apart from the influence exerted by his fiancée, there were other compelling elements in his transformation from cloistered academician to social activist. He described them this way: "I had had a continuing smoldering fury about the treatment of Jews in Germany. I had relatives there, and was later to help in extricating them and bringing them to this country. I saw what the Depression was doing to my students. Often they could get no jobs, or jobs which were wholly inadequate. And through them, I began to understand how deeply political and economic events could affect men's lives. I began to feel the need to participate more fully in the life of the community." His activism was far-ranging, but he consistently denied that he was ever a member of the Communist party ("I never accepted Communist dogma or theory"), and no substantial evidence was ever adduced to refute him.

Dr. Arthur H. Compton, the Nobelist, brought Oppenheimer informally into the atomic project in 1941. Within a year he had convinced Compton and military authorities that to build a bomb it was essential to concentrate qualified scientists and their equipment in a single community under a unified command. He also impressed Lieutenant General Leslie R. Groves, in charge of the $2-billion Manhattan Engineer District, as the bomb project was code-named, who selected him for the post of director and who ordered him cleared for the job despite Army counterintelligence qualms over his past associations. This action placed Oppenheimer in Groves's debt. With the general, Oppenheimer selected the Los Alamos site for the laboratory. "To recruit staff," he said later, "I traveled all over the country talking with people who had been working on one or another aspect of the atomic-energy enterprise, and people in radar work, for example, and underwater sound, telling them about the job, the place that we were going to, and enlisting their enthusiasm." His persuasiveness and qualities of leadership were such that he gathered a star scientific staff that numbered nearly four thousand by 1945 and lived, often amid frustrations and under quasi-military rule, in the hastily built houses of Los Alamos. Among the staff were Dr. Enrico Fermi and Niels Bohr, two physicists of immense world stature.

In the two exciting, tension-filled years that it took to construct the bomb, Oppenheimer displayed a special genius for administration, for handling the sensitive prima-donna scientific staff (often he spent as much time on personal as on professional problems), and for coordinating their work. He drove himself at breakneck speed, and at one time his weight dropped to a precarious 115 pounds. But under the whiplash of the war he always managed to surmount whatever problem arose, and it was for this stupendous task that he was exalted as "the father of the atomic bomb."

His security troubles had their fateful genesis while he was director at Los Alamos. Because a security-risk potential was imputed to him on account of past associations, he was dogged by Army agents, his phone calls were monitored, his mail was opened, and his every footstep was watched. In these circumstances his overnight visit with his former fiancée—by then no longer a Communist—on a trip to San Francisco in June 1943, aroused the interest of the Counter-Intelligence Corps. The following August, for reasons that still remain obscure, Oppenheimer volunteered to a CIC agent that the Russians had tried to get information about the Los Alamos project. George Eltenton, a Briton and a slight acquaintance, had asked a third party to get in touch with some project scientists. In three subsequent interrogations Oppenheimer embroidered his story, but he declined to name the third party who had approached him or to identify the scientists. In one interrogation, however, he gave the CIC a long list of persons he said were Communists or Communist sympathizers in the San Francisco area, and he offered to dig up information as to former Communists at Los Alamos. Finally, in December 1943, Oppenheimer, at Groves's direct order, vouchsafed the third party's name as Haakon Chevalier, a French teacher at Berkeley and a longtime close and devoted friend of the Oppenheimer family. At the security hearing in 1954, the scientist recanted his espionage account as a "cock-and-bull story," saying only that he was "an idiot" to have told it. He never gave a further explanation.

There was some basis for Oppenheimer's original story, according to him and Chevalier. The professor said that Eltenton had indeed approached him in late 1942 or early 1943 with a nebulous notion about getting scientific information and had been quickly rebuffed. Chevalier said that he had recounted the episode to Oppenheimer and that both had dismissed the matter. This part of the incident was corroborated by Oppenheimer in his testimony at his security hearings.

(Just how much of Oppenheimer's spy-attempt story the CIC believed is difficult to judge in the light of the fact that neither Chevalier nor Eltenton was interrogated until May 1946. Neither was prosecuted. Indeed, Chevalier was an interpreter on the United States staff at the Nuremberg War Crimes Trial in 1945. Twenty years later he wrote *Oppenheimer: The Story of a Friendship,* in which he charged that the scientist had betrayed him out of ambition for fame and to stay in the CIC's good graces. A CIC operative who had questioned Oppenheimer suggested to his Army superiors that an unimpeachable assistant be assigned to the scientist. The operative's memo included this sentence: "It is the opinion of this office that subject's [Oppenheimer's] personal inclinations would be to protect his own future and reputation and the high degree of honor which would be his if his present work is successful, and, consequently, it is felt that he would lend every effort to cooperation with the Government in any plan which would leave him in charge.")

Another of the charges pressed against Oppenheimer in 1954 also had its origin at Los Alamos. It involved the hydrogen, or fusion, bomb and Oppenheimer's relations with Dr. Edward Teller over that superweapon, of which the Hungarian scientist was a vociferous proponent. At Los Alamos, Teller was passed over for Dr. Hans Bethe as head of the Theoretical Physics Division, so he worked furiously on problems of fusion. At the war's end, when most of the Los Alamos scientists returned to their campuses, hydrogen-bomb work was generally suspended. In 1949, however, when the Soviet Union exploded its first fission bomb, the United States considered pressing forward immediately with building and testing a fusion device. The matter came to the Atomic Energy Commission's general advisory board, headed by Oppenheimer. On the ground that manufacturing a hydrogen bomb was not technically feasible at the moment, the board unanimously recommended that thermonuclear research be maintained at the theoretical level only. Oppenheimer, who also thought a hydrogen bomb morally dubious, played a leading role in this proposal, and it did not endear him to Teller. In 1950, President Harry S Truman overruled the Oppenheimer board and ordered work pushed on the fusion bomb. Teller was given his own laboratory and within a few months the hydrogen bomb was perfected with the aid of a technical device he suggested.

It was charged at the security hearings that Oppenheimer was not sufficiently diligent in furthering the hydrogen bomb and that he influenced other scientists against participating in work on it. Teller testified that, apart from giving him a list of names, Oppenheimer had not assisted "in the slightest" in recruiting scientists for the project. Teller, moreover, went on record as being opposed to restoring Oppenheimer's security clearance, saying: "In a great number of cases I have seen Dr. Oppenheimer act—I understand that Dr. Oppenheimer acted in a way which for me was exceedingly hard to understand. I thoroughly disagreed with him in numerous issues and his actions frankly appeared to me confused and complicated. To this extent I feel that I would like to see the vital interests of this country in hands which I understand better, and therefore trust more. In this very limited sense I would like to express a feeling that I would personally feel more secure if public matters would rest in other hands."

Oppenheimer, for his part, vigorously denied that he had been dilatory or neglectful in supporting the hydrogen bomb, once Truman had acted. "I never urged anyone not to work on the hydrogen-bomb project," he declared. He insisted, too, that his board had materially assisted Teller's work.

If Oppenheimer had stirred Teller's animosity in 1949, he also aroused strong feelings in Dr. Edward U. Condon of the National Bureau of Standards for different reasons. In an appearance before an executive session of the House Un-American Activities Committee, Oppenheimer described a fellow atomic scientist as a former German Communist. When quotations from the testimony were printed in the newspapers, Condon and a number of other scientists were shocked. "It appears that he is trying to buy personal immunity from attack by turning informer," Condon wrote. Subsequently, Oppenheimer wrote a public letter in which he attested to the atomic scientist's patriotism, but the incident perplexed a number of his friends.

The security hearings for Oppenheimer were triggered late in 1953 when William L. Borden, former executive director of the Joint Congressional Committee on Atomic Energy, wrote an unsolicited letter to J. Edgar Hoover, director of the Federal Bureau of Investigation. Borden gave it as his opinion that the scientist had been "a hardened Communist" and that "more probably than not he has since been functioning as an espionage agent." Hoover wasted little time in sending the letter and an FBI report to the White House and other agencies. It was then that Eisenhower cut Oppenheimer off from access to secret material. Lewis L. Strauss (pronounced Straws), then chairman of the Atomic Energy Commission, gave him the option of resigning his consultantship with the commission or asking for a hearing. He chose a hearing.

The action against Oppenheimer dismayed the scientific community and many other Americans. He was widely pictured as a victim of McCarthyism who was being penalized for holding honest, if unpopular, opinions. The AEC, Strauss, and the Eisenhower administration were accused of carrying out a witch-hunt in an attempt to account for Soviet atomic successes and to feed public hysteria about Communists. The personnel security board of the AEC, consisting of Gordon Gray, an educator, chairman, Thomas A. Morgan, a businessman, and Dr. Ward V. Evans, a chemist, held hearings in Washington from April 12 to May 6, 1954. They considered a long list of specific charges, one batch dealing with Oppenheimer's past associations, another with the Haakon Chevalier incident, and another with the hydrogen bomb. Oppenheimer testified in his own behalf, and forty great names in American science and education offered evidence of his loyalty. However, by a vote of two to one (Evans dissented) the board declined to reinstate its consultant's security clearance. After asserting as "a clear conclusion" that he was "a loyal citizen," the majority report said that it had "been unable to arrive at the conclusion that it would be clearly consistent with the security interests of the United States to reinstate Dr. Oppenheimer's clearance. . . ."

The report listed the following as controlling its decision:

1. We find that Dr. Oppenheimer's continuing conduct and associations have reflected a serious disregard for the requirements of the security system.

2. We have found a susceptibility to influence which could have serious implications for the security interests of the country.

3. We find his conduct in the hydrogen-bomb program sufficiently disturbing as to raise a doubt as to whether his future participation, if characterized by the same attitudes in a government program relating to the national defense, would be clearly consistent with the best interests of security.

4. We have regretfully concluded that Dr. Oppenheimer has been less than candid in several instances in his testimony before this board.

On appeal to the commission Oppenheimer lost by a vote of four to one. After declaring that he had "fundamental defects in his character," the majority said that "his associations with persons known to him to be Communists have extended far beyond the limits of prudence and self-restraint."

With the commission ruling, Oppenheimer returned to Princeton and the institute he headed. He lived in quiet obscurity until April 1962, when President John F. Kennedy invited him to a White House dinner for Nobel Prize winners. By this time, Oppenheimer was perceived in much less hostile light than had been the case in 1954. The worst cyclones of McCarthyism had passed, and many men and women were beginning to feel ashamed that they had bent to its winds; the issue of communism or the matter of a "Communist conspiracy" that had haunted the American fifties was now viewed as essentially false. In this changed climate of opinion, Oppenheimer was seen as the victim of zealotry and foolish apprehensions; and, although some of his friends remained disquieted by his ethics, they also joined the larger scientific community in greeting Kennedy's symbolic reversal of the verdict against him.

Further evidence of official forgiveness came in December 1963, when President Lyndon B. Johnson handed Oppenheimer the highest award of the Atomic Energy Commission, the $50,-000 Fermi Award, named for Enrico Fermi, the distinguished nuclear pioneer. In his acceptance remarks, the scientist alluded to his security hearings, saying wryly, "I think it is just possible, Mr. President, that it may have taken some charity and some courage for you to make this award today."

About two years later, and dying of cancer, he retired as director of the Institute for Advanced Study, but continued to live quietly in Princeton.

—————————————— ✣ ——————————————

ANDRÉ MAUROIS

Master of a pellucid and colorful prose style, prolific and versatile, André Maurois, who died in Paris at the age of eighty-two, was a literary professional. He was a jack of all genres—biography, history, fiction, essays, and criticism of manners; biography, though, was his true métier and the basis for his reputation. He displayed an affinity for such literary and political greats of the nineteenth century as Victor Hugo, George Sand, Lord Byron, and Disraeli, and his craftsmanship improved with his years; his masterwork, *Prometheus: The Life of Balzac,* was produced at the age of eighty. Although Maurois was undoubtedly French in his sensibilities, the appeal of his writing was international. He was read and admired in Britain and the United States as well as on the Continent;

everywhere his biographies were excellent sellers; his following, especially in the United States, was devoted. He regarded biography as a creative art, and to it he brought a sophisticated and vivacious mind and the keen perceptions of human frailty that had served him as a novelist earlier in his career.

"Except in those rare cases in which [the biographer] is writing the history of a man whose life happens to have constructed itself, he is obliged to take over a shapeless mass, made up of unequal fragments and prolonged in every direction by isolated groups of events which lead nowhere," he once remarked of his craft. "There are deserts in every life, and the desert must be depicted if we are to give a fair and complete idea of the country. It is [also] true that these long periods of empty monotony sometimes throw up the color of the livelier periods into greater relief.

"Balzac was not afraid of deserts in his novels. But the biographer will never have the luck to find a life perfectly grouped around a single passion. Thus the biographer has greater difficulty than the novelist in composition. But he has one compensation: To be compelled to take over the form of a work ready-made is almost always a source of power to the artist. It is painful, it makes his task more difficult; but at the same time it is from this struggle between the mind and the matter that resists it that a masterpiece is born."

Another of Maurois's precepts was never consciously to think about morals. "Every biographer should write on the first page of his manuscript: Thou shalt not judge," he said. "Moral judgment may be hinted at; but as soon as it is formulated, the reader is recalled to the sphere of ethics and the sphere of esthetics is lost to him."

To a marked degree Maurois chose his biographical subjects because they reflected problems or predicaments associated with his life. "The need to express oneself in writing springs from a maladjustment to life, or from an inner conflict, which the adolescent (or the grown man) cannot resolve in action," he said. Elaborating this dictum with me in the spring of 1967 in his sumptuously furnished Paris apartment, Maurois explained: "My first biography—*Ariel: The Life of Shelley*—I did because it was an expression of one of my conflicts. Shelley had come from a family from which he wanted to escape, and so did I. The problem of Shelley was also my problem."

The writer was alluding to a family that had not had much sympathy with his literary aspirations.

"My personality was also expressed in *Disraeli*," he went on in his precise tenor. "He was Jewish. I was Jewish myself. He was for me an example of how to get on with a Christian society." Turning slightly away from his desk in his cushioned swivel chair, Maurois paused to review his other selections. "Proust, Chateaubriand, and Balzac I did because I admired them as writers," he said after a moment. "The choices were guided by my inner feelings, whether I can get on with this man or this woman. I couldn't accept the idea of spending three years of my life with someone I didn't like."

Maurois's habit was to absorb himself in his subject. "It is arduous, hard work to do research," he commented; and he entrusted the task to no one but himself and his wife. This perfectionism carried over to his writing. He worked with a fountain pen on unlined white paper and made frequent revisions. "Words flow easily," he said, "but not when first written." Because he was able to produce so consistently and on such a diversity of subjects (some of his books and essays were serious criticism, some were fripperies about love and marriage), there were critics who wrote him off as superficial. Harold J. Laski, the British Socialist leader, once remarked that Maurois "ministers to those who want the elements of culture without the need to stir the muddy waters of scholarship." Other critics thought of him as a literary factory; and, in a way, he was. "I get up at seven and am at my desk at eight and work all day long," he told me. "I write every day except for Sunday, either here or at my country home in the Périgord region. The job of a writer is to write."

In Périgord, his house was atop a high hill. "From my window," he said, "I look out on nothing but tree- and heather-covered slopes, with cows grazing in the meadows and farm carts laden with hay, while far away is the village with its church steeple. There I escape from the agitation of Paris." In Paris, his study was a large, square, booklined room on the Boulevard Maurice-Barrès overlooking the Bois de Boulogne. He dressed each day as if he were going out to a business office. Typically, he wore a blue serge suit with a vest and a neatly knotted four-in-hand tie. His sole concession to informality was a pair of expensive brown leather slippers. One of the least bohemian of writers, he relished the comforts of life—a pleasant dinner, truffles, noble wines, good table talk, an evening at the cinema or the theater, a walk every day. Maurois's pen earned him a great deal of money, which he was not ashamed to spend on his own pleasure.

André Maurois was born into well-to-do circumstances. His name was actually Emile Herzog, but he changed it legally in 1947. His father, Ernest, was an Alsatian who had moved his textile factory to Normandy after the Franco-Prussian war of 1871. Emile was born in Elbeuf, near Rouen, on July 26, 1885. The boy was a brilliant student. He took many prizes at the Elbeuf secondary school, at the Lycée Corneille in Rouen, and at the University of Caen, where he studied philosophy under Emile Chartier, better known by his pseudonym of Alain. "I wanted to write, but I did not know if I should be able to do it," Maurois recalled. "My father wished me to enter his factory. The man who had the greatest influence on my life [Alain] advised me to do what my father wanted. 'If you wish to write,' he told me, 'nothing will be more useful to you than to have lived first, to have employed yourself in a trade and to have known responsibility.' The greatest influences of my youth were, first, that of Alain, who was himself a remarkable writer, and next, among books, those of Anatole France, the great French classics, and also the works of Kipling, whose philosophy of action pleased me."

Maurois remained at the family factory until World War I. Since he knew English, he was attached first as an interpreter, then as a liaison officer, to the British Army in France. As he had been doing for years, he wrote for his own pleasure, describing what came under his eye, and his notes were read by a fellow French officer, who took it upon himself to have them published. "These notes formed my first book, *Les Silences de Colonel Bramble* (The Silence of Colonel Bramble)," he recalled. "This book, partly because of the circumstances—it was published in 1918 in the midst of the war—had a great popular and critical success, so that I found myself, from one day to the next, transformed from a factory official and an officer into an author. After that I was naturally only too happy to continue a career that had been since my childhood the object of my desires."

The name Maurois, that of a French village, was signed to the first book mostly because the author liked its somber sound. He continued to use it with his other books. Now a man of letters, he began in earnest to pursue his profession. Although he wrote his biography of Shelley in 1924, it was as a novelist that he first achieved renown. In addition to *The Silence of Colonel Bramble,* he wrote in the twenties *Bernard Quesnay* and *Climate,* both of which had enormous sales in Europe. "My novels are better known in France and Europe than my biographies," Maurois said in his eighty-second year. "*Climate* sold two million copies in France, but it was not a success in the United States, where only forty thousand were sold. As to why *Climate* and my other novels were not so well received in the United States, the ideas of love and marriage are not the same in France as in America. The hero of *Climate* was a sentimental man. Americans don't like to talk about emotion; they prefer physical love, what goes on behind the bedroom door. For the French it is what precedes the bedroom door that counts. 'Every beginning is lovely' is a saying that fits the case perfectly."

In between novels and biographies Maurois wrote short stories, which, he said, "may turn out to be the best things I have written." These, too, had to do with emotional and romantic situations in the bourgeois world. It was a limitation that he recognized. "In my novels and short stories I wrote about a rather limited world," he said in retrospect. "The difference between me and Balzac is that Balzac knew all classes of French society, gangsters and bankers. My type of life made me know bourgeois society much better. I don't know the underworld and can't write about it."

Following his life of Shelley, Maurois dealt in 1927 with Benjamin Disraeli, the nineteenth-century British prime minister. Still in an English mood, he did Byron in 1930. In that decade he wrote some of his major biographies: those of Marshal Louis Hubert Lyautey, a close friend and the pacifier of French Morocco; of Voltaire, King Edward VII, Charles Dickens, and François de Chateaubriand, the poet and statesman who was also a notable lover. Honors fell upon him in the thirties, as each new book added to his luster. He was made a knight of the Order of the British Empire, a commander of the Legion of Honor, and, as a climax, he was elected to the French Academy in 1938. "I like the French Academy," he said in 1967. "It's a nice place and I enjoy meeting my friends there once a week on Thursday. They are the companions of my life." These included François Mauriac and Jules Romains, both novelists of his age.

In World War II, Maurois became a captain in the French Army, attached to British General Headquarters. After the fall of France in 1940, he and his wife came to the United States, living in New York and in Kansas City, where he taught at the University of Kansas City. He described his temporary exile in two autobiographical volumes, *I Remember, I Remember* and *From My Journal.* Published after the war was his *History of the United States.* Reviewers found it "pleasantly styled" and sympathetic, but neither profound nor particularly illuminating. In 1943, Maurois went to North Africa as a volunteer in the French forces. He returned to his Paris apartment and his Périgord farm after the Germans had been thrown out of France. One of his first books was *Eisenhower, the Liberator,* and it was quickly followed by *Franklin: The Life of an Optimist* and *Washington: The Life of a Patriot.* None of these was among his more memorable biographies.

Maurois hit his stride again, however, in the fifties and early sixties with *Proust: Portrait of a Genius, Lélia: The Life of George Sand, Olympio: The Life of Victor Hugo, The Titans: A Three-Generation Biography of the Dumas,* and his biography of Balzac.

Of this last Orville Prescott wrote in *The New York Times:* "His book is enriched by much enlightening criticism of all Balzac's books separately and with a brilliant exposition of *La Comédie Humaine* as a whole. Maurois recognizes minor flaws in Balzac's novels and certain clumsinesses in Balzac's style; but his fervent enthusiasm is eloquent and persuasive." Francis Steegmuller, another critic, hailed the book as "the most engrossing chronicle conceivable of a literary genius."

Maurois's graceful style survived translation into English, as this passage from his life of Balzac indicates: "He [Balzac] read a great many books on these matters [medicine]. The medical profession at the time was divided into three schools: the vitalists, who believed that a man possessed a 'life force,' which was another name for the soul; the mechanistic-chemical school, which scorned all metaphysical concepts and saw only organs, actions, and reactions; and the 'eclectic' school, which advocated the empirical approach. There was Dr. Virey, a vitalist, whose theories broadly corresponded with Honoré's beliefs—that longevity was to be attained by husbanding the vital forces; that these were squandered no less by intellectual labor than by dissipation, and that chastity led to the accumulation of a reserve of energy which, concentrated in thought, produced physical results. To these principles Balzac added the one with which he had always been obsessed, namely, that man is able, by the use of his will, to control his own vital force and project it beyond himself. Hence the magnetic healing which he practiced, like his mother, by the laying-on of hands."

Critics also thought highly of *The Titans.* His purpose, its author said, was "to study, through three generations, the successive manifestations of a temperament so fantastic as to have become legendary." It began with Alexandre Dumas, the mulatto son of a Frenchman of gentle birth and a black slave girl of Santo Domingo, who rose from private to general in the wars of the French Revolution. The second in line, writer of some of the most popular plays and novels in European history, was a man who, according to Maurois, "loved women en bloc." The third, of course, wrote hugely popular plays, chiefly problem melodramas.

In addition to his biographies, Maurois kept up a steady stream of serious comment in literary reviews, and, in a less weighty mood, he wrote often in women's magazines as a sort of counselor on love and marriage. He was a favorite with editors because his witty articles, on virtually any subject, emerged with a swiftness that never missed a deadline.

In his later years more honors were showered on him. He received the Grand Cross of the Legion of Honor; he was made a grand officer of the British Empire; he got the Prix des Ambassadeurs for his writings in general; and he became an honorary doctor of such universities as Oxford, Edinburgh, and Princeton. Unlike some of his colleagues, Maurois refused to subordinate literature to the fierce political debates of the times. Although he took exception to Jean-Paul Sartre's militant leftist politics, Sartre was his choice for the Nobel Prize in 1964, and Maurois supported his subsequent refusal of it.

Maurois was twice married. His first wife, whom he wed in 1912, was Jeanne-Marie Wanda de Szymkiewicz. The couple had three children, Michelle, Gerald, and Oliver. After her death he married Simone de Caillavet in 1926. They had a daughter, Françoise, who died in 1930. Even in old age Maurois, a slight man with a sharp face and a long nose, did not give the appearance of venerability. His face was virtually unlined, his mind was keen, and his blue-gray eyes were quick. He felt sad, though, that his life was behind him. "I don't like being old; it's unpleasant," he said. "I hope there are not too many more years for me."

———————————————✜———————————————

FRANCIS J. SPELLMAN

From his appointment as archbishop of New York in 1939 until his death in 1967 at the age of seventy-eight, Francis Joseph Spellman was the preeminent leader of forty-five million Roman Catholics in the United States. He was the best-known, most widely traveled, and most publicized member of the American hierarchy of about 250 prelates; and of the American cardinals, he was the dean as well as the first among equals. He dominated his church in the United States as no other person had, so much so that he was often thought of as a kind of American pope.

Many of the cardinal's accomplishments were tangible—the new churches, schools, and hospitals built for a congregation that had doubled since 1939 to almost two million. His brick and mortar, spread over an archdiocese of 4,717 square miles, was valued at more than a half-billion dollars. His ecclesiastical jurisdiction included Manhattan, Staten Island, and the Bronx in New York City, plus the suburban counties of Westchester, Putnam, Dutchess, Orange, Rockland, Sullivan, and Ulster. His prominence and influence in American life arose from a combination of related circumstances. These consisted of his pervasive power at the Vatican, especially in the reign of his close friend Pius XII; the immense wealth of his see and its location at the communications center of the United States; the millions he collected yearly for the papal treasury; the number of American bishops and cardinals elevated from among his protégés and on his recommendation; his assiduously cultivated friendships at the uppermost levels of American government, society, business, industry, and banking; his extraordinary skill as a behind-the-scenes diplomat; his key position as military vicar to the Armed Forces; the tireless care with which he attended his churchly duties; and, of course, his personality. In addition, the emergence of Catholics as a more accepted segment of American society and the vastly increased role of United States Catholics in their global church tended to enhance the cardinal's importance and the respect he was accorded.

On the whole he exercised his power unobtrusively, making his views and desires known through others. He personally spoke out from time to time in favor of federal aid to parochial education, on motion pictures, and on communism, generating ill feeling on some of these occasions: his acerbic dispute with Eleanor Roosevelt over church-state relations; his calls to boycott certain films as salacious or sacrilegious; his endorsement of Senator Joseph R. McCarthy's allegations; his breaking of a gravediggers' strike; and his support of the United States war in Vietnam. In these instances of assertion of his authority he seemed to be ungenerous and narrowly partisan.

The cardinal traveled hundreds of thousands of miles, many of them as head of the military ordinariate. This was, in effect, a second archdiocese that extended all over the world, wherever

American troops were stationed. Beginning with World War II, he visited training camps, fleets at sea, air forces at their bases, and fighting fronts. It was his custom to pass the Christmas season with troops overseas. These personal visits, his battlefield masses, and his supervision of nearly two thousand Catholic chaplains, brought the church to a great number of American youths, including many reared to be suspicious of Catholicism. In an indirect way, his activity helped to generate an increasing toleration for his church. At the same time he widened his friendships among high-ranking military men, a great many of whom on their visits to New York regularly checked in at 452 Madison Avenue, the cardinal's residence, for luncheon or conversation.

A genuinely warm and friendly man, Spellman possessed a gentle smile and sly Irish wit. These attributes endeared him to important people in ecclesiastical and temporal life—among them President Franklin D. Roosevelt. He was Roosevelt's "favorite bishop," who helped to bring about a rapprochement between the Vatican and the United States in 1939. He was also on amicable terms with President Harry S Truman, President Dwight D. Eisenhower, President John F. Kennedy, and President Lyndon B. Johnson.

He was indeed a gregarious man, at home with a great variety of persons. This characteristic puzzled some of his friends, who could not understand how he could enjoy, seemingly equally, the company of a serious intellectual and that of a fun-loving, yacht-owning lawyer.

The fact was that the cardinal delighted in the rare moments of informality that his position afforded. These were the times he could sit and chat with old school and family friends, to whom he was either Frank or Spelly. Such occasions were an echo from his youth or his less burdened Roman days. He enjoyed listening to songs, Irish ballads in particular. A favorite was "Danny Boy," and a monsignor on his staff, possessed of a good tenor, was often called upon to sing it and other sentimental lilts. He was rarely without guests for breakfast, luncheon, or supper at the large oval table in his dining room. In the course of a week he talked to diplomats, travelers, men of affairs, potential contributors to charitable causes, and others whose knowledge might somehow be useful. These gatherings were scarcely ever solemn, for the cardinal had a spontaneous humor. He could turn a phrase or make a sally. His accent, even after years in Italy and New York, betrayed its Massachusetts origin. "New Yorkers still think I speak English with a foreign accent," he said after twenty-five years as head of the archdiocese.

The cardinal was a tireless worker. His day began at seven or earlier with mass in his private, oak-paneled chapel on the third floor of the residence; it often ended at midnight or later. (Like all priests, he devoted an hour a day to saying his office.) Although he delegated many responsibilities to members of his staff and officials of the chancery, he was personally involved in most diocesan activities. For example, he appeared for years at every Catholic college commencement in the archdiocese, handed out the diplomas that he had signed, and shook hands with each graduate and his parents. For good measure he sometimes took in a couple of high-school graduations.

The public saw the cardinal most frequently as a ceremonial figure—presiding at the ten o'clock Sunday mass at St. Patrick's Cathedral, reviewing parades from the cathedral steps facing Fifth Avenue, appearing at school commencements, cornerstone-layings, parish events, formal luncheons, dinners, and charity affairs. At these times he seemed almost swallowed up in the Renaissance magnificence of his clerical robes, an impression accentuated by his stature of just over five feet. But what was memorable amid the opulence of his garb was his face. It was round, benign, shining, almost cherubic. The forehead was high, the ears large, the nose a mite pointed, and the dark blue eyes, peering through old-fashioned rimless spectacles, were steady. The face conveyed a sense of cheerfulness that even long hours of ceremony rarely seemed to dull.

The cardinal's unaustere demeanor was best revealed when he

dressed in unadorned black, which he did as often as he could. In a house cassock he was indistinguishable from a rotund parish priest. For his walks, which he took almost nightly in his younger years, he also dressed in black. As a stroller, he was known to hundreds of policemen and taxicab drivers, who singled him out from other priests because of his face. On his trips to troop concentrations he dressed in his khaki uniform as a military vicar, but he often wore his shirt collar open and sported an overseas cap. He liked to mingle and banter with service men and women. Once, in the early days of World War II, a G.I. said to him, "How come, Archbishop, that you're not a cardinal?" "Our T.O. calls for seventy," he replied, "but promotions have been frozen during the war."

In matters of charity Spellman was generous to a fault. When he visited another bishop's diocese, he almost always left a check for a worthy cause. Passing through Genoa once, he pressed a check for $1,000 on its astonished ordinary. Other clergymen, recipients of his bounty, looked upon him as something of a Santa Claus. On his seventy-fifth birthday he made a gift of $75,000 to Pope Paul VI; and there was $10,000 here and $10,000 there for other public or nonchurch causes.

Criticism of the cardinal, in the church and outside it, amounted to a small industry. Although he was generously praised for his piety, his charity, his building program, and for helping to bring Catholics more into the mainstream of American life, his critics called him narrow in his outlook and halting in his leadership. He inspired, they said, a theological airlessness in the American church. Conservative was the word most frequently employed. His voice, it was said, was unmistakably clear in condemning movies and plays that he disliked, but less vehement on such social issues as political corruption and slum housing. Of the few occasions on which he appeared in the cathedral pulpit, three were attacks on communism, one was a call to boycott so-called indecent movies, one marked his accession as archbishop, and another welcomed an apostolic delegate to the United States. This record, obviously, did not reflect the currents of concern in the world.

Rather than displaying largeness of mind in confronting the public and church issues of his time, Spellman concentrated on buttressing conventional attitudes on morals, divorce, birth control, mixed marriages, and Americanism. Complex political, economic, and moral issues were turned into easy choices between good and evil, patriotism and treachery. "The only grave sins the cardinal recognizes are Hollywood, sex and communism," one critic remarked. It was conceded that he did indeed issue statements or make speeches about racial equality, social justice, and interfaith goodwill. But what was lacking, his critics insisted, was vigorous, crusading leadership. He was too prudent, too bland, too soft, and not basically interested in such matters as the encyclicals of Pope John XXIII.

Spellman's defenders, for their part, said that his lack of flamboyance did not imply ineffectiveness in keeping the church in step with the times or passivity in promoting interfaith goodwill and social goals. "The Boss," said one priest, using the nickname by which the cardinal was universally known in his archdiocese, "did not believe in change just to change, nor did he believe in thrashing out church problems in public. He preferred to work quietly in the background, encouraging change when and where it would do the most good." This priest suggested that the cardinal was also a traditionalist. "The imprint on him from the church and its liturgy as he experienced them in his formative years was very strong," he said. "You would not expect him in his late years to become a flaming liberal."

Another priest, sympathetic to the cardinal, insisted that he should be viewed in the context of the history of the Catholic church in this country. "The American church was shaped by a strong Irish component, fresh from persecution in Ireland," the priest said. "It was fiercely self-protective, preoccupied with maintaining doctrinal purity and attaining a measure of social respectability. The cardinal, with his Irish background, was molded by this history so that his Catholicism was more akin to straitlaced Irish Catholicism than it was to the more easygoing Catholicism of the church in France or Italy. He was basically more Puritan than Catholic."

In his own archdiocese and through selection of his protégés for church office, the cardinal was said to have singled out men of Irish background for preferment. On the other hand, he was interested in meeting the religious and educational needs of Puerto Ricans in New York. Newly ordained priests were sent to Georgetown University for Spanish studies and to the Catholic University in Puerto Rico for language and cultural instructions. In addition, teaching nuns and brothers received background training in Puerto Rico.

In temporal affairs the cardinal wielded a degree of power that was difficult to measure precisely. His residence and the chancery across Madison Avenue were usually referred to in political circles as "the powerhouse;" and it was rumored that mayors, governors, and sometimes presidents harkened to "word from the powerhouse." Although documented instances of political influence were rare, it was generally conceded that no New York politician was foolhardy enough to engage the cardinal head-on and that no piece of legislation inimical to the church was likely of passage. A priest close to the cardinal for many years once remarked that he exercised less direct political muscle than he was given credit for. "The cardinal's views—or rather the church's attitude—seep down," this priest said. "The days when 'the powerhouse' ran the city went out with Tammany Hall in the early thirties."

Within the church, Spellman ran a tight ship. Restless priests who ventured out of line on social and economic issues could find obstacles to their careers. A glaring instance of this involved the Reverend George Ford, former Catholic chaplain at Columbia University and pastor of Corpus Christi Church. An outspoken political liberal and ecumenist, Father Ford was at one time forbidden to speak outside his parish. The cardinal's ban, once strict, was quietly abandoned after many years, though never explicitly revoked; and when the priest retired from his church he and the cardinal composed their differences.

Other priests were not so fortunate; offenders were often banished to uncongenial parishes or passed over for promotion. One of those who fell into dire disfavor was the Most Reverend Fulton J. Sheen, once auxiliary bishop of New York. For some years Sheen was high in the cardinal's esteem, but, according to reliable sources, he slipped in a difference of opinion over money raised for Catholic missionary work. Their poor relations were an open secret, and the bishop was eased out of the archdiocese.

Priests who dealt directly with the cardinal found him difficult to gauge. "The Boss can be brusque and impassive in bawling out a subordinate," one priest recalled, "yet when the interview is over he is on his feet helping the errant man into his overcoat and making pleasantries. You never know what to make of him. If a priest who has displeased The Boss then does something he likes, he does not hold the past against him."

Although the cardinal was known to be displeased from time to time with *Commonweal,* a liberal Catholic magazine, and with *The Catholic Worker,* a Socialist monthly, he did not interfere with them. He could be irked by what they printed, and subside after a while in seeming benevolence. One example involved *The Foundling,* a novel the cardinal published in 1951. The signed review that appeared in *Commonweal* was quite unflattering to the cardinal's literary craftsmanship, and he passed the word that the reviewer had forever incurred great displeasure. Fourteen years later the reviewer received an award for Catholic journalism. Not only did the cardinal present the citation publicly, but he avowed privately that the journalist was a splendid chap.

As an author of inspirational religious and patriotic poetry, including *What America Means to Me and Other Poems and Prayers,* the cardinal stirred less criticism. The half-million dollars in royalties from all his books—they were brisk sellers in New York—was given to various charities.

When the future cardinal, then only a bishop, was named archbishop of New York, he announced: "I shall pray as if everything depended on God. I shall work as if everything depended on me."

This formula, with its emphasis on strenuous practical activity, re-flected Francis Joseph Spellman's life and rise in the church.

He was born May 4, 1889, in Whitman, Massachusetts, a small shoe-manufacturing town southeast of Boston. He was the first of five children of William and Ellen Conway Spellman. His mother named him for two saints—Francis of Assisi and the husband of the Virgin Mary. William's father, Patrick, was a bootmaker who had come from Ireland. Mrs. Spellman's father was a farmhand, also an immigrant from Ireland. Both families lived in an area with a sparse Catholic population, and they very quickly assimilated the dominant Yankee ways of thrift and frugality. Although Catholics in other parts of the country were then subject to persecution, the Spellmans, the Conways, and their coreligionists escaped searing manifestations of bigotry.

William Spellman was the proprietor of a "cash grocery" when his eldest son was born. It became such a successful enterprise that he was able to buy a fine house, set off in five acres of lawn and trees, and also to expand his store. Frank worked there in his spare time from the age of eight, selling provisions or delivering them in a horse-drawn wagon. His father had a dry wit. "Son," he used to tell the boy, "always associate with people smarter than yourself, and you will have no difficulty finding them."

The father was also a cautious man with a penny. When his son came home one evening from college to announce that he had won a scholastic medal, William Spellman's comment was, "Did you put out the light downstairs?" Frank's mother, on the other hand, was indulgent, gentle, and easygoing. A picture of her hung prominently in the cardinal's study, and he established an endow-ment fund in her memory at Whitman High School.

As a student at Whitman, Frank was not outstanding, although he won two prizes for essays, one on the Battle of Gettysburg and the other consisting of his suitably patriotic impressions of a visit to Washington. His out-of-school interests were photography, boxing, ice hockey, horseshoe pitching, and baseball. On graduat-ing from high school in 1907, Frank was sent, largely at his mother's urging, to Fordham, a Jesuit college in the Bronx. His four years there were passed inconspicuously, although he showed competence in English composition, Latin, and scientific studies. Disappointed in not making the baseball team (he was a good infielder, but a light hitter), he learned to play tennis. He also tried his hand at poetry and oratory.

On the day of his graduation, Frank Spellman told his parents that he wanted to be a priest. His mother was overjoyed; his father asked only if he was certain. On his assertion that he was, the family agreed to back him in his desire to attend the North American College in Rome. "In those days you did not have to be bright to go to the North American College," the cardinal said in later life. "The only qualification was financial." That was not quite the case, for he had to obtain the consent of his clerical superiors, including the Most Reverend William O'Connell, archbishop of Boston and later a cardinal.

Arriving in Rome in the fall of 1911 with camera in hand, Frank Spellman donned his seminarian's uniform—a black cassock with blue piping and buttons and a maroon sash—and went for his interview with the college officials. He did not make a favorable impression, with the result that for five years he was never an officer of his house, a sacristan, or a beadle; moreover, he was not permitted to go for a walk alone.

If his superiors were frosty, the seminarian's fellow students were not, and some of them became his lifelong friends. Another lifelong friendship was with one of his teachers, Francesco Borgongini-Duca, later to be an influential cardinal and Vatican official. Frank Spellman also sharpened his instinctive ability for pleasing people of high rank. Visiting a new cardinal with a group of seminarians, Frank persuaded the dignitary to pose for his camera; then he asked if he might call again to deliver the finished photographs. The cardinal agreed, and before long Frank had acquired a powerful patron.

The seminarian received his doctorate in sacred theology after a thesis in sacramental theology and was ordained a priest May 14,

1916. He said his first mass the following morning at the Tomb of St. Peter.

When he returned to the United States and to the archdiocese of Boston, Father Spellman received a cool welcome from Cardinal O'Connell, a crusty, blunt, and powerful prelate. In the nine years that Father Spellman spent in the Boston chancery he appears never to have been in the cardinal's favor. Some students of the situation have said that there was a clash of personalities between a strong-minded superior and a young man who seemed to be in a hurry. Others have said that the young priest lacked humility after his exalted experiences in Rome. In any event, Spellman's first appointment was as chaplain for a home for aged women. This was followed by a routine assignment as second curate at the Church of All Saints in Roxbury, where, in addition to sick calls, parlor duty, and preaching every Sunday, he was in charge of the Holy Name Society, the First Communion class, the Confirmation class, the Sunday school, and the baseball team.

With United States entry into World War I, Spellman delivered fervent patriotic speeches and received O'Connell's permission to volunteer as a Navy chaplain. Turned down by the Navy, he was accepted by the Army and was on the point of departure to camp when O'Connell abruptly ordered him to promote subscriptions to *The Pilot,* the diocesan newspaper. For the next four and a half years Spellman visited a different church each Sunday, preaching at all the masses and drumming up sales of *The Pilot.* It was humdrum work, and to relieve the monotony and for intellectual exercise, Spellman studied Spanish and translated into English two devotional books written in Italian by his old professor, Borgongini Duca. This endeared him to the monsignor, who, at an opportune time, was able to get Spellman out of Boston. Meanwhile he had become a general handyman on *The Pilot,* reading proofs and writing headlines and an occasional editorial. In 1922 he was made an assistant in the chancery, where he studied accounting and canon law and gained experience in the procedures of diocesan administration. He apparently did not please his cardinal, however, for he was demoted to archivist and given an office in the basement of the chancery office.

The turning point in Spellman's career came in 1925, a jubilee year in Rome. O'Connell and his chancellor, Monsignor Richard J. Haberlin, led a pilgrimage of Boston Catholics to the Eternal City early in the year. While the chancellor was away his brother died, and Spellman comforted the family. On his return, the chancellor thanked the young priest and asked what he could do to repay his kindness. Spellman replied that he would like to go to Rome on the second pilgrimage. Haberlin was able to arrange this, and Spellman sailed for Italy as secretary to the bishop leading the pilgrims—over the bishop's protests. When the party arrived in Rome there was an immediate and dramatic change in Spellman's status, for on hand to greet him at the railroad station was Borgongini-Duca of the Vatican secretariat of state. The monsignor made it plain to the Boston bishop and to the pilgrims that Spellman was his friend.

During the pilgrimage he was introduced to Pope Pius XI, and pleased him by translating several of his addresses to pilgrim groups. Also during the visit, Borgongini-Duca arranged for him to take charge of a playground project in Rome that had been initiated by the Knights of Columbus. The appointment was confirmed by the pope himself, and Spellman was effectively detached from the Boston archdiocese for the next seven years. Technically, he was made an attaché in the first section of the Vatican secretariat of state—the first American to hold such a job. There he enlarged his circle of friendships to include Pietro Cardinal Gasparri, the secretary of state, as well as other members of the Roman curia, or governing body of the church. His playground duties were not so onerous that he could not spend a part of each day in the secretariat. When prominent Americans came to pay their respects to the pope, it was Spellman who made the arrangements and who came into contact with the American embassy in Rome.

Among the Americans in Rome with whom the black-haired, good-looking priest became intimate were the Nicholas F. Bradys, who owned a villa, Casa del Sole, on Janiculum Hill. Nicholas and

Genevieve Brady were immensely wealthy and immensely interested in partaking of the Vatican's social life. To their villa came all the important cardinals, and one of these, John Cardinal Bonzano, brought along Spellman. Very shortly he was the Bradys' private chaplain and good friend. "After mass in the morning, I play tennis with Mr. Brady and then take a shower and get to work at 10:30 or 11," Spellman wrote his family at the time. "It does him good and I am certain it does me worlds of good." Another letter to Whitman, Massachusetts, reported: "Yesterday Cardinal Gasparri, Monsignor Borgongini, Monsignor Pizzardo and Mr. Brady and I had a 150-mile ride in the country. . . . We all had a great time. I suggested to Mr. Brady to give Cardinal Gasparri a new Chrysler Limousine 82 and he said, 'Sure.' Both Mr. Brady and the Cardinal are delighted." Somewhat later Spellman obtained three Graham-Paige motor cars for the pope through a former classmate at Fordham.

Three years after his arrival at the Vatican, Spellman became a monsignor and then a domestic prelate. Meanwhile he had made the acquaintance of John J. Raskob, the American industrialist, and had persuaded him to give $45,000 for a papal project. For this he was personally commended by the pope. In 1929 Spellman met Monsignor Eugenio Pacelli, then the papal nuncio in Berlin and later to be a cardinal and Pope Pius XII. "He is a wonderful man," Spellman wrote of their first meeting. The friendship that developed was intimate and profound. After Pacelli returned to Rome as Vatican secretary of state, he and Spellman spent their vacations together in Switzerland, and, of course, the two men saw much of each other through their duties in the church. Over the years the friendship flourished. It was Eugenio Pacelli who consecrated Spellman a bishop, who appointed him archbishop of New York, and who named him a cardinal, bestowing upon him his own red hat. As Pope Pius XII, Pacelli recognized his friend as the chief American cardinal. When Spellman had Vatican business to transact, he went directly to the pope rather than through normal bureaucratic channels; he was able to get the pope directly on the telephone from New York; and he was able to lunch with the pope, a privilege permitted no other cardinal. In turn, the cardinal performed delicate diplomatic tasks for the pope, raised money for papal projects, and advised him on his relations with the United States.

In 1931 a bishopric opened in the Boston archdiocese, and the following summer Spellman was named to fill it. He wrote to his family: "On Monday evening, July 25th, Cardinal Pacelli sent for me. I went into his big room and he at once came towards me and before saying a word he embraced me. Then he said, 'I have something to communicate to you, something joyful and something sad, sad because it means you will leave me, joyful because it will be for the welfare of the Church and because it is clearly God's will—the Holy Father has named you Auxiliary Bishop of Boston."

Spellman was consecrated in St. Peter's Basilica in September 1932. He was named titular bishop of Sila and auxiliary bishop of Boston. He was the first American to receive episcopal consecration at the basilica's high altar. His ring, a gift of Borgongini-Duca, now an archbishop, was a sapphire surrounded by diamonds with a fragment of the true cross set in gold. His vestments were those that Pacelli, his consecrator, had worn when he himself had been consecrated a bishop. Afterward, he was received privately by Pope Pius XI, who suggested to him his episcopal motto, Sequere Deum, or Follow God. After a short holiday with Pacelli in France and Switzerland, Spellman departed for Boston. He was forty-three years old and on the verge of a new career.

In seven years he had served a diplomatic apprenticeship open to few priests. He had copied orders, translated encyclicals, arranged broadcasts, drafted documents, carried out diplomatic missions, obtained a global perspective on Vatican affairs, and met every American bishop who visited Rome. He had, moreover, achieved every mark of the Vatican's approbation. Spellman's return to Boston was less cordial than he might have hoped. His official greeting was a radiogram, delivered to him on shipboard. It read: "Welcome to Boston. Confirmations begin on Monday. You are expected to be ready. Cardinal O'Connell." The cardinal was as frosty as his message, for he did not receive his new auxiliary for more than five months. He then appointed him parish priest of the debt-burdened Sacred Heart Church in Newton Center. He remained there until his appointment to New York in 1939.

As a parish priest, Spellman won the affection and respect of his congregation, increased its size, erased its debt by skillful fundraising, including a horse show, and built up an excellent parish school. At the same time, he traveled about the United States, seeing and talking with other members of the American hierarchy, playing host to visiting Vatican dignitaries, and maintaining a flow of correspondence with Vatican officials. Some of this correspondence had to do with American affairs, beginning in 1933 when United States recognition of the Soviet Union was under way. An entry in his diary for November 7, 1933, read: "Had a letter from Mr. [Enrico] Galeazzi [a Vatican intimate] saying that the Pope wished him to tell James Roosevelt to ask his father to request some guarantee for freedom of religion in Russia before recognition. Sent letter to Apostolic Delegate."

Spellman edged further into Vatican–United States diplomacy in 1936. In that election year, when the Reverend Charles E. Coughlin, a Michigan priest, was berating President Roosevelt as "anti-God" and as "a scab President," Pacelli, the Vatican secretary of state, accepted an invitation to spend his vacation as a guest of Mrs. Nicholas Brady, by then a papal duchess, at Inisfada, her Long Island estate. This raised the possibility of delicate complications: To what political leaders, if any, should the cardinal pay his respects? What should he say if he was asked to comment on Father Coughlin? What should he say if he was asked about an American-Vatican diplomatic tie? Spellman stepped into the situation with characteristic energy, and became the cardinal's guide and mentor on his visit, which, it was stressed, was purely personal and ecclesiastical. The cardinal gave no interviews on his 8,000-mile tour of the country. The fact that a little-known Boston prelate was Pacelli's host-in-fact was not lost on observers, especially when Spellman escorted the cardinal to a post-election meeting with President Roosevelt at Hyde Park. The interview had been arranged by Joseph P. Kennedy, a Catholic layman and a friend of the bishop's.

The cardinal's obvious confidence in the bishop led President Roosevelt to consult increasingly with Spellman on national and international affairs. He became, indeed, the principal avenue of communication between the White House and the Vatican, and the president termed him "my favorite bishop." To the end of the president's life in 1945, the prelate and Roosevelt were on good terms. He was a frequent White House guest, and his advice was solicited on great and small matters. He was consulted, for example, when Supreme Court Justice Hugo Black was disclosed to have been a member of the Ku Klux Klan; when Roosevelt considered paying a call on George Cardinal Mundelein of Chicago; when the president was dickering for a diplomatic tie with the Vatican. In 1939, shortly after his appointment to New York, Spellman arranged the final steps whereby Roosevelt sent Myron C. Taylor as his personal representative to the Vatican. It was a momentous diplomatic accord, the first United States recognition of the Holy See since 1866. Arguments for even limited relations with the Vatican had, in the 1930's, excited many in the Protestant community, who felt that the Vatican was not properly a state, and it took all Roosevelt's skill to assuage fears that recognition implied an alliance with a religious organization. Spellman's role was discreet and behind-the-scenes in bringing the Vatican and the president together in such a manner that recognition in fact was accomplished comparatively innocuously.

During World War II, when he was also military vicar and traveling the world to war theaters, Spellman and the president were in communication on policy matters regarding Europe. Coolness in his support began to develop, however, with the Allied bombing of Rome and Vatican property in 1943 and 1944. On several occasions he intervened with the president to protest American and British tactics in battling the Germans in and near

Rome. And when Rome finally fell to the Allies on June 4, 1944, the president yielded to the archbishop's importunings and agreed to a virtual demilitarization of the city. Subsequently, the archbishop was instrumental in obtaining speedy economic relief for Italy. In other areas, also, his enthusiasm for the president waned. He came to disagree with the policy of unconditional surrender for Germany; he was disenchanted by the Yalta agreements with the Soviet Union on the ground that Roosevelt had conceded too much, especially in Catholic Eastern Europe, to the Russians. There was no public break, of course, and when Roosevelt died the cardinal said a votive mass in St. Patrick's.

The way had been opened for Spellman's further rise in the hierarchy by the death of Patrick Cardinal Hayes in New York in September 1938. Although Spellman received some initial consideration for the vacancy, archdiocesan officials favored the Most Reverend Stephen J. Donahue, auxiliary bishop of New York, and Pope Pius XI was said to have decided on the Most Reverend John T. McNicholas, archbishop of Cincinnati. Before the designation papers could be signed the pope died in February 1939. He was succeeded by Pacelli as Pius XII, and one of his first acts was to send a personal cablegram to Spellman. This was followed, in April, by his designation of his old friend to the New York post. "The news broke at 7 o'clock [April 24]," the bishop wrote at the time. "I said mass in the convent at 6:30 and told the nuns after mass. . . . I wrote a letter to the Holy Father, to President Roosevelt and I went to see Cardinal O'Connell. It was quite an interview. He was very nice. Of course he knew the past, and also the immediate past, and I knew the past and also the immediate past. . . ." O'Connell's public statement was a model of praise, but his private comments were caustic. "Francis epitomizes what happens to a bookkeeper when you teach him to write," he remarked to a Catholic journalist. He also cautioned a group of New York priests, "Don't you believe a word he says."

Coming to New York, Spellman impressed himself on the public as a busy and civic-minded prelate. He appeared at public receptions, dinners, and dedications, considerably in contrast to his more retiring predecessor. He also took steps to overhaul the administrative machinery of the archdiocese, which he found $28 million in debt. Curtailing the fiscal autonomy of parishes, he centralized and refinanced the debt, consolidated insurance coverage, centralized purchasing, created an archdiocesan bank, and established firm controls over spending and building. In carrying out these policies, with a talent that amounted to genius, he came to work closely with bankers, builders, industrialists, and corporation executives. "There's nothing abstract about Spellman," a financial man who collaborated with him once remarked. "He tells you exactly what he wants and then lets you do it."

Spellman was nominated to the college of cardinals in December 1945, and was raised to it in Rome on February 18, 1946. The red hat that he received from the pope was the one Pius XII had himself received when he became a cardinal. The pope also gave the new cardinal his own pectoral cross and assigned him his own titular church of SS. John and Paul in Rome.

In his New York years the prelate was involved in several public disputes. The four most notable concerned films, a gravediggers' strike, Mrs. Roosevelt, and McCarthyism. In 1941, he condemned *Two-Faced Woman,* a slight comedy starring Greta Garbo, as dangerous to the morals of Catholics. Ten years later he attacked Roberto Rossellini's *The Miracle,* a story of an idiot girl seduced by a stranger she believed to be Saint Joseph. When a child was born, the girl considered a miracle had occurred. Calling for a nationwide Catholic boycott of the movie, the cardinal termed it sacrilegious and "a despicable affront to every Christian." Catholic pickets were mobilized to march at the New York theater where it was showing and the film was quickly banned by New York State. The ban was thrown out, however, by the United States Supreme Court in 1952 in a landmark ruling that condemned capricious censorship.

The cardinal's personal involvement in a labor dispute came early in 1949 when 240 members of the United Cemetery Workers Union, a CIO affiliate, struck for a five-day week and a basic wage of $77.23. The gravediggers, virtually all of whom were Catholics and who began their meetings with a Hail Mary and a prayer, declined to dig graves at Calvary Cemetery in Queens. The cardinal broke the strike by enlisting as gravediggers divinity students at St. Joseph's Seminary, Dunwoodie, Yonkers, and by leading them through union picket lines.

"I admit to the accusation of being a strikebreaker," he said, "and I am proud of it. If stopping a strike like this isn't a thing of honor, then I don't know what honor is." Eventually the strikers joined an AFL union and the cardinal approved a contract with it for an 8.3 percent raise over the prestrike weekly wage of $59.40. Looking back on the strike, the cardinal remarked that it had confronted him with "one of the most difficult, grievous, heartbreaking issues that has ever come within my time as Archbishop of New York, and it will be my daily prayer that if ever again the workingmen of this Archdiocese must make their choice between following their faith or faithless leadership, they will of their own free and immediate choice, choose—God!"

In mid-1949 the cardinal also fell out with Mrs. Roosevelt over whether parochial schools were entitled to federal aid. Mrs. Roosevelt regarded such help as a threat to the constitutional separation of church and state. The cardinal wanted funds for nonreligious textbooks, bus transportation, and health aids. The dispute began with a single reference to the cardinal in one of Mrs. Roosevelt's "My Day" columns. It said: "The controversy brought about by the request of Francis Cardinal Spellman that Catholic schools should share in Federal aid funds forces upon the citizens of the country the kind of decision that is going to be very difficult to make."

His response was a long, emotion-charged letter in which he accused Mrs. Roosevelt of waging a "personal attack" and of mounting an "anti-Catholic campaign." The letter concluded by calling Mrs. Roosevelt "unworthy" as "an American mother." The letter shocked many Americans and public criticism was immediate. Acting through Edward J. Flynn, a Catholic layman and a Democratic leader, the cardinal thereupon got in touch with Mrs. Roosevelt and the rough edges of the episode were eventually smoothed over. In later years he shunned discussion of the incident. "I don't like to have any hard feelings," he said in explanation. "I want to be charitable with everybody."

Spellman usually avoided an open expression of his political preferences. This neutralism, however, did not extend to Senator McCarthy and his investigations of alleged subversive activities. He came to McCarthy's defense in 1953 by asserting, "No American uncontaminated by Communism has lost his good name because of Congressional hearings on un-American activities." The following April he appeared at the annual communion breakfast of the police department's Holy Name Society and, to the cheers of some five thousand policemen, shook hands with McCarthy. He never retreated from his defense of the senator even after McCarthy was censured by the Senate. Indeed, the cardinal maintained a friendship with one of the senator's coworkers and most contentious investigators, Roy M. Cohn.

On the subject of communism the cardinal was one-dimensional; he saw its perils and threats almost everywhere in American and international life. According to Father Gannon, his biographer, the cardinal's all-inclusive hatred of communism led him to deplore "the indifference of the United Nations to Divine Guidance, their exclusion of Ireland and Spain and every civilized country that might prove embarrassing to the Kremlin, and above all, their cynical attitude toward the liquidation of Poland, Estonia, Latvia, Lithuania and the Atlantic Charter."

Spellman was on his way home from a pilgrimage to Lourdes when Pope Pius XII died in 1958. He flew to Rome, took part in the funeral rites of his old friend, and attended the conclave that elected Angelo Cardinal Roncalli as Pope John XXIII. The two were on friendly terms. Similarly, he was on friendly terms with Pope Paul VI, whom he had met when both were in the Vatican secretariat of state. The pontiff honored him when he celebrated his seventy-fifth birthday and twenty-fifth anniversary as archbishop of New York at a dinner in May 1964. On that occasion the pope, through a representative, gave the cardinal a jeweled clasp that had been worn by Pope Pius XII. It was inscribed in Latin with words meaning "to our beloved son." Later that year the pontiff, through the cardinal, gave his jewel-studded crown to the United States "to express gratitude for the goodness of all people of America." After being exhibited at St. Patrick's Cathedral the triple tiara was placed on display at the National Shrine of the Immaculate Conception in Washington.

A climactic honor came to the cardinal on October 4, 1965, when he was host to Pope Paul on his visit to New York. From the moment of his arrival at Kennedy Airport until his departure, the cardinal was at his side. The honor paid the cardinal was enhanced by the fact that it was the first visit of any pope to the United States. Nonetheless, the cardinal's influence in the Vatican and his power in the United States had diminished considerably by 1965. Having so often "jumped channels" when Pius XII was pope, he had annoyed many in the curia, and the political pendulum now swung against him. At the same time, the Vatican paid less heed to the cardinal's advice on American affairs.

In May 1966, the cardinal marked his fiftieth anniversary as a priest. There was an elaborate ceremony at St. Patrick's Cathedral attended by four other cardinals and the apostolic delegate to the United States. In the glow of the celebration the cardinal seemed to have mellowed and to have withdrawn from the arena of public dispute. This belief was accentuated by his offer, in September, to resign as archbishop and as military vicar because he was over seventy-five. A month later he announced the offer (and its rejection by the pope) in one of his rare appearances in the pulpit at St. Patrick's. "I accept this decision of His Holiness as God's will for me," he said.

But any thought that the cardinal might have eschewed controversy was dispelled when he traveled to South Vietnam at Christmastime. Addressing American troops, he asserted, "This war in

Vietnam is, I believe, a war for civilization." He went on to say that "less than victory is inconceivable." These words, uttered as the pope was attempting a Vietnam peace, evoked denunciation from without and within the church. He was even chided by the Vatican newspaper, which remarked that all Catholics had a duty to give loyalty to the pope's peace efforts. The cardinal later sought to modify his stand by insisting that he, too, wanted peace in Southeast Asia.

Francis Spellman had a dazzling career as a churchman. Once it was under way, he proved himself an adept institutional administrator; his legacy of bricks and mortar was a visible symbol of his diligence in building a solid Roman Catholic church in New York and, by extension, in the United States. His strengths were many, while his weaknesses were the results of the rigidities of doctrine. He exemplified these in full measure just as he symbolized the church's institutional power.

HELEN KELLER

When Helen Keller died in Westport, Connecticut, at the age of eighty-seven she was truly of that select company whose achievements made her legendary in her own time. Her extraordinary life, almost beyond praise but not beyond foibles, demonstrated how much is possible to the person who stubbornly struggles to attain "impossible" goals. Better described than explained, Helen Keller's life was a phenomenon. For its first eighteen months she was a normal infant who cooed and cried, learned to recognize the voices of her mother and father, found joy in looking at their faces and at objects about her home. "Then," as she later recalled, "came the illness which closed my eyes and ears and plunged me into the unconsciousness of a newborn baby." The illness, perhaps

65

scarlet fever, vanished as quickly as it struck, but it erased not only the child's vision and hearing, but also her power of articulate speech. Her life thereafter, as a girl and then as a woman, became a hard-won triumph over crushing adversity and shattering affliction; in time, she learned how to circumvent blindness, deafness, and muteness; she could "see" and "hear" with exceptional acuity, and she even learned how to talk passably well. Her remarkable mind unfolded, and she was in and of the world, a happy participant in life.

What set Miss Keller apart was that no similarly afflicted person before had done more than acquire the simplest skills. But she was graduated from Radcliffe; she became an artful and subtle writer; she led a vigorous life; she developed into a crusading humanitarian who espoused socialism; and she energized movements that revolutionized help for the blind and the deaf. Her tremendous accomplishments and the force of assertive personality that underlay them were released through the devotion and skill of Annie Sullivan Macy, her teacher through whom in large degree she expressed herself. Mrs. Macy was succeeded, at her death in 1936, by Polly Thompson, who died in 1960. Afterward several specially trained communicators took her place. Miss Keller's life was so long and so crowded with improbable feats—from riding horseback to learning Greek—and she was so serene yet so determined in her advocacy of beneficent causes, that she became a great legend. She always seemed to be standing before the world as an example of unquenchable will. Many who observed her—and to some she was a curiosity and a publicity-seeker—found it difficult to believe that a person so handicapped could acquire the profound knowledge and the sensitive perceptions and writing talent that she exhibited when she was mature; yet no substantial proof was ever adduced that she was anything less than she appeared—a person whose character impelled her to perform the seemingly impossible. With the years, the skepticism, once quite overt, dwindled as her stature as a heroic woman increased.

Miss Keller always insisted that there was nothing mysterious or miraculous about her achievements. All that she was and did, she said, could be explained directly and without reference to a "sixth sense." Her dark and silent world was held in her hand and shaped with her mind. Concededly, her sense of smell was exceedingly keen, and she could orient herself by the aroma from many objects; on the other hand, her sense of touch was less finely developed than in many other blind people. Tall, handsome, gracious, poised, she had a sparkling humor and a warm handclasp that won her friends easily. She exuded vitality and optimism. "My life has been happy because I have had wonderful friends and plenty of interesting work to do," she once remarked. "I seldom think about my limitations, and they never make me sad. Perhaps there is just a touch of yearning at times, but it is vague, like a breeze among flowers. The wind passes, and the flowers are content."

This equanimity was scarcely foreshadowed in her early years. She was born Helen Adams Keller on June 27, 1880, on a farm near Tuscumbia, Alabama. Her father was Arthur Keller, an intermittently prosperous country gentleman who had served in the Confederate Army. Her mother was Kate Adams. After Helen's illness, her infancy and early childhood were a succession of days of frustration, manifested by outbursts of anger and fractious behavior. "A wild, unruly child" who kicked, scratched, and screamed was how she afterward described herself.

Her distracted parents were without hope until Mrs. Keller came across a passage in Charles Dickens's *American Notes* describing the training of the blind Laura Bridgman, who had been taught to be a sewing teacher by Dr. Samuel Gridley Howe, director of the Perkins Institution in Boston. Howe, husband of the author of "The Battle Hymn of the Republic," was a pioneer teacher of the blind and the mute. Shortly thereafter the Kellers heard of a Baltimore eye physician who was interested in the blind, and they took their daughter to him. He said that Helen could be educated and put her parents in touch with Dr. Alexander Graham Bell, the inventor of the telephone and an authority on teaching speech to the deaf. After examining the child, Bell advised the

Kellers to ask Howe's son-in-law, Michael Anagnos, director of the Perkins Institution, about obtaining a teacher for Helen. The teacher he selected was twenty-year-old Anne Mansfield Sullivan. Partly blind, Miss Sullivan had learned at Perkins how to communicate with the deaf and blind through a hand alphabet signaled by touch into the patient's palm.

"The most important day I remember in all my life is the one on which my teacher came to me," Miss Keller wrote later. "It was the third of March, 1887, three months before I was seven years old. I stood on the porch, dumb, expectant. I guessed vaguely from my mother's signs and from the hurrying to and fro in the house that something unusual was about to happen, so I went to the door and waited on the steps."

Helen, her brown hair tumbled, her pinafore soiled, her black shoes tied with white string, jerked Miss Sullivan's bag away from her, rummaged in it for candy, and, finding none, flew into a rage. Of her savage pupil, Miss Sullivan wrote. "She has a fine head, and it is set on her shoulders just right. Her face is hard to describe. It is intelligent, but it lacks mobility, or soul, or something. Her mouth is large and finely shaped. You can see at a glance that she is blind. One eye is larger than the other and protrudes noticeably. She rarely smiles."

It was days before Miss Sullivan, whom Miss Keller throughout her life called "Teacher," could calm the rages and fears of the child and begin to spell words into her hand. The problem was of associating words and objects or actions: What was a doll, what was water? Miss Sullivan's solution was a stroke of genius. Recounting it, Miss Keller wrote: "We walked down the path to the well-house, attracted by the fragrance of the honeysuckle with which it was covered. Someone was drawing water and my teacher placed my hand under the spout. As the cool stream gushed over one hand she spelled into the other the word 'water,' first slowly, then rapidly. I stood still, my whole attention fixed upon the motions of her fingers. Suddenly I felt a misty consciousness as of something forgotten—a thrill of returning thought; and somehow the mystery of language was revealed to me. I knew then that 'w-a-t-e-r' meant the wonderful cool something that was flowing over my hand. That living word awakened my soul, gave it light, hope, joy, set it free! There were barriers still, it is true, but barriers that in time could be swept away."

Miss Sullivan had been told at Perkins that if she wished to teach Helen she must not spoil her. As a result, she was soon locked in physical combat with her pupil. This struggle was to thrill theater and film audiences many years later when it was portrayed in *The Miracle Worker* by Anne Bancroft as Annie Sullivan and Patty Duke as Helen. The play was by William Gibson, who based it on *Anne Sullivan Macy: The Story Behind Helen Keller* by Nella Braddy, a friend of Miss Keller. Opening in New York in October 1959, it ran for 702 performances.

Typical of the battles between child and teacher was a dinner-table struggle in which Helen, uttering eerie screams, tried to jerk Miss Sullivan's chair from under her. "She pinched me and I slapped her face every time she did," Miss Sullivan wrote. "I gave her a spoon which she threw on the floor. I forced her out of the chair and made her pick it up. Then we had another tussle over folding her napkin. It was another hour before I succeeded in getting her napkin folded. Then I let her out into the warm sunshine and went to my room and threw myself on the bed, exhausted."

Once Helen became more socialized and once she began to learn, her hunger for knowledge was insatiable. In a few hours one April day she added thirty words to her vocabulary. Abstractions—the meaning of the word "love," for example—proved difficult, but her teacher's patience and ingenuity prevailed. Helen's next opening into the world was learning to read. "As soon as I could spell a few words my teacher gave me slips of cardboard on which were printed words in raised letters," she recalled. "I quickly learned that each printed word stood for an object, an act, or a quality. I had a frame in which I could arrange the words in little sentences; but before I ever put sentences in the frame I used to make them into objects. I found the slips of paper which represented, for example, 'doll,' 'is,' 'on,' 'bed' and placed each name on its object; then I put my doll on the bed with the words is, on, bed arranged beside the doll, thus making a sentence of the words, and at the same time carrying out the idea of the sentence with the things themselves." Helen read her first connected story in May 1887, and from that time "devoured everything in the shape of a printed page that has come within the reach of my hungry finger tips."

After three months with her pupil, Miss Sullivan wrote to Anagnos in Boston, "Something tells me that I am going to succeed beyond all my dreams." Helen's progress was so rapid that in May 1888 she made her first trip to the Perkins Institution, where she learned to read braille and to mix with other afflicted children. For several years she spent the winters in the North and the summers with her family. It was in the spring of 1890 that Helen was taught to speak by Sarah Fuller of the Horace Mann School.

"Miss Fuller's method was this," Miss Keller recalled. "She passed my hand lightly over her face, and let me feel the position of her tongue and lips when she made a sound. I was eager to imitate every motion and in an hour had learned six elements of speech: M, P, A, S, T, I. I shall never forget the surprise and delight I felt when I uttered my first connected sentence: 'It is warm.' " Even so, it took a long time for the child to put her rushing thoughts into words. Most often Miss Sullivan or Miss Thompson was obliged to translate the sounds, for it took a trained ear to distinguish them accurately. When Miss Keller spoke very slowly and employed monosyllabic words, she was fairly readily understandable. At the same time the child learned to lip-read by placing her fingers on the lips and throat of those who talked with her. But one had to talk slowly with her, articulating each word carefully. Nonetheless, her crude speech and her lip-reading facility further opened her mind and enlarged her experience.

Each of the young girl's advances brought pressure on her from her elders for new wonders and this inevitably fed public skepticism. This was intensified when, in 1892, a story appeared under her name that was easily identified as similar in thought and language to an already published fable. Although she denied the charge of plagiarism, the episode hurt Miss Keller for many years. In that period, she was also exploited through such incidents as publicized trips to Niagara Falls and visits to the World's Fair of 1893 in the company of Bell.

When she was fourteen, in 1894, Miss Keller undertook formal schooling, first at the Wright-Humason School for the Deaf in New York and then at the Cambridge (Massachusetts) School for Young Ladies. With Miss Sullivan at her side and spelling into her hand, Miss Keller prepared herself for admission to Radcliffe, which she entered in the fall of 1900. It was indeed an amazing feat, for the examinations she took were those given to unhandicapped applicants; but it was no more astonishing than her graduation cum laude in 1904, with honors in German and English. Miss Sullivan was with her when she received her diploma, which she obtained by sheer stubbornness and determination. "I slip back many times," she wrote of her college years. "I fall, I stand still. I run against the edge of hidden obstacles. I lose my temper and find it again, and keep it better. I trudge on, I gain a little. I feel encouraged. I get more eager and climb higher and begin to see widening horizons."

While still in Radcliffe, Miss Keller wrote, on her Hammond typewriter, her first autobiography. *The Story of My Life* was published serially in the *Ladies' Home Journal* and, in 1902, as a book. It consisted largely of themes written for the English composition course conducted by Professor Charles Townsend Copeland, Harvard's celebrated Copey. Most reviewers found the book well written, but some critics, including that of *The Nation,* scoffed. "All of her knowledge is hearsay knowledge," *The Nation* said, "her very sensations are for the most part vicarious and she writes of things beyond her power of perception with the assurance of one who had verified every word."

Miss Keller's defenders replied that she had ways of knowing things not reckoned by others. When she wrote of the New York subway that it "opened its jaws like a great beast," it was pointed out that she had stroked a lion's mouth and knew whereof she spoke. At a circus zoo she had also shaken hands with a bear, patted a leopard, and let a snake curl itself around her. "I have always felt I was using the five senses within me, that is why my life has been so full and complete," Miss Keller said at the time. She added that it was quite natural for her to use the words "look," "see," and "hear" as if she were seeing and hearing in the full physical sense.

After college Miss Keller continued to write, publishing *The World I Live In* in 1908, *The Song of the Stone Wall* in 1910, and *Out of the Dark* in 1913. Her writings, mostly inspirational articles, also appeared in national magazines of the time. And with Miss Sullivan at her side she took to the lecture platform. After her formal talks—these were interpreted sentence by sentence by Miss Sullivan—Miss Keller answered questions such as "Do you close your eyes when you go to sleep?" Her stock response was, "I never stayed awake to see."

Meanwhile Miss Keller was developing a largeness of spirit on social issues, partly as a result of walks through industrial slums, partly because of her special interest in the high incidence of blindness among the poor, and partly because of her conversations with John Macy, Miss Sullivan's husband, a social critic. She was further impelled toward socialism in 1908 when she read H. G. Wells's *New Worlds for Old*. These influences, in turn, led her to read Marx and Engels in German braille, and in 1909 she joined the Socialist party in Massachusetts. For many years she was an active member, writing incisive articles in defense of socialism, lecturing for the party, supporting trade unions and strikes, and opposing American entry into World War I. She was among those Socialists who welcomed the Bolshevik Revolution in Russia in 1917. Although Miss Keller's Socialist activities diminished after 1921, when she decided that her chief life work was to raise funds for the American Foundation for the Blind, she was always responsive to Socialist and Communist appeals for help in causes involving oppression or exploitation of labor. As late as 1957 she sent a warm greeting to Elizabeth Gurley Flynn, the Communist leader, then in jail on charges of violating the Smith Act.

When literary tastes changed after World War I, Miss Keller's income from her writings dwindled, and, to make money, she ventured into vaudeville. She, with Miss Sullivan, was astonishingly successful; no Radcliffe graduate ever did better in variety than she. Harry and Herman Weber, the entrepreneurs, presented her in a twenty-minute act that toured the country between 1920 and 1924. (Although some of her friends were scandalized, Miss Keller enjoyed herself enormously and argued that her appearances helped the cause of the blind.) In the Keller-Sullivan act, the rising curtain showed a drawing room with a garden seen through French windows. Miss Sullivan came on stage to the strains of Mendelssohn's "Spring Song" and told a little about Miss Keller's life. Then the star parted a curtain, entered, and spoke for a few minutes. *The New York Times* review of her debut at the Palace said: "Helen Keller has conquered again, and the Monday afternoon audience at the Palace, one of the most critical and cynical in the world, was hers." On the vaudeville tour, Miss Keller, who had already met scores of famous people, formed friendships with such celebrities as Sophie Tucker, Charlie Chaplin, Enrico Caruso, Jascha Heifetz, and Harpo Marx.

In the late twenties, Miss Keller, Miss Thompson (who had joined the household in 1914), Miss Sullivan, and her husband moved from Wrentham, Massachusetts, to Forest Hills, Long Island. She used this home as a base for her extensive fund-raising tours for the American Foundation for the Blind, of which she was counselor until her death. In this effort she talked in churches, synagogues, and town halls. She not only collected money but also sought to alleviate the living and working conditions of the blind. In those years the blind were frequently ill-educated and maintained in asylums; her endeavors were a major factor in changing these conditions. A tireless traveler, Miss Keller toured the world with Miss Sullivan and Miss Thompson in the years before World War II. Everywhere she went she lectured in behalf of the blind and the deaf; and, inevitably, she met everyone of consequence. She also found time for writing: *My Religion* in 1927; *Midstream—My Later Life* in 1930; *Peace at Eventide* in 1932; *Helen Keller's Journal* in 1938; and *Teacher* in 1955. The *Journal,* one of her most luminous books, disclosed the acuity and range of Miss Keller's mind in the thirties. In her comments on political, social, and literary matters, she condemned Hitlerism, cheered the sit-down strikes of John L. Lewis's Committee for Industrial Organization, and criticized Margaret Mitchell's *Gone with the Wind* as overlooking the brutalities of Southern slavery.

Although she did not refer to it conspicuously, Miss Keller was religious but not a churchgoer. While quite young she was converted to the mystic New Church doctrines of Emanuel Swedenborg. The object of his doctrine was to make Christianity a living reality on earth through divine love, a theology that fitted her sense of social mission. Although her serenity was buttressed by her religious faith, she was subjected, in adulthood, to criticisms and crises that sometimes unsettled her. Other people, she discovered, were attempting to run her life, and she was helpless to counter them. The most frustrating of these episodes occurred in 1916 during an illness of Miss Sullivan's. For a while the household was broken up. Miss Thompson was ministering to Miss Sullivan in Puerto Rico, and Miss Keller was left in the Massachusetts house with Peter Fagan, a twenty-nine-year-old newspaperman, who was her temporary secretary, and her mother. Miss Keller, then thirty-six, fell in love with Fagan, and they took out a marriage license, intending a secret wedding. But a reporter found out about the license, and his witless article on the romance horrified the stern Mrs. Keller, who ordered Fagan out of the house and broke up the love affair. "The love which had come, unseen and unexpected, departed with tempest on his wings," she wrote in sadness, adding that the love remained with her as "a little island of joy surrounded by dark waters." For years her spinsterhood was a chief disappointment. "If I could see," she said bitterly, "I would marry first of all."

With Miss Sullivan's death in 1936, Miss Keller and Miss Thompson moved from New York to Westport, Connecticut, Miss Keller's home for the rest of her life. She made friends with Westport's artists (Jo Davidson executed a sculpture of her) and writers (Van Wyck Brooks wrote a biographical sketch). With Mr. and Mrs. Davidson, Miss Keller and Miss Thompson toured France and Italy in 1950, where Miss Keller saw great sculptures with her fingers under Davidson's tutelage. "What a privilege it has been," Mrs. Davidson remarked to a friend, "to live with Helen and Polly. Every day Helen delights us more and more— her noble simplicity, her ability to drink in the feel of things, and that spring of joyousness that bubbles up to the surface at the slightest pressure."

In her middle and late years Miss Keller's income was derived from her book royalties and a stipend from the Foundation for the Blind. After Miss Thompson's death in 1960, a trustee conducted most of her affairs. For her work in behalf of the blind and the deaf, in which she was actively engaged up to 1962, Miss Keller was honored by universities and institutions throughout the world—the universities of Harvard, Glasgow, Berlin, and Delhi among them. She was received in the White House by every president from Grover Cleveland to John F. Kennedy.

Despite the celebrity that accrued to her and the air of awesomeness with which she was surrounded in her later years, Miss Keller retained an unaffected personality, certain that her optimistic attitude toward life was justified. "I believe that all through these dark and silent years God has been using my life for a purpose I do not know," she said. "But one day I shall understand and then I will be satisfied."

❖

NORMAN THOMAS

When Norman Thomas was eighty years old, in 1964, bent and hobbled by arthritis, hard of hearing and so troubled in sight that he could not read without a powerful magnifying glass, several thousand friends gave him a birthday reception in New York. At its conclusion, a young reporter asked the gaunt, dignified, white-haired guest, "What will you do now, sir?" The reply was unhesitating. "The same thing I've always done." For Thomas, "the same thing" was to serve as the Isaiah of his times, the zealous and moralistic prophet who for a half-century had warned his countrymen of the inherent evils of capitalism while pointing out to them the pathways of social, economic, and political justice. Once scorned as a visionary, he lived to be venerated as an institution, a patrician rebel and idealist who refused to despair, a moral man who declined to permit age to mellow him. When he died at the age of eighty-four he was accounted one of a very few Americans who had kept a lifelong faith in the ultimate democratic decency of his countrymen. He was not a political philosopher and his specific judgments were not always sound, but on the big moral issues he was often the lonely voice of conscience talking about the nation's soul rather than its hedonistic balance sheet.

Times changed, but Norman Thomas appeared steadfast. He spoke to the mind; he appealed to ethical sensibilities; he thundered at malefactors; he counseled with doubters; he goaded the lethargic and chided the faint of heart; he rallied the committed. If his moralism was stern, his manner was gentle and his words were good-humored. But the message—and he always had a message—was the need for reformation of American society.

The general toleration, even acceptance and respectability, that he achieved in his long career had a number of explanations. Passionate critic though he was, he lived within the accepted social order and conformed to most of its standards of propriety; he used perfect English, had excellent table manners, lived in or near fashionable Gramercy Park, had a family life that was a model of decorum, and possessed a captivating personality. Esteem for him was personal to the point where he conferred a certain cachet on dissent. A further explanation was that, although he was the voice of the mute and the tribune of the disenfranchised, his brand of socialism was mild. It shunned class conflict, the dictatorship of the proletariat, and the turbulence of revolution. It was to Marxism what Muzak is to Mozart. In Leon Trotsky's celebrated gibe, "Norman Thomas called himself a Socialist as a result of misunderstanding."

Thomas, who was anti-Communist and anti-Soviet to a marked degree, wrote extensively on what he regarded as the shortcomings of Marxism. One of his favorite arguments was expressed in question form: "Can a generation which has had to go far beyond Newtonian physics or atomic chemistry or Darwinian biology be expected to find Marx, who was also the child of his time, infallible?" In his own philosophy, he seemed ultimately to lean to democracy, albeit a radical one by some standards. "For the believer in the dignity of the individual," he once declared, "there is only one standard by which to judge a given society and that is the degree to which it approaches the ideal of a fellowship of free men. Unless one can believe in the practicability of some sort of anarchy, or find evidence there exists a superior and recognizable governing caste to which men should by nature cheerfully submit, there is no approach to a good society save by democracy. The alternative is tyranny."

There was irony in the fact that Thomas lived to see many of his specific prescriptions for social ills filled by other parties. Running for president in 1932, in one of six such races, he called for such Depression remedies as public works, low-cost housing, slum clearance, the five-day week, public employment agencies, unemployment insurance, old-age pensions, health insurance for the aged, the abolition of child labor, and minimum wage laws. Each of these then-radical proposals is now an accepted part of the fabric of American life. He once acknowledged this state of affairs. "It was often said by his enemies that [Franklin D.] Roosevelt was carrying out the Socialist party platform," he said in a bitter moment. "Well, in a way it was true—he carried it out on a stretcher."

Thomas later explained what he had in mind. "You know, despite the fact that the New Deal took over many of the ideas we Socialists campaigned for, I have been profoundly disappointed," he said. "Some of our major concepts have not been accepted, but time has not changed my advocacy of them. I still heartily yearn for the nationalization of the steel industry, for example. In fact, I'm for public ownership of all natural resources. They belong to all the people and should not be for the private enrichment of the few." He summed up his alternative to capitalism as "the cooperative commonwealth." Its main features were public ownership and democratic control of the basic means of production as well as long-range economic planning.

Because he campaigned for both his long-term and his short-term reforms so assiduously and yet with so little likelihood of winning office, critics accused him of lacking realism. To these he said, "Vote your hopes and not your fears," or "Don't vote for what you won't want and get it." He was also criticized for being too professorial. According to a sketch of him in 1932, he "looks like a cultivated aristocrat, with his high-domed head, his thin gray hair, his narrow nose, firm lips and thoughtful blue-gray eyes. He belongs to the Woodrow Wilson type, depending more upon logic than upon emotions, and his manner is faintly academic." That appraisal appeared in the old *New York Sun,* an impeccably Republican newspaper.

In the opinion of the late F. O. Matthiessen, the social historian, Thomas "never served to do much more than educate some middle-class intellectuals." Echoing that assessment, a fellow Socialist told him: "Most of your time is devoted to the LID [League for Industrial Democracy, an educational organization] instead of to the workers in the factories, mines, and mills. I suppose Karl Marx must have said, 'Students, lawyers, doctors, ministers of the world, unite!' instead of 'Workers of the world, unite!' " He tended to be wry with his critics, one of whom was President Roosevelt. Twitting the Socialist leader at a White House tête-à-tête in 1935, Roosevelt said, "Norman, I'm a damned sight better politician than you." "Certainly, Mr. President," Thomas shot back, "you're on that side of the desk and I'm on this."

It was not for want of trying that he was always on the visitor's side of the desk. He campaigned for the presidency at four-year intervals from 1928 through 1948; he ran for governor of New York, for mayor twice, for state senator, for alderman, and for Congress. He also lectured two or three times a week (for a fee whenever possible) and wrote innumerable articles. His subjects were world peace, anticommunism, civil liberties, black rights, and all manner of specific causes that he believed had a place under the umbrella of social justice.

Thomas had a truly awesome capacity for work. "Some of my friends and members of my family wanted me to go slow during the recent presidential campaign," he said at the age of eighty. "How could I? Oh, I wasn't all the way with LBJ—only most of the way—but I was all the way against Barry Goldwater, a dangerous man, the prophet of war. So I made speeches from Massachusetts to Hawaii." Almost two years later he was still going about the country, living out of a battered duffel bag, lecturing to campus groups, talking at sit-ins, voicing moral indignation over United States military involvement in Vietnam and Southeast Asia. Young people ordinarily skeptical of anybody over thirty flocked to hear him, to watch his years fall away as he denounced the Vietnam conflict as "an immoral war ethically and a stupid war politically." "We are ruining a country and ourselves in the process," he said; but he declined to incriminate President Lyndon B. Johnson, whom he described as "a sincere man" who had been "caught in the meshes of an inherited system."

Arguing against militarism and war in the 1960's, he even softened his anticommunism. "If you cannot learn to live with Communists," he told his audiences, "then you might begin to think about dying with them." His fears were of thermonuclear war. "Kennedy said that if we had nuclear war we'd kill 300 million people in the first hour," he would declare in a typical thrust. Then there would be a rhetorical pause and this clincher: "McNamara, who is a good businessman and likes to save, says it would be only 200 million!"

Those who saw and heard Thomas in his declining years could still gather some impression of the man in his prime, for he was tall, he had presence and self-command. Murray B. Seidler, a friend and biographer, once described him this way: "He can communicate warmth and friendliness to widely varying types of people. The handshaking art of politics . . . comes easily to him because he likes people and is interested in the problems of individuals as well as those of mankind en masse. Although he is probably more keenly sensitive to the problems of society than to problems confronting individuals, it is not difficult to address him as Norman; most of his political associates have done so."

He was probably one of the finest platform orators of his day. Having learned the art before electronics altered the nature of speaking to large masses of people, he strongly resembled in his style such virtuoso spellbinders as William Jennings Bryan, Eugene Victor Debs, Woodrow Wilson, Billy Sunday, and Franklin Roosevelt. He possessed a booming, virile, organ-roll voice that he could modulate from a roar to a whisper. And part of the magic of his eloquence resided in his gestures—the pointing finger, the outflung arm, the shaking of the head. H. L. Mencken heard him in the campaign of 1948. "It was extempore throughout, and swell stuff indeed," he wrote. "It ran on for more than an hour, but it seemed far shorter than an ordinary political speech of twenty minutes. It was full of adept and memorable phrases, some of them apparently almost new. It shined with wit and humor. The speaker poked gentle but devastating fun at all the clowns in the political circus, by no means forgetting himself. There was not a trace of rancor in his speech, and not a trace of Messianic bombast. His voice is loud, clear, and a trifle metallic. He never starts a sentence that doesn't stop, and he never accents the wrong syllable in a word or the wrong word in a sentence."

In his battles Thomas frequently had the support of many men of intellectual substance—John Dewey, John Haynes Holmes, Rabbi Stephen S. Wise, Reinhold Niebuhr, to mention but a few—but he lacked in quantity. Congratulated on the lofty caliber of his campaigns, his reply was, "I appreciate the flowers; only I wish the funeral weren't so complete." On another occasion he said, "While I'd rather be right than be president, at any time I'm ready to be both." But his presidential vote was always slender. In 1928, in his first White House bid, he was credited with 267,420 votes. In 1932 the votes counted for him soared to 884,781—his record. Four years later the tally slipped to 187,342. In 1940 it was 116,796; and in 1944 a total of 80,518 votes were recorded for him. In his final race, in 1948, his supporters numbered 140,-260. When the results were in that year, showing President Harry S Truman returned to office over Governor Thomas E. Dewey of

New York, a prominent New York Democrat remarked: "The best man lost."

"You mean Dewey?" a listener asked. "No, Thomas."

The feeling that Thomas was "the best man" was widely shared, and many who were not Socialists voted for him because of disenchantment with what he called "the Tweedledum and Tweedledee" choice offered by the two major parties. On the other hand, there were many who believed such a protest vote was wasted because his chances at the polls were obviously so slim. He himself was very aware of this situation. In 1932, with the Depression searing the nation, many supporters predicted a vote of perhaps two million; but he knew better. Sitting with his associates on election eve, he said: "I want to tell all of you that I'm not going to get a big vote tomorrow. It's going to be a lot smaller than anybody thinks. For instance, at my wonderful meeting in Milwaukee last Saturday, hundreds came to shake my hand. One young man came up to me with tears in his eyes and said, 'I believe in everything you say and I agree entirely with your principles, but my wife and I can't vote for you. The country can't stand another four years of Hoover.' You can multiply that couple by thousands, if not millions. I can't help but sympathize with the feelings of that young man, but our vote will be small."

In the race of 1932, as in every other, Thomas campaigned earnestly. He toured the country by auto and train (sleeping in an upper berth to save money) and he spoke to whatever crowds could be drummed up. Apart from the needle trades workers in New York, however, he did not get the labor vote, a painful anomaly for a professed Socialist. But the truth was that he was not a trade-union figure, although a number of his close associates—David Dubinsky, Walter Reuther, Victor Reuther, and Emil Rieve—were union officials. Unlike Eugene Debs, his predecessor as a party leader, Thomas did not have a working-class or trade-union background. His natural idiom and style, moreover, were those of the sack suit, not overalls. His intellectualism and his moralism were part of his heritage and of his own early life. Both his grandfathers had been Presbyterian ministers, as was his father; and he himself remained a clergyman until 1931.

He was born November 20, 1884, in Marion, Ohio, where his father, Welling Evan Thomas, had a pastorate. His mother was Emma Mattoon, whose surname was her son's middle name. Norman, the eldest of six children, attended the local schools and earned pocket money by delivering Warren G. Harding's *Marion Star*. In 1901 the Thomas family moved to a new pastorate in Lewisburg, Pennsylvania, where Norman entered Bucknell. After a year he transferred to Princeton when an uncle offered to pay four hundred dollars of his yearly expenses. He was graduated in 1905 as class valedictorian. Still basically conservative in his outlook, Thomas was jolted by the urban blight he saw in his first job—that of a social worker at the Spring Street Presbyterian Church and Settlement House in New York. After a world trip he continued his social service as a pastoral assistant at Christ Church in New York. Then, while serving as an associate at the Brick Presbyterian Church, he attended Union Theological Seminary, from which he received his divinity degree in 1911.

At the seminary he was influenced by the writings of Dr. Walter Rauschenbusch, who taught a theology that accented the Protestant churches' social responsibility. This helped to prepare him for pastoral work among Italian immigrants in East Harlem, where he lived and worked for the next several years.

Meantime, in 1910, he had married Frances Violet Stewart, who came from an aristocratic banking family and who shared his social-service work. Their union was extremely happy. Until her death in 1947, Violet Thomas, as she was known, devoted her life to her husband and to the rearing of their children. The Thomases were the parents of six: Norman Jr. (who died in childhood), William, Polly, Frances, Becky, and Evan. The family lived on a basic income of about ten thousand dollars a year that was provided to Mrs. Thomas through a legacy. This was supplemented by sums she earned by breeding cocker spaniels at the family summer home in Cold Spring Harbor, Long Island, and by Thomas's fees from lectures and writing. For many years Thomas had his office in his New York home. This permitted him to take a greater part in family life than his otherwise crowded schedule might have allowed.

A number of developments helped to bring him to socialism. In his introduction to *A Socialist's Faith,* published in 1951, he wrote: "I had come to socialism, or more accurately to the Socialist Party, slowly and reluctantly. From my college days until World War I my position could have been described, in the vocabulary of the times, as 'progressive.' Life and work in a wretchedly poor district in New York City drove me steadily toward socialism, and the coming of the war completed the process. In it there was a large element of ethical compulsion."

His initial overt step was taken toward the end of 1916, when he joined the Fellowship of Reconciliation, a Christian pacifist group. Shortly afterward he became a member also of the American Union Against Militarism, in which social workers and intellectuals were active. "War and Christianity are incompatible," he said at the time, and this was the theme of scores of speeches. In his activities he met Socialists, read their books and articles, and was impressed by the party's opposition to American entry into the war. In 1917, when Morris Hillquit ran for mayor of New York on a Socialist antiwar platform, Thomas supported him.

A year later, in October 1918, he joined the Socialist party with this statement: "I am sending you an application for membership in the Socialist Party. I am doing this because I think these are the days when radicals ought to stand up and be counted. I believe in the necessity of establishing a cooperative commonwealth and the abolition of our present unjust economic institutions and class distinctions based thereon." Meanwhile, he had resigned his church post to work full time for the Fellowship of Reconciliation and to edit *The World Tomorrow,* its monthly magazine. He was also active, with Roger Baldwin, in the National Civil Liberties Bureau, which became the American Civil Liberties Union in 1920. He was a leading figure in that organization for the rest of his life, and a tireless advocate of individual rights. To this end he helped to organize or joined hundreds of committees over the years that sought justice for persons of all political views. Some were futile, some were frivolous, but many were effective.

Although Thomas was primarily an evangelist, he never hesitated to join a picket line in a good cause no matter what the personal risk. He was active, for example, in the famous textile workers' strike in Passaic, New Jersey, in 1919 and again in 1926. In the latter strike he was arrested and jailed until bail could be raised, but a grand jury declined to indict him. In 1922 he became codirector, with Harry W. Laidler, of the League for Industrial Democracy, a post he held until 1937. The LID, the educational arm of the Socialist party, sponsored thousands of his speeches. Through them he preached socialism across the country, becoming in the process the recognized leader of the party, the successor to Eugene Debs after his death in 1926. In this capacity he was the presence and spokesman for the party rather than an organizer or administrator. Nonetheless, he undoubtedly drew into it thousands of native-born Americans and helped it to outgrow its ethnic and European origins.

Thomas made his first bid for public office in 1924 as the Socialist candidate for governor of New York. Running against Governor Alfred E. Smith, a popular liberal who was also a friend of labor, he polled 99,854 votes. A year later he was campaigning for mayor of New York against James J. Walker, the Democrat, and Frank Waterman, Republican. The Socialist platform called for city-owned housing and public ownership of the transit system. Thomas trailed the field, of course, with only 39,083 votes. He ran again in 1928 with the endorsement of the Citizens Union and amassed 175,000 votes. A major issue was corruption, but Mayor Walker won easily.

In the early 1930's, Thomas turned his tremendous energies to causes growing out of the Depression. He spoke in behalf of the unemployed; he helped set up the Workers Defense League; he was an active sponsor of the Southern Tenant Farmers Union, a sharecropper organization; and he marched in countless picket lines and signed countless petitions. He was nonetheless a critic of the New Deal, although he conceded in after years that "we would have had very bad times" if Roosevelt had not been elected in 1932. "In retrospect, I wouldn't change many of the criticisms I then made," he said. "Yet the net result was certainly the salvation of American capitalism, and it produced peacefully, after some fashion not calculated by Roosevelt, the welfare state and almost a revolution." Chiefly, the Socialist leader regarded the New Deal as a device to bail out capitalism; he considered President Roosevelt too facile; and he liked to note that full employment was not achieved until the nation entered World War II. Many Socialists, especially labor-union officials, disagreed with their leader's assessment. The result was a party split, in which such unionists as David Dubinsky and Sidney Hillman broke away to support the New Deal on the ground that labor could bargain with Roosevelt to its advantage.

At the same time Thomas was beset by the Communists. Prior to 1936 he was denounced "as a social Fascist" for reputedly being too soft on the New Deal. Then, during a united front period, he was wooed in the name of workers' unity against fascism. Next, he was assailed as anti-Soviet; but in the final period of his life, when he was opposing the Vietnam War, he was viewed more leniently. He was stoutly anti-Communist. "The differences between us preclude organic unity," he said in 1936 of the Communist party. "We do not accept control from Moscow, the old Communist accent on inevitable violence and party dictatorship, or the new accent on the possible good war against fascism and the new Communist political opportunism." And after a disillusioning visit to the Soviet Union in the late thirties, he said: "More and more it becomes necessary for Socialists to insist to the whole world that the thing which is happening in Russia is not socialism and it is not the thing which we hope to bring about in America or in any other land."

Thomas was involved in several free-speech incidents, perhaps none more dramatic than that in Jersey City in 1938 against

Mayor Frank Hague. Hague, who once boasted, "I am the law," declined to sanction a Socialist May Day rally in his city. Thomas showed up anyhow to the cheers of a crowd in Journal Square. The police roughed him up, shoved him in a car, and "deported" him to New York with a warning never to return. He was back later that evening and was again ejected. He went to nearby Newark a few weeks later to thunder at "Hagueism" from that quarter. He also initiated court action and instigated a Federal Bureau of Investigation inquiry into Hague's affairs. The result of these actions, and complementary ones by the Committee for Industrial Organization, was a federal court ruling against Jersey City. Thomas immediately returned to Journal Square and made a speech to a big throng.

With the gathering of war clouds in Europe in 1938–39, Thomas tried to stem the trend to United States involvement. With his most passionate feelings aroused, he helped to set up the Keep America Out of War Congress. "We who insist that Americans must keep out of war," he said, "do not do it because we condone fascism, but because American participation in war will bring new horrors and sure fascism to America without curing fascism abroad." To the dismay of many of his friends, he also spoke to audiences of the America First Committee, an isolationist group, in 1940–41.

When the United States entered the war Thomas felt it a personal setback. "Pearl Harbor meant for me the defeat of the dearest single ambition of my life: that I might have been of some service in keeping my country out of a second world war," he said. During the war he led his party in a program of what he termed "critical support" of American actions. He was afraid that whichever side triumphed democracy would suffer, but he ultimately decided that the "lowest circle of hell" would be a Fascist victory. On the home front he protested the internment of Japanese-Americans in 1942 and in the presidential campaign of 1944, he argued against the Roosevelt policy of unconditional surrender, calling instead for a statement of democratic peace terms.

In the strongest terms he denounced the atomic bombing of

Hiroshima and Nagasaki in 1945. "Proof of the power of atomic energy did not require the slaughter of hundreds of thousands of human guinea pigs," he said. "We shall pay for this in a horrified hatred of millions of people which goes deeper and farther than we think." To the end of his life he spoke out earnestly for proposals to restrict—or, better, in his view—to outlaw nuclear war; he pleaded for disarmament "down to the police level" and called for an end to conscription. As a step toward these goals he helped to establish the Post War Council, an organization that was concerned "with matters of foreign policy and, especially, with a crusade for universal disarmament under effective international control, coupled with a war on the world's poverty, in which lie the seeds of true world government."

Even though he was accounted a visionary for his antiwar views, Thomas enjoyed more sympathy for them after World War II than he had received in pre-Pearl Harbor days. The antihumanitarian menace of Hitlerism was real, and there was substantial feeling that defeating it by force of arms was morally justified. In opposing that war, he put himself in the ambiguous position of lining up with the most conservative and right-wing forces in American life; after the war, however, his attitude was less ambiguous, since yesterday's isolationists became today's advocates of nuclear warfare. Times changed, and Mr. Thomas's antiwar philosophy placed him among those who sought to forestall American nuclear bellicosity. It was the chief threat to world peace in the last twenty years of his life; and his recognition of that situation made him seem more the realist than those who peddled dreams of nuclear glory in an Armageddon with the Soviet Union.

Although he stopped running for office, Thomas did not relinquish his basic role as a social philosopher, nor did his zest diminish. "I enjoy sitting on the sidelines and Monday-morning quarterbacking other people's performances," he said. However, he was so busy bouncing around the country that he rarely sat. He was among the leading opponents of McCarthyism and of the government's loyalty-security program to screen alleged subversives.

And in speeches and articles he maintained a drumfire of comment on current events, especially topics having to do with foreign affairs, black rights, the John Birch Society, and individual freedoms. He was a prolific writer, the author of twenty books, scores of pamphlets, and almost numberless newspaper and magazine articles. He also served as editor or associate editor of a variety of Socialist publications.

Toward the end of his life, he was asked what he thought he had achieved. His reply was this: "I suppose it is an achievement to live to my age and feel that one has kept the faith, or tried to. It is an achievement to be able to sleep at night with reasonable satisfaction.

"It is an achievement to have had a part, even if it was a minor one, in some of the things that have been accomplished in the field of civil liberty, in the field of better race relations, and the rest of it.

"It is something of an achievement, I think, to keep the idea of socialism before a rather indifferent or even hostile American public. That's the kind of achievement I have to my credit, if any. As the world counts achievement, I have not got much."

—————————❖—————————

JOHN L. LEWIS

For forty years, and especially during the turbulent thirties, forties, and early fifties, John Llewelyn Lewis, a pugnacious man of
righteous wrath and rococo rhetoric, was a dominant figure in the
American labor movement. He aspired to national political and
economic power, but they both eluded his grasp except for fleeting moments. He nudged greatness as a labor leader only to end in
isolation from the mainstream of trade unionism. And when he
died in Washington at the age of eighty-nine, it was generally
agreed that, save for a few magnificent years when he had tran-
scended himself, he lacked any broad vision of labor's role in society; even his own union reflected his narrowness, being less
strong at his death than it had been thirty years earlier. But in his

headline years Lewis, with his black leonine mane, his bushy reddish eyebrows, and his outthrust-jaw stubbornness, was an idol without peer to millions of American workers and the symbol of blackest malevolence to millions in the middle and upper classes. Gruff and unsmiling in public, his broad-brimmed fedora tilted over his eyes, he reveled in the dramatic tensions he helped to create, and he sparkled whether he was in the center stage or whether he was the deep stentorian voice from the wings. As the thunderer for labor he was unsurpassed.

Starting in 1935, when coal was the country's kingpin fuel and he was president of the United Mine Workers of America, Lewis shattered the complacent craft-union American Federation of Labor by setting up the Committee for Industrial Organization to organize workers into single unions for each big industry. He went on to lead convulsive sit-down strikes, to humble the auto industry and Big Steel, to endorse and then to break bitterly with President Franklin D. Roosevelt, to defy the government in coal-mine disputes during World War II, to battle with President Harry S Truman in two coal strikes (in which Lewis was twice held in contempt of federal court and fined), to ease the way for mechanization of bituminous mining, and to pioneer in the establishment of a pension and welfare fund for wage workers. Once denounced for balking the authority of the government, he later received the Medal of Freedom, the highest civil honor a president can bestow. It was given to him in 1964 as one of "the creators" in American life.

In the course of tumultuous labor politics, Lewis's wealthy and influential union left the American Federation of Labor and then rejoined it after leaving the Congress of Industrial Organizations, the successor to the Committee for Industrial Organization. Finally, Lewis took his union out of the AFL in the late 1940's and went it alone. Although he wrote history for all labor, and with seldom a dull line, the mine union, which he ruled with fierce pride, held his steadiest focus.

Addressing the miners, he summed up his efforts in their behalf:

"I have never faltered or failed to present the cause or plead the case of the mine workers of this country. I have pleaded your case not in the quavering tones of a mendicant asking alms, but in the thundering voice of the captain of a mighty host, demanding the rights to which free men are entitled." Soot-smirched miners heeded him without question. If he called for a shutdown, the pits were deserted. If he wanted the mines run on a three-day week, as he did during contract talks in 1949–50, that was the way they were operated. For their unswerving loyalty the miners received periodic wage increases, vacation pay, pensions at age sixty, pay for underground travel time, improved mine safety, and many other benefits. There was, however, little or no democracy within the union; Lewis did not like to have his judgments questioned or challenged. It was his besetting weakness.

In the larger context of American life, Lewis, by force of personality, was able to bend public officials to his will. Perhaps the most notable instance of this occurred during the sit-down strike in 1937 at General Motors plants in Flint, Michigan. The strikers had ignored an injunction to leave the factories, and Governor Frank Murphy was about to declare a state of insurrection and order the National Guard to evict the workers. The governor took a copy of his order to Lewis at his Detroit hotel in an eleventh-hour effort to get him to end the strike. After he had refused, Murphy asked him what he would do if the Guard were called out. Following a suitable pause Lewis replied: "You want my answer, sir? I give it to you. Tomorrow morning, I shall personally enter General Motors plant Chevrolet No. 4. I shall order the men to disregard your order. I shall then walk up to the largest window in the plant, open it, divest myself of my outer raiment, remove my shirt and bare my bosom. Then when you order your troops to fire, mine will be the first breast those bullets will strike. And as my body falls from that window to the ground, you listen to the voice of your grandfather [he had been hanged in Ireland by the British for rebellion] as he whispers in your ear, 'Frank, are you sure you are doing the right thing?' "

Color draining from his face and his body quivering, the governor left the room. The order was not issued. The next day General Motors capitulated.

Lewis was also the master of the oblique approach, which he demonstrated in dealings in 1937 with Myron Taylor, chairman of the United States Steel Corporation. He charmed the industrialist by chatting with him in his Fifth Avenue mansion about Gothic tapestries and statuary. He flattered Mrs. Taylor. He also convinced Taylor, in a series of conversations, that Big Steel would be wise to recognize the Steel Workers Organizing Committee of the CIO. Taylor, in turn, persuaded other steelmen to deal with Lewis. The result was a stunning victory for the CIO.

A superb orator with a bass-baritone that could shake an auditorium without electrical amplification or that could be muted to a whisper audible in the last rows, Lewis swayed thousands of emotion-hungry audiences. Describing him in his prime, one observer said: "He can use his voice like a policeman's billy or like a monk at orisons. He can talk an assemblage into a state of eruption. He can translate a group of people into a pageant of misery and back again." With mine operators in wage negotiations, Lewis was equally effective. C. L. Sulzberger, in his *Sit Down with John L. Lewis,* related this episode from contract talks in the early thirties:

"Lewis began to walk up and down. Back and forth he went, deftly, stolidly, with a peculiar, light-footed stride, throwing his chest forward. He stuck a cigar in his mouth, folded his nubby hands behind him.

" 'Gentlemen,' he said, speaking in a slow, tricky way. 'Gentlemen, I speak to you for my people. I speak to you for the miners' families in the broad Ohio Valley, the Pennsylvania mountains and the black West Virginia hills.

" 'There, the shanties lean over as if intoxicated by the smoke fumes of the mine dumps. But the more pretentious ones boast a porch, with the banisters broken here and there, presenting the aspect of a snaggly toothed child. Some of the windows are wide open to flies, which can feast nearby on garbage and answer the family dinner call in double quick time. But there is no dinner call. The little children are gathered around a bare table without anything to eat. Their mothers are saying "We want bread."

" 'They are not asking for more than a little. They are not asking for a $100,000 yacht like yours, Mr. _____,' suddenly pointing his threatening cigar, 'or for a Rolls-Royce limousine like yours, Mr. _____,' transfixing him with his beetle-browed gaze. 'A slim crust of bread . . .' "

The operators, according to Sulzberger's book, squirmed, and one of them muttered, "Tell him to stop. Tell him we'll settle."

On other contract occasions he could be more blunt. In 1949 talks, A. H. Raskin of *The New York Times* reported, he intransigently told the chief negotiator for the operators: "You need men and I have all the men and they are in the palm of my hand; and now I ask, 'What am I bid?' "

Many thought Lewis merely theatrical. In a sense he was, for his histrionics were in the grand manner; but when he was speaking from a position of strength there was nothing hollow about his acting. On the other hand, when he lacked public sympathy, as in his court battles in the late forties, he tended to bombast. Those who crossed him discovered there was sting to his tongue. When, in 1939, John Nance Garner, then the vice-president, took exception to some of the labor leader's views, Lewis called him "a labor-baiting, poker-playing, whiskey-drinking, evil old man." Of William Green, the president of the AFL, he once said: "I have done a lot of exploring of Bill's mind and I give you my word there is nothing there." He characterized Walter Reuther, head of the United Automobile Workers Union, as "an earnest Marxist chronically inebriated, I think, by the exuberance of his own verbosity." George Meany, president of the AFL-CIO, was dismissed as "an honest plumber trying to abolish sin in the labor movement."

Lewis's showmanship sometimes tended to obscure his matchless fund of knowledge about coal production and marketing. In appearances before congressional committees he was the professor lecturing sophomores on fuel economics. He was also exceedingly well read in the classics of English literature, in the Bible, in Napoleonic lore, in American history, and in labor-industry problems. His speeches and even his conversations were laced with literary allusions.

Lewis was often pictured as a radical, especially by those who opposed his type of trade unionism. Basically, however, his economic and political views tended to be comfortably conservative. A Republican in the twenties, he was twice considered for appointment as secretary of labor. He supported Roosevelt in 1936 and was on close personal terms with him until the outbreak of World War II in Europe in 1939, when, fearing American involvement, he switched to Wendell L. Willkie, the Republican candidate. He later fell out with President Truman, and, although he never again became an ardent Republican, neither was he a staunch Democrat. He backed Democrats perfunctorily in 1956, 1960, and 1964.

Although much of the public may have equated Lewis with bellicosity, he was actually an amiable and courtly person, possessed of a nimble wit and a pleasant laugh. In private he was also gracious and conciliatory; he talked congenially and temperately on a wide range of subjects; and he was hospitable, even to those with whom he disagreed. "I am not disappointed about anything," he remarked toward the close of his active union leadership, when it was suggested that he had failed to exercise enduring labor and political influence. "When you see those editorials about me being a bitter, disappointed old man, just remember that I do my laughing in private."

Lewis, whose salary rose by steps to fifty thousand dollars a year plus expenses, was not a flashy liver. He had a modest, book-lined house on a quiet street in Alexandria, Virginia, and shunned most Washington parties. Fastidious about the trim of his hair and his sartorial appearance, he had a fondness for well-tailored suits and excellent shirts and ties. He liked to travel in high-powered motor cars and he liked to lunch at the Sheraton-Carlton in Washington; but he passed up choice viands for steak or roast beef and potatoes, topped off with banana cream pie, which accounted for his weight of 230 pounds in his earlier years. He occasionally sipped a glass of sherry or a weak highball for sociability's sake. He smoked Havana cigars, or sometimes chewed them unlighted.

John Lewis was born to the coal mines and to unionism. His father was Thomas Lewis, a miner who had emigrated from Wales to Lucas, Iowa. His mother, Louisa Watkins, was also Welsh and the daughter of a miner. John, their first child—there were in all six sons and two daughters—was born February 12, 1880, in Lucas. For his role in a Knights of Labor strike Thomas Lewis was blacklisted for several years; talk of militant trade unionism and of the miners' hazardous and besooted lot filled John's childhood. The youngster left school after the seventh grade and was toiling in the mines at fifteen. In his leisure time he organized and managed both a debating and a baseball team; and he read, at first planlessly and then guided by Myrta Bell, the daughter of a Lucas physician, who became his wife in 1907. But before that, when John was twenty-one, he left Lucas and wandered the West as a casual laborer for five years. He mined copper in Montana, silver in Utah, coal in Colorado, gold in Arizona. He also was one of the rescue squad in a Wyoming coal mine disaster in which 236 men were killed. Returning to Lucas and a mine job, he was elected a delegate to the national convention of the United Mine Workers, which traced its history to 1849. It was his first step to union leadership. The next was to move to Panama, Illinois, with his five brothers. In a year he was president of the local mine union.

Shortly he became Illinois lobbyist for the union and, in 1911, he was named general field agent for the AFL by Samuel Gompers, then its president. This gave him a chance to travel and to get to know the ins and outs of labor politics, of which Gompers was a master. One result was that he built a large personal following in the mine union, for which he became chief statistician in 1917 and later that year vice-president. Two years later he was acting president, and president in 1920. He did not relinquish that office for forty years.

In World War I he sat on the National Defense Council, where he successfully opposed proposals for government operation of the mines. His first major confrontation with the government oc curred in 1919 in a strike of four hundred thousand miners; it was denounced by President Woodrow Wilson, and Lewis sent his men back to the pits after the government obtained an injunction. All through the twenties, Lewis worked to consolidate his power in the union and to enlarge its membership. He fought the opera-tors on the one hand and the Communists on the other. He earned a reputation as a Red-baiter and for denouncing "Moscow plots." He purged his union opponents from time to time on, it was said, flimsy charges. His attitude toward the Communists softened in the thirties, when party members were among the most active or-ganizers of the CIO. Chided, he retorted: "Industry should not complain if we allow Communists in our organization. Industry employs them."

The genesis of the CIO was in the plague years of the De-pression, when unemployment mounted to 15 million workers. Union working and wage standards were toppled, and the AFL lost thousands of members, and with them, its effectiveness. The mine union itself shrunk to a hundred thousand members. At the same time, it became evident that organization of workers by skilled crafts, which was the basis of the AFL, was unrealistic in most major industries, where unskilled or semiskilled workers constituted the bulk of employees. This situation led to the CIO's efforts to organize the unorganized.

That was made possible in part by section 7A of the National Industrial Recovery Act, adopted in 1933 as part of President Roosevelt's attempt to reverse the Depression. Section 7A, often called labor's Magna Charta, gave workers the right to organize and bargain collectively through representatives of their choice. It was Lewis who was instrumental in getting the section into the NIRA. With its adoption, he sent scores of organizers into the coalfields with the cry, "The president wants you to join the union," and in two years membership rose to 400,000.

The CIO came into being after the AFL convention of 1935,

at which tensions between industrial and craft unions erupted in a fist fight between William Hutcheson of the Carpenters Union and Lewis. As soon as the convention adjourned, Lewis met to form the CIO with, among others, Charles P. Howard of the Typographical Union; David Dubinsky of the International Ladies Garment Workers Union; Max Zaritsky of the Hat, Cap and Millinery Workers; Thomas McMahon of the Textile Workers; and Sidney Hillman of the Amalgamated Clothing Workers. Subsequently these and other unions backing the CIO were expelled from the AFL, but it was an empty gesture, for, virtually from the outset, workers responded to the CIO campaigns in the basic industries. First the automotive industry capitulated, then Big Steel, then others, until 4 million workers were enrolled in CIO unions; but the steady procession of successes was interrupted in late 1937 by Little Steel, the small fabricators, and especially by Tom Girdler of Republic Steel.

The Little Steel strike, an old-fashioned walkout, was marked by violence; in Chicago on Memorial Day the police shot and killed ten strikers and sympathizers, and there was sporadic shooting elsewhere. In the course of the strike, which was lost, President Roosevelt was asked what he thought of the dispute. "A plague on both your houses," he replied, a remark that enraged Lewis, whose union had contributed $500,000—$120,000 as an outright gift—to the president's 1936 campaign. His retort was: "It ill behooves one who has supped at labor's table and who has been sheltered in labor's house to curse with equal fervor and fine impartiality both labor and its adversaries when they become locked in deadly embrace." Lewis followed this excoriation with others equally acerbic in the campaign of 1940, in which he sought to rally organized labor against Roosevelt's third-term bid. "Sustain me now, or repudiate me," he said in accusing the president of Caesarism. After Roosevelt won the election, Lewis resigned as head of what was then the Congress of Industrial Organizations, and Philip Murray, a pliant Lewis lieutenant, took over. In 1942, however, Lewis broke with Murray, his "former friend," and the mine union left the CIO.

Lewis's moment of national influence, waning since 1940, concluded at that point; but from 1935 to 1940, when he symbolized the CIO, he helped to bring millions into the ranks of organized labor. Alone among highly industrialized nations in 1930, the United States was without a strong union movement, and the time for one was overripe. Workers, particularly those in the basic industries, were virtually defenseless against exploitation, which grew worse as wages were driven down in the Great Depression. A desire to organize was present, but the means and the form were lacking. Lewis's special contribution was to provide them; his union's treasury put up the money for organizing costs and he saw the merits of industrial unionism, a concept with a history that went back at least to Eugene V. Debs and the American Railway Union of the 1890's.

It does not diminish Lewis's stature to say that he articulated the needs of inchoate masses of workers; that he was a bold champion in the cause of higher wages, better working conditions, and union recognition. For the five years when he appeared larger than life itself, he stirred hopes among those who toiled in textile mills, steel plants, in automobile, tire, and rubber factories, on shipboard, in brass foundries, in glassworks and even on the farms. In this respect, he was the creature of a vitalized labor movement, not its autocrat—as he found to his dismay in 1939–40 when he attempted to draw union votes away from President Roosevelt. Having allied the CIO to the New Deal in 1935 and having thus foreclosed independent politics, he discovered that workers could be inspired but not pushed. His charismatic power was virtually gone when he took his union out of the CIO.

Four years later he and the mine union were back in the AFL, but the reunion lasted less than two years. Again there was an exchange of broadsides, this time over a provision of the Taft-Hartley Act requiring union officials to take a non-Communist oath. The AFL (along with a much-tamed CIO) was willing to accept the oath; Lewis was not. To him the law was "damnable, vicious, unwholesome, and a slave statute." As for the AFL, it had "no head, its neck just growed and haired over." The mine union then went its independent way. Meantime, Lewis was tangling with the government in a show of miners' muscle.

A series of wartime strikes won substantial wage increases, including portal-to-portal (or underground travel time) pay. Then in the spring of 1946 he called a soft-coal strike in a bid for royalties on each ton mined, the money to go into the union's health and welfare fund. President Truman ordered the mines seized and the strike ended with a wage increase and a royalty arrangement. A hard-coal strike followed almost immediately, but it ended quickly on about the same terms as had been obtained in the bituminous fields. Peace, however, was short-lived. In November 1946, Lewis denounced the contract under which the government had been running the mines. Quickly, on motion of the government, federal Judge T. Alan Goldsborough issued an order restraining Lewis from maintaining the contract-termination notice. President Truman ordered the Justice Department to seek a contempt citation if Lewis disobeyed the court. When the union chief made no move to halt the walkout, the judge found him and the union guilty of civil and criminal contempt. A fine of $10,000 was imposed on Lewis and $3.5 million on the union, despite his oration to the court.

Three days later, Lewis sent the miners back to work pending an appeal of the contempt ruling to the Supreme Court. In a seven-to-two decision in March 1947, that tribunal upheld the contempt judgment and the fine against Lewis. The fine against the union was reduced, however, to $700,000, with $2.8 million more to be assessed if a strike occurred during the government's operation of the mines. Lewis complied with the court and purged himself and the union of contempt. In 1948, after the government had returned the mines to the operators, Lewis was once again in court. The miners were idle in a pension dispute, and Judge Goldsborough ordered him and the union to end the walkout. He declined and was fined $20,000 and the union $1.4 million. The fines were eventually paid.

At the mine union convention in 1948, Lewis stormed against Truman for persecuting the union. "He is a man totally unfitted for the position," he said of the president. "His principles are elastic. He is careless with the truth. He is a malignant, scheming sort of individual who is dangerous not only to the United Mine Workers but dangerous to the United States of America." He added that Truman had been "too cowardly" to put him in jail. The two men composed their differences before the end of Truman's tenure, and in 1952 the president reversed a ruling of his Wage Stabilization Board to permit a wage increase that Lewis had negotiated for the miners.

As a result of the royalty fees that Lewis negotiated with the mine operators, his union initiated a pension program in 1948 that became a model for other unions. He also built a number of hospitals in the coal areas, but these were less successful than the welfare and pension arrangement. Some were obliged to close and others were sold.

By his flair for dramatizing the problems of his miners Lewis also won a long struggle for federal mine inspection in 1952. When 119 miners perished in the West Frankfort, Illinois, mine explosion in 1951, he flew to the scene, inspected the shafts, and assailed Congress for failing to enact safety legislation. In dramatic testimony before a Senate subcommittee, he called on Congress to give the federal government power to close unsafe mines. The Federal Mine Safety Law was enacted. It set up a board of review of which the union's safety director was a member; to ensure its passage, Lewis called a ten-day "memorial" stoppage. In 1953 he was powerful enough to block President Dwight D. Eisenhower's choice of J. B. Lyon as director of the Bureau of Mines. The fight brought out that Lyon had a five-thousand-dollar-a-year pension from the Anaconda Copper Mining Company, had no experience in coal mining, and was opposed to the safety law.

In the fifties coal lost its dominance as a fuel; oil and gas became competitive. To meet the situation Lewis cooperated with the operators in introducing mechanization into coal production; this made it possible in 1952, for example, for 375,000 bituminous miners to produce more coal than double that number could have dug thirty years before. He also convinced the operators that it was wise to close uneconomic mines and pay high wages in the efficient ones. This was done quietly, in contrast to his former tactics, and by 1955 the miners' daily scale was $20.25—well above the standard in other mass industries. When he stepped down as union chief in 1960 the scale was $24.25 a day. By that time the welfare and pension fund had collected $1.3 billion, had a reserve of $130 million, and had aided more than a million persons. Miners were enabled to retire at sixty with a pension of $100 a month. In 1960, a total of 70,000 were receiving these retirement benefits.

In the last years of the fifties, Lewis clamped down on unauthorized strikes. Laying down the law at the union convention of 1956, he warned fractious miners that "you'll be fully conscious that I'm breathing down your necks" if they struck. When he announced late in 1959 that he was preparing to retire, the operators expressed regret. They praised him both for his "outstanding ability" and as "an extraordinarily fine person." In his farewell to his union he said: "The years have been long and the individual burdens oppressive, yet progress has been great.

"At first, your wages were low, your hours long, your labor perilous, your health disregarded, your children without opportunity, your union weak, your fellow citizens and public representatives indifferent to your wrongs.

"Today, because of your fortitude and your deep loyalty to your union, your wages are the highest in the land, your working hours the lowest, your safety more assured, your health more guarded, your old age protected, your children equal in opportunity with their generation, and your union strong with material resources."

He retired on an annual pension of $50,000 and was voted the title of president emeritus. He remained chairman of the welfare and retirement fund to his death. He lived alone, except for a housekeeper, in the boyhood home of Robert E. Lee. His wife died in 1942 and his daughter, Kathryn, died in 1962. A son, John, a physician, lived in nearby Baltimore.

——————————————✦——————————————

MIES VAN DER ROHE

More than to any other architect of our time, we owe to Mies van der Rohe the glassy skyscrapers and sleek-walled buildings typical of twentieth-century cities. By the time of his death in Chicago at the age of eighty-three, he was admired for his uncompromisingly spare design and for the innovations he had incorporated in scores of structures expressing what he conceived to be the spirit of an industrial civilization. His style, which was widely if not always well copied, was the product of a mind that knew exactly what it wanted to do. "Architecture is the will of an epoch translated into space," he remarked in a talkative moment. Pressed to elaborate his own pathfinding role—a matter on which he was as shy as he was on most others—he said: "I have tried to make an architecture for a technological society. I have wanted to keep everything reasonable and clear—to have an architecture that anybody can do." A building, he was convinced, ought to be "a clear and true statement of its times"—cathedrals for an age of pathos, glass and metal cages for an age of advanced industrialism.

He thought, for example, that the George Washington Bridge in New York was an outstanding example of a structure expressing its period, and he used to go to admire it whenever he visited the city. "It is the most modern building in the city," he remarked in 1963. He was fond of the bridge because he considered it beautifully proportioned and because it did not conceal its structure. Mies liked to see the steel, the brick, the concrete of buildings show themselves rather than be concealed by ornamentation. A twentieth-century industrial building had to be pithy, he believed.

Mies's stature rested not only on his lean yet sensuous business and residential buildings, but also on the profound influence he exerted on his colleagues and on public taste. As the number of his structures multiplied in the years after World War II and as their stunning individuality became apparent, critical appreciation flowed to him in torrents, and his designs and models drew throngs to museums where they were exhibited. It became a status symbol to live in a Mies house, to work in a Mies building—or even to visit one.

His name had already been established among architects long before he came to the United States in 1937. In 1919 and 1921 in Berlin he designed two steel skyscrapers sheathed in glass from street to roof. Although never carried out, the designs are now accepted as the origin of today's glass-and-metal skyscrapers. In 1922 he introduced the concept of ribbon windows, uninterrupted bands of glass between the finished faces of concrete slabs, in a design for a German office building. It has since become the basis for many commercial structures. Mies, in 1924, produced plans for a concrete villa that is now regarded as the forerunner of the California ranch house. He is also said to have previsioned the return of the inner patio of Roman times in an exhibition house built in 1931; to have started the idea of space dividers, the use of cabinets or screens instead of walls to break up interiors; and to have originated the glass house, with windows and glass sliding panels extending from floor to ceiling that permit outside greenery to form the visual boundaries of a room.

Apart from simplicity of form, what struck students of his buildings was their painstaking craftsmanship, their attention to detail. "God is in the details," he liked to say. In this respect the buildings reflected the man, for Mies was fussy about himself. A large, lusty man with the massive head of a Dutch burgher topping a five-foot ten-inch frame, he dressed in exquisitely hand-stitched suits of conservative hue, dined extravagantly well on haute cuisine, sipped the correct wines from the proper goblets, and chain-smoked hand-rolled cigars. For a man so modern in his conceptions, he had more than a touch of old-fashionedness. It showed up in such things as the gold chain across his waistcoat to which was attached his pocket timepiece. Rather than live in a contemporary building or one of his own houses (he briefly contemplated moving to a Mies apartment, but feared fellow tenants might badger him), he made his home in a high-ceilinged, five-room suite on the third floor of an old-fashioned apartment house on Chicago's North Side. The thick-walled rooms were large and they included, predictably, a full kitchen with an ancient gas range for his cook. The apartment contained armless chairs and furniture of his own design as well as sofas and wing chairs—in which he preferred to sit. The walls were stark white; but the apartment had a glowing warmth, given off by the Klees, Braques, and Schwitterses that dotted its walls. Paul Klee was a close friend, and his collection of Klees was among the finest in private hands.

Mies's chairs were almost as well known as his buildings, and they were just as spare. He designed his first chair, known as the MR chair, in 1927. It had a caned seat and back and its frame was tubular steel. There followed the Tugendhat chair, an armless affair of leather and steel that resembled a square S; the Brno chair with a steel frame and leather upholstery that looked like a curved S; and the Barcelona chair, an elegant armless leather and steel design in which the legs formed an X. The bottoms of all these chairs were uniformly wide, a feature that puzzled furniture experts until one of them asked Mies for an explanation. It was simple, he said; he had designed them with his own comfort in mind.

Mies did not receive wide public recognition in the United States until he was over fifty. Up to 1937 he lived in Aachen, Germany, where he had been born on March 27, 1886. Emigrating to Chicago, he had to wait for the postwar building boom before many of his designs were translated into actuality. At his death examples of his work were in Chicago, Pittsburgh, Des Moines, Baltimore, Detroit, Newark, New York, Houston, Washington, Mexico City, Montreal, Toronto, and West Berlin. All his buildings were dissimilar, although the same basic principles were employed in each. These principles centered on a demand for order, logic, and clarity. "The long path through function to creative work has only a single goal," he said, "to create order out of the desperate confusion of our time."

One Mies structure, counted among his outstanding works, is the thirty-eight story dark-bronze and pinkish-gray glass Seagram building on New York's Park Avenue between Fifty-second and Fifty-third Streets. Called by appreciative critics the city's most tranquil tower and "the most beautiful curtain-walled building in America," it emphasizes pure line, fine materials, and meticulous detailing outside and in. (Mies designed the room numbers, doorknobs, elevator buttons, bathroom fixtures, and mail chutes, as well as the furniture.) The building's grace is enhanced by its setting in a half-acre fountained plaza of pink granite. It was begun in 1955 and completed two years later at a cost of $35 million. It was, at the time, the city's most costly office building. Not everyone who gazed upon it or watched the aging of its extruded bronze was convinced of its beauty. Acerbic nonarchitectural critics pointed out that the tower rises 520 feet without setbacks and that it is unornamented. It is too sparse, they said. One critic likened it to an upended glass coffin. Those who worked in the building were put off at first by its floor-to-ceiling windows and the illusion of giving off into space that they created; but once they became adjusted to the sensation they did not mind looking out the windows.

The Seagram building ranked third in Mies's offhand list of his six favorites, chosen to illustrate his most notable concept—"Less is more." (By this Delphic utterance he meant achieving the maximum effect with the minimum of means.) First on the list was the Illinois Institute of Technology's Crown Hall. This is a single glass-walled room measuring 120 feet by 220 feet and spanned by four huge trusses. The structure appears to do no more than to enclose space, a feeling reinforced by its interior movable partitions. It was one of twenty buildings that Mies designed for the school's hundred-acre campus on Chicago's South Side. Crown Hall is as good an example as any of his "skin-and-bones architecture," a phrase he once used to describe his point of view. The Chicago Federal Center, his largest complex of high- and low-rise buildings, was his second favorite. He considered its symmetry symbolic of his lifelong battle against disorder.

Another Chicago creation was fourth—two twenty-six-story apartment house towers at 860 and 880 Lake Shore Drive that overlook Lake Michigan. The facades are all glass. Tenants had to accept the neutral gray curtains that were uniform throughout the buildings and that provided the only means of seeking privacy and excluding light. No other curtains or blinds were permitted lest they mar the external appearance. He was also the architect of the Promontory Apartments in Chicago, in which he used brick and glass in an exposed frame. His fifth favorite was a project for a Chicago convention hall, a place for fifty thousand persons to gather in unobstructed space under a trussed roof 720 feet square. The project, however, never materialized. The final pet on the architect's list was the since-destroyed German Pavilion at the 1929 International Exposition at Barcelona. It was, one critic said, "a jewel-case structure employing the open planning first developed by Frank Lloyd Wright that combined the richness of bronze, chrome, steel, and glass with free-standing walls."

In addition to the Seagram building, the architect was represented in the New York area by Pavilion Apartments and Colonnade Apartments, both in Colonnade Park, Newark. He also devised a master plan for a twenty-one-acre development in New Haven, Connecticut. His last building, the National Gallery in Berlin, opened in September 1968. It is a templelike glass box set atop a larger semibasement, and serves as a museum. Although many accolades were bestowed on Mies for these and other works, there were also brickbats. "Unsparing," "grim," the work of "barren intellectualism," and "brutal in its destruction of individual possessions and the individual," were some of the phrases his detractors used. "Less is less," they also said, turning his aphorism against him.

Ludwig Mies, who added the van der Rohe from his mother's name because of its sonority, learned the basics of architecture from his father, a German master mason and stonecutter, and from studying the medieval churches in his native Aachen (Aix-la-Chapelle). He attended trade school and became a draftsman's apprentice before setting off for Berlin at the age of nineteen to take instruction from Bruno Paul, Germany's leading furniture designer. Two years later, eager to experiment, he built his first house, a wooden structure on a sloping site in suburban Berlin; its style, oddly, harked back to the eighteenth century. Then, in 1909, he apprenticed himself to Peter Behrens, a German architect of modernist views who had also taught Le Corbusier and Walter Gropius; and he was put in charge of carrying out Behrens's design for a new German embassy building in St. Petersburg. Going to the Netherlands three years later, he designed a house near the Hague for Mrs. H. E. L. J. Kröller, the well-to-do owner of the Kröller-Muller collection of modern paintings. Although the house was never built, its architect absorbed significant lessons in design by erecting a full-scale canvas and wood mockup on the site.

Mies returned to Berlin in 1913 and opened a professional office, but with the outbreak of World War I in 1914 his life was disarrayed; for four years he was attached to the German Army, designing and building bridges and roads in the Balkans. When peace arrived at last, he returned to civilian life as the architectural director of the Novembergruppe, an organization devoted to promoting modern art; and in his own work he was marked out for employing brick. Often he would go to the kilns to select one by one the bricks he fancied. He used brick for the monument (now destroyed) to Karl Liebknecht and Rosa Luxemburg, the German Communist leaders; for suburban villas for wealthy businessmen; and for low-cost housing for the city of Berlin.

At times, friends recalled, he would describe with unrestrained enthusiasm the quality of brick and stone, their texture, pattern, and color. "Now a brick, that's really something," he once remarked. "That's really building, not paper architecture." For him the material was always the beginning. He used to talk of primitive building methods, where he discerned the "wisdom of whole generations" stored in every stroke of an ax, every bite of a chisel. For his students in the United States and Germany it meant that they were obliged to learn the fundamentals of building before they could start to consider questions of design. He taught them, first, how to build with wood, then stone, then brick, and finally with concrete and steel. Each material had specific characteristics that had to be understood. "New materials are not necessarily superior," he would say. "Each material is only what we make it."

This point of view matured from 1926 to 1932, when he was first vice-president of the Deutscher Werkbund, formed to integrate art and industry in design. He directed the group's second exposition, the Weissenhof housing project erected in Stuttgart in 1927, which, in addition to houses designed by Mies, included examples of the work of Gropius, Le Corbusier, Oud, Stam, Behrens, Hilberseimer, Polzig, and Tauts. Mies's contribution was a four-story apartment complex built around a steel skeleton—the basic design principle of all his American apartment buildings. The peak achievements of his European career were the German Pavilion he designed for the Barcelona exposition of 1929 and the Tugendhat house in Brno, Czechoslovakia, in 1930. A. James Speyer, a critic for *Art News,* extolled them both as "among the most important buildings of contemporary architecture and the most beautiful of our generation." The pavilion consisted of a rectangular slab roof supported by steel columns, beneath which free-standing planes of Roman travertine, marble, onyx, and glass of various hues were so placed as to create the feeling of space beyond. The Tugendhat house permitted space to flow in a similar fashion.

In 1930 Mies took over direction of the Bauhaus, a laboratory of architecture and design in Dessau, Germany. It was closed three years later after the Nazis attacked the architect as "degenerate" and "un-German." At the urging of Philip C. Johnson, the New York architect and a close friend, he emigrated to the United States to head the School of Architecture at the Armour (now Illinois) Institute of Technology in Chicago. He retired from the post in 1958. He designed a new plant for the institute, but only a dozen of the research, laboratory, and residence buildings of the twenty from his drawing board were completed. Crown Hall was among them.

As a teacher Mies did not deliver formal lectures, but worked, seminar fashion, with groups of ten or twelve students. His method of teaching, according to a former student, was "almost tacit." "He was never wildly physically active, and he did not do much talking," this student recalled, adding that Mies, sitting Buddhalike, would frequently puff through a whole cigar before commenting on a student sketch. Abandoning the Beaux Arts system based on competition for prizes, he sternly told his students, "First you have to learn something; then you can go out and do it." He was not one to tolerate self-expression among his students. One of them once asked him about it. Silently he handed the student a pencil and paper and told her to write her name. This done, he said, "That's for self-expression. Now we get to work." Another former student thought of him as a "great teacher because he subjects himself to an extraordinary discipline in thinking and in his way of working, and because what he is teaching is very clear to him."

Mies himself was quite confident of his influence. "I don't know how many students we have had," he said a couple of years before his death, "but you need only ten to change the cultural climate if they are good."

In the years that he was with the institute and later, he was a constantly busy designer. Ideas and projects streamed from his Chicago office, some of them never built but all of them provocative. Nevertheless, he worked slowly, using sketch pads to draft his ideas. The result was not a rough drawing but a precise delineation, with each detail filled in. In his later years, when he was slowed by arthritis, he worked mostly at home. He would frequently sit so wrapped in thought that he neglected to answer the telephone. He was also unresponsive to letters.

Despite seclusiveness during the day, Mies liked company in the evening, especially that of old friends. Talking in German-accented English, he could be the life of a party. His shyness was with strangers, and then it was painful, for he could usually find nothing to say. They came away persuaded that he was unpersonable. He was well-to-do, but not wealthy. He received the usual architect's fee of six percent of the gross cost of a building, but he was not a very careful manager of his income, according to his friends. He was considered generous with his office staff and on spending for designs that were unlikely to see the light of day. He received three noteworthy honors—the Presidential Freedom Medal and the gold medals of the Royal Institute of British Architects and of the American Institute of Architects. He was also a member of the National Institute of Arts and Letters.

❖
―――――――――――――――――――――――――

HO CHI MINH

Among twentieth-century revolutionary leaders, Ho Chi Minh was remarkable both for the tenacity and patience with which he pursued his goal of Vietnamese independence and for his success in blending communism with nationalism. By the time of his death in Hanoi at the age of seventy-nine, he had demonstrated how an ideal—in his case national freedom—could seize a man and become his whole life; he had also demonstrated how it was possible to lay the foundations for the defeat of a mighty imperial invader by sapping its technological military superiority through popular-based guerrilla warfare. From his youth he espoused freedom for the French colony of Vietnam; he persevered through years when his chances of attaining his objective were so remote as to seem ridiculous; he went on to organize the defeat of the French in 1954 in the historic battle of Dienbienphu, a triumph of guerrilla strategy; his ultimate triumph, which he did not live to witness, was the discomfiting of the United States and its puppet regime in southern Vietnam, an epic event that took place in 1975 after more than twenty years of difficult struggle.

In the war, in which the United States became increasingly involved, especially after 1964, Ho maintained an exquisite balance in his relations with the Soviet Union and the People's Republic of China. These Communist countries, at ideological sword's points, were his principal suppliers of foodstuffs and war goods. It was a measure of his diplomacy that he kept on friendly terms with each.

To the nineteen million people north of the seventeenth parallel and to other millions below it, the small, frail, aged-ivorylike figure of Ho, with his long ascetic face, goatee, sunken cheeks, and luminous eyes, was a patriarch, the George Washington of his nation. Although his name was not attached to public squares, buildings, factories, airports, or monuments, his magnetism was undoubted, as was the affection that the average citizen had for him. He was universally called "Uncle Ho," a sobriquet also used in the North Vietnamese press. Before the exigencies of war confined him to official duties, he regularly visited villages and towns; simply clad, he was especially fond of dropping into schools and chatting with the children. Westerners who knew him were convinced that, whatever his guile in larger political matters, there was no pose in his expressions of feeling for the common people. Indeed, his personal popularity was such that it was generally conceded, even by his political foes, that Vietnam would have been unified under his leadership had the countrywide elections, pledged at Geneva, taken place. As it was, major segments of South Vietnam were effectively controlled by the National Liberation Front despite the presence of hundreds of thousands of American troops.

Intelligent, resourceful, dedicated, he created a favorable impression on many of those who dealt with him. One such was

Harry Ashmore of the Center for Democratic Studies, former editor of *The Arkansas Gazette.* Ashmore and William C. Baggs, editor of *The Miami News,* were among the last Americans to talk with Ho at length when they visited Hanoi in early 1967. The chief of state conversed with the two men in the Presidential Palace (the former governor general's residence), in the servants' quarters, in which he lived. "Ho was a courtly, urbane, highly sophisticated man with a gentle manner and without personal venom," Ashmore recalled. At the meeting he was dressed in his characteristic high-necked white pajama type of garment, called a cu-nao, and he wore open-toed rubber sandals. He chain-smoked American-made Salems. Their hour-long conversation started out in Vietnamese, Ashmore said, but soon shifted to English. Ho astonished Ashmore by his adeptness in English, which was one of several languages—the principal others were French and Russian—in which he was fluent. At one point he reminded Ashmore and Baggs that he had once been in the United States. "I think I know the American people," he said, "and I don't understand how they can support their involvement in this war. Is the Statue of Liberty standing on her head?"

This was a rhetorical question that he also posed to other Americans in an effort to point up what to his mind was an inconsistency: a colonial people who had gained independence in a revolution were fighting to suppress the independence of another colonial people.

Ho's knowledge of American history was extensive, and he put it to advantage in the summer of 1945 when he was writing the Declaration of Independence of the Democratic Republic of Vietnam. He remembered much of the American Declaration of Independence, but not its precise wording. From an American military mission then working with him he tried in vain to obtain a copy of the document, and when none could supply it, Ho paraphrased it from recollection. Thus his declaration begins, "All men are created equal; they are endowed by their Creator with certain unalienable Rights; among these are Life, Liberty, and the pursuit of

Happiness." After explaining that this meant that "all the peoples on the earth are equal from birth, all the peoples have a right to live, to be happy and free," he went on to enumerate, in the manner of the American declaration, the grievances of his people and to proclaim their independence.

Apart from Americans, Ho struck a spark with many others who came in contact with him over the years. "Extraordinarily likable and friendly" was the description of Jawaharlal Nehru, the Indian leader. Paul Mus, the French orientalist who conducted political talks with Ho in 1946 and 1947, found him an "intransigent and incorruptible revolutionary, in the manner of Saint-Just." A French naval commander who observed the slender Vietnamese for the three weeks he was a ship's passenger concluded that he was an "intelligent and charming man who is also a passionate idealist entirely devoted to the cause he has espoused," and a man with "naive faith in the politico-social slogans of our times and, generally, in everything that is printed."

Ho was an enormously pragmatic Communist, a doer rather than a theoretician. His speeches and articles were brought together in a four-volume *Selected Works of Ho Chi Minh* issued in Hanoi between 1960 and 1962. The late Bernard B. Fall, an American authority on Vietnam, published a collection of these in English in 1967 under the title *Ho Chi Minh on Revolution*. They are simply and clearly worded documents, most of them agitational or polemical in nature and hardly likely to add to the body of Marxist doctrine.

Like Mao Tse tung, Ho composed poetry, some of it considered quite affecting. One of his poems, written when he was a prisoner of the Chinese Nationalists in 1942–43, is called "Autumn Night" and reads in translation:

In front of the gate, the guard stands with his rifle.
Above, untidy clouds are carrying away the moon.
The bedbugs are swarming around like army tanks on maneuvers,
While the mosquitoes form squadrons, attacking like fighter planes.

My heart travels a thousand li toward my native land.
My dream intertwines with sadness like a skein of a thousand
   threads.
Innocent, I have now endured a whole year in prison.
Using my tears for ink, I turn my thoughts into verses.

Ho's rise to power and world eminence is not a fully documented story. On the contrary, its details are imprecise at some crucial points. This led at one time to the suspicion that there were two Hos, a notion that was discounted by the French Sûreté when they compared photographs of the early and the late Ho. One explanation for the confusion is that Ho used about a dozen aliases, of which Ho Chi Minh (Ho, the Shedder of Light) was but one. Another was Ho's own reluctance to disclose biographical information. "You know, I am an old man, and an old man likes to hold on to his little mysteries," he told Fall. "Wait until I'm dead," he continued, with a twinkle. "Then you can write about me all you want." Nonetheless, before he left Hanoi Fall received a brief, unsigned summary of Ho's life "obviously delivered on the old man's instructions."

Despite Ho's apparent self-effacement, he did have a touch of personal vanity. Fall recalled having shown the Vietnamese leader a sketch of him by Mrs. Fall. "Yes, that is very good. That looks very much like me," he said. He took a bouquet of flowers from a nearby table and, handing it to Fall, said, "Tell her for me that the drawing is very good and give her the bouquet and kiss her on both cheeks for me."

Although there is some uncertainty over Ho's birth date, the most reliable evidence indicates that he was born May 19, 1890, in Kimlien, a village in Nghe-An Province in central Vietnam. Many sources give his true name as Nguyen Ai-Quoc, or Nguyen the Patriot. However, Wilfred Burchett, the Australian-born correspondent who knew Ho well, believes (and it is now generally accepted) that Ho's birth name was Nguyen Van Thanh, or Nguyen Who Will Be Victorious. He was said to be the youngest of three children. His elder brother died in 1950 and his sister in

1953. His father, who lived into the 1930's, was only slightly better off than the rice peasants of the area, but he was apparently a man of some determination, for by rote learning he passed mandarinal examinations that gave him a job in the imperial administration just when the French were taking over. An ardent nationalist, the father refused to learn French, the language of the conquerors, and joined anti-French secret societies. Young Ho got his first underground experience as his father's messenger in an anti-French network. Shortly, the father lost his government job and became a healer, dispensing traditional Oriental potions. Ho's mother was believed to have been of peasant origin, but he never spoke of her.

He received his basic education from his father and from the village school, going on to a few years of high school at the Lycée Quoc-Hoc in the old imperial capital of Hué. That institution, founded by the father of Ngo Dinh Diem, was designed to perpetuate Vietnamese national traditions. It had a distinguished roster of graduates that included Vo Nguyen Giap, the brilliant guerrilla general, and Pham Van Dong, who became the premier of Vietnam. Ho left the school in 1910 without a diploma and taught, briefly, at a private institution in a South Annam fishing town. It was while he was there, according to now accepted sources, that he decided to go to Europe. As a step toward that goal, he went in the summer of 1911 to a trade school in Saigon, where he learned the duties of a kitchen boy and pastry cook's helper, skills in demand by Europeans of that day. (His training, incidentally, gave him an epicure's palate, which he liked to indulge, and an ability to whip up a tasty dish, which he delighted to do when he could.) For the immediate moment, though, his training enabled him to sign aboard the *Latouche-Treville* as a kitchen boy, a job so menial that he worked under an alias, Ba. In his travels, he visited Marseilles and ports in Africa and North America. Explaining the crucial significance of these voyages for Ho's education as a revolutionary, Fall wrote in *The Two Vietnams:* "His contacts with the white colonizers on their home grounds shattered any idea of his illusions as to their 'superiority,' and his association with sailors from

Brittany, Cornwall, and the Frisian Islands—as illiterate and superstitious as the most backward Vietnamese rice farmer—did the rest. Ho still likes to tell the story of the arrival of his ship at an African port where, he claims, natives were compelled to jump into the shark-infested waters to secure the moorings of the vessels and were killed by the sharks under the indifferent eyes of passengers and crew. But his contacts with Europe also brought him the revelation of his own personal worth and dignity; when he went ashore in Europe in a Western suit, whites, for the first time in his life, addressed him as 'monsieur,' instead of using the deprecating 'tu,' reserved in France for children, but used in Indochina by Frenchmen when addressing natives, no matter how educated."

In his years at sea, Ho read widely—Shakespeare, Tolstoy, Marx, Zola. He was even then, according to later accounts, an ascetic and something of a Puritan, who was offended when prostitutes clambered aboard his ship in Marseilles. "Why don't the French civilize their own people before they pretend to civilize us?" he is said to have remarked. (Ho, incidentally, is believed to have been a bachelor, although the record on this point is far from clear.)

With the advent of World War I, he went to live in London, where he worked as a snow shoveler and as a cook's helper under Escoffier, the master chef, at the Carlton Hotel. Escoffier, it is said, promoted Ho to a job in the pastry kitchen and wanted to teach him the art of cuisine. The twenty-four-year-old Vietnamese was more interested in politics. He joined the Overseas Workers Association, composed mostly of Asians, and agitated, among other things, for Irish independence. Sometime during the war, he gave up the Carlton's kitchen for the sea and journeyed to the United States. He is believed to have lived in Harlem for a while. Ho himself often referred to his American visit, although he was hazy about the details. According to his close associate, Pham Van Dong, what impressed Ho in the United States were "the barbarities and ugliness of American capitalism, the Ku Klux Klan mobs, the lynching of Negroes." Out of his American experiences came a pamphlet, issued in Moscow in 1924, called *La Race Noire* (The

Black Race), which assailed racial practices in America and Europe.

About 1918 Ho returned to France and lived in a tiny flat in the Montmartre quarter of Paris, eking out a living by retouching photos under the name of Nguyen Ai-Quoc. He subsisted on a diet of rice, sausage, and fish as he made friends in the French Socialist party and among the thousands of Vietnamese exiles in the city. At the Versailles Peace Conference of 1919, he emerged as a self-appointed spokesman for his native land. Seeing in Woodrow Wilson's proposal for self-determination of the peoples the possibility of Vietnam's independence, Ho, dressed in a hired black suit and bowler hat, traveled to the Palace of Versailles to present his case. He was, of course, not received, although he offered a program for Vietnam. Its proposals did not include independence, but basic freedoms and equality between the French rulers and the native population.

Whatever hopes he may have held for French liberation of Vietnam were destroyed in his mind by the failure of the Versailles Conference to settle colonial issues. His faith was transferred to Socialist action. Indeed, his first recorded speech was at a congress of the French Socialist party in 1920, and it was a plea, not for world revolution but "against the imperialists who have committed abhorrent crimes on my native land." He bid the party "act practically to support the oppressed natives." At this congress he became, fatefully, a founding member of the French Communist party because he considered that the Socialists were equivocating on the colonial issue, whereas the Communists were willing to promote national liberation. "I don't understand a thing about strategy, tactics, and all the other big words you use," he told the delegates, "but I understand well one single thing: the Third International concerns itself a great deal with the colonial question. Its delegates promise to help the oppressed colonial peoples to regain their liberty and independence. The adherents of the Second International have not said a word about the fate of the colonial areas."

A similar pragmatism was evident in an article he wrote in

1960, "The Path Which Led Me to Leninism," that traced the roots of his communism. In it he said: "At first patriotism, not yet communism, led me to have confidence in Lenin, in the Third International. Step by step, along the struggle, by studying Marxism-Leninism parallel with participation in practical activities, I gradually came upon the fact that only socialism and communism can liberate the oppressed nations and the working people throughout the world from slavery."

With his decision to join the Communists, Ho's career took a marked turn. For one thing, he became the French party's resident expert on colonial affairs and edited *La Paria* (The Outcast), the weekly paper of the Intercolonial Union, which he was instrumental in founding in 1921. This group was a conglomeration of restless Algerian, Senegalese, West Indian, and Asian exiles in Paris who were united by a fervid nationalism and, to a lesser extent, by a common commitment to communism. For another thing, the fragile-looking Ho became an orator of sorts, traveling about France to speak to Vietnamese soldiers and war workers who were awaiting repatriation. It was a stimulating departure for a book-oriented revolutionary. And for a third thing, he gravitated to Moscow, then the nerve center of world communism. He went there first in 1922 for the Fourth Comintern Congress, where he met Lenin and became a member of the Comintern's Southeast Asia bureau. By all accounts, he was vocal and energetic, helping to organize the Krestintern, or Peasant International, for revolutionary work among colonial peoples and meeting all the reigning Communists.

After a brief sojourn in France, Ho was back in Moscow, his base for many years thereafter. He attended the University of the Toilers of the East, receiving formal training in Marxism and the techniques of agitation and propaganda. Then (and later) he steered clear of intraparty doctrinal disputes, and this probably saved his life in the Stalinist purges of the thirties.

Following his studies in Moscow, Ho was dispatched to Canton, China, in 1925 as an interpreter for Michael Borodin, one of the leaders of the Soviet mission to help Chiang Kai-shek, then in Communist favor as an heir of Sun Yat-sen. Once in Canton, Ho set about spreading the spirit of revolution in the Far East. He organized Vietnam refugees into the Vietnam Revolutionary Youth Association and set up the League of Oppressed Peoples of Asia, which soon became the South Seas Communist Party, the forerunner of various national Communist groups including Ho's own Indochinese Communist party of 1930. For two years, until July 1927, when Chiang turned on his Communist allies, Ho sent apt Vietnamese to Chiang's military school at Whampoa while conducting a crash training course in political agitation for his compatriots. Some of the best of them he sent to Moscow for more advanced schooling. One of his students and a graduate from Whampoa was Pham Van Dong, who remained loyal to his preceptor. But there were those who faltered and many of these, it is said, were picked up and liquidated by French colonial agents in Vietnam. His critics have charged that this was his way of dealing with defectors.

Following the break between Chiang and the Communists, Ho fled to Moscow by way of the Gobi. His life immediately thereafter is not clearly known, but it is believed that he lived in Berlin for a time (he spoke some German and seemed to know the geography of Berlin) and traveled in Belgium, Switzerland, and Italy, using a variety of aliases and passports. After 1928 he turned up in eastern Thailand, disguised as a shaven-headed Buddhist monk. He traveled among Vietnamese exiles and organized political groups and published newspapers that were smuggled over the border into Vietnam. In 1930, on advice from the Comintern, he was instrumental in settling the vexatious disputes that had arisen among Communists in Indochina and in organizing the Indochinese Communist party, which later became the Vietnamese Communist party and, still later, the Vietnamese Workers party.

In that same year a peasant rebellion, which the Communists backed, erupted in Vietnam. On its suppression by the French, Ho was sentenced to death in absentia. At the time he was in a British jail in Hong Kong, having been arrested there in 1931 for subversive activities. The French sought his extradition, but he argued that he was a political refugee not subject to extradition. The case, which was handled in London by Sir Stafford Cripps in a plea to the Privy Council, was decided for Ho. He was released, and fled Hong Kong in disguise (this time as a Chinese merchant) and made his way back to Moscow. There he attended Communist schools—the Institute for National and Colonial Questions and the celebrated Lenin School. He was, however, back in China in 1938, now as a communications operator with Mao Tse-tung's renowned Eighth Route Army. Subsequently, he found his way south and entered Vietnam in 1940 for the first time in thirty years.

The timing was a master stroke, for the Japanese, virtually unopposed, had taken effective control of the Indochina peninsula and the French administrators, most of them Vichy adherents, agreed to cooperate with the Japanese. With great daring and imagination, Ho took advantage of World War II to piece together a coalition of Vietnamese nationalists and Communists into what was called the Viet Minh, or Independence Front. The Viet Minh created a ten-thousand-man guerrilla force, "Men in Black," that battled the Japanese in the jungles with notable success.

Ho's actions projected him onto the world scene as the leading Vietnamese nationalist and as an ally of the United States against the Japanese. "I was a Communist," he said then, "but I am no longer one. I am a member of the Vietnamese family, nothing else." In 1942 Ho was sent to Kunming, China, for military training, reportedly at the request of his American military aides. He was arrested there by Chiang Kai-shek's men and jailed until September 1943, when he was released, it has been said, by American request. On his release, according to Fall, Ho cooperated with a Chinese Nationalist general in forming a wide Vietnamese freedom group. One result of this was that in 1944 Ho accepted a portfolio in the Provisional Republican Government of Vietnam.

That government was largely a paper affair, but it permitted him to court vigorously the American Office of Strategic Services. Thus, when his Viet Minh took over Hanoi in 1945, senior American military officials were in his entourage. It was in this period that he took the name of Ho Chi Minh.

With the end of World War II, Ho proclaimed the independence of Vietnam, but it took nine years for his declaration to become effective. First, under the Big Three agreement of Potsdam, the Nationalist Chinese occupied Hanoi and the northern sector of Vietnam. Second, the French (in British ships) arrived to reclaim Saigon and the southern segment of the country. And third, Ho's nationalist coalition was strained under pressure of these events.

Forming a new guerrilla force around the Viet Minh, Ho and his colleagues, according to most accounts, dealt summarily with dissidents unwilling to fight in his fashion for independence. Frequent assassinations were reported. Meanwhile, as the Chinese withdrew from the North and the French advanced from the South, Ho negotiated with the French to save his nationalist regime. In a compromise that he worked out in Paris in 1946, he agreed to let the Democratic Republic of Vietnam become a part of the French union as a free state within the Indochina federation. The French recognized Ho as chief of state and promised a plebiscite in the South on the question of a unified Vietnam under him.

By the start of 1947, the agreement had broken down, and Ho's men were fighting the French army. The Viet Minh guerrillas held the jungles and the villages, the French the cities. For seven years the war raged as Ho's forces gathered strength, squeezing the French more and more. For most of this time Ho was diplomatically isolated, for he was not recognized by Communist China nor by the Soviet Union until his victory over the French was virtually assured. In an effort to shore up their political forces, the French resurrected Bao Dai, the Japanese puppet who held title as emperor. Corrupt and pleasure-loving, he soon moved with his mistresses to France, leaving a weak and splintered regime in Saigon. This, of course, proved no support for the French army, which was also sapped by General Giap's guerrilla tactics. Finally, on May 8, 1954, the French were decisively defeated at Dienbienphu. The Indochina War ended officially in July at a cost to the French of 172,000 casualties and to the Viet Minh of perhaps three times as many.

The cease-fire accord was negotiated on July 21, 1954, in Geneva. It represented far less than Ho's hopes. But by that time the United States was involved in Vietnam on the French side through $800 million a year in economic aid. Fear of Communist expansion in Asia dominated Washington, with Vice-President Richard M. Nixon saying, "If, to avoid further Communist expansion in Asia, we must take the risk of putting our boys in, I think the executive branch has to do it."

The Geneva accord divided Vietnam at the seventeenth parallel, creating a North and a South Vietnam. It removed the French from the peninsula and provided for all-Vietnam elections in 1956, the winner to take all the country. Although a party to the Geneva accord, the United States declined to sign it. On this ground, South Vietnam refused to hold the elections. Meanwhile, the United States built up its military mission in Saigon and its support of the Ngo Dinh Diem regime there as a counter to continued National Liberation Front guerrilla activity, which became pronounced after 1956. The front, technically independent of Ho Chi Minh in the North, increased its sway into the 1960's. It supplied itself from captured American arms and from matériel that came through from the North. Beginning in 1964, thousands of American troops were poured into South Vietnam to battle the Viet Cong and then to bomb North Vietnam. Various attempts were made to end the war, which by 1967 was clearly a conflict between the United States on the one hand and the people of South Vietnam and Ho's Democratic Republic of North Vietnam on the other. On several occasions Ho was said to be willing to discuss a settlement if the United States would halt its bombing of the North and deal also with the Viet Cong or the National Liberation

Front as a party to the war. Throughout, Ho was serenely confident of victory. In 1962, when the war was still a localized conflict between the South Vietnamese forces and eleven thousand American advisers and a smaller guerrilla force, he told a French visitor: "It took us eight years of bitter fighting to defeat you French and you knew the country and had some old friendships here. Now the South Vietnamese regime is well armed and helped by the Americans. The Americans are much stronger than the French, though they know us less well. So it perhaps may take ten years to do it, but our heroic compatriots in the South will defeat them in the end."

Ho was still confident in January 1967, when he talked with Ashmore and Baggs. "We have been fighting for our independence for more than twenty-five years," he told them, "and of course we cherish peace, but we will never surrender our independence to purchase a peace with the United States or any party." At the close of his conversation, he clenched his right fist and said emotionally, "You must know of our resolution. Not even your nuclear weapons would force us to surrender after so long and violent a struggle for the independence of our country."

NOVEMBER 18, 1969

---❖---

JOSEPH P. KENNEDY

With single-minded perseverance, Joseph Patrick Kennedy devoted himself to founding a family political dynasty. To that end he devoted an extraordinary talent for making money, a capacity for making the right friendships, and his unquestioned position as a paterfamilias. By his death in Hyannis Port, Massachusetts, at the age of eighty-one, he had indeed started a dynasty, only to see it all but obliterated by assassinations; to these he was a silent witness, having been rendered virtually speechless by a stroke in 1961. His final withered years were a tragic capstone to a life of aggressive upward mobility and the amassing of a fortune that totaled about $500 million, much of it acquired by shrewdness in short-term investments. As rich as he became, he tended to discount his wealth, saying, "The measure of a man's success is not the money he's made; it's the kind of family he's raised." As platitudinous as that sounds, Joseph Kennedy meant it with profound conviction, for he was a strong and forthright father who insisted upon contributing his own success drives to the development of his children. He valued power and realized that in American society politics was one important avenue to that goal.

Kennedy was candid about his own contribution. He had nurtured his eldest son, Joseph Jr., for a political career that he hoped would culminate in the White House; but the young man was killed in World War II. He then turned his attention to John, his second son. "I got Jack into politics, I was the one," he said in 1957 of his son, then a United States senator who hoped to become president. "I told him Joe was dead and that it was his responsibility to run for Congress. He didn't want to. He felt he didn't have the ability and he still feels that way. But I told him he had to."

"It was like being drafted," John F. Kennedy said later. "My father wanted his eldest son in politics. 'Wanted' isn't the right word. He demanded it. You know my father."

Later, with John in the White House and Robert, another son, appointed attorney general, Kennedy insisted that Edward M., his youngest son, have his share of public office, a senatorship from Massachusetts. He laid down the law in a conversation with the president and the attorney general: "You boys have what you want and everybody worked to help you get it. Now it's Teddy's turn. I'm going to see that he gets what he wants." In 1962 Edward got the Senate seat, but without the active participation of his father, who had been paralyzed by a stroke in December 1961.

Kennedy's pride in his sons was immense. John's election to the presidency—he was the first Roman Catholic to sit in the White House—gave his father unexampled satisfaction. The beam on his face in photographs at the time reflected the sweet triumph he felt. Afterward, when his son was assassinated in November 1963, he met the tragedy with stoic fortitude. For the fulfillment of his family ambitions, he would have to look to Edward and to Robert, the elder surviving son, in whose election to the Senate from New York in 1964 Kennedy took pleasure. This was cut short on June 5, 1968, when Robert, only minutes after he had won the California primary for the Democratic presidential nomination, was shot by an assassin in a Los Angeles hotel.

Kennedy had nine children. Three of his four sons predeceased him, as did a daughter, Kathleen, who was killed in an air accident in 1948. Rosemary, another daughter, had been in an institution since the 1940's as mentally retarded. Of the three other daughters, Jean was married to Stephen Smith, later active in the Kennedy financial dealings; Eunice was married to Sargent Shriver, manager of the Kennedys' Merchandise Mart in Chicago and later director of the Peace Corps and the Office of Economic Opportunity, and ambassador to France; and Patricia was married to Peter Lawford, the British actor. They were divorced in February 1966.

Kennedy equaled his success as a dynast in the realm of finance. He enjoyed making money, and was very good at it. He coined millions in stock speculation, the movies, liquor importing, real estate, oil ventures, and corporate reorganizations. Sharp and canny, he was not primarily interested in industry and production, but rather in stocks and securities. Of these he was an astute analyst, so keen, in fact, that he developed a prescience of what the stock market would do. His exquisite sense of timing gave him an edge over many other speculators. In explaining his success in the stock market, Richard J. Whalen wrote in *The Founding Father:* "He mixed well in all kinds of company, against every background. He was equally at ease with hard-eyed manipulators like [Ben] Smith and Wall Street patricians like Jeremiah Milbank, with corporation bosses as different as Paramount's [Adolph] Zukor and GE's Owen D. Young, with bantering newspapermen and press lords like William Randolph Hearst, Colonel Robert R. McCormick, and Joseph M. Patterson. He could enjoy the companionship of celebrities at the Ziegfeld Roof and of roistering theatrical unknowns at Bertolotti's in Greenwich Village. Kennedy moved through many worlds, and only the keenest observer would detect the profound detachment of this gregarious man who belonged to no world but his own."

Although Kennedy was, in his heyday, a hail-fellow-well-met with important friends in corporate and financial and political positions, he was not accepted socially by the entrenched families. He was blackballed when he sought membership in the Cohasset Country Club in Massachusetts, which was run by Boston's old families; in New York he fared a little better, but he and his family were never really taken into the city's society, Catholic or Protestant. In Hollywood, where he passed time in the late 1920's, his status was higher, but he was still uncomfortable. He resented the doors closed against him, and he eventually took opulent refuge in Palm Beach, Cap d'Antibes on the Riviera, and Cape Cod.

His eagerness to make money was so strong that many observers considered him brusque and unfeeling in his use of economic power. As one example, shortly after buying control of the Keith-Albee-Orpheum theater chain in 1928, he responded to a business suggestion from E. F. Albee, the chain's titular president, by telling him: "Didn't you know, Ed? You're washed up, you're through."

At one time Kennedy harbored political ambitions for himself. He served with distinction as first chairman of the Securities and Exchange Commission; he supported President Franklin D. Roosevelt when other business leaders reviled him; he headed the Maritime Commission; but he lacked political gracefulness, and a sense of the public mood. These shortcomings were illustrated when he was named ambassador to Britain in 1938. There, during the crisis over Czechoslovakia at Munich, he made known his support of Prime Minister Neville Chamberlain's appeasement policy. "It is true," Kennedy said then, "that the democratic and dictator countries have important and fundamental divergencies of outlook. But there is simply no sense, common or otherwise, in letting these differences grow into unrelenting antagonism. After all, we have to live together in the same world, whether we like it or not." War, in his view, was a fearsome catastrophe. "Joe thought war was irrational and debasing," a confidant said. "War destroyed capital. What could be worse than that?"

In 1940, after war had broken out, he sought to explain his view in a letter to a friend in the United States. "I always believed that if England stayed out of war it would be better for the United States and for that reason I was a great believer in appeasement," he wrote. "I felt that if war came, that was the beginning of the end for everybody, provided it lasted for two or three years. I see no reason yet for changing my mind one bit." Meanwhile, he expressed somewhat similar views in public in the United States. "As you love America," he told one Boston audience in 1939, "don't let anything that comes out of any country in the world make you believe you can make a situation one whit better by getting into the war. There is no place in this fight for us."

These remarks caused Kennedy to lose prestige abroad and at home, for in the climate of those times his isolationism was unrealistic. He had misjudged the thrust of events and had voiced opinions that proved to be political liabilities not only to himself but also to his son John. After John began to rise in politics, his father's isolationism was pushed into the background. At the time there were whispers that he was anti-Semitic. These reports were based in part on his habit of referring in conversation to Jews as "sheenies" and "kikes." (He was, it was pointed out in his defense, equally inelegant about Italians—he called them "wops"—and the Irish—who were "micks" to him.) In part, the whispers were also based on documents in the Nazi archives, among them dispatches from Herbert von Dirksen, the German envoy in London. In one message allegedly covering a long talk with Ambassador Kennedy, von Dirksen wrote: "The Ambassador then touched upon the Jewish question. In this connection it was not so much the fact that we wanted to get rid of the Jews that was so harmful to us, but rather the loud clamor with which we accomplished this purpose." Kennedy denied the authenticity of the interview and said that the views attributed to him were "complete poppycock." In later years he was careful to criticize publicly Hitler's persecution of the Jews.

Joseph P. Kennedy's independence and his fierce will to succeed were bred into him as a child. His father, Patrick J. Kennedy, was born in an East Boston slum, but he became a "lace curtain" Irishman, with a comfortable income derived from ownership of saloons, a wholesale liquor business, and an interest in a bank. Patrick was determined that his son, who was born on September 6, 1888, should rise high in the world. With this in mind, he sent Joseph to Boston Latin School and to Harvard, schools that few Boston Irish Catholics attended in those years. There the young man experienced the hauteur of the established families. He got to know the well-connected at Harvard (his class was 1912), but he was not a member of the best clubs. (Kennedy's connections with the university were never cordial, and they became positively frigid when he was turned down for an honorary degree later in life.) In addition to giving his son educational advantages that most Roman Catholic boys of his day did not enjoy, Patrick Kennedy endowed Joseph with a political heritage that was to come in handy for his sons. Patrick was a power in Boston politics, serving five terms as a state representative and one as a state senator. He was also a member of the famous Board of Strategy, the inner circle of Boston Irish ward leaders.

Quiet-spoken, Patrick had little in common temperamentally with the ebullient John F. (Honey Fitz) Fitzgerald, the maternal grandfather of the thirty-fifth President. In fact, Pat Kennedy found Honey Fitz, who served three terms in Congress and was mayor of Boston, a barely tolerable buffoon, much given to singing "Sweet Adeline." But the families were on social terms and, in 1914, Joseph P. Kennedy married Rose Fitzgerald, daughter of Honey Fitz.

Joseph was at that time a lanky youth with pale blue eyes and sandy-red hair who had showed business acumen by earning five thousand dollars operating a tourist-bus enterprise during summer vacations at Harvard. He told friends that he would be a millionaire before he was thirty-five. Within two years of his graduation he was president of a bank, the Columbia Trust Company, of which his father was a director. He and Mrs. Kennedy moved to Brookline, then a moderately fashionable suburb of Boston. The family expanded rapidly—five babies in six years, nine in all. John F., their second child, was born in the Brookline house on May 29, 1917. Shortly after his birth, the father accepted Charles M. Schwab's offer of a wartime executive job at the Bethlehem Steel Company's big Fore River plant in Quincy, Massachusetts. At the end of the war, he joined an investment banking firm in Boston. He foresaw the beginning of a wild financial boom and soon he was in Wall Street, trying his luck as a lone-wolf operator.

During the 1920's he dabbled in show business. He bought a chain of New England movie houses, got control of a small producing company, and finally flourished as a board chairman, special adviser, or reorganizer of five film, vaudeville, and radio companies: Paramount, Pathé, First National, Keith-Albee-Orpheum, and the Radio Corporation of America. He is said to have made $5 million in three years in the motion-picture business. In pursuit of his motion-picture ventures, Kennedy spent considerable time on the West Coast, leaving the day-to-day rearing of the family to his wife. It was she who ruled the children in her husband's name and saw to it that, absent though he was, he retained their respect.

Among the movie stars Kennedy backed was Gloria Swanson, whose banker, adviser, and intimate friend he was for several years. The end of their relationship was abrupt. "I questioned his judgment," Miss Swanson recalled. "He did not like to be questioned." Earlier, however, she had named her adopted son for him. All the while Kennedy was managing Miss Swanson's fortunes and making money in Hollywood, he was busy in Wall Street. When the crash came in 1929 he was largely out of the market, having taken his winnings early and in cash. "Only a fool," he said at the time, "holds out for the top dollar." He also made money in the crash itself by selling stocks short.

By 1916, his varied business interests were concentrated so exclusively in New York that he decided to uproot his family from the Boston scene. The move was made in style—a private railroad car brought the family from Brookline to their new home in the Riverdale section of the Bronx. Later the family moved to Bronxville, New York, where he purchased an eleven-bedroom redbrick mansion surrounded by spacious lawns. This was the family homestead until World War II.

Kennedy entered national politics in 1932. Through dealings with William Randolph Hearst, the publisher, he was of significant help in obtaining the Democratic presidential nomination for Roosevelt. Moreover, he gave $25,000 to his campaign fund, lent it $50,000, and raised $100,000 for it from friends. He had a hope of being named secretary of the treasury, but President Roosevelt chose him as the first chairman of the Securities and Exchange Commission. In this post he was responsible for writing the regulations that outlawed wild buying on margin and protected investors from sharp Wall Street practices. Just before taking the government job, he made a million dollars or more by cornering the important franchise for several Scotch whiskeys and a British gin. With repeal imminent, he obtained a government permit to import thousands of cases of his whiskey and gin for medicinal purposes. Kennedy warehouses were bulging and ready to flow when repeal came. The franchise had cost $118,000. He sold it thirteen years later for $8.5 million. Just before his appointment to the SEC, he was questioned by President Roosevelt in the presence of Raymond Moley, a New Deal adviser. In the conversation, Moley told Kennedy that "if anything in your career in business could injure the President, this is the time to spill it."

In his book, *After Seven Years,* Moley recalled what happened next: "Kennedy reacted precisely as I thought he would. With a burst of profanity he defied anyone to question his devotion to the public interest or to point to a single shady act in his whole life. The President did not need to worry about that, he said. What was more, he would give his critics—and here again the profanity flowed freely—an administration of the SEC that would be a credit to the country, the President, himself, and his family—clear down to the ninth child." And indeed, liberals who had protested his appointment were obliged to concede that he did a splendid job at the commission. He was a good administrator—conscientious, outspoken, thorough. He resigned in 1935, but was recalled to Washington as chairman of the Maritime Commission, a post in which he served with distinction in an attempt to reorganize the nation's merchant navy.

In 1936, when many business leaders were joining the Liberty League to battle the New Deal, Kennedy supported Roosevelt's second-term bid, writing an effective tract, *I'm for Roosevelt,* that argued that the New Deal was saving the capitalist economic structure. His reward this time was the post of ambassador to the Court of St. James's. He was to represent the United States in London at one of the most crucial periods of Anglo-American relations—1938 through the outbreak of World War II and until his resignation in the fall of 1940. His honeymoon with the British press was short-lived. A chill also quickly developed between the ambassador and the White House. In London he had become a close and frequently consulted friend of Prime Minister Chamberlain and other leading appeasers of Hitler in the government—Sir Horace Wilson and Sir John Simon. Like them, he felt that Munich assured "peace in our time." He made a widely quoted speech at the British Navy League dinner in 1938 in which he said that the world was big enough for the democracies and the dictatorships and there was no reason why they couldn't get along together without war.

President Roosevelt had not yet taken an open stand against the Munich agreement, but he found Kennedy's words hard to swallow. Shortly after the Navy League speech, the ambassador was in the news again with a plan to remove 600,000 Nazi-persecuted Jews from Germany and resettle them in sparsely populated parts of the world. In Washington, President Roosevelt and Secretary of State Cordell Hull, clearly annoyed, said they knew nothing of the Kennedy plan.

The war years were grim for the Kennedys. Kennedy's eldest son and namesake went to war as a Navy pilot, and was killed when his plane exploded over the English Channel on August 12, 1944. His death cut off a political career that had begun in 1940 when he was a twenty-five-year-old delegate to the Democratic National Convention. Joseph Kennedy was emotionally shattered, for at that time his son John, also a Navy lieutenant, was in Chelsea Naval Hospital, Boston, recovering from severe injuries suffered when a Japanese destroyer rammed his PT boat in the Solomon Islands. Only a few weeks after the death of Joseph Jr., Kennedy lost his son-in-law, the Marquess of Hartington, the husband of Kathleen; he was killed while leading an infantry charge in Normandy. (Four years later Kathleen was killed in a plane crash in France.)

After the war, Kennedy concentrated on increasing his fortune by Texas oil investments and the purchase of real estate in New York, Palm Beach, and Chicago. He bought Chicago's Merchandise Mart, then the world's largest commercial building, from Marshall Field in 1945 for $12.5 million, putting up only $800,000 in cash, and promptly mortgaged it for $18 million. By the end of 1945 Kennedy owned real estate in New York with an assessed valuation of $15 million. His transactions were spectacular. He bought a property at Fifty-first Street and Lexington Avenue for $600,000 and sold it for $3,970,000; another at Forty-sixth Street and Lexington for $1.7 million, selling it for $4,975,000, and another at Fifty-ninth and Lexington for $1.9 million that skyrocketed in value to more than $5.5 million. As fast as he moved into real estate, he got his money out by mortgaging his properties to the hilt. Much of the money he made went into oil ventures offering depletion allowances for tax purposes. He joined syndicates backing wildcat wells, and although his luck ran hot and cold he managed to earn high profits. At least one of his enterprises served his acquired taste for haute cuisine; his behind-the-scenes financing of Henri Soulé's Le Pavillon restaurant in New York. The elegant eating place, which rapidly became celebrated for the perfection of its kitchen, rarely returned

---

big profits, but Kennedy was partial to it all the same. "I always wanted a restaurant," he said, "where I didn't have to make a fuss for a good table, good service, and good food."

In 1946, John F. Kennedy was persuaded to get into politics. A family council decided that he should make his debut in a race for the House of Representatives from the Eleventh Massachusetts District, which embraced Harvard University, slum areas, and middle-class Irish and Italian wards in Boston. At the time, the elder Kennedys were not legal residents of Massachusetts and John was not a registered Democrat, a qualification he met as the deadline was about to expire. The primary in June 1946 was crucial since the district was solidly Democratic. Ten aspirants sought the nomination, but only one had Joseph P. Kennedy for a father, whose command post was a suite in Boston's Ritz-Carlton Hotel. "I just called people," Kennedy said modestly in after years. "I got in touch with people I knew. I have a lot of contacts." Describing Kennedy's role in that campaign more accurately, Whalen wrote in *The Founding Father:* "The telephone was the instrument and symbol of Kennedy's power. That a man with his enormous wealth enjoyed influence was not unusual; but the scope of his influence was extraordinary. He knew precisely whom to call to move the levers of local political power. Jack's campaign had two separate and distinct sides. On display before the voters was the candidate, surrounded by clean-cut, youthful volunteer workers, the total effect being one of wholesome amateurism. At work on the hidden side of the campaign were the professional politicians whom Joe Kennedy had quietly recruited. In his hotel suite and other private meeting places, they sat with their hats on and cigars aglow, a hard-eyed, cynical band, brainstorming strategy."

The result was that John Kennedy's district was saturated with his name, and he himself went from door to door soliciting votes. His brothers and sisters also pitched in. Joseph Kennedy did not believe in leaving politics to chance; his cash outlay, according to Whalen, was $50,000. His son won easily. Once in office,

Representative Kennedy was reelected handily in 1948 and 1950. As early as 1949, however, John (and his father) had an eye on Henry Cabot Lodge's Senate seat, which would be up for contest in 1952. Every weekend John was in Massachusetts on speaking engagements in preparation for his campaign. "We're going to sell Jack like soap flakes," his father said. Again in 1952 Kennedy moved into the Ritz-Carlton, recruited campaign personnel, and worked out of the public view. How much he spent was never disclosed, but the cost of the Kennedy campaign was estimated to exceed $500,000.

The campaign against Lodge and his defeat had overtones for Kennedy. In 1916, Lodge's grandfather had barely beaten Fitzgerald, his wife's father. Moreover, since 1936, Lodge, the quintessence of brahminism, had defeated James M. Curley, Joseph Casey, and David I. Walsh, three popular Irish politicians who had sought the senatorship. A few weeks before the election *The Boston Post* switched support from Lodge to his opponent. Six years later a House investigating committee discovered that Joseph Kennedy had lent John Fox, owner of *The Post,* $500,000. The loan was made after the election and Kennedy insisted that it was "simply a commercial transaction."

This was a time, too, when Senator Joseph R. McCarthy, Republican of Wisconsin, was at the height of his power in Washington. Kennedy contributed to McCarthy's campaign. It was later alleged that one purpose of the contribution was to keep the senator from coming into Massachusetts and campaigning for Lodge. Whatever the truth of this, the fact was that McCarthy stayed out of Massachusetts. And John F. Kennedy suppressed any faint urge he might have had to attack McCarthy.

But when he ran for president in 1960 his father was definitely an albatross. At the Democratic convention in Los Angeles, supporters of Adlai E. Stevenson charged that Joseph P. Kennedy had attempted to buy the nomination for his son and had tried to influence delegates, notably from New York and New Jersey. Eleanor Roosevelt, who had never liked Joseph Kennedy, wondered in public about the father's influence on the son. And just a few hours before John won the nomination, Senator Lyndon B. Johnson of Texas, a leading contender, made a bitter attack on the father. "I was never any Chamberlain umbrella policy man," he said. "I never thought Hitler was right." If the Johnson slur angered Senator Kennedy, political expediency dictated an overnight healing of wounds. Next day he said he wanted Johnson as his running mate and, to the astonishment of many, Johnson accepted.

The naive idea that John Kennedy seldom, if ever, agreed with "Old Joe" on political issues was carefully nurtured by the Democrats in the campaign and by the candidate himself. "Dad is a financial genius, all right," his son once said, "but in politics he is something else." Joseph Kennedy was more than three thousand miles from American shores, in a villa at Cap d'Antibes, when his son won the nomination. He stayed there most of the summer. He was back in his rambling beachfront home at Hyannis Port on Cape Cod in time for the election. "I just think it's time for seventy-two-year-old men like me to step aside and let the young people take over," he told a reporter who hunted him out on the Riviera. Rose, his wife, had another explanation: "He has been rather a controversial figure all his life and he thinks it's easier for his sons if he doesn't appear on the scene."

He surfaced quickly when the election had been won. Shortly after Richard M. Nixon, the Republican candidate, had conceded, the Kennedys gathered for news photographers at Hyannis Port. The photos included a beaming Joseph Kennedy, sitting at the right of the new president. Subsequently, until his crippling stroke, he was prominent in photos and articles on the activities of the First Family at the White House, Palm Beach, and Cape Cod. Afterward, he lived in virtual seclusion either at Palm Beach or in Hyannis Port.

---❖---

BERTRAND RUSSELL

"Three passions, simple but overwhelmingly strong, have governed my life: the longing for love, the search for knowledge, and unbearable pity for the suffering of mankind." In those words Bertrand Arthur William Russell, the third Earl Russell, described the motive forces of his extraordinarily long—he was ninety-seven when he died in Wales—provocative, and complex life. Only one yearning, however, was fully satisfied, that for love, he said, and only when he was eighty and married to his fourth wife, Edith Finch, then a fifty-two-year-old American. Of his search for knowledge, he reflected, "a little of this, but not much, have I achieved." And as for pity: "Echoes of pain reverberate in my heart: Children in famine, victims tortured by oppressors, helpless old people a hated burden for their sons, and a whole world of loneliness, poverty, and pain make a mockery of what human life should be. I long to alleviate this evil, but I cannot, and I too suffer."

Russell's self-assessment scanted his lifelong passionate skepticism, which provided the basis for his intellectual stature. Possessing a mind of dazzling brilliance, he made significant contributions to mathematics and philosophy for which, alone, he would have been renowned. Two works, *The Principles of Mathematics* and *Principia Mathematica,* both published before World War I, helped to determine the direction of modern philosophy. Russell's name, as a result, was linked with those of such titans of modern thought as Alfred North Whitehead and Ludwig Wittgenstein. Largely for his role as a philosopher, Russell received the Nobel Prize for Literature in 1950. A year earlier, he had been named by King George VI to the Order of Merit, whose British membership is limited to twenty-four persons. These honors cast into strange relief the fact that in 1940 a New York State Supreme Court justice ruled him unfit to teach at City College in New York.

Unlike some generative thinkers, Russell epitomized the philosopher as a public figure. He was the Voltaire of his time, but lacked the Sage of Fernay's malice. From the beginning to the end of his active life, he engaged himself with faunlike zest in the great issues of the day—pacifism, rights for women, civil liberty, trial marriage, new methods of education, communism, the nuclear peril, and war and peace—for he was at bottom a moralist and a humanist. He set forth his views on moral and ethical matters in such limpidly written books as *Marriage and Morals, Education and the Social Order,* and *Human Society in Ethics and Politics.* He posed awkward questions and gave answers that some regarded as less than commonsensical. However, from his first imprisonment (as a pacifist in World War I) to his last huzzah of dissent (as a Zola-like accuser of the United States for its involvement in Vietnam) he scorned easy popularity and comfortable platitudes. He was, indeed, untamable, for he had a profound faith in the ultimate triumph of rationality, which he was certain he represented in undidactic fashion. "I don't think, taking it generally, that I have a dogmatic temperament," he insisted. "I am very skeptical about most things and I think that skepticism in me is deeper than positive statements. But, of course, if you get into propaganda you have to make positive statements."

His active involvement in causes (and the scores of positive declarations he made in their behalf) earned him a good deal of abuse and even ridicule. "England's wisest fool," was what his deriders said. Some of the severest criticism was directed at him for his condemnation of United States policy in Vietnam and for his attempts to show this country guilty of crimes against humanity there. Oddly, the criticism came not only from war partisans but also from the Soviet Union—a professed ally of North Vietnam—which Russell believed lacked staunchness because it was under the thumb of the United States. His idiosyncratic views on Vietnam stemmed from concern over the possibility of a nuclear conflict. Although he had once suggested the threat of a preventive nuclear war as a means to impose disarmament on the Soviet Union, his views sobered in the mid-fifties, and through the Committee of One Hundred in Britain he strove to arouse mass opposition to atomic weaponry. For his part in a demonstration against nuclear arms in London's Trafalgar Square in 1961, he went unrepentantly to jail. He was eighty-nine at the time. Later, at the height of the Cuban missile crisis in 1962, he dispatched letters to President John F. Kennedy and Premier Nikita S. Khrushchev, bidding them hold summit talks to avert war. Although he was curtly rebuffed by Mr. Kennedy, Russell was convinced that he had been instrumental in settling the dispute peacefully. *Unarmed Victory,* published in 1963, included this correspondence as well as letters he addressed to U Thant, Jawaharlal Nehru, and Chou En-lai, among others, about the Chinese-Indian border conflict, for the settlement of which he also took some credit.

No Communist ("I dislike communism because it is undemocratic and capitalism because it favors exploitation"), Russell was a relentless critic of the Soviet Union until after the death of Stalin in 1953. He then softened his attitude because he considered the post-Stalin leadership more amenable to world peace. In the Vietnam conflict he was certain that the United States acted from sinister economic and political motives—a grasping for Southeast Asian raw materials and an itching for war with China. He took the position that the United States, "the excessive power in the world," had escalated a war for which it bore "total responsibility." He compared American actions to the German occupation of Czechoslovakia, French terror in Algiers, and Soviet suppressions in Hungary. "Whatever happens," he told a visitor in his wafer-thin voice in the spring of 1967, "I cannot be a silent witness to murder or torture. Anyone who is a partner in this is a despicable individual. I am sorry I cannot be moderate about it. What I hope is that the Americans will arouse so much opposition that in their own minds they will start to think that it is not worth the trouble."

Convinced by data collected for him in Vietnam that the United States was committing war crimes, he organized and helped finance a mock trial of this country's leaders. The War Crimes Tribunal, presided over by Jean-Paul Sartre and Isaac Deutscher, met in Stockholm in May 1967, and issued a detailed indictment of United States military practices. Although the State Department discounted the testimony adduced by the tribunal, Russell was impressed by the evidence. The tribunal, in the end, caused only a minor stir, in part because the Communist press in Europe boycotted its proceedings.

Because of the stridency of his views, some charged that Russell was senile and a dupe of one of his secretaries, Ralph Schoenman, who was also for a time secretary of the Bertrand Russell Peace Foundation and active in the War Crimes Tribunal. Dispassionate reporters who traveled to Russell's home overlooking the winding Glaslyn River at Penrhyndeudraeth, Wales, found the frail philosopher very alert. As to Schoenman, he said, "You know, he is a rather rash young man, and I have to restrain him."

A gentle, even shy man, Russell was delightful as a conversationalist, companion, and friend. He was capable of a pyrotechnical display of wit, erudition, and curiosity, and he bubbled with anecdotes about the world's greats. Despite his title, he was "Bertie" to all. His charm, plus his assured position in the upper reaches of the British aristocracy, created for him a worldwide circle of friends. They were a heterogeneous lot, ranging over the years from Tennyson to Graham Greene to Sartre. They included philosophers such as Whitehead and Wittgenstein; scientists such as Einstein, Niels Bohr, and Max Born; writers such as P. G. Wodehouse, Joseph Conrad, D. H. Lawrence, E. M. Forster, T. S. Eliot, Ezra Pound, George Bernard Shaw, Maxim Gorky, and H. G. Wells; and political figures such as Sydney and Beatrice Webb, Harold Laski, Lenin, and Trotsky. They numbered in the hundreds, and Russell maintained a lively correspondence with them. Someone calculated, in fact, that he wrote one letter for every thirty hours of his life.

As a young man, gaunt and black-haired, Russell favored a flowing mustache and high, starched collars. In his autumnal years his spareness became frailty and, mustache discarded, he resembled a frost-famished sparrow. His glittering eyes and half-smile, combined with a shock of white hair, gave him the appearance of a sage, at once remote and kindly. It was a visage cartoonists delighted to draw.

Although he wrote a book about the mysteries of relativity, he humorously admitted that he could not change a light bulb or understand the workings of an automobile engine. However, he had a reason for everything. William Jovanovich, the American publisher, recalled that as a Harvard student he ate in a cafeteria where the food was cheap and not very good. "I would sit at a long public table where on many occasions also sat the philosopher Bertrand Russell," Jovanovich said. "One day I could not contain my curiosity. 'Mr. Russell,' I said, 'I know why I eat here. It is because I am poor. But why do you eat here?' 'Because,' he said, 'I am never interrupted.' "

In his last years Russell lived on liquids, a food concentrate, soups, puddings, tea, and seven double Red Hackle scotches a day—because an intestinal kink had been discovered when he was in his eighties and surgery was ruled inadvisable. He said that he had started drinking scotch as a pacifist in World War I. "King George V took the pledge because he thought he could save money and use the money to kill Germans, so I drank," he explained with a twinkle.

Russell's eccentricity, or, as he would have it, his independence of mind, was familial. He was born at Ravenscroft, Monmouthshire, on May 18, 1872. He was the youngest of three children of Lord Amerley and Katharine Stanley, daughter of Baron Stanley of Alderley. His paternal grandfather was John Russell, the first earl, who was twice prime minister and a leader in obtaining passage of the Reform Bill of 1832, which liberalized election to the House of Commons. One of Bertrand's maternal uncles became a Roman Catholic and a bishop in partibus infidelium; another became a Moslem and made the pilgrimage to Mecca; a third was a combative agnostic. His mother campaigned for votes for women and was a friend of Mazzini, the Italian revolutionary. His father was a freethinker. Together they shocked society by arranging a ménage à trois with the tutor of their elder son, Frank. Bertrand's mother died when he was two and his father about a year later. Lord Amerley left the guardianship of his sons (the third child, a daughter, had died) to the tutor and another man, both atheists. Their guardianship was broken, however, by Lord John Russell, and Bertrand was reared, after his grandfather's death in 1878, by the dowager Lady Russell, a woman of puritanical moral views. In the first volume of *The Autobiography of Bertrand Russell*, published in 1967, the philosopher candidly disclosed his mixed feelings for his grandmother. He thought her overly protective; on the other hand, he admired (and profited from) one of her favorite Bible texts, "Thou shalt not follow a multitude to do evil."

Russell's childhood, as he recalled it, was a lonely one, for most of his companions were adults and he had a succession of German and Swiss governesses. He was rescued, however, by geometry. "At the age of eleven, I began Euclid, with my brother [seven years his senior] as my tutor," he wrote. "This was one of the great events of my life, as dazzling as first love. I had not imagined there was anything so delicious in the world. From that moment until Whitehead and I finished *Principia Mathematica,* when I was thirty-eight, mathematics was my chief interest and my chief source of happiness." As an adolescent he read widely, advanced in mathematics, and speculated about religion. At seventeen he became convinced that there was no life after death, "but I still believed in God because the 'First Cause' argument appeared to be irrefutable," he wrote. "At the age of eighteen, however, I read [John Stuart] Mill's *Autobiography,* where I found a sentence to the effect that his father had taught him that the question 'Who made me?' cannot be answered since it immediately suggests the further question 'Who made God?' This led me to abandon the 'First Cause' argument and to become an atheist." Russell's *Autobiography* recites in detail the painful intellectual struggle that he waged with himself over theology, in the course of which he wrote out in his journal the argumentation that led to his conclusions.

Entering Trinity College, Cambridge, at eighteen, Russell was soon in the company of its brightest minds—G. Lowes Dickinson, G. E. Moore, John Maynard Keynes, Lytton Strachey, Charles Sanger, Theodore Davies, John McTaggart, and Whitehead. Among them he became less and less solemn while continuing his devotion to philosophy and mathematics. "What I most desired," he said, "was to find some reason for supposing mathematics true." Graduating with highest honors, he married Alys Pearsall Smith, a pretty American Quaker five years his senior. The marriage lasted from 1894 to 1921, but it was terminated in fact in 1901. "I went out bicycling one afternoon and suddenly, as I was riding along a country road, I realized that I no longer loved Alys," he recalled. Subsequently, Russell had several love affairs, including a celebrated liaison with the flamboyant Lady Ottoline Morrell and another with Lady Constance Malleson. His second marriage, in 1921, was to Dora Winifred; his third was to Patricia Helen Spence in 1936; and his fourth, to Edith Finch, took place sixteen years later. After Russell's first marriage he and his wife traveled on the Continent, where he studied economics and German social democracy, and thence to the United States, where he lectured on non-Euclidian geometry at Bryn Mawr College and the Johns Hopkins University. Meanwhile, he became a Fellow at Trinity.

The year 1900 was one of the most important of his life. In July he attended an international congress of philosophy in Paris and met Giuseppe Peano, an originator of symbolic logic. He devoured Peano's work. Recounting his exhilaration, he wrote, "For years I had been endeavoring to analyze the fundamental notions of mathematics, such as order and cardinal numbers. Suddenly, in the space of a few weeks, I discovered what appeared to be definite answers to the problems which had baffled me for years. And in the course of discovering these answers, I was introducing a new mathematical technique, by which regions formerly abandoned to the vagueness of philosophers were conquered for the precision of exact formulae."

In October he sat down to write *The Principles of Mathematics*, putting down two hundred thousand words in three months. Its purpose was "first to show that all mathematics follows from symbolic logic, and, secondly, to discover, so far as possible, what are the principles of symbolic logic, itself." With its publication in 1902, he plunged into an eight-year task of elucidating the logical deductions of mathematics that became *Principia Mathematica*. Reducing abstractions to paper was a grueling intellectual task. "Every morning I would sit down before a blank sheet of paper," he said. "Throughout the day, with a brief interval for lunch, I would stare at the blank sheet. Often when evening came it was still blank." As time went on and the agony of effort increased, Russell "often wondered whether I should ever come out of the other end of the tunnel in which I seemed to be." Several times he contemplated suicide, but he persevered. "My intellect never quite recovered from the strain," he said. "I have been ever since definitely less capable of dealing with difficult abstractions than I was before."

Principia Mathematica, one of the world's great rationalist works, cost Russell and Whitehead, his collaborator, fifty pounds each to publish. Despite its complexities, the book took the mystery out of mathematical knowledge and eliminated any connection that might have been supposed to exist between numbers and mysticism. The Russell philosophy, which he called "logical atomism," freed logical analysis from the tyranny of ordinary grammar or syntax. One illustration of the point is his theory of descriptions, which he first developed in 1905, and which has to do with the problem of the meaning of existence. He explained it this way: "Suppose I say 'The golden mountain does not exist,' and suppose you ask 'What is the golden mountain?' It would seem that, if I say 'It is the golden mountain,' I am attributing some sort of existence to it. 'The golden mountain does not exist' means there is no entity c such that 'x is golden and mountainous' is true when x is c, but not otherwise." Thus, he argued, "existence" can only be asserted of descriptions.

In the years when Russell was writing his imposing volumes, he continued his interest in social problems by participating in the woman suffrage movement and Fabian Society activities. World War I mobilized his concern for world affairs. A jingoist in the early stages of the Boer War, he later changed his mind and became an anti-imperialist; and in 1914 he was a pacifist, but not a pro-German. He wrote such books as *War—the Offspring of Fear, Principles of Social Recognition,* and *Justice in Wartime.* "But of all the evils of war," he wrote, "the greatest is the purely spiritual evil: the hatred, the injustice, the repudiation of truth, the artificial conflict." He was jailed for six months for his writings, spending his sentence writing and studying in a comfortable cell in Brixton prison.

His pacifism alienated many of his friends, and in his loneliness he entered into an intense love affair with the actress Colette

O'Niel. "Colette's love was a refuge to me, not from cruelty itself, which was inescapable, but from the agonizing pain of realizing that that is what men are," he recalled. "I became for the first time deeply convinced that puritanism does not make for human happiness," he said. "I became convinced that most human beings are possessed by a profound unhappiness venting itself in destructive rages, and that only through the diffusion of instinctive joy can a good world be brought into being."

After the war, he visited the Soviet Union and met Lenin, Trotsky, and Gorky. He expressed sympathy for the aims espoused by the Communists, but he also voiced misgivings about the Soviet regime. In *The Practice and Theory of Bolshevism,* published in 1920, he wrote: "I am compelled to reject bolshevism for two reasons: First, because the price mankind must pay to achieve communism by Bolshevik methods is too terrible; and secondly because, even after paying the price, I do not believe the result would be what the Bolsheviks profess to desire."

In the twenties, after his second marriage, the Russells established the Beacon Hill School to promote progressive education. Of the children there Russell wrote: "We allow them to be rude and use any language they like. If they want to call me or their teachers fools, they call us fools. There is no check on irreverence toward elders or betters." The school's concepts had a wide influence in Britain and the United States, where they were the foundation for scores of similar institutions and practices. However, Russell revised his views about Beacon Hill, saying in later years, "I feel several things were mistaken on the principles on which the school was conducted; young children in a group cannot be happy without a certain amount of order and routine."

Russell became the third Earl Russell in 1931 on the death of his brother, John Francis Stanley Russell. Two years later his wife, Dora, who had borne him two children, announced that her third child had been sired by another man. The couple's divorce suit was a nine days' wonder in the press. After the decree was granted, Russell married his secretary, Patricia Spence, and the couple had a child in 1937. With the rise of Hitler, Russell denounced Nazi methods, but opposed any steps that might lead to war. His attitude changed in 1939 after the German invasion of Czechoslovakia and Poland. In *Unarmed Victory* he explained his shift from pacifism: "I had hoped until after the time of Munich that the Nazis might be persuaded into not invading other countries. Their invasions proved that this hope was in vain, and at the same time evidence accumulated as to the utterly horrible character of their internal regime. The two factors led me reluctantly to the conviction that war against the Nazis was necessary."

Meantime, in 1938, Russell began an extended visit to the United States, teaching first at the University of Chicago and then at the University of California at Los Angeles. He also gave a lecture series at Harvard, and in 1949 he received an appointment to teach at tax-supported City College in New York. The step loosed a storm of protest from politicians now forgotten and from the Right Reverend William T. Manning, a bishop of the Episcopal Church in New York. The bishop charged that Russell was "a recognized propagandist against religion and morality and who specifically defends adultery." The registrar of New York County suggested that the philosopher be "tarred and feathered and run out of the country." A city councilman called him "a bum." Among other things that incensed critics was a sentence from *Education and the Social Order* that read: "I am sure that university life would be better, both intellectually and morally, if most university students had temporary childless marriages." Amid guffaws from the intellectual community, state Supreme Court Justice John E. McGeehan vacated the appointment on the ground that Russell was an alien and an advocate of sexual immorality. He said Russell would be occupying "a chair of indecency" at City College.

For a brief time Russell found himself publicly taboo. "Owners of halls refused to let them if I was to lecture," he recalled in the third volume of his autobiography, "and if I had appeared anywhere in public, I should probably have been lynched by a Catholic mob, with the full approval of the police." Although he undoubtedly overstated the case, he did have trouble earning money for a while. He was rescued from this situation by Dr. Albert C. Barnes, the inventor of Argyrol and the millionaire art collector and creator of the Barnes Foundation, who gave him a five-year appointment to lecture at his museum in Merion, Pennsylvania. In the fall of 1940, he also gave the William James lectures at Harvard, and over the next four years he spoke at various institutions and put the finishing touches on his *History of Western Philosophy,* the chief source of his income for many years.

Returning to Britain in 1944, he wrote and lectured; and, in 1948, gave the first Reith Lecture for the British Broadcasting Corporation. His reputation then, as in former years, was mixed. He was thought to be wise, yet he was ridiculed for uttering his maxims oracularly. He was recognized as a brilliant logician but a deficient politician—as when he wanted to take advantage of Western atomic superiority to bring the Soviet Union to heel. He was lecturing at Princeton in 1950 when he was awarded the Nobel Prize "in recognition of his many-sided and significant writings, in which he appeared as a champion of humanity and freedom of thought."

After the middle fifties Russell devoted most of his seemingly inexhaustible energies to campaigns against nuclear war. In taking his stand, he proposed that Britain be neutral in the East-West conflict. He urged the withdrawal of United States nuclear weapons from British soil. "For my part, both as a patriot and as a friend of humanity," he said, "I would wish to see Britain officially neutral. The patriotic argument is very obvious to me. No sensible man would wish to see his country obliterated. And as things stand, so long as Britain remains allied to America, there is a serious threat of extermination without the slightest advantage either to America or to the Western way of life." In furtherance of his views he took part in a sit-down demonstration in London and was arrested for breach of peace. The eighty-nine-year-old man was jailed for seven days in Brixton prison after replying "No, I won't" to a magistrate's request that he pledge himself to good behavior.

Although some thought Russell meddled in the Cuban crisis in 1962, the main point of his activity, as conveyed in letters to world leaders, appeared to be that no national objective justified a crisis that might lead to world destruction. "If people could learn to view nuclear war as a common danger to our species," he wrote, "and not as a danger due solely to the wickedness of the oppressing group, it would be possible to negotiate agreements which would put an end to the common danger."

His attitude toward the Vietnam War flowed from his desire to advance the cause of world peace, which he saw endangered by United States imperialism. He believed that a rebuff for the United States, indeed a military defeat, would dampen war fires.

Russell had a rather pixie sense of humor about himself and death, and in 1937 he composed his own obituary as he imagined it might appear in *The Times* of London. He disclosed his article in a later interview. It read in part: "In his [Russell's] youth, he did work of importance in mathematical logic, but his eccentric attitude toward the first World War revealed a lack of balanced judgment, which increasingly infected his later writings. His life, for all its waywardness, had a certain anachronistic consistency, reminiscent of that of the aristocratic rebels of the early nineteenth century. His principles were curious, but such as they were they governed his actions. In private life, he showed none of the acerbity which marred his writings but was a genial conversationalist, not devoid of human sympathy."

ROCKWELL KENT

At various (and frequently simultaneous) periods of his long life the protean Rockwell Kent, who died at the age of eighty-eight, was an architect, painter, illustrator, lithographer, xylographer, cartoonist, advertising artist, carpenter, dairy farmer, explorer, trade-union leader, and political controversialist. "He is so multiple a person as to be multifarious," Louis Untermeyer, the poet, once observed.

It was as a painter and graphic artist, however, that Kent established his reputation. His romantic realist oils were hung in the Metropolitan Museum of Art, the Whitney Museum of American Art, the Brooklyn Museum, the Corcoran Gallery of Art in Washington, the Art Institute of Chicago, the Pushkin Museum in Moscow and the Hermitage in Leningrad. They were also part of many private collections, including that of Joseph H. Hirshhorn. In addition, Kent's murals were on the walls of several public buildings.

His clean, precise graphic art was known to thousands who were stirred by his illustrations for editions of the works of Shakespeare, as well as for *The Bridge of San Luis Rey, Moby-Dick, Beowulf, The Canterbury Tales, Leaves of Grass, Paul Bunyan, Faust, The Decameron,* and *Candide.* Kent also illustrated his own books, among them *Voyaging Southward from the Strait of Magellan, N by E, Greenland Journal,* and *It's Me O Lord,* his 617-page, 300,000-word autobiography.

Kent's paintings, watercolors, lithographs, and woodcuts often depicted the stark and rugged aspects of nature—bleak and icy mountains and lonely shacks and frozen wastes. They reflected his adventurous life in Maine, Greenland, Arctic Alaska, Tierra del Fuego at the tip of South America, and in other wilderness areas of this continent. His style was distinctive, vigorous, and simple, yet his people were portrayed with the subtle compassion of one who knew their secrets.

Although Kent had a stern appearance, his manner was gentle and humorous except when he was aroused over some wrong. Standing five feet nine inches, he was lean and sinewy. He was prematurely bald, and his long, square-jawed face was dominated by burning gray eyes under bushy brows. He wore a thin mustache that whitened with the years.

A man of strongly individual opinions, he was once asked why he felt obliged to be "different." "Be yourself as a painter; be yourself as a man," he responded. In this spirit he rarely bothered to bow to conformity. "I have only one life and I'm going to live it as nearly as possible as I want to live it," he remarked a few years before his death, adding: "Life has always been and, God help me, always will be so exciting that I'll want to talk about it. I rate even my being an artist and a writer by being heart and soul a revolutionist. I think that the ideals of youth are fine, clear, and unencumbered; and that the real art of living consists in keeping alive the conscience and sense of values we had when we were young."

Expressing the dramaturgy of his art in his life, Kent seemed to relish his political battles with the prevailing establishment. In one of the first of these, in 1937, he enraged patriotic societies by "defiling" federal property. He had executed a mural for the Post Office Building in Washington, part of which depicted a United States mailman delivering a letter to a native of Puerto Rico, then an American dependency. The letter contained this message, written in minuscule script in Kuskokwims, an obscure Eskimo dialect: "PuertoRicomiunun Ilapticnum: Ke ha chimmeulakut engayscaacut, amna ketchimmi attunim chuli waptictun itticleoraatigut." A newspaperman spotted the words and got Vilhjalmur Stefansson, the Arctic authority, to translate them. They read: "To the people of Puerto Rico, our friends: Go ahead, let us change chiefs. That alone can make us equal and free." Postmaster General James A. Farley had the offending message expunged, but paid Kent his $3,000 fee.

Kent blandly denied that he had engaged in partisanship. "The cause of independence in Puerto Rico needs no propaganda," he remarked. "Everybody knows that the majority of people down there are in favor of it."

Beginning in the late twenties, the artist joined a score or more of committees and organizations that espoused causes also advocated by Communists. He was active in such groups for the rest of his life. Among them was the 162,000-member International Workers Order, a fraternal society of which he was president and that was dissolved in 1950 by a New York court order as "Communist-dominated."

As a consequence of his activities and associations, Kent was frequently called a Communist, a charge he denied. The House Committee on Un-American Activities heard the charge in 1939, then made by a former Communist party official. In 1949 the committee topped its list of Americans who belonged to "subversive" organizations with his name. It said he had been affiliated with at least eighty-five such groups.

In 1953, the artist refused, on Fifth Amendment grounds, to say whether or not he was a Communist when he was questioned on this point by Senator Joseph R. McCarthy. Outside the hearing, however, Kent again insisted he was not a party member. He made no effort, though, to disguise his social and political beliefs, saying: "When I was a young fellow I was very much disturbed by there being some people with lots of money and lots of people with no money. I thought a lot about it and I read a lot about it, so that when I voted for the first time, I voted Socialist. I'm still disturbed by the fact that there are some people with a lot of money and a lot of people with no money and a few million with no jobs, and that the world is rich in resources and that people are starving to death, and that all the people in the world want to live and yet a good part of the time they're busy killing each other."

In flaunting these views, often crustily and cantankerously, Kent found himself ignored as an artist, and his reputation in the United States declined in the fifties and sixties. It rose, however, in the Socialist-bloc countries, where his revolutionism was accounted a virtue.

In the 1950's the State Department sought to deny him a passport on the suspicion he was a Communist. Kent sued and won in the United States Supreme Court in a landmark case. He summed up his feelings by saying, "I'm an American who doesn't want his corns stepped on."

Kent's American roots traced to Thomas Kent, who migrated here from England early in the eighteenth-century. Zenas Kent, the artist's great-grandfather, was a mercantile banker and business partner of John Brown, the abolitionist. His grandfather built the New York, Pennsylvania and Ohio Railroad. Rockwell Kent was born June 21, 1882, in Tarrytown Heights, New York, the son of Rockwell and Sara Holgate Kent. His father was a mining engineer and a lawyer.

His formal schooling was somewhat hit-or-miss. "I was sent to school, and then another school, and then another school, and then to college," he recalled. "One school I didn't like, so I ran away. Latin I didn't like so they tried to break me. My teachers gave up." What the youth enjoyed was painting and drawing, which he studied assiduously in vacation times with William Merritt Chase and then nights with Kenneth Hayes Miller, Robert Henri, and Abbott H. Thayer while he was attending the Columbia School of Architecture.

For a dozen years after leaving college he practiced architecture, but in 1904 he went to live on Monhegan Island, Maine, where he built a house and supported himself by manual labor while painting. In the next ten years he wandered, working as an architect and union carpenter in New Hampshire, Connecticut, and Minnesota. He went to Newfoundland in 1914 and was expelled on suspicion of being a German spy.

His paintings in those years won him his first recognition as a serious artist. The National Academy displayed two of them when he was twenty-two. His Maine experiences produced, among others, "Winter," which was done in 1907 and was later acquired by the Metropolitan Museum of Art. In Newfoundland he did "The Seiners," the first modern American painting to be hung in the Frick. In those days his paintings sold for less than five hundred dollars, not enough to support him.

Wanting to go to Alaska to paint the mountains and the sea and the wilderness, he had himself incorporated in 1916 as Rockwell Kent, Incorporated, selling shares to his friends; and with the proceeds he managed to live for a year on Fox Island in Resurrection Bay. His products—oils and black-and-white drawings—were exhibited in 1920 and created a sensation for the vivid impression they conveyed of the cold north wind, the chill of the sea, and the barrenness of the rocks. The works sold well, enabling Rockwell Kent, Incorporated, to pay a twenty percent dividend. Sales also permitted the artist to buy out the company and to dissolve it.

The Alaska art, moreover, created a demand for his illustrations, some of which he did in his own name and some as Hogarth, Jr. Under that pseudonym he did satirical and humorous drawings for *Vanity Fair* and other magazines as well as commercial art work, including advertisements for Rolls-Royce motor cars; but wanderlust again afflicted him, and in 1923 he beat his way around Cape Horn in a small sailboat and spent a year in the desolation of Tierra del Fuego.

Kent's illustrated account of his adventures, *Voyaging Southward from the Strait of Magellan,* won him fresh acclaim. After a pause of six years he voyaged to Greenland. His chronicle of that trip, which included a shipwreck, was published (with his illustrations) as *N by E* in 1930 and was widely distributed by the Literary Guild. Meanwhile Kent edited *Creative Art,* a periodical about modern art; and he was hailed, because of his aggressiveness, as a dynamic force among his contemporaries.

In the thirties he wrote and illustrated *Salamina,* another book about Greenland, to which he returned in 1931 and 1934, and did the illustrations for his edition of Shakespeare and other classics. In the thirties also Kent cut a figure in the newspapers for his political activities. He sought to organize an artists' union for the Congress of Industrial Organizations; he was vocal in his support of the Loyalists in the Spanish Civil War; he backed Earl Browder, the Communist presidential candidate in 1936; he headed an American-Soviet friendship group; and he wrote *This Is My Own,* an ebullient account of his life and controversies that was published in 1940.

Kent also purchased a 200-acre farm near Ausable Forks, New York, which he called Asgaard, the Norse name for the home of the gods. He operated a dairy there until 1948, when he gave it to his two employees, charging that his milk had been boycotted because he supported Henry Wallace, the Progressive party presidential candidate that year.

In the forties and fifties Kent continued to paint, to draw, and to write. His lengthy, lushly written, and extroversive autobiography came out in 1955, and *Greenland Journal,* an account of his 1931 trip to that island, was issued in 1962.

Age did not mellow Kent's caustic attitudes. In giving 80 landscapes and 800 drawings to the Soviet Union in 1960, he explained that he had been spurned by his native country for his political beliefs. And in accepting the Lenin Prize in 1967, he announced that he was giving his monetary award to the people of North Vietnam. The State Department complained that such an action constituted trading with the enemy, but since the award was made in Moscow and in Soviet currency, the complaint came to nothing.

Kent was not in fact so completely shunned in his own country as he claimed. *The American Book Collector,* a magazine, devoted a special issue to him in 1964 that contained unstinted praise for his art and his personality. "To many he may be a mystery, but not to his friends and associates who know him best," Dan Burne Jones, the critic, wrote in his essay. "He is of dauntless courage and boundless energy, of strong and forceful will, and once fired into thought and action that thought is often immediately followed by the accomplished fact."

———————————————❖———————————————

BENNETT CERF

Bennett Cerf was one of those personalities better known to the American public for their avocations than for their professions; yet what sustains him in reputation was his half-century as a book publisher, not his more popular identity as a television celebrity, raconteur, joke teller, author, lecturer, and partygoer. When he died at the age of seventy-three, It was his importance as a publisher of such disparate writers as James Joyce, John O'Hara, and Marcel Proust that made his life noteworthy, for, as a publisher, he helped to shape the country's literary and cultural life. That was the serious side of Bennett Cerf, an extrovert who could not be contained in an unusually introverted profession. For fun (and money) he not only retailed quips and puns, most of them outrageous, but he also appeared for sixteen years as a weekly panelist on the television parlor-game show *What's My Line?* with Arlene Francis, the actress; Dorothy Kilgallen, the gossip columnist; and John Daly, the actor—all diverting lightweights. It was a big leap from associating with Miss Kilgallen to friendship with William Faulkner, but Cerf managed to jump with ease. He took to the unfettered life with zest.

With a flair for commerce and advertising promotion, he was something of a blithe spirit in the book world—a man quite different from the staid, tweedy gentlemen-publishers who dominated American book houses prior to the 1920's. Whereas such publishers tended to insist that all their books should have literary merit, Cerf had a keen eye for the sales chart and the balance sheet. He published Plato and Franz Kafka and Eugene O'Neill along with many writers who catered to more transient public whims. In other important respects he also differed from both his ivory-tower predecessors and his contemporaries. One of these was his larky engagement in nonpublishing activities, chiefly *What's My Line?* on which he first appeared in 1951. The show, in which panelists attempted to guess the occupations of various guests, made Cerf a national entertainer. "I have to remind people I'm a publisher," he once said as he was being sought out for his autograph.

Questioned a few years ago by Geoffrey Hellmann of *The New Yorker* about his desire for celebrity, Cerf explained: "Everyone has a streak of pure unadulterated ham. Many won't admit it. I revel in it."

With fame, or at least attention, focused on him, the publisher appeared in newspaper and slick magazine advertisements endorsing such products as Yuban coffee, L&M cigarettes, Bostonian shoes, and Schiaparelli's Snuff, an after-shave lotion. In one ad for Heublein's bottled martinis he was shown dueling with Moss Hart, the Broadway playwright. Reproved by his wife for flagrant exhibitionism and for taking money he didn't need, he replied: "Everyone needs money. Besides, I like the publicity and I'm all dressed up in a dueling outfit in the ad." Although most of his commercial endorsements were passed off by his friends as "Bennett having fun again," his unbecoming membership on "the Guiding Faculty" of the Famous Writers School of Westport, Connecticut, a mail-order outfit that purported to teach writing, was less charitably perceived. It was one thing to earn a fee for something so nonsensical as prepared martinis, his friends told him sharply, and quite another to lend his name to a correspondence school that could trap the unwary. After some prodding, particularly from Jessica Mitford, he saw the point.

Another activity that set Cerf apart from his fellow bookmen was his subtrade as a jokesmith. Jokes concocted or recounted by him appeared in *The Saturday Review* for many years and, until his death, in newspapers that carried his syndicated column. Not one to let a joke die, he collected them in more than twenty books that had astonishing sales—more than five million copies in all. His last book was *Sound of Laughter,* which he introduced by saying: "It is aimed straight at your jocular vein, and I can only hope that detractors will be limited to a Boeing 747." Savoring his own wit (he laughed harder than his listeners), he telephoned his jokes to a select list of friends almost every working day.

Cerf's jokes included these:

"Have you heard about the sultan who left a call for seven in the morning?"

"A maker of eyeglasses has just moved his shop to an island off Alaska and is now known as an optical Aleutian."

"A wealthy manufacturer regarded the young man pleading for his daughter's hand with deep suspicion. 'I wonder,' he mused, 'if you'd be so anxious to marry my Rosalie if I didn't have a penny?' 'I think I'd love her twice as much,' vowed the suitor fervently. 'Get out,' cried the manufacturer. 'We've got enough idiots in the family already!' "

"The usual worried husband invaded the office of the usual society psychoanalyst to plead, 'You've got to help my wife, doctor. She's convinced she's an elevator.' 'An elevator?' echoed the surprised analyst. 'You'd better send her right up to see me.' 'I can't do that,' demurred the husband. 'She's an express elevator, and doesn't stop on your floor.' "

The fame accruing to Cerf from his noncultural roles gave him yet another occupation, as a lecture-platform personality. He appeared at colleges, clubs, and conventions, speaking on such topics as "Modern Trends in Literature and Humor" and "Authors I Have Known." Describing the publisher at the lectern, Hellmann wrote in *The New Yorker* in 1959: "He chats in a confidential nasal drawl, easy of stance, hands in pockets, feeding his audience puns, anecdotes and such teasing remarks as (in toto) 'John O'Hara was in our office the other day. I could tell you stories about him by the hour.' "

Tall, brown-eyed and bespectacled, flawlessly tailored, Cerf looked the dandy, but was saved from foppishness by his boyish, cheerful, unsophisticated manner. He was genuinely warmhearted and likable, and hardworking, and much of his display—his lavish houses, his devotion to Cadillacs, his dining at Toots Shor's, his self-publicity—was forgiven him. He was, after all, Bennett Cerf, and he made very few pretenses about his love of pleasure and fun. Yet he was an extraordinarily industrious and shrewd publisher, who actually read many of the books he issued and who was liked and respected by most of his authors. He had an uncommon ability for inspiring friendship; he was, for example, on close terms with both John Hersey and John O'Hara—not to mention such unliterary types as Frank Sinatra.

Friendships and a taste for writing brought him into publishing. Born in Harlem on May 25, 1898, Bennett Alfred Cerf was the only child of Gustave Cerf, a lithographer, and Fredericka Wise Cerf. The elder Cerf was a French Jew. Bennett's maternal grandfather was a wholesale tobacco distributor who bequeathed him a trust fund of $100,000; this came to him when he was sixteen and an honors graduate of Townsend Harris High School in New York. He entered Columbia in 1915 and became both a columnist for *The Daily Spectator,* the student newspaper, and editor of *The Jester,* the college humor magazine. After receiving his degree along with a Phi Beta Kappa key, he got a job as a clerk in the Wall Street brokerage house of which he was a customer. At lunch one day in 1923 with Richard L. Simon, a Columbia contemporary who was on the staff of Boni and Liveright, the book publishers, Simon confided that he was about to leave his job and, with Max Schuster, set up a new publishing venture.

Cerf, who was bored with brokerage, quit his job by telephone and went to see Horace Liveright, who offered him a vice-presidency at $50 a week in return for a $10,000 investment in the firm. Two years later, on his twenty-seventh birthday, he bought the Modern Library, a successful series of reprinted classics that Liveright (with Albert Boni) had set up in 1918. His partner in the purchase was his best friend, Donald S. Klopfer, then twenty-three. After getting Rockwell Kent and Elmer Adler to redesign the books and after binding them in cloth, the partners went out to peddle them, and with such success that by 1927 they had recouped their investment of $210,000. The Modern Library series, one of the forerunners of the paperback, has since become a staple of Random House. Vastly expanded from its original 109 titles, it now includes more than 400 books, the gross sales of which rarely falter.

With Modern Library doing well, Cerf and Klopfer established a subsidiary to publish limited editions; since its titles would be chosen at random, they called it Random House. Cerf was president, a post he held until 1965, when he became chairman of the board. He stepped down in December 1970, and was succeeded by Klopfer.

Early Random House books included a Kent-illustrated *Candide* and a lavishly printed *Adventures of Tom Sawyer*. By 1933 the Depression put an end to the market for such luxuries, and Random House turned to trade books by acquiring the rights to Eugene O'Neill's plays and the works of the poet Robinson Jeffers. Cerf sealed the O'Neill deal by flying to Sea Island, Georgia, where the playwright was staying. The fact that the two had met worked in Cerf's favor. Out of the O'Neill acquisition came the decision to hire Saxe Commins, who was Random House's chief editor until his death in 1958. With Commins's counsel and Cerf's instincts, the company began to grow into one of the giants of the book business. One of its early ventures—and among its most significant—was the publication, in 1934, of the unabridged *Ulysses.* Cerf had to go to court to upset the federal ban on the James Joyce masterpiece, which was officially regarded as obscene. With Morris Ernst as counsel, he won a notable victory over government censorship that benefited the entire publishing industry.

In 1936, Random House bought Harrison Smith and Robert Haas, Incorporated, a merger that added to Cerf's list William Faulkner, Isak Dinesen, Edgar Snow, Angela Thirkell, and the Babar books. Over the years he added Sinclair Lewis, W. H. Auden, Gertrude Stein, William Saroyan, James Michener, John O'Hara, Robert Penn Warren, Truman Capote, Kathleen Winsor, and Robert Jay Lifton. There was, as well, a roster of Broadway playwrights. He assembled a corps of editors that included, in addition to Commins, Albert Erskine, Jr. and Jason Epstein. He gave them pretty much free rein, while he took charge of major advertising campaigns and financial dealings with the authors. He appeared to run a happy shop, which was housed, until 1969, in the palatial old Villard House, a now vandalized landmark on Madison Avenue just behind St. Patrick's Cathedral. The company then moved to a nondescript skyscraper, where Cerf had a more impersonal and less grand office.

That he had the qualities of an impresario did not bother his coworkers. "Bennett runs Random House as a conservative branch of show business," Mr. Epstein conceded a few years ago. "The company is vulgar to a degree. But what makes the difference with Bennett is how important he feels it is to have Philip Roth and William Styron on the list. Some other publishers would know a thousand ways to get rich without having one author like that. Bennett Cerf doesn't."

One of his biggest and most financially rewarding was *The Random House Dictionary of the English Language,* a 2,059-page volume issued in 1966 after a decade of preparation costing $3 million. In the 1950's, he branched out into young people's books, publishing works on American and world history, nature, and science. Under the title of Beginner Books, he also published the works of Dr. Seuss, a perennial favorite.

His multiple activities, cultural and otherwise, brought him about $375,000 a year, much of which he spent on the full life. This included a townhouse on New York's East Side and a forty-two-acre estate in Mount Kisco. Many of his evenings were given over to dinner parties, either as a guest or as a host. "It's Bennett's theory," his wife said, "that if you're going to have two people for dinner you might as well have forty."

His offhand infectiousness could hardly have been in greater contrast to that of Alfred A. Knopf, whose manner and appearance resembled that of a Cossack sergeant. Yet, in 1960, Cerf bought out Knopf for about $3 million and the two men got along well, with Knopf operating his fiefdom under Random House overlordship. This was followed six years later by the purchase of the Random House complex by the Radio Corporation of America for about $40 million. Cerf, in his turn, became a count with a fiefdom. If he minded the loss of his sovereignty, he kept it to himself.

Cerf had liberal political sympathies. He was, for example, a partisan of Republican Spain and visited that country during the Civil War. He published books exposing South Africa's apartheid long before such exposures were fashionable; one of these books, a collection of photographs, was doomed to lose money, but he was proud of having "paid his dues" to a good cause. He also published one of the few early books to criticize the Federal Bureau of Investigation at a time when its image for purity was unalloyed. The FBI's response, of course, was to investigate him, an experience that made him fume, even years later.

The publisher was twice married. His first wife was Sylvia Sidney, the film actress, whom he courted with romantic flamboyance in the thirties. His second wife was Helen Nichols, who as a child actress had changed her name to Phyllis Fraser. They were married in New York in 1940 with Mayor Fiorello H. La Guardia officiating. Phyllis Cerf later became a successful editor of children's books at Random House.

One man who lunched with Bennett Cerf from time to time was always delighted by his candor. He was a man of pride utterly lacking in pretension. The luncheon companion once asked him about his life as a publisher. "I have enjoyed every moment of it," he replied with a grin. "I had a small talent, and it was fun to expand it to its maximum."

———————————— ✤ ————————————

MAURICE CHEVALIER

No French entertainer was so jaunty, so debonair, so burnished yet so saucy, so much the elegant boulevardier of an idealized Paris as Maurice Chevalier. When he died in Paris on New Year's Day at the age of eighty-three, he recalled an older generation, a carefree time, for he was the epitome, in the blurred mind's eye of nostalgia, of a happy hedonism. Attired in a one-button dark suit, sporting a springtime boater and singing and talking in his magical Gallic accent, he was America's No. 1 Frenchman, the personification of a bubbling glass of champagne. He was also France's No. 1 chanteur, whose renditions of "Ma Louise," "Mimi," "Valentine," "Ma Pomme," "Ça Va, Ça Va," "Place Pigalle," and "Paris Oui Oui" reflected the bittersweet of life and the careless rapture of the 1920's and 1930's. Chevalier was, moreover, ageless: a headliner at the Folies-Bergère in 1909, he was still without peer as a revue artist almost sixty years later. "Le Grand Maurice" he was called in the fall of 1966 when he appeared, full of zest in his seventy-ninth year, in the Empire Room of New York's Waldorf-Astoria Hotel. Although the years had etched his once-smooth face with lines and creases, once he started to perform he became in the twinkling of an eye a well-preserved man of no more than sixty. His voice was full and strong, his step was spry, and his light-blue eyes shimmered. His way with an audience was unaffected and unforced; he enchanted them by being their Maurice, and when he departed the stage waving his boater after an hour of songs and gentle patter about the joys of senescence, it was to a spontaneous and standing ovation.

"I believe in the rosy side of life," Chevalier said in explanation of his artistic longevity. "I know that life has many dark sides for everybody. It has been for me at many moments of my life. But I believe in bringing to people the encouragement of living, and I think I am lasting so long in the interest of the people through something that comes out of my personality and out of my work, which is just to be sort of a sunshine person, see."

At his best in songs and skits in which his joie de vivre and personality sparkled, Chevalier was only somewhat less renowned as a motion-picture actor. In the thirties he starred at $20,000 a week in such Hollywood romantic classics as *The Love Parade* and *The Merry Widow,* directed by the redoubtable Ernst Lubitsch. In these he was the gay, sophisticated, and irresistible lover, leading man to such actresses as Jeanette MacDonald, Claudette Colbert, and Evelyn Brent. There was a ten-year hiatus in his film career that ended with the French movie *Le Silence Est d'Or* in 1947, which won the grand prize at the Brussels World Film Festival.

His comeback in American films—as a dramatic and character actor—occurred in 1957 in *Love in the Afternoon.* Playing with Leslie Caron in 1958, he stole the show as the aging ladies' man in *Gigi,* a film that added the song "Thank Heaven for Little Girls" to his repertory. His performance won him an honorary Oscar. There followed character roles in *Can-Can, Fanny, Jessica,* and *The Castaways* that gained him additional acclaim. In all, he appeared in forty films, the first released in 1914, with remarkably few clinkers among them. He was a hard and self-centered worker. "I could never say that working with him was anything more than agreeable," Miss MacDonald remarked of their associ ation. "All he cared about was his career and his mother." Once when Chevalier was in Hollywood, he was a houseguest of Mary Pickford. "He would go out on the lawn every day with his straw hat and rehearse his entire music-hall act," the actress recalled. "He leaves nothing to chance."

Although he made a lot of money in the movies and reached a world audience through skillful acting in them, his true métier was the revue and the one man show. In these he mesmerized his audiences, who were transfixed by his long underlip, his dancing eyes, and roguish smile. American and English listeners might suspect that his fractured English was a shade too carefully preserved and that his Gallic accent was too perfect, but such skepticism melted before his warmth. Indeed, his appeal was so irresistible that he once persuaded the august Charles de Gaulle, president of France, to join him, at a charity ball, in a refrain of "Ma Pomme." As a singer, Chevalier was no great shakes. He could carry an uncomplicated tune, phrase a line, and be sly at the proper time, but that was about all. By unending practice, however, he converted his vocal deficiencies into assets. "Thank God, it was my good luck not to have any voice," he said. "If I had, I would have tried to be a singer who sings ballads in a voice like a velvet fog, but since I am barely able to half-talk and half-sing a song, it made me look for something to make me different from a hundred other crooners who are neither good nor bad. If I had any voice, I would have been content to rest on my voice and learn nothing else. Since I had no voice, I had to find something that would hold the interest of the public."

"Any third-rate *chanteur de charme* [crooner] has a better voice than I," he remarked on another occasion. "But they sing from the throat while I sing from the heart." Chevalier's handling of a song, as well as the songs themselves, contributed to the spell he cast on the stage or in supper clubs. A favorite was "Ma Louise," written for him in the twenties; another was "Ça Va, Ça Va," which he wrote for himself in the forties; still another was "Valentine." It is the story of a girl who was so little and so sweet; the years go by and Valentine is encountered again, but she is no longer petite and she has a double chin. "It is a very human story," he said of the song; and by accenting that quality he gave it a special character. Audiences never seemed to tire of it.

As an entertainer Chevalier considered himself in the tradition of Sir Harry Lauder, the great Scotch balladeer of the early part of the century, and Al Jolson, the American song-and-dance man. He admired them both for the intimacy they established with their audiences and for their artistic intensity. A similar intensity appeared to account for his reluctance to retire. "Often people ask me how it feels to be seventy-eight," he said shortly after he reached that age. "And I say wonderful, considering the alternative." Another time he said, "I'm traveling through old age without being unhappy, without being forgotten. I get my energy from the audience."

Energy, ambition, and drive for stage success characterized Maurice Chevalier from early childhood. Born September 12, 1888, in a Paris working-class quarter, he was the youngest of nine children. His father was a ne'er-do-well house painter who deserted the family when his son was eight, and his mother was a lacemaker to whom he was devoted throughout her life. Her death in 1932 was a severe emotional blow, but he kept her memory alive by naming his villa outside Paris "La Louque," a nickname he had given her. Maurice ended his formal schooling at the age of ten, when he was apprenticed to an engraver, and he later worked briefly in a tack factory. But he wanted above all to be an entertainer, first as an acrobat with his brother Paul, and then as a singer. An accident nipped his acrobatics, and he made his vocal debut in a neighborhood café on amateur night. It was *un grand succès d'hilarité,* because he was laughed off the stage for singing in a different key from that of the pianist. Unfazed, the ragamuffin persisted until he began to sing in the hurly-burly variety halls and *cafés-concerts* in Paris and in the provinces. His comic effects were based on his youth, his extravagant attire, and the earthiness of his songs. When he was fifteen he began to appear in the boulevard revues as a singing comedian, billed as Le Petit Jésus [The Wonder Boy]. "Records and radio and movies did not exist at that time," Chevalier later said of those hansom-cab-and-gaslight days. "It took years of traveling and playing to a few hundred people a night to build a reputation."

His big break came in 1909, when he was twenty-one. He was hired by the Folies-Bergère to be the legendary Mistinguett's partner in a revue. Mistinguett had begun life as a flower girl and she achieved fame on account of her pungent personality, her slender, sexy legs, and a song called "Mon Homme." When Chevalier met her she was thirty-six and at the apex of her career. The two did something called "The Flooring Waltz," in which they rolled themselves up in a carpet, fell to the stage, and rose and unrolled. One evening early in the revue's run, they were a little slower than usual in unrolling, and they emerged from the carpet in love. "She was very attractive and I loved her madly," Chevalier said later of their liaison. "People have said that she made me a star. That is not true. I was already a star of the younger generation. However, I learned much from her because she was a great artiste. She also brought me the dearest and biggest love a man can have."

Called up for compulsory military duty in late 1913, Chevalier was at Mélun when World War I broke out; in the German invasion he was hit in the right lung by shrapnel and captured. After twenty-six months in a prisoner-of-war camp in Germany, during which he learned English from a fellow inmate, he was released in a prisoner exchange and went home to Mistinguett and a Croix de Guerre. Overcoming his lung wound, he played at the Olympia in

Paris, returned to the Folies-Bergère, and appeared at the Théâtre Femina and the Casino de Paris. In most of his roles since 1910 he had appeared in a full dress suit and top hat, but a trip to London in 1919 changed all that. "One day I saw a young fellow in a tuxedo and a straw hat," he recalled. "He looked so smart that I thought, I do not need to look further. There is my hat. It's a man's hat. It's a gay hat. It's the hat to go with a tuxedo." From that moment I was never without a straw boater if I could help it, even when those hats went out of fashion."

Back in Paris, he played in a musical, did a further stint at the Folies-Bergère with Mistinguett, and then appeared in a song-and-dance revue with Yvonne Vallée, to whom he was subsequently married for about six years. After playing the lead in the operetta *Dédé,* he was brought to the United States by Charles B. Dillingham, the New York producer, but he was too frightened or too overawed to perform. His first working visit began in 1928, and in the following seven years he made twelve films. His Hollywood stint ended in 1935 when Irving Thalberg, the producer, wanted to give Grace Moore, a singer, top billing in a Chevalier picture. "I told Thalberg I had never been second on any bill since I was twenty," he recounted. "I left for Paris. It was the end of my first American movie career." Between pictures, however, he had made his New York debut at the New Amsterdam Roof Garden and played the Fulton Theater. His song repertory even then captivated New Yorkers.

Back in France, Chevalier was again a hit in the music halls. He entertained King George VI and Queen Elizabeth on their state visit in 1938 and was decorated as a Chevalier of the Legion of Honor. By 1940, when World War II embroiled France, he was living with Nita Raya, a young actress; fearing Nazi persecution because Miss Raya was a Jew, the couple moved to Chevalier's villa in Cannes, in the free zone. His later conduct during the war suggested a degree of collaboration with the Nazis, as the documentary film *Le Chagrin et la Pitié* (The Sorrow and the Pity) demonstrated. In it he could be seen and heard in a sequence in which he defended his performing during the Nazi occupation. He contended that he never sang for the Germans, never in Germany, and only before German-held French prisoners. These incidents were investigated at the time, and his collaboration was dismissed as not serious. In any event, he returned to the Paris stage after the war without any noticeable decline in his popularity.

After touring Belgium, the Netherlands, Switzerland, and the Scandinavian countries, Chevalier brought his one-man show to New York in 1947. Critical acclaim was undiminished, and he toured the United States and Canada for almost a year. He planned to return in 1951, but he was refused a visa because he had signed the Stockholm appeal, a plea against the use of nuclear armaments. On the ground that Communists had been energetic in circulating the appeal, the State Department adjudged the entertainer potentially dangerous to the security of the United States. The matter was considered of such moment that Secretary of State Dean Acheson, a Cold War liberal, sought personally to justify the visa ban. Despite Chevalier's protest that he had subscribed to the Stockholm document out of a sense of humanity, the ban on him was not lifted until 1954. After that he was in this country several times, either to make films or to play theater and club dates. He also appeared in several televison shows, none of lasting note.

Offstage Chevalier lived a relatively quiet and unostentatious life. In his early years he liked to box and sparred from time to time with Georges Carpentier, the French heavyweight and a close friend. Later, he kept his five-foot eleven-and-a-half-inch frame in trim with calisthenics and by playing golf. With advancing years, he also practiced moderation. "Until the age of fifty," he told a friend, "I lived from the belt down to the heels; since then I have oriented myself toward that part that lies between belt and the head." In the late sixties, he began a series of farewell, or "last," recitals; perhaps the truly final one took place when he was eighty. Appearing in a Paris theater, he said it had been his aim to "pay homage to Paris after sixty-eight years of good and loyal service" to its glory. In the last couple of years before his death he also made a phonograph record or two and appeared quite often in public—at opening nights and major horse-racing events—striking people as jaunty and fit.

In the fifties, he donated his Cannes villa to the French Society of Authors and Composers; he lived in a long, low white house on the outskirts of Paris, with a companion many years his junior. The house itself contained a museum of his show-business souvenirs, including photographs of friends and associates. One of Marlene Dietrich, signed "Marlinou," said, "I have always known you were the greatest. But since I have invaded your profession I am on my knees." There were also paintings—a Utrillo scene of Ménilmontant and oils by Cézanne, Matisse, Dufy, and Picasso. Statuettes of himself in various stage poses stood against the walls; metal ashtrays, shaped and colored like his straw hats, were much in evidence. Egocentric though he may have been, Maurice Chevalier had the wit to be diverting. In the early sixties, a writer, meeting him for the first time, had occasion to drive with him from Marseilles to Paris. For much of the distance, Chevalier entertained his guest with a virtually nonstop recital of his repertory, and the writer was completely charmed. Chevalier was doing what he liked best—entertaining. It was this essential characteristic that led Jean Cocteau to call him "le grand sympathique." He was indeed all of that.

For those who have never heard Maurice Chevalier in person, his recordings can be searched out in almost any conscientious record shop.

MARIANNE MOORE

A writer with a dazzling ability to describe things as if she were observing them for the first time and with a remarkable talent for subtle imagery, Marianne Craig Moore was one of the country's most laureled poets and among its most ingenuous talkers and public personalities. Her final years were dimmed by a series of strokes that all but stilled her pen and tongue until her death at eighty-four. Nonetheless, she permitted an occasional visitor, to one of whom she confided, "I'm all bone, just solid, pure bone. I'm good-natured, but hideous as an old horn toad."

Miss Moore, the Pulitzer Prize poet, often took a back seat to Miss Moore, the personality, for she was an inveterate frequenter of concerts, balls, parties, fashion shows, unveilings, public receptions, lecture platforms, grocery shops, department stores, subway trains, baseball parks, boxing exhibitions, and literary salons. A slight, frail woman five feet three-and-a-half inches tall, with luminous, inquisitive blue-gray eyes, she was immediately recognizable wherever she went for her invariable attire—a tricorn hat, a cape, and a suit. "I like the tricorn shape," she once explained, "because it conceals the defects of the head." It also was her insigne: Thousands of New Yorkers who had never read a line of her poetry knew that the tricorn hat was borne by Marianne Moore, the poet, and they made way for her.

Her tricorn (she had dozens) was, after middle age, perched on a braid of gray hair that she wrapped around her head and held in place with a celluloid hairpin. Her face, likened to that of an angelic Mary Poppins, was once round and soft, and although lines of age creased it over the years, it never lost its glow.

Her conversation, which tended to breakneck monologue, was notable for its diversity. Sometimes it seemed that she was as discursive and as superficial as a teenager; but this was deceptive, for her associative mode of thought had a way of coming to a profound (or at least important) point by the time she stopped talking. Her remarks, delivered in a Middle Western drawl, charmed and enthralled persons as disparate as Casey Stengel, E. E. Cummings, and John Hay Whitney, about whose horse Tom Fool she wrote a poem. It read in part:

"You've the beat of a dancer to a measure/or harmonious rush of a porpoise at the prow/where the racers all win easily."

Although T. S. Eliot, expressing a generally held view, once remarked that "her poems form part of the small body of durable poetry written in our time," and although W. H. Auden confessed to pilfering from her, Miss Moore did not think of herself as a poet in the popular sense, one who wrote resonant sonnets, epics, and odes. She was "an observer," she said, who put down what she saw. "In fact, the only reason I know for calling my work poetry at all is that there is no other category in which to put it," she remarked on one occasion, adding: "I'm a happy hack as a writer."

Few agreed with this self-disparagement, for Miss Moore was a painstaking craftsman whose verse, which she composed in a spidery hand, was notable for its rhythms and for its use of homely speech. "I think the thing that attracted me to put things in verse was rhythm," she told an interviewer on her seventy-fifth birthday in 1962. "Someone said the accents should be set so it would be impossible for any reader to get them wrong. If you can read it in ten different ways, it's no good. That's very important to me.

"There are patterns in verse, just as you have restatement after contrast in music—as you have in Bach particularly. Also, I admire the legerdemain of saying a lot in a few words."

Miss Moore's poems utilized rhythms to create moods as well as to convey her admiration of such no-nonsense virtues as patience, firmness, courage, loyalty, modesty, and independence. Much of her writing in this vein was a wry but gentle criticism of human conduct, literature, and art, sometimes presented in unusual or baffling typographical arrangements. She made her point obliquely, for animals and plants rather than people were usually the formal subjects of her verse. Some thought her poetry cold and austere because it seemed so detached from human life, but Miss Moore insisted that she wrote with affection. "She is a naturalist without pedantry, and a moralist without harshness," was the verdict of Louise Bogan, the critic.

Miss Moore's compact verse was not always easy to read or to comprehend, even though she professed "a burning desire to be explicit"; but for those who might have preferred the obvious she had this answer: "It ought to be work to read something that was work to write." She took pride in catching attention with the first lines of her poems. "I am very careful with my first lines," she advised a questioner. "I put it down. I scrutinize it. I test it. I evaluate it."

One of her poems, "Values in Use," illustrates her concept of a catchy opening, as well as her economy of phrase and her use of aphorism to make an ironic and faintly pessimistic thrust. It reads:

I attended school and I liked the place—
grass and little locust-leaf shadows like lace.

Writing was discussed. They said, "We create
values in the process of living, daren't await

their historical progress." Be abstract
and you'll wish you'd been specific; it's a fact.

What was I studying? Values in use,
"judged on their own ground." Am I still abstruse?

Walking along, a student said offhand,
" 'Relevant' and 'plausible' were words I understand."

A pleasing statement, anonymous friend.
Certainly the means must not defeat the end.

In some of her other verse the poet celebrated the weak as standing off a hostile natural environment, as in this fragment from
"Nevertheless":

> The weak overcomes its
>   menace, the strong over-
>   comes itself. What is there
> like fortitude! What sap
>   went through the little thread
>   to make the cherry red!

As poets go, Miss Moore was unprolific. Only 120 poems, occupying 242 pages, were in *The Complete Poems of Marianne
Moore,* published by Viking Press and Macmillan for her eightieth
birthday in 1967. In addition to this fruit of more than fifty years,
there were nine translations in verse from *The Fables of La Fontaine.* Miss Moore was not a writer-to-order. "I don't believe in
substituting conscious expression for spontaneous devotion," she
once said in response to a request from her church—the Lafayette
Avenue Presbyterian in Brooklyn—for a special benediction for
ceremonial occasions. She labored to compose ("fiddling," she
called it), going over and over each poem until she was satisfied of
its perfection. This accounted for much of the intricate detail in

the verse, its quality of seeming like an exquisite needlepoint embroidery.

Miss Moore's gift for magical words was enlisted in 1955 by the Ford Motor Company in a quest for a name "for a rather important new series of cars." In the exchange of letters, subsequently published in *The New Yorker*, she suggested the Ford Silver Sword, Hurricane Hirundo, The Impeccable, The Ford Fabergé, The Resilient Bullet, The Intelligent Whale, The Arcenciel, Regna Racer, Varsity Stroke, Cresta Lark, Chaparral, and The Turtletopper.

The final letter in the exchange from Ford said:

"We have chosen a name [that] fails somewhat of the resonance, gaiety and zest we were seeking. But it has a personal dignity and meaning to many of us here. Our name, dear Miss Moore, is—Edsel. I hope you will understand." (Edsel was a son of Henry Ford, founder of the company. The car that bore his name failed for lack of sales.)

For thirty-seven years, from 1929 to 1966, the poet lived in a snug fifth-floor apartment at 260 Cumberland Street, in the Fort Greene section of Brooklyn. It was crammed with books and bric-a-brac—porcelain and ivory animals, a walrus tusk, prints and paintings, shells and feathers, old coins. The kitchen, though, was sparsely furnished ("I cook only the essentials—meat and potatoes. I've never baked a pie.") but it contained a vegetable squeezer in which Miss Moore made her own carrot juice, a libation of which she was fond. "Carrot juice increases vigor," she explained.

As Miss Moore's renown increased, her apartment was seldom without visitors—poets, artists, critics, admirers. Reluctantly, when the neighborhood became unsafe, she moved to Ninth Street in Greenwich Village in June 1966, where she lived until her death.

Miss Moore's rise to eminence was slow. She was the daughter of John Milton and Mary Warner Moore and was born in Kirkwood, Missouri, a suburb of St. Louis, on November 15, 1887.

She never knew her father, a construction engineer, who was institutionalized before her birth. After a brief stay with relatives, Mrs. Moore took Marianne and John, her elder son, to Carlisle, Pennsylvania, where the mother taught in Metzger Institute, now a part of Dickinson College. Marianne was sent to Bryn Mawr, where for lack of aptitude in English she studied biology and contributed some ephemeral verse to the literary monthly. Upon graduation in 1909 she took courses in typing and shorthand at the Carlisle Commercial College and then got a job teaching these subjects at the Carlisle Indian School. One of her pupils, before she resigned in 1916, was Jim Thorpe, the athlete.

Miss Moore moved to Chatham, New Jersey, to help keep house for her brother, a Presbyterian minister and later a Navy chaplain. In 1918, when he joined the Navy, she and her mother went to New York, where they lived for eleven years in an apartment on St. Luke's Place in Greenwich Village. After a stint as secretary to a girls' school, Miss Moore became, in 1921, assistant librarian at the Hudson Park branch of the New York Public Library, a post she filled until 1925.

Meanwhile, her first serious verse was published in *The Egoist,* a London magazine in which the imagists were influential, and in Harriet Monroe's *Poetry* magazine in Chicago. The poems had a select but impressed readership, and in 1921 H.D. (Hilda Doolittle) and Bryher (Winifred Ellerman), the historical novelist, collected and published these works in a small volume called *Poems.* It was issued in London without Miss Moore's knowledge. The poems, with some later additions, were printed as *Observations* in the United States in 1925, winning for their author her first literary prize, the Dial Award, and enthusiastic critical notices. Edwin Seaver's review in *The Nation,* which was typical, said, "In respect to her work Miss Moore hews to an ideology that is aristocratic and severe and pure. Against the commonplace and the easy her subtlety of sarcasm is devastating."

Now an established writer, Miss Moore left her library job to join the staff of *The Dial,* first as acting editor and then as editor.

She remained with the magazine, one of the storied literary periodicals of the day, until it expired in 1929. After moving to Brooklyn that year with her mother, Miss Moore devoted herself to writing and published *Selected Poems* in 1935, winning the Ernest Hartsock Memorial Prize. The verses, *The New York Times* said, were "positive and exhilarating."

More encomiums greeted *What Are Years* when it appeared in 1941. Malcolm Cowley, for example, described the title poem as "among the noblest lyrics of our time." With each succeeding slim book, Miss Moore fattened the list of her awards—the Harriet Monroe Poetry Award in 1944, a Guggenheim Fellowship in 1945, a joint grant from the American Academy of Arts and Letters and the National Institute of Arts and Letters in 1946, the Bollingen Prize in Poetry in 1952, the National Book Award for Poetry and the Pulitzer Prize the same year, the M. Carey Thomas Memorial Award in 1953, the Gold Medal of the National Institute of Arts and Letters in 1953, the MacDowell Medal in 1967. In addition, France gave her the Croix de Chevalier des Arts et Lettres for her translation of *The Fables of La Fontaine*. She also held honorary degrees from at least eight colleges.

Despite all these honors, Miss Moore remained unaffected, saying, "There's nothing very special about me." She played tennis with neighborhood children in Fort Greene Park, rode the subway to and from appointments, and became a fiery rooter for the Brooklyn Dodgers baseball team, whose feats she extolled in verse. When the Dodgers deserted Brooklyn for Los Angeles she changed her allegiance to the Yankees. Miss Moore had become hooked on the Dodgers (and on baseball) after a friend had taken her to Ebbets Field in 1949. "These men are natural artists," she recalled in 1962. "Why, I remember Don Zimmer playing at third base. He was moving toward the home plate when a fly came toward him. He had to get back to third and he backhanded it with his left hand."

Miss Moore delighted to entertain in moderation. Her guests

received tea and cookies, a glimpse of her watercolors (insects, flowers, and landscapes executed with minute care), and the offer of a subway token for the trip home. The token was proffered because she worried about her friends' financial health, just as she was concerned, in a mother-hen way, about their physical state. Guests were also likely to experience one of her monologues. Winthrop Sargeant described one of them in an article for *The New Yorker* in 1957. The starting point was a label on a sherry bottle. Mr. Sargeant wrote:

"At an afternoon gathering in her apartment a couple of months ago, the label led her to a consideration of other labels (though she might just as easily have veered in the direction of rabbits or quail), and this, in turn, led her to comment on grocery-store stocks, specifically on the stocks of the S. S. Pierce store in Boston.

" 'Very discriminating grocers,' she went on. 'Even if they do carry cigars and wine and cosmetics along with their cheese, jam, cakes, soups and all kinds of crackers. I can't abide dilutions or mixtures, but I like candy. If I drank whiskey, I would drink it straight. I have a lethal grudge against people who try to make me drink coffee. My friend Mrs. Church grinds her own coffee from French and American beans. Her husband's grandfather was a chemical inventor who invented a brand of bicarbonate of soda. His wife is a Bavarian. Mrs. Church, I mean. She had a house at Ville-d'Avray with a big cedar of Lebanon and a dog named Ti-quot. They had a gardener who also drove the car. They wouldn't have begonias on the place. They did have a few geraniums, though. Mr. Church was a close friend of Wallace Stevens, who wrote "The Necessary Angel." He reprinted an anecdote about Goethe wearing black woolen stockings on a packet boat. I like Goethe. My favorite language is German. I like the periodic structure of the sentences. "And Shakespeare inspires me, too. He has so many good quotations. And Dante. He has a few, too." That's from Ruth Draper. At Monroe Wheeler's once, we played a game called "Who would you rather be except Shakespeare?" I wouldn't mind being La Fontaine, or Voltaire. Or Montaigne? No. I wouldn't be Montaigne—too sombre. I have always loved the vernacular. It spites me that I can't write fiction. And that book of essays I wrote [*Predilections*], I let myself loose to do my utmost, and now they make me uneasy. The critics didn't care a great deal for them, but their reviews weren't really vipish. Those readings of my verse I made for the phonograph—well, they're here forever, like the wheat in the pyramids. I'm fond of Bach and Pachelbel and Stravinsky. I'm also fond of drums and trumpets— snare drums. If I find that a man plays the trumpet I am immediately interested. . . .'

". . . one of the guests finally reached the point of exhaustion, and exclaimed, 'Marianne, don't jump around so in your conversation!'

"Miss Moore paused, turned pityingly toward the heretic, and replied with spirit, 'It isn't jumping around. It's all connected.' Then she was off again."

Miss Moore was as cryptic a lecturer as she was a conversationalist, and she appeared to enjoy herself immensely, whether she talked at Harvard or to a woman's club. At one woman's club meeting she read some of her verse that included a line dealing with "metaphysical newmown hay." Afterward, a listener demanded to know what sort of hay that was. In a patient tone of voice, the poet replied: "Oh, something like a sudden whiff of fragrance in contrast with the doggedly continuous opposition to spontaneous conversation that had gone before."

Miss Moore took her advanced age with equanimity. "I look like a scarecrow, like Lazarus awakening. I look permanently alarmed," she told a visitor. "I aspire to be neat. I try to do my hair with a lot of thought to avoid those explosive sunbursts, but when one hairpin goes in, another comes out.

"My physiognomy isn't classic at all, it's like a banana-nosed monkey. Well, I do seem at least to be awake, don't I?"

❖

WALTER WINCHELL

"Other columnists may print it—I make it public," said Walter Winchell, the creator of modern gossip writing. His forthright self-assessment, typical of his brash, egotistical manner, was remarkably accurate, for in the twenty years of his heyday, from 1930 to 1950, he was by all odds the country's best-known and most widely read journalist as well as among its most influential.

Millions read "On Broadway," his syndicated daily column, and more millions listened to the weekly radio broadcasts that he addressed, in a staccato voice, to "Mr. and Mrs. America—and All the Ships at Sea." Yet when Winchell died of cancer at the age of seventy-four, his assertiveness, his glamour, and his personal style all seemed old hat. He was nonetheless generously thought of as the fast-talking song-and-dance man who had evoked an era as a newspaperman.

Left unsaid, or whispered, were recollections of his uneasy friendships in the late twenties and early thirties with important members of the underworld. He soft-pedaled those associations, preferring, especially in his prime, to portray himself as a hard-working reporter with access to inside information about personalities and events, which he summarized as "items" in his columns or broadcasts.

"WW," as he often styled himself, or "Mrs. Winchell's little boy, Walter," purveyed a mélange of intimate news about personalities, mostly in show business and politics; backstairs items about business and finance; bits and pieces about the underworld; denunciations of Italian and German fascism; diatribes against Commu niom; puffs for people, stocks, and events that pleased him; and a large smattering of innuendos.

Although Winchell was often demonstrably inaccurate or hyperbolic, he was implicitly believed by many of his readers and auditors. In clumsier hands, his "news" might not have made much impact, but he imparted a certain urgency and importance to what he wrote and said by the frantic and almost breathless style of his presentation. His column items were usually short and separated by dots and cast in breezy neologisms, while his broadcasts, delivered in a barking voice at the rate of 227 words a minute, sounded as compelling as the clicking telegraph key that accompanied them.

Not only did Winchell contrive the modern gossip column, but also he devised a language to go with it. "Inasmuch as he is chiefly concerned with the life of Broadway and its circumambient night life, his inventions have largely to do with the technics and hazards of its ethnology," H. L. Mencken reported in *The American Language*. Thus, in Winchellese, a person could start life as "a bundle from Heaven," attend "moom pitchers" in his youth, then be "on the merge" or "on fire" and "middle-aisle it" or be "welded" to a "squaw." Later on, the couple might "infanticipate" and be "storked" and perhaps have a "dotter," which could be the occasion for imbibing "giggle-water" along the "Bulb Belt." Still later, the couple's "pash" could dim and they would "phewd," "phfft" and employ "profanuage." Ultimately, they would be "renovated," but if they were sophisticated they still might attend a "revusical" together and gaze at its "terpischorines" and their comely "shafts."

Although Winchell was often thought lacking in taste, he had friends in high and low places. Among those in exalted places were President Franklin D. Roosevelt and J. Edgar Hoover, director of the Federal Bureau of Investigation. From the outset of the New Deal, the columnist was a fervent backer of Roosevelt, and early in his second term Winchell was invited to the White House for the first of several private conversations. At one press conference, the president made his feelings evident. "Walter, I've got an item for you—stick around," he said.

Winchell kept the president supplied with the latest Broadway jokes, and Roosevelt countered with news tidbits and encouragement for the columnist's vitriolic attacks on the "Ratskis," his name for the German Nazis and their American followers. These attacks, incidentally, infuriated the Nazis, who publicly excoriated their author as "a new hater of the New Germany." They also disquieted William Randolph Hearst, Winchell's boss, who ordered his editors "to leave out any dangerous or disagreeable paragraphs."

Hoover, another top-level friend, was chronicled admiringly in the column, and he and Winchell were frequent companions at Sherman Billingsley's Stork Club, a restaurant the columnist single-handedly made famous. Winchell's praise for Hoover (and his agents) developed into an enduring relationship. "Dear Walter," the FBI chief wrote in one letter that was signed "John," "Just a note to say hello. Do take good care of yourself and don't overdo because you are far too valuable to the country."

At the nether end of the scale, Winchell was on cordial terms with Frank Costello, a mob "don" who slipped him items from time to time; Al Capone, the Big Fellow of organized crime; and Owney Madden, a New York Hell's Kitchen roughneck known as The Killer, who had a big stake in the Manhattan booze business during Prohibition's last years. According to Tom Clark's *The World of Damon Runyon,* when Winchell was still a neophyte columnist in the twenties, Madden sought him out one day in a barbershop and said, "I like your stuff, kid."

"Thereafter," Clark wrote, "the two were constantly seen together in public, in nightclubs and restaurants, and at the [Madison Square] Garden on fight nights."

Although Winchell was never as sycophantic about mobsters as some other columnists, he was often "summoned" to audiences with them. "In 1929 he got a call from Capone in Florida," according to Clark. "He caught the first train to Miami and met with the Big Fellow at his Palm Island estate. Scarface . . . had a grumble about the newspapers. He griped to Winchell about 'phony inside-stuff writers who claim to know me.' . . . 'There's lots of grief attached to the limelight,' the Big Guy complained. . . . He demanded his tribute of respect from the scribes, and Winchell was delegated to make the commandment known. . . .

"Walter showed deep sympathy and promised to do what he could. And, of course, he did. Who needed a broken head?"

Later on, in the fifties, Winchell told Herman Klurfeld, an early and friendly biographer, that he had "secretly despised" his hoodlum associates. "The mobsters were wild," Winchell is quoted. "They could be as polite as headwaiters one minute and kill you the next." At the time, however, according to Klurfeld, the mob rulers "courted him, appointed themselves his bodyguards, believed it to be a mark of distinction to be seen in his presence and hoped he would mention them—or their girls—in his column."

It was through Frank Costello, his apartment-house neighbor, that Winchell was the hero in one of the most spectacular episodes of his career, the surrender of Louis (Lepke) Buchalter to the FBI's Hoover in 1939. Wanted in New York on capital charges and by the federal government for narcotics smuggling, Lepke was induced by Costello to telephone Winchell, offering to give himself up to Hoover if the columnist were present.

The result was that Winchell picked up the gangster on a Manhattan street corner and delivered him to Hoover a few blocks away.

"Mr. Hoover," said the columnist, "this is Lepke."

"How do you do," said Hoover.

"Glad to meet you," said the hoodlum.

In his prime years as a columnist, Winchell made the rounds of Broadway on the prowl for news. Of medium height, he was carefully tailored, and his cherubic face and blue eyes were set off by a snap-brim gray fedora that was his newspaperman's trademark. He loved to respond to police and fire calls (he had a police-band radio), often arriving at the scene first. His car, courtesy of the police, was outfitted with a siren and a red light.

At a crime, according to Bob Thomas's authoritative *Winchell,* he "interviewed victims and interrogated suspects, some of whom spilled out confessions because of awe over meeting" the columnist.

Winchell hustled for many of his items, but as time went on he came to rely more and more on press agents, some of whom were employed for their known or presumed ability to get their client's name in the column. These press agents came to Table Fifty in the Stork Club's Cub Room—Winchell's throne—to pay homage.

Press agents were rewarded for their gossip or their printable jokes or their suggestions by plugs for their clients. To one press agent who invented the word "neWWsboy," the columnist said in thanks, "I owe you five plugs." But press agents whose items proved unreliable or who in other items crossed Winchell were placed on his "DD," or drop-dead list, and were curtly banished from his presence (and his column) for varying periods. It was a dread experience.

Two press agents were enormously helpful to Winchell. One of them, Irving Hoffman, contributed what Thomas called "large portions" of the column while receiving film studio retainers for his ability to inspire Winchell's "orchids," or praise, for certain movies. Ernest Cuneo, a lawyer with connections in Washington, reportedly prepared a number of Winchell columns about public affairs. Some of the columns entitled "Things I Never Knew Till Now" were supplied by press agents, one of whom, Herman Klurfeld, was on the columnist's payroll. Many of the cloying verses that appeared over the signature of "Don Wahn" were spun from the pen of Philip Stack, a clerk at the Brooklyn Edison Company. With the exception of the poems, most Winchell columns bore his imprint, for he did edit, to a greater or lesser degree, the submissions of others.

Contrary to a widespread belief, "My Girl Friday," one of the most popular of the regular columns, was Winchell's and not that of Ruth Cambridge, his first secretary, or Rose Bigman, who succeeded her in 1935. The column was a potpourri of his secretary's notes to him and it contained occasional apologies and retractions.

Winchell lived and worked in a free-spending atmosphere to which he himself was immune. Save for a Westchester house he bought to please his wife, "he lavished money on nothing," Thomas reported, adding: "He hadn't the slightest inclination to art and other possessions. He owned eight suits, no more. He lived with utmost simplicity in an apartment which was useful only for sleeping. Every restaurant and nightclub owner in New York was eager to entertain him." He kept his money in cash in bank vaults. On becoming a millionaire in 1937, he had the Colony Club cater him an elegant meal, which he ate alone.

The plates and napery of that lunch were far removed from the poverty in which the columnist was reared. Born April 7, 1897, near the corner of Madison Avenue and 116th Street, in New York, Walter Winchell was the elder son of Jacob and Janette Bakst Winchel—the son later added a second "l" to the name. Jacob left the family when Walter was young, and the boy was obliged to learn the lessons of survival early.

He picked up his first money as a street-corner newsboy. When he was twelve he made his debut in the entertainment world.

George Jessel's mother urged the manager of the Imperial Theater to hire her son and Walter as ushers, but the boys persuaded the manager to try them out as singers. Their success was only middling, but it was sufficient for Walter to quit P.S. 184 in the sixth grade, which was the sum of his formal education.

That was an era of child performers, and Gus Edwards added the boys and Jack Wiener, another youngster, to his song revue, billing them as the Imperial Trio. Walter toured the country for two years with the Edwards revues in company with young Jessel, Eddie Cantor, Lila Lee, and Georgie Price. It was not an easy life, and Walter received a thorough knockabout education in the petty chicaneries of show business.

In 1915 Walter teamed in a vaudeville act with Rita Green, an act that once played for a week at the American Roof in New York. There was time out for World War I, in which Winchell, a volunteer in the Navy, served as an admiral's receptionist in New York. Returning to second-rate vaudeville after the war, Winchell began his column in embryo. He was with a Pantages road show in 1919, and he began typing and posting a bulletin that contained the gossip of the troupe. It was called "Newsense."

Winchell and Miss Green were married in 1920—the union lasted two years—and he began to submit show-business gossip columns to *Billboard,* an entertainment weekly, and later to *The Vaudeville News,* for which he went to work in 1922 as a combined reporter and advertising salesman. His column, "Stage Whispers," attracted attention, and he himself became known around Broadway as a bright and eager and very brash hustler who took notes with a left-handed scrawl.

In his rounds, he met June Magee, a red-haired dancer, whom he married in 1923. She died in 1970, reunited with her husband after a long estrangement.

After about two years on *The Vaudeville News,* Winchell demanded a larger field for his talents. He managed an introduction to Fulton Oursler of *The Evening Graphic,* a bizarre tabloid that had been founded in 1924 by Bernarr Macfadden, an eccentric millionaire food faddist and physical-culture advocate. Winchell was hired to write a column and play reviews and to serve as drama editor, amusement editor, and ad solicitor. His pay was $100 a week.

The Graphic was a freewheeling paper, but at first Winchell's column (it was then weekly) was curiously staid in the midst of its surrounding sensationalism. One day in 1925, with no jokes or poems for his column, he sat down and typed out a clutch of gossip notes he had acquired on his theatrical beat. The first few items read:

"Helen Eby Brooks, widow of William Rock, has been plunging in Miami real estate.... It's a girl at the Carter de Havens.... Lenore Ulric paid $7 income tax.... Fanny Brice is betting on the horses at Belmont.... S. Jay Kaufman sails on the 16th via the Berengaria to be hitched to a Hungarian.... Report has it that Lillian Lorraine has taken a husband again...."

It was the prototype of Winchell columns for almost forty years. Shortly "Your Broadway and Mine," the column's title then, was the backbone of *The Graphic*'s circulation.

There had been columnists before Winchell, notably Colonel William d'Alton Mann, a dashing scalawag who wrote about society personalities for the weekly *Town Topics*. But none indulged in saucy gossip, nor wrote with piquancy. These were Winchell's contributions to the genre. Others sought to emulate him in New York and other cities, but none managed to capture his special flavor. For this reason, "making Winchell"—being mentioned in his column—was a badge of almost unbearable distinction.

Winchell's years at *The Graphic*—they ended in 1929—were filled with tensions. He and Emile Gauvreau, the hard-driving managing editor, frequently exchanged shouted abuse in the city room. At *The Graphic*, the columnist also began his long feud with Ed Sullivan, a fellow reporter. Its origins were trivial, but its proportions and its vituperativeness grew with years as Sullivan and Winchell became rival columnists. Their differences were ultimately patched up after Winchell had retired.

Leaving *The Graphic* after an explosive display of temper and exchange of invective, Winchell transferred himself and his column to William Randolph Hearst's morning tabloid, *The Daily Mirror*. His first column appeared there June 10, 1929, and he was paid the then-astronomical sum of $500 a week, testimony to his ability to draw circulation.

His *Mirror* columns set off a number of flurries in teacups, always to the advantage of newsstand sales. For example, he enraged Earl Carroll, the producer, by panning his shows. (Slyly, he quoted Groucho Marx as saying of one of them, "I saw it at a disadvantage—the curtain was up.") Other columns offended the Shuberts, powerful theater owners and producers, who barred him briefly from their premises. Winchell's barbs also got under the skins of Westbrook Pegler, the sportswriter and conservative Scripps-Howard columnist; Eleanor (Cissy) Patterson, owner of *The Washington Times-Herald;* and various congressional targets of convenience. In those years Winchell, often to the distaste of his employer, was accounted a New Dealer, which explains the verve of his attacks on such as Mrs. Patterson.

For one so much around and about, Winchell had few intimates, but among them was Damon Runyon, a fellow Hearst writer and night owl, whose classic Broadway tales included a transparent and teasing portrait of Winchell as Waldo Winchester. Their friendship became particularly close in 1944 after Runyon had lost his power of speech. "Walter and I make the ideal companions," Runyon wrote. "He loves to talk, and I can't do anything but listen."

Not only did Runyon become a welcome habitué of Table Fifty at the Stork Club, but he also accompanied Winchell in his restless predawn patrols of New York streets in pursuit of police and fire calls. The two loners, together at least eight hours a day, were called, somewhat tritely, Damon and Pythias. On Runyon's death of throat cancer in 1946, his friend, genuinely grief-stricken, established a cancer research fund, which by 1970 had collected and disbursed $32 million, with no skim for administrative costs.

The awesome power and influence of Winchell's column started to wane in the late forties. He did not hit it off with President Harry S Truman, and anti-Truman items began to sprinkle the column, a situation that did not sit well with liberal New Yorkers, the backbone of his popularity. He countenanced an episode of discrimination against Josephine Baker, the black entertainer, and wrote columns disparaging to her; and he feuded with Dorothy Schiff, publisher of *The New York Post,* as well as with Leonard Lyons, one of its columnists.

These were all signals of a political turnabout that took the columnist to the far right, resulting in his championship of Senator Joseph R. McCarthy and his investigations and in screeching anti-Communist columns.

Moreover, appearing on television, Winchell dealt in horse tips, as he had formerly, over the radio, and touted stocks. Communications executives became wary of him because he devoted so much of his time to his feuds and vendettas. His column slipped from 800 papers to 175, and it virtually disappeared with the demise in 1963 of *The Mirror,* whose circulation he had sustained for many years. For a while he saw print one day a week in *The World Journal Tribune,* but that paper, too, folded.

He tried syndication himself without much luck. The king of the columnists was now a commoner, a victim of his own excesses and of changing public taste. "Let's face it," said Robert Sylvester, a New York *Daily News* columnist, in 1967, "the decline of Broadway meant the decline of the Broadway column. Broadway was once a great, glamorous street. Now look at it. It's shoddy. You can't be the historian of something that no longer exists."

A perceptive press agent also noted that although the public was still interested in scandal, a new life-style had taken over. "Look, you have glamorous stars now openly living with each other," he said. "You get people going on TV and talking about the most intimate things. You get magazine articles that are incredibly blunt.

"Everything's changed. No one's shocked any more."

A measure of Winchell's decline was his seventieth birthday party in New York. Only a few prominent entertainers showed up, among them Jimmy Durante. The columnist moved away from the city in 1965 for the West, where he lived either in Los Angeles or Arizona. For the last several years he stayed at the Ambassador in Los Angeles, a lonely figure. His son, Walter Jr., committed suicide in 1967.

The bounce had gone out of him. "I have stopped seeing everyone," he wrote Thomas in 1970. "There is nothing I want to discuss about my career. I leave it to you historians to deal with."

EDMUND WILSON

Edmund Wilson, who wrote with erudition and a passion for excellence about literature, history, anthropology, and economics, died at the age of seventy-seven in a very old stone house in Talcottsville, an upstate New York village that had served as the setting of his last published book, *Upstate: Records and Recollections of Northern New York*. Like its predecessors in a remarkable oeuvre, the book reflected its author's penetrating intelligence and felicity of style. But of all the mediums in which he labored, literary criticism seemed most to become him, and the appellation "literary critic" was the one most frequently applied to him. He would have preferred to be thought of as a man of letters, yet by common consent he was the most wide-ranging, most productive, most finicky, and most dyspeptic critic of his time. He was certainly among the most didactic and most influential, although his work did not encompass the black and feminist writers of the sixties, nor many of the post-World War II literary figures. Even so, there was no question of his devotion to American letters generally and to the humanism that literature represents.

For fifty years Wilson, who regarded literature as "a history of man's ideas and imaginings in the setting of the conditions which have shaped them," wrote elegantly, chiefly for the intellectually elite; yet such was the force of his judgments that he conferred reputations on writers and fashioned, as a result, the reading tastes of millions, to whom he himself was but a shadowy figure.

Like Samuel Johnson and his own mentor, Hippolyte Taine, the nineteenth-century French historian and critic, and like Charles Sainte-Beuve, also a nineteenth-century French critic, Wilson was a man of letters in the broadest sense. Besides being a critic, he was a novelist, short-story writer, playwright, poet, historian, Bible authority, essayist, literary quarreler, self-interviewer, and autobiographer. Having learned as an adult to read German, Russian, Hebrew, and Hungarian, and versed from adolescence in Greek, French, and Italian, he ranged effortlessly through Western literature and culture. From his well-furnished mind he was able to draw apposite allusions and examples to illuminate his diverse writings, the bulk of which, however, were essentially critical.

"For me," he once remarked, "literary criticism has always meant narrative and drama as well as an establishing of comparative values. On the comparative side, my function has, I think, been to make an effort to see in relation to one another, to bring into the same cultural sphere, a number of literary fields which have been in some cases hardly aware of one another."

Four of Wilson's books represented direct attempts to apply his humanist and historical values to writers and the culture that nurtured them. These were *Axel's Castle* in 1931, *To the Finland Station* in 1940, *The Wound and the Bow* in 1941, and *Patriotic Gore* in 1962. The first analyzed the work of Yeats, Eliot, Pound, and Joyce in terms of the French symbolist movement; the second dealt with Vico, Saint-Simon, Michelet, Taine, Marx, Engels, Lenin, and Trotsky in terms of the revolutionary tradition in Europe; the third concerned the dualism of Dickens, Kipling, Casanova, Edith Wharton, Hemingway, and Joyce; and the fourth treated Harriet Beecher Stowe, Lincoln, Grant, Sherman, and a number of others who left a record of their experiences leading up to or during the Civil War.

In other words the critic paid his respects to many of his contemporaries—Fitzgerald, Steinbeck, Faulkner, Aldous Huxley, Louis Bromfield, Katherine Anne Porter, Dorothy Parker, John O'Hara, Thornton Wilder, Malraux, and Sartre, among others. Contemplating O'Hara, Wilson found that his work derived from Hemingway and James M. Cain, but that "his writing really belongs to a different category of fiction."

"O'Hara," he declared, "is primarily a social commentator [who] subjects to a Proustian scrutiny the tight-knitted social web of a large Pennsylvania town, the potpourri of New York night life in the twenties, the nondescript fringes of Hollywood. In all this he has explored for the first time from his peculiar semisnobbish point of view a good deal of interesting territory."

Wilson bestowed his approval on Faulkner, but it was not unalloyed. Reviewing *Intruder in the Dust,* he remarked bluntly that "it ought to be said that, from the point of view of the writing, this is one of the more snarled up of Mr. Faulkner's books." But Wilson did not limit his criticism to the kind of writers usually discussed in literary journals. He wrote of Emily Post and her etiquette books, and in an essay entitled "Who Cares Who Killed Roger Ackroyd?" he reported his conclusion that detective stories were a waste of an intelligent reader's time. He had worked his way, with characteristic thoroughness, through dozens of popular successes in that genre.

He would discuss writers long forgotten and others who had never been much known. The writing was always direct and pungent. He began an essay called "What Became of Louis Bromfield?" this way: "In the days of 'The Green Bay Tree' and 'The Strange Case of Miss Annie Spragg,' Mr. Louis Bromfield used to be spoken of as one of the youngest writers of promise. By the time he had brought out 'Twenty-Four Hours,' it was more or less generally said of him that he was definitely second rate. Since then, by unremitting industry and a kind of stubborn integrity that seems to make it impossible for him to turn out his rubbish without thoroughly believing in it, he has gradually made his way into the fourth rank, where his place is now secure."

His books of criticism brought Wilson his renown; a collection of six stories satirizing suburban manners and morals, *Memoirs of Hecate County,* earned him notoriety. Published in 1946, the book was banned in New York State as obscene, chiefly for one story, "The Princess With the Golden Hair." The story, told in the first person, contrasted the sex life of a suburban matron with that of a city working girl. Its love scenes, tame by today's standards, shocked the court of special sessions.

Reflecting a general attitude toward him in the 1960's, Sherman Paul, author of a book on Wilson, wrote: "We think of Wilson, as he probably intended us to, when we read in *Patriotic Gore* of the old Romans of the old America." Professor Paul had in mind Wilson's reputation for incorruptibility; but he could also have been describing his physical appearance and his patrician attitudes. Of medium height and tending to paunchiness, his body was dominated by a massive head. His features—a high forehead and a slightly jutting jaw, resembled those of a bulldog in repose. He was, though, not so much pugnacious as he was disdainful or impatient with lesser intellects. Some of this was reflected in a letter he once sent to the British weekly *The New Statesman.* "I read your journal mostly with admiration," he wrote, "but I do wish you would not so often confuse 'titillate' with 'titivate.' "

Another facet was shown in a self-interview in *The New Yorker* in 1962 that dealt with a trip to Britain. It read in part: "INTERVIEWER: What brings you to England, Mr. Wilson?

"WILSON: I wanted to dine at the Café Royal. I have never been able to get any English friend to go there with me. They always say that it isn't what it used to be. But I want to see it all the same. That's one reason, and another is that I want to get a set of Ackermann's 'London' at a somewhat cheaper price than they ask for it in the United States. I feel that when I've achieved those two objectives, I need never come to London again."

And later in the "interview," when Wilson was asking himself his opinions of various British writers, he wrote: "INTERVIEWER: And Anthony Powell [the novelist]—have you read him?

"WILSON: I don't see why you make so much fuss about him. He's just entertaining enough to read in bed late at night in summer, when his books usually reach me. If Evelyn Waugh is the Shakespeare of this school, Powell is the Middleton or Day. It's a pity he never dipped into Proust—and that goes for Durrell, too, though of course Durrell did more than dip, he saturated himself completely. Durrell is even better to read in bed."

Inevitably, as his writing gained attention, Wilson was beset, even beleaguered, by appeals to his limited supply of good nature. To fend them off he devised a printed postcard that read in full:

"Edmund Wilson regrets that it is impossible for him to: Read manuscripts, write articles or books to order, write forewords or introductions, make statements for publicity purposes, do any kind of editorial work, judge literary contests, give interviews, take part in writers' conferences, answer questionnaires, contribute to or take part in symposiums or 'panels' of any kind, contribute manuscripts for sales, donate copies of his books to libraries, autograph works for strangers, allow his name to be used on letterheads, supply personal information about himself, supply opinions on literary or other subjects."

Alas, the postcard was self-defeating, for people wrote him just to get a copy of it. The critic's desire to be left in peace was understandable in view of the care and diligence with which he worked. He often called himself a journalist and, in fact, many of his essays appeared in their first form in such magazines as *The*

New Republic, The New Yorker, and *The New York Review of Books.* These he expanded and burnished for his books, and this required enormous concentration. Partly, too, he disliked dealing with strangers because of his stutter and his absentmindedness. He thus accumulated a reputation for bad manners. Richard Chase, a Melville scholar, once wrote:

"People who write about Edmund Wilson are likely to include a note on how badly he acted when they saw him at a party. So I had better add that when I saw him at a party he was amenable enough. He made a point of sitting beside me like a benign if somewhat nettled uncle, and he asked me about Melville's poems, which he was reading at that time. The great man somewhat confounded me, and I forgot most of whatever I knew about Melville's poems. We talked about Whitman, and Wilson emphatically pronounced him the greatest of our classic writers ('The Scarlet Letter,' on the other hand, was a 'fraud'). Wilson seemed rather baffled by me and soon retired to a corner with the host, who helped him puzzle out a Yiddish newspaper that had been sticking out of his pocket when he entered the house."

Chase did not catch Wilson at small parties he gave in his apartment or at his home on Cape Cod. On these occasions, he delighted his guests with his skill at puppetry, especially Punch and Judy shows, and with his aptitude for magic, which he picked up in Italy when he was a boy.

A command of culture came naturally to Edmund Wilson, for it was a world into which he was born and in which he was reared. The only child of Edmund and Helen Mather Kimball Wilson, he was born May 8, 1895, in Red Bank, New Jersey. His father, a successful lawyer, served a term as attorney general of New Jersey. His mother, also of professional background, put store by books and art as household equipment. When the boy was thirteen his parents took him to Europe for a thorough tour of the cultural sights of Italy, Austria, Germany, France, and Britain. A year later he was sent to the Hill School in Pottstown, Pennsylvania, where his first months were agonizing and rebellious. "My mother, with characteristic lack of tact, had called me 'Bunny' when she brought me on and, at a first get-together in my rooming-house, this was taken up by the boys," Edmund explained later with some asperity. "I tried to fight everybody who did this, but was outnumbered, and the house-master broke it up. I have been saddled with this nickname all my life. When I later asked my mother why she had called me that, she gave me the even more embarrassing explanation that she used to say about me as a baby that, with my black eyes, I 'looked just like a plum-bun.' "

Throughout his life Wilson endured his nickname, but barely. Use of it to his face was a certain invitation to disfavor. "Bunny," though, was freely employed behind his back. Edmund began to practice his métier at Hill with a story for the school magazine, of which he became editor. At Princeton, which followed Hill from 1912 to 1916, the young man continued to display literary and critical abilities. On the staff of *The Nassau Literary Magazine*, he encouraged his friend and fellow student, F. Scott Fitzgerald, to contribute. It was the start of a novelist's career on which Wilson had an enduring influence. The association of the two Princetonians lasted beyond Fitzgerald's life. Two years after Fitzgerald died in 1940, Wilson edited his friend's autobiographical memoir, *The Crack-Up*. For the dedication he wrote a poem that began:

> Scott, your last fragments I arrange
>   tonight,
> Assigning commas, setting accents right,
> As once I punctuated, spelled and
>   trimmed,
> When passing in a Princeton spring—how
>   dimmed
> By this damned quarter century and
>   more!—
> You left your Shadow Laurels at my
>   door.

He also edited his friend's posthumous novel *The Last Tycoon* and gave it its title. Both tasks were performed without fee.

Majoring in literature, Wilson was stimulated by Professor

Christian Gauss and by the writings of H. L. Mencken, Shaw, and James Gibbons Huneker, the American critic. He also traveled abroad in these years, soaking up more of Europe on each trip. His humanism and interest in European cultures, encouraged by Gauss, were enhanced by a postgraduate summer at Columbia, where he studied sociology and economics, and by a stint as a reporter on *The Evening Sun* in New York.

After World War I, in which Wilson served successively as a private, a hospital attendant in France, and a member of the Intelligence Corps, he joined the staff of *Vanity Fair* and was its managing editor in 1920–21. Recalling him as an editor, Zelda Fitzgerald described him as "beautiful and bloodless." Her husband, Scott, was less cryptic. He wrote of his friend "walking briskly through the crowd [in New York] wearing a tan raincoat over his inevitable brown get-up," cane in hand, confident, "wrapped in his own thoughts and looking straight ahead." In those years Wilson also wrote essays on Fitzgerald, Willa Cather, Pound, Byron, Poe, O'Neill, Hemingway, Lardner, Stephen Crane, and William James. In addition, he collaborated with John Peale Bishop, a Princeton friend, on *The Undertaker's Garland*, a book of satiric verse and prose about death and funerals.

From 1926 to 1931, Wilson was associate editor and principal book reviewer for *The New Republic*. In addition to commenting on the literary scene and introducing, among many others, John Dos Passos as a gifted writer, he wrote *Discordant Encounters*, imaginary dialogues between men of contrasting opinions, and *Poets Farewell!*, a volume of lyrics and verse sketches, mostly satirical. He also published, in 1929, his only novel, *I Thought of Daisy*, a book about Greenwich Village with characters that some readers insisted on recognizing. He revised it for republication in 1967, and in his introduction to that edition he was at pains to disabuse those who saw the narrator of the first-person story as Wilson. "Nothing annoys me more than to have the characters and incidents which figure in my works of fiction represented as descriptions of real people and events," he wrote. "In the case of a still living writer, such guesses are something of an impertinence." Nonetheless, he did transmute some of his experiences into stories, though the incidents were rearranged and disguised.

Of his articles for *The New Republic* the most political was "An Appeal to Progressives," published in 1931, about a year after the onset of the Depression. In it Wilson attacked the myth of a prosperous American society and the hopes of liberals that it might be gradually reformed. "The present depression," he said in urging liberals to become concerned, "may be one of the turning points in our history, our first real crisis since the Civil War." In suggesting a radical approach to the country's plight, he invited intellectuals to consider the American Communist party. He found its dogmas narrow, but said radicals "must take Communism away from the Communists, and take it without ambiguities, asserting that their ultimate goal is the ownership by the Government of the means of production." And in an article the following year he issued a virtual call to arms, saying: "So, American intelligentsia—scientists, philosophers, artists, engineers—who have been weltering so long in prostitutions and frustrations, that phase of human life is done. Stagger out of the big office, the big mill—look beyond your useless bankrupt fields and pastures!"

Finally, in the presidential election of 1932, he was one of a number of writers who supported the Communist ticket of William Z. Foster and James W. Ford. By this time he had already established himself with *Axel's Castle* as one of the nation's foremost critics; and he added to that reputation with *The American Jitters,* a collection of articles on American politics and society during the slump. In 1935 Wilson traveled and studied in the Soviet Union under a Guggenheim Fellowship. He was generally disillusioned by the experience, though he found many things of which he approved.

Meanwhile he had been working on a long book, *To the Finland Station* (1940), his study of the revolutionary tradition in Europe. With his customary scholarship he prepared himself by reading not only all of Marx and Engels, but also such nineteenth-century social theorists as Lasalle and Bakunin. After tracing the development of this tradition, he concluded in the final paragraph of the book that it was unlikely that Marxist formulas would be able to lead to "a society in which the superior development of some is not paid for by the exploitation, that is, by the deliberate degradation, of others."

In 1938 Wilson, then forty-three, had married Mary McCarthy, the twenty-five-year-old book critic for *The Nation*. He had been married twice previously. His first marriage, to Mary Blair, had ended in divorce; his second wife, Margaret Canby, had died in an accident. The union with Miss McCarthy, which lasted seven years, tended to be troubled, at least in his wife's recollection. She found him domineering in his views, so that everything that came under his hand was shaped into "an authorized version." She also reported that at one point Wilson said, " 'I think you've got a talent for writing short stories.' So he put me off in one free room with a typewriter and shut the door."

The forties were fruitful years. He published *The Boys in the Back Room* in 1941, *The Wound and the Bow* also in 1941, *Notebooks of Night* in 1942, *The Shock of Recognition* in 1943, *Memoirs of Hecate County* in 1945, and *Europe Without Baedeker* in 1947. His apparent slacking off after 1944 was illusory, for in that year he became book reviewer for *The New Yorker*. His almost weekly treatment of new books was demanding, long-range, and scholarly, an attitude that irritated some readers accustomed to the blander criticism of Clifton Fadiman, Wilson's predecessor. Although Wilson ceased to be a regular contributor to the magazine in 1948, he continued for years to submit book reviews and feature articles. For example, from his *New Yorker* articles emerged "The Scrolls From the Dead Sea" in 1955. This book, rationalist in tone, brought him into conflict with orthodox interpreters of the theological implications of the scrolls. It was, however, based on an enormous body of archeological information that he had amassed in visits to the Middle East. Also from his magazine articles he shaped *Apologies to the Iroquois,* issued in 1949, which was both an account of his life among the Iroquois Indians and a discussion of how to right the injustices done to them over the years.

The significant book of Wilson's later life was *Patriotic Gore,* on which he worked off and on for fifteen years. Critics called it a masterly study of the literature of the Civil War, at once encyclopedic and profound. In 1963, a year after its publication, the writer underwent an experience that puzzled him deeply. He published a polemic, *The Cold War and the Income Tax,* a detailed recital of his troubles with the Internal Revenue Service and an indictment of federal spending for the war in Vietnam and for defense. "I have finally come to feel that this country, whether or not I live in it, is no longer any place for me," he wrote. Almost simultaneously he was awarded the Presidential Medal of Freedom, the nation's highest civilian honor. The citation acclaimed him as a "critic and historian [who] has converted criticism itself into a creative act, while setting for the nation a stern and uncompromising standard of independent judgment." He did not leave the United States. Instead he continued to live, as he had for many years, with Elena von Mumm Thornton, his fourth wife, in virtual seclusion in Wellfleet on Cape Cod, in Talcottville, and in the Caribbean.

In the years after 1963 Wilson got into at least two furious quarrels. One was with Vladimir Nabokov over the latter's translation of Pushkin from the Russian. The other was with the Modern Language Association over its scholarly editions of American authors. Wilson considered these editions pedantic to the point of uselessness.

A month before he died *The Times Literary Supplement* of London, in a cover essay on Wilson and his book *Upstate,* praised the scope and scale of the author's interests. "Only the European panoptic scholars come near matching Wilson for learning, and for sheer range of critical occupation there is no modern man to match him," the weekly said. The book is a personal and elegiac diary of a man growing old in the place where as a child he had first learned he was capable of "imaginative activity and some sort of literary vocation."

Generous honors came to Wilson in the late sixties. He won the

National Medal for Literature in 1966 and, with it, $5,000. The award, he said, was "all the more welcome for being, as I understand it, tax-free, so that not a penny of it will be demanded for the infamous war in Vietnam and for our staggering appropriations in the interest of so-called defense, which, when I last examined the budget in 1964, amounted, together with space programs and the cost of past wars, to seventy-nine percent of the total." Two years later he received the Aspen Award for his contributions to the humanities. With it went $30,000 also tax-free. At that time, in a rare public appearance, Wilson commented on his studies in Greek and Russian and on his examinations of the Dead Sea Scrolls and American Indian lore. "Now, I am far from an authority on any of these subjects but, out of a volatile curiosity and an appetite for varied entertainment, I have done reading in all of them; and I have been working, as a practicing critic, to break down the conventional frames, to get away from academic canons, that always tend to keep literature provincial."

He could have fashioned no more apposite epitaph.

PABLO PICASSO

The Pablo Picasso who died at the imposing age of ninety-two at his villa above Cannes on the Riviera was an artist of multiple skills and changeable personal traits. There was Picasso the neoclassicist; Picasso the cubist; Picasso the surrealist; Picasso the modernist; Picasso the ceramist; Picasso the lithographer; Picasso the sculptor; Picasso the superb draftsman; Picasso the political partisan; Picasso the effervescent and exuberant; Picasso the saturnine and surly; Picasso the faithful and faithless lover; Picasso the crafty financial man; Picasso the publicity seeker; Picasso the recluse; Picasso the smoldering Spaniard; Picasso the joker and mime; Picasso the generous; Picasso the miser; even Picasso the playwright.

A genius for the ages possessing virtually boundless fecundity, a man who initiated wonderful yet sometimes outrageous changes, Pablo Picasso remains without doubt the most original, the most protean, and the most forceful personality in the visual arts in the first three quarters of this century. He took a prodigious gift and with it transformed the universe of art. Henri Matisse and Georges Braque, two painters with assured stature in modern art and both his close friends, were also original; but both developed a style and worked within its confines, whereas Picasso, with a feverish creativity and lavish talent lasting into old age, was a man of many styles whose artistic life was a continuous process of exploration. In a sense, he created his own universe, peopling it with humans of his own devising and his own forms of beasts, birds, and flora and investing them all with his own mythopoetry.

"For me, a picture is neither an end nor an achievement, but rather a lucky chance and art experience," he once explained. "I try to represent what I have found, not what I am seeking. I do not seek—I find." On another occasion, however, he saw his work in a different light. "Everything I do," he remarked at seventy-six, "is only one step on a long road. It is a preliminary process that may be achieved much later. Therefore my works must be seen in relation to one another, keeping in mind what I have already done and what I will do."

For all his guises, or disguises, Picasso had an amazing fertility of imagination that permitted him to metamorphize a mood or an idea into a work of art with bewildering quickness. He was, in André Malraux's phrase, "the archwizard of modern art," a man who, as a painter alone, produced well over six thousand pictures. Some he splashed off in a few hours; others took weeks. In 1969, his eighty-eighth year, he produced out of his volcanic energy a total of 165 paintings and 45 drawings, which were exhibited at the Palace of the Popes in Avignon, France. Crowding the walls of that venerable structure, the Picasso array drew exclamatory throngs and moved Emily Genauer, the critic, to say, "I think Picasso's new pictures are the fire of heaven." Explaining the source of this energy, Picasso said as he neared ninety, "Everyone is the age he has decided on, and I have decided to remain thirty."

The painter was so much known for works that blurred or obliterated conventional distinctions between beauty and ugliness and for depersonalized forms that he was accused of being an antihumanist. That appraisal disturbed him, for he regarded himself, with all his vagaries, as having created new insights into a seen and unseen world in which fragmentation of form was the basis for a new synthesis. "What is art?" a visitor once asked him. "What is not?" he replied. And he substantiated this point once by combining a bicycle seat and a pair of handlebars to make a bull's head.

"Whatever the source of the emotion that drives me to create, I want to give it a form that has some connection with the visible world, even if it is only to wage war on that world," he explained to Françoise Gilot, one of his mistresses and herself a painter. "Otherwise," he continued, "a painter is just an old grab bag for everyone to reach into and pull out what he himself has put in. I want my paintings to be able to defend themselves, to resist the invader, just as though there were razor blades on all surfaces so no one could touch them without cutting his hands. A painting isn't a market basket or a woman's handbag, full of combs, hairpins, lipstick, old love letters, and keys to the garage.

"Valéry used to say, 'I write half the poem. The reader writes the other half.' That's all right for him, maybe, but I don't want there to be three or four thousand possibilities of interpreting my canvas. I want there to be only one and in that one to some extent the possibility of recognizing nature, even distorted nature, which is, after all, a kind of struggle between my interior life and the external world as it exists for most people. As I've often said, I don't try to express nature; rather, as the Chinese put it, to work like nature. And I want that internal surge—my creative dynamism—to propose itself to the viewer in the form of traditional painting violated."

In the long course of upending traditionalism, Picasso became a one-man history of modern art. In every phase of its turbulent (and often violent) development he was either a daring pioneer or a gifted practitioner. The sheer variousness of his creations reflected his probings of modern art for ways to communicate the multiplicity of its expressions; and so Picasso could not be categorized as belonging to this or that school, for he opened and tried virtually all of them. In his peripateticism he worked in oils, watercolors, pastels, gouaches, pencil and ink drawings, and aquatints; he etched, made lithographs, sculptured, fashioned ceramics, put together mosaics, and constructed murals.

One of his masterpieces was "Guernica," painted in 1937 and on loan for many years to the Museum of Modern Art in New York. An oil on canvas 11¼ feet high and 25½ feet long, it is a majestic, stirring indictment of the destructiveness of modern war. By contrast, another masterpiece was a simply and perfectly drawn white pigeon, "The Dove," which was disseminated around the world as a symbol of peace. But whether masterpiece or something not so exalted, virtually all Picassos were interesting and provocative. Praised or reviled, his work never evoked quiet judgments. The artist, however, held a different view. "There is no such thing as a bad Picasso," he said. "Some are less good than others."

Exhibitions of his work, especially in his later years, were sure-fire attractions. The mention of his name was sufficient to lure thousands, many of them only barely acquainted with any art, to museums and galleries and benefits. Reproductions and prints were hung up in homes all over the Western world, a mark of the owner's claim to culture. Originals were widely dispersed, both in museums and in the hands of collectors wealthy enough to meet Picasso's prices—and they were steep. In 1965 he charged London's Tate Gallery $168,000 for "Les Trois Danseuses," a painting he did in 1925. For the last fifty years there has been no such thing as a cheap Picasso. Leo and Gertrude Stein and Ambroise Vollard, a Paris dealer, may have been the last to get a Picasso for $30, and that was in 1906 and 1907.

As Picasso's fame grew, so did his income, until it got so that he could manufacture money by sketching a few lines on a piece of paper and tacking on his dramatic signature. He was probably the world's highest paid pieceworker, and there were many years in which he garnered more than a million dollars. "I am rich enough to throw away a thousand dollars," he told a friend with some glee.

The artist, however, was canny about money, driving hard bargains with his dealers and keeping the bulk of his work off the market. He released for sale about forty of his paintings a year out of a production of hundreds, so that the market was never glutted. What he did not sell (and he said that many of these constituted the best from his palette) he squirreled away in bank vaults, studios, in a castle not far from the Riviera, and in empty rooms in his villa near Cannes. Picasso did not exactly hide his collection, for on occasion he permitted special friends to see it, to photograph it, and to publish the results. Toward the close of his life he donated eight hundred to nine hundred of his finest early works to a Barcelona museum. Worth a multimillion-dollar fortune, his works represented his Spanish period and were given in memory of Jaime Sabartès, his longtime secretary. In 1971 he gave an early constructed sculpture, "Guitar," to the Museum of Modern Art in New York.

Mostly, though, Picasso took a merchant's delight in acquiring money. "Art is a salable commodity," he once observed. "If I want as much money as I can get for my art, it is because I know what I want to do with it." Contrary to Miss Gilot's suggestion that Picasso was tightfisted, he gave large sums to the Republican side in the Spanish Civil War and then to refugee groups that cared for the defeated Republicans who had fled to France.

"He was a very generous man," Daniel-Henry Kahnweiler, his principal dealer since 1912, said of him. "He supported for many years more than a dozen indigent painters, most of whom would have been living in poverty but for his help. And whenever he was asked to help some charities, he always gave something." He was surprisingly openhanded, in a quiet fashion, with the women of his past. One of these was Fernande Olivier, who was his mistress for a number of years until 1912 and whose book about her experiences with him was not flattering. However, when Picasso heard that her funds were running low, he saw to it that she was supplied with money.

His generosity, like his temperament, could be mercurial. Once, when the faking of Picassos was a small industry, a friend brought the painter a small work belonging to a poor artist for authentication so that it could be sold. "It's false," said Picasso. From a different source the friend brought another Picasso, then a third. "It's false," Picasso said each time. "Now listen, Pablo," the friend said of the third painting. "I watched you paint this with my own eyes."

"I can paint false Picassos just as well as anybody," Picasso replied. And then he bought the first Picasso at four times the amount the poor artist had hoped it would fetch.

As for himself, Picasso, from the time he began to take in appreciable sums until his death, lived like an Okie, albeit one who never had to worry about where his next meal or his next pair of trousers was coming from. "I should like to live like a poor man with a lot of money," he had said in the days when he was desperately poor and burning some of his canvases for heat. All his studios and homes—even the eighteen-room rambling La Californie at Cannes—were crammed and cluttered with junk—pebbles, rocks, pieces of glass, a hollow elephant's foot, a bird cage, African drums, wooden crocodiles, parts of old bicycles, ancient newspapers, broken crockery, bullfight posters, old hats, weird ceramics. Picasso was a compulsive collector of oddments, and he never threw any of them away, or permitted anyone to move any object once he had dropped it, tossed it, or placed it somewhere. To compound the chaos inside La Californie, the villa's lawn was home to clucking chickens, pigeons, at least one goat, dogs, and children. They all disported among bronze owls, fountains, and statuary scattered about the grounds. Freedom for animals and children was a cardinal belief. In later years this villa became a weekend residence, while his main home was Notre Dame de Vie in nearby Mougins.

Despite the disorganization with which he surrounded himself, Picasso was a most methodical man. When he drove to Cannes or to Arles he invariably followed the same route; and when he lived in Paris he walked or rode the same streets in a fixed order. When his Paris studio was at 7 rue des Grand-Augustins on the Left Bank, he almost always dined at La Brasserie Lipp on the Boulevard Saint-Germain and then crossed the street to the Café Flore to join friends for mineral water and conversation before going home. One Picasso day was, in outline, much like the next. He rose late, usually around ten or eleven, devoted two or three hours to friends, conversation, business, letters, and lunch; then, at three or four, he would go to his studio to work in Trappist silence, often for twelve hours at a stretch, breaking off only for dinner around ten-thirty. Afterward, he sometimes worked until two or three in the morning.

When Miss Gilot was living with Picasso in Paris, she found that one of her most difficult tasks was to get him started on his day. "He always woke up submerged in pessimism, and there was a definite ritual to be followed, a litany that had to be repeated every day," she recalled in her book, *Life With Picasso*. The rigmarole, as Miss Gilot recounts it, had largely to do with reassuring Picasso that his lamentations were falsely based. "Well, I do despair," he would say in Miss Gilot's reconstruction. "I'm pretty nearly desperate. I wonder, really, why I bother to get up. Why should I paint? Why should I continue to exist like this? A life like mine is unbearable."

Eventually Picasso would permit himself to be convinced that the world was not in conspiracy against him. Part of his maledicent mood could perhaps be traced to the physical aspects of his bedroom. "At the far end was a high Louis XIII secretary," according to Miss Gilot, "and, along the left-hand wall, a chest of the same period, both completely covered with papers, books, magazines and mail that Pablo hadn't answered and never would, drawings piled up helter skelter, and packages of cigarettes. Above the bed was a naked electric light bulb. Behind the bed were drawings

Pablo was particularly fond of, attached by clothespins to nails driven into the wall. The so-called more important letters, which he didn't answer either but kept before him as a permanent reminder and reproach, were pinned up, also with clothespins, onto wires that stretched from the electric-light wire to the stovepipe. There was almost no other furniture, except a Swedish chair in laminated wood."

By early afternoon, Picasso, amid the chirm of the household and friends who came to pay him court, was bubbly and sunny. He liked not so much to converse as to talk, and his monologues were usually witty. His agile mind leaped from subject to subject, and he had almost total recall.

He always had several projects in hand at the same time, and to each he seemed equally lavish with his talent. "Painting is my hobby," he said. "When I am finished painting, I paint again for relaxation."

"He used no palette," Miss Gilot wrote of his working habits. "At his right (as he addressed his easel) was a small table covered with newspapers and three or four large cans filled with brushes standing in turpentine. Every time he took a brush he wiped it off on the newspapers, which were a jungle of colored smudges and slashes. Whenever he wanted pure color, he squeezed some from a tube onto the newspaper. At his feet and around the base of the easel were cans—mostly tomato cans of various sizes—that held gray and neutral tones and other colors that he had previously mixed.

"He stood before the canvas for three or four hours at a stretch. He made almost no superfluous gestures. I asked him if it didn't tire him to stand so long in one spot. He shook his head. 'No,' he said. 'That is why painters live so long. While I work I leave my body outside the door the way Moslems take off their shoes before entering the mosque.'

"Occasionally he walked to the other end of the atelier and sat in a wicker armchair. He would cross his legs, plant one elbow on his knee and, resting his chin on his fist, would stay there studying the painting without speaking for as long as an hour. After that he would generally go back to work on the portrait. Sometimes he would say, 'I can't carry that plastic idea any further today,' and then begin to work on another painting. He always had several half-dry unfinished canvases to choose from.

"There was total silence in the atelier, broken only by Pablo's monologues or an occasional conversation; never an interruption from the world outside. When daylight began to fade from the canvas he switched on two spotlights and everything but the picture surface fell away into the shadows. 'There must be darkness everywhere except on the canvas, so that the painter becomes hypnotized by his own work and paints almost as though he were in a trance,' he said. 'He must stay as close as possible to his own inner world if he wants to transcend the limitations his reason is always trying to impose on him.' "

Mood was a vital ingredient of Picasso. Everything he saw, felt, or did was for him an incomplete experience until it had been released and recorded. Once he was lunching on sole and happened to hold up the skeleton so that he could look at it. He got up from the table and returned almost immediately with a tray of clay in which he made an imprint of the skeleton. After lunch he drew colorful designs around the filigree of the bones, and the eventual result was one of his most beautiful plates. Here, as in other art areas, when the inspiration was upon him he worked ceaselessly and with such concentration that he could, for example, paint a good-sized picture in three hours.

Just as intensely, Picasso loved to mime, to clown, to play charades, to joke. To amuse his friends (and himself) he would don a tuxedo, red socks, and funny hats; or he would put on Chaplin-esque garb and engage in horseplay. "The moment when disguises are called for most urgently is on the arrival of visitors, especially those from abroad," Roland Penrose, a British friend, wrote in his *Picasso: His Life and Work.* "The less known or the more intimidating the guest may be, the more likely it is that he will find himself confronted by the master not as he expected to find him but as a burlesque little figure wearing perhaps a yachting cap with horn-rimmed spectacles, a red nose and black side-whiskers and brandishing a saber."

Picasso was a short, squat man with broad, muscular shoulders and arms. He was most proud of his small hands and feet and of his hairy chest. In old age his body was firm and compact; and his cannonball head, which was almost bald, gleamed like bronze. Set into it were deep black eyes of such penetration and alertness that they became his hallmark. Photographs from his younger years showed him a handsome man with jet-black hair. Apart from the absence of hair, the description by Miss Olivier, his first long-term mistress, could have applied to the artist of later years. "Small, dark, thickset, unquiet, disquieting, with somber eyes, deep-set, piercing, strange, almost fixed," she wrote. "Awkward gestures, a woman's hands, ill-dressed, careless. A thick lock of hair, black and glossy, cut across his intelligent, obstinate forehead. Half bohemian, half workman in his clothes; his hair, which was too long, brushing the collar of his worn-out coat."

Although at various times in his life Picasso dressed as a dandy, he was never comfortable in conventional clothes. He preferred corduroy or heavy velvet jackets, a T-shirt and heavy trousers made of a blanket type of wool. These, after he could afford them, were custom-made in odd designs. Sometimes he varied his getup by wearing a striped jersey pullover and sometimes he just walked around in shorts. It was all a matter of mood.

Women were one of Picasso's most persistent preoccupations. Apart from fleeting affairs, there were seven women significant in his personal and artistic life. He married two of them, but his relationships with the five others were well recognized. Two of his companions bore three of his four children. The artist's wives and mistresses served as his models, organized the domestic aspects of his household so far as that was possible, petted him, suffered his mercurial moods, and greeted his friends.

In Picasso's early days in Paris, his mistress was Miss Olivier, a young painter and teacher, who lived, as he did, in the Bateau-

Lavoir—a Montmartre building given its name by the poet and painter Max Jacob because it swayed like a creaky Seine laundry boat. "I met Picasso as I was coming home one stormy evening," Miss Olivier recalled. "He had a tiny kitten in his arms, which he laughingly offered me, at the same time blocking my path. I laughed with him. He invited me to his studio." Their liaison lasted until 1912, when Picasso met Marcelle Humbert, the mistress of a sculptor friend. The two ran off together, and there followed a series of superb canvases expressing the artist's happiness. He called Miss Humbert "Eva" and signed two of his works "J'aime Eva." Miss Humbert died in 1914.

In Rome, early in 1917, he met Olga Khoklova, a ballerina with Sergei Diaghilev's Ballets Russes. He painted her in a Spanish mantilla, and he and Olga were married in 1918. Three years later a son, Paolo— Italian for Pablo or Paul—was born. The marriage broke up in 1935, and Olga died in southern France twenty years later. The couple were never divorced; one reason, it is said, was that they had been married under a community property arrangement that would have obliged Picasso to divide his fortune with her. At the time of the separation Picasso's mistress was his blond model, Marie-Thérèse Walter, who bore him a daughter, Marie de la Concepcion, in 1935. A portrait of the girl, known as Maia, was one of Picasso's most fetching naturalist studies.

Dora Maar, a young Yugoslav photographer, was the painter's next mistress. Their companionship lasted until 1944. The same year, when Picasso was sixty-two, he began an eleven-year liaison with Françoise Gilot. Their children were Claude, born in 1947, and Paloma, born in 1949. His final attachment was to Jacqueline Roque, who became his mistress in 1955, and his wife in 1961, when she was thirty-five and he was seventy-nine. Miss Roque had a rather wry sense of her role in the painter's life. A member of a movie crew asked her quite innocently who she was. "Me, I'm the new Egeria," she replied.

Amid the bohemian clutter in which he lived and thrived, despite the concomitant disarray of his personal affairs, Picasso maintained a strong, consistent, and lasting emotional bond to the country of his birth. This bond influenced his painting and, after 1936 and the Spanish Civil War, propelled him for the first time into politics. His attachment to Spain was romantic and passionate; and the fact that he shunned Generalissimo Francisco Franco's Spain yet kept his Spanish nationality was an expression of his umbilical feeling for the country. There were two principal consequences of this bond: One was "Guernica" and the other was his membership in the French Communist party, which he joined in 1944. "Up to the time of the Spanish Civil War, Picasso was completely apolitical," Kahnweiler, his agent, recalled. "He did not even know the names of the different parties. The Civil War changed all that."

Previously, Picasso's insurgency had been that of every artist against the constrictions of conventional life. But with the outbreak of conflict in his homeland, Picasso became instinctively an aroused partisan of the Republican government. In January 1937, he began etching the two large plates of "Sueno y Mentira de Franco" ("The Dream and Lie of Franco"). These showed the rebel leader as a perpetrator of symbolic horrors—himself ultimately transformed into a centaur and gored to death by a bull. Countless copies of these etchings were dropped like propaganda leaflets over Franco territory. But it took the bombing of the Basque town of Guernica y Luno on April 26, 1937, to drive Picasso to the heights of his genius. At four-thirty on that cloudless Monday afternoon, German airmen, who had been provided to Franco by Adolf Hitler, descended on Guernica, a town of no military importance, in a test of the joint effect of explosive and incendiary bombs on civilians. The carnage was enormous, and news of it appalled the civilized world.

At the time Picasso had been engaged by the Republican government to paint a mural for its pavilion at a Paris fair later that year. The outrage at Guernica gave him his subject and in a month of furious and volcanic work he completed his great and stunning painting. The monochromatic mural, stark in black, gray, and white, was retained by the artist in trust for the Spanish nation.

Picasso painted two other major historical pictures, "The Korean Massacres" and "War and Peace." The two large compositions are in an old chapel in Vallauris, France. Both were intended to arouse the conscience of mankind to the horrors of war, but neither was as widely known or as powerful as "Guernica."

Toward the close of World War II the artist joined the Communist party, and *L'Humanité*, the French party daily, marked the occasion by publishing an almost full-page photograph of him. Although his decision seemed clearly motivated by the Spanish war and the ensuing World War, there were many who thought at first that the action was another of Picasso's caprices. He responded to such charges with a statement published in *Les Lettres Françaises*, which said in part: "What do you think an artist is? An imbecile who has only his eyes if he is a painter, or his ears if a musician, or a lyre at every level of his heart if he is a poet, or, if he is merely a boxer, only his muscles?

"On the contrary, he is at the same time a political being, constantly alert to the heartrending, burning, or happy events in the world, molding himself in their likeness. How could it be possible to feel no interest in other people and, because of an ivory-tower indifference, detach yourself from the life they bring with such open hands?

"No, painting is not made to decorate apartments. It is an instrument of war, for attack and defense against the enemy."

But Picasso's brand of communism was not Moscow's, at least not in the Kremlin's Stalinist period. In 1948 his works were denounced by Vladimir Kemenov, a Soviet art critic, as an "apology for capitalistic esthetics that provokes the indignation of the simple people, if not of the bourgeoisie. His pathology has created repugnant monstrosities," Kemenov went on. "In his 'Guernica' he portrayed not the Spanish republic but monsters. He treads the path of cosmopolitanism, of empty geometric forms. His every canvas deforms man—his body and his face." Picasso was pained but unmoved by the attack. "I don't try to advise the Russians on economics. Why should they tell me how to paint?" he remarked to a friend.

About that time, according to one account, an orthodox Soviet painter said to Picasso on being introduced, "I have known of you for some time as a good Communist, but I'm afraid I don't like your painting." "I can say the same about you, comrade," Picasso shot back.

After Kemenov's appraisal, Moscow's attitude to the artist fluctuated. "The Dove" helped, quite unintentionally, to create a thaw, which came about this way. One day in 1949 Matisse came to visit Picasso, bringing a white fantail pigeon for his friend's cote. Virtually on the spot, Picasso made a naturalistic lithograph of the newcomer; and Louis Aragon, the Communist poet and novelist, who saw it shortly afterward, realized its possibilities at once. The lithograph, signed by the artist, was first used as a poster at a world peace conference. From that introduction it flew around the world, reproduced in all sizes and in all media as a peace symbol.

The man who so largely created the special esthetic of modern art was born on the night of October 25, 1881, in Málaga, on Spain's southern coast. Picasso's father was José Ruiz, an Andalusian who taught for small pay in the local school of arts and crafts. His mother was Maria Picasso, a Majorcan. Pablo could draw as soon as he could grasp a pencil, but as a pupil in the ordinary sense he preferred looking at the clock to doing sums and reading. Save for art, he managed to avoid all but the rudiments of formal schooling. Picasso often accompanied his father to the bullfights. These made an indelible impression, for throughout his life bullring scenes and variations on them were a significant part of his work, recurring more persistently than any other single symbol; his first oil, at the age of nine, was of the bullring.

In 1895 the family moved to Barcelona, where Pablo's father taught at the School of Fine Arts. By that time the youngster's talent was truly Mozartean, so that his father solemnly presented him with his own palette and brushes. The confidence was justified when Pablo, at fifteen, competed for admission to the art school; a month was ordinarily allowed, but he completed his picture, a male nude, in a single day and was admitted to classes in 1896. He remained there for a year before going to Madrid for further study. During an illness he lived among the peasants of Catalonia, the poverty and barrenness of whose lives appalled him. From them and from the countryside, he said later, he learned "everything I know."

Late in 1898, the young artist dropped his father's name from the signature "P. Ruiz-Picasso" for reasons that have never been made clear. (His full baptismal name had been Pablo Diego José Francisco de Paula Nepomuceno Paria de los Remedios de la Santisima Trinidad Ruiz Picasso). He paid his first visit to Paris in 1900 and after three more visits settled there in 1904. On one of these visits he met Max Jacob, who was, next to Pierre Reverdy, his most appreciative friend until Jacob's death in a Nazi concentration camp. Picasso also became acquainted with Berthe Weill, the art dealer, who purchased some of his paintings, and Petrus Manach, another dealer, who was to support him briefly at the rate of $37.50 a month. Meanwhile his "blue" pictures had established him as an artist with a personal voice. This period, ending about 1904, was characterized by his use of the color blue to depict the haunting melancholy of dying clowns, most of them in catatonic states, and agonized acrobats. "La Mort d'Arlequin" is one of the most widely known of these.

When the artist moved into the Bateau-Lavoir, his rickety and drafty studio became an important meeting and talking place for persons later to be famous in arts and letters. In addition to Max Jacob there were Guillaume Apollinaire, the poet; André Salmon, the writer; Matisse; Braque; Le Douanier Rousseau; Juan Gris, the Spanish painter; Cocteau; Dufy; Gertrude and Leo Stein; Utrillo; Lipschitz; and Marcoussis. Apollinaire, Picasso's spiritual guide in those days, introduced him to the public with a long article in a Paris review in 1905.

One of Picasso's lifelong habits, painting at night, started during this time, and for the simple reason that his day was frequently absorbed by friends and visitors. It was also the time of his two-year "rose period," generally dated from 1904 to 1906, so-called because hues of that color dominated his pictures. Near the close of this period, he was taken up by the Steins, American expatriates in Paris. Leo and Gertrude did not so much discover the painter as popularize him. He, in turn, did a portrait of Gertrude with a face far from representational. When Miss Stein protested that she didn't look like that, Picasso replied, "But you will," and, indeed, in her old age Miss Stein came to resemble her picture.

The year 1907, the end of a very brief "Negroid" or "African" period, was a milestone for the painter, for it marked the birth of cubism in an oil of five distorted nudes called "Les Demoiselles d'Avignon." With cubism, Picasso—along with Braque—rejected light and perspective, painting not what he saw, but what he represented to himself through analysis. (The name "cubism" was coined afterward, and it was based on the cube forms into which Picasso and Braque tended to break up the external world.) "When we painted as we did," Picasso said later, "we had no intention of creating cubism, but only of expressing what was inside us. Cubism is neither a seed nor a fetus, but an art which is primarily concerned with form, and, once a form has been created, then it exists and goes on living its own life."

This was also the case when Picasso added a new dimension to cubism in 1911 or 1912 by inventing the collage; he glued a piece of imitation chair caning to a still life. Later he went on to an even less academic cubism, sometimes called rococo cubism. These expressions in the cubist manner were not Picasso's total output in the years from 1907 to 1917, for at the same time he was painting realistically. His first substantial recognition came in this period through an exhibition in New York in 1911 and one in London in 1912. His pictures began to fetch high prices—almost $3,000 for "Acrobats" in 1914.

From his marriage to the ballerina Olga Khoklova until about

1925, Picasso was a costume designer and scenery painter for the
Ballets Russes, all the while painting for himself, mostly in a neo-
classic and romantic manner. "The Woman in White" is among
the best known of these pictures. With the advent of the surrealist
movement in the middle of the twenties, the artist's work turned
to the grotesque. Some of his figures were endowed with several
heads, displaced noses, mouths, and eyes, overenlarged limbs.
Turbulence and violence seemed to be at the bottom of his feelings. Then, in 1929, he returned somewhat abruptly to sculpture,
of which he had done little for fifteen years. But again it was not a
full occupation, and he was soon attacking his easel, this time with
variations within a distinctive generally surrealistic framework.
One typical picture was "Young Woman with a Looking-glass,"
painted in 1932.

With these and other pictures in a similar genre, the artist's renown and income reached new heights. Life was also quieter for
him, especially after 1935 when Dora Maar helped put routine
into his daily existence. She was the model for a notable series of
portraits in which the Mercator projection principle was applied to
the human face. Serenity, or as much of it as ever was possible for
Picasso, persisted until the fall of Paris in 1940. He rejected an opportunity to escape to the United States, and instead remained in
Paris throughout the war, painting industriously amid considerable
personal hardship and the prying of Nazi soldiers. It was forbidden
to exhibit his pictures or to print his name in the newspapers.

After the war, he became enchanted by lithography, which he
taught himself. In a short period he turned out more than two
hundred lithographs. He was at the same time painting, in Paris
and in Antibes, and restlessly investigating pottery. Ceramics en-
tranced him, and his work with clay created an industry for the
town of Vallauris, not far from the Riviera. In a single year he
made and decorated six hundred figures and vessels, all different.
Even this concentration on one medium seemed not to diminish
the intensity with which he painted, sculptured, and illustrated
books.

His painting style, although it had moments of naturalism, contained wild reinventions of anatomy, but in such an idiosyncratic way that surrealism or any other "ism" did not appear to apply. Picasso had isolated an idiom for himself.

Toward the close of his life he also produced a number of seascapes and paintings as a composer would write variations on another's theme. Among Picasso's more notable variations were ten on Cranach's "David and Bathsheba," fifteen on Delacroix's "Femmes d'Alger," and forty-four on Velázquez's "Las Meninas." He also painted scores of portraits of his wife in a variety of poses—on a bed fondling a cat, seated nude in his studio, reading. They were portraits only in the sense that they were vaguely representational of Jacqueline Roque, for the figure and the face were almost always distorted.

Popular acclaim for Picasso seemed to mount with his age. In 1967, when he was eighty-six, "Homage to Picasso," an exhibition of some of his works, drew throngs to museums here and abroad. His sculpture was given a special exhibition at the Museum of Modern Art in New York. One example of his sculpture, "Bust of Sylvette," is a sixty-ton, sandblasted work that rests in University Plaza, in downtown New York.

The painter did not often leave his hilltop villa in his last years. He seemed to feel the world slipping away from him, especially when his old friends died one after another. He shut himself up, refusing to answer the telephone, for example, to mourn Ilya Ehrenburg in September 1967. But for the most part he painted. Rather than stand, he sat down, bending almost in half over his canvas. Age lines in his face underscored an intensity of purpose hardly abated by time. And as he painted his nostrils flared, his eyes widened, he frowned, and all the while his hand was never still. He was, in the words of a friend, "like a sturdy old oaken tub brimful of the wine of life."

"You would think," another friend said, "he is trying to do a few more centuries of work in what he has left to live."

———————————————— ✦ ————————————————

PABLO CASALS

"I think it goes like this," a cello student struggling with a Johann Sebastian Bach suite once told Pablo Casals.

"Don't think," the master cellist replied. "It is better to feel."

With this emphasis on an inner sensitivity to a composer's intentions, Casals was able to demonstrate what luminescent and human music could be drawn from the strings of a rather awkward instrument. He was active musically almost to his death at the age of ninety-seven. In concerts and recordings over some seventy-five years, he provoked awe and applause for the profundity of his insights, the felicity of his playing, and, above all, for the soaring purity of his interpretations of baroque and classical composers. Bach was his specialty, but he was also at home with Boccherini,

Mozart, Brahms, Beethoven, Schumann, and Dvorak. At the same time Casals (he pronounced the name KaaSAALS) won much admiration and acclaim as a man of probity and principle for his humanitarianism, his personal musical "crusade for peace," and his lifelong stand against the regime of Francisco Franco in his native Spain. Few musicians achieved in their own time his international renown and respect.

Part of this fame, in the United States at least, came very late in life and rested on his talents in conducting, which he fancied as his real métier and which he had practiced, mainly in Europe, since 1920. Conducting gave him a sense of fulfillment, he said, because orchestras, with their human teamwork, are "the greatest of all instruments." Early in his career, on his first American tour in 1901, a falling rock injured the fingers of his left hand. His first thought, as he recalled it, was, "Thank God, I won't have to play the cello any more." He associated that reaction with his desire to conduct.

After a period of semiactivity in Europe starting in 1945, Casals went to Puerto Rico to live in 1956. He was then seventy-nine years old and seemed spent. The next year, however, he started the Festival Casals, which became an annual springtime series of concerts. He had a heart attack just before the opening of the first festival, but he recovered buoyantly in the following years, using an orchestra brought together by Alexander Schneider, the violinist and an old friend. The concerts drew thousands of mainlanders and introduced the post-World War II generation of music lovers to Casals. Then in 1961 he joined Rudolf Serkin's Marlboro Music Festival in Vermont, where each July he conducted the orchestra and gave master cello classes; and, beginning in 1962, he conducted a choral work in New York every year. His first presentation was his own oratorio, *El Presebre* (The Manger), a lengthy composition dedicated "to those who have struggled and are still struggling for the cause of peace and democracy." In this resurgence, he also gave a widely publicized cello recital at the United Nations in New York in 1958 to mark that organization's thirteenth anniversary. Three years later he played to a distinguished gathering at the White House on the invitation of President John F. Kennedy.

The public attention that Casals generated in those years helped also to swell sales of his cello recordings, and this, in turn, created new esteem for his wizardry with the bow. Thousands who never saw him came to know him intimately. Another element of his appeal was his apparent refusal to age or grow stale. "Sometimes I feel like a boy," he told an interviewer in 1964. "Music does that. I can never play the same piece twice in the same way. Each time it is new." Watching him rehearse an orchestra when he was eighty-nine, an astonished student exclaimed: "When the maestro came onto the stage he looked seventy-five! When he stepped on the podium he seemed even ten years younger. And when he began to conduct he could have been a youngster ready to chase Easter eggs."

In the musical world, Casals's enduring reputation was associated with two accomplishments: his restoration to the repertory of Bach's cello music, especially the six magnificent unaccompanied suites; and his innovations in bowing and fingering that gave the instrument a new and striking personality in orchestral and solo works. He greatly lightened the work of the left hand, for example, by changes of finger positions, thus adding to its mobility. He also showed that it was possible to attain fresh subtleties in tone by freer bowing. His own style was aristocratic. He made the most difficult passages seem simple yet luscious, all the while shunning pyrotechnics.

Casals came upon the Bach suites by accident when he was thirteen years old and browsing with his father in a Barcelona music shop. "I forgot entirely the reason of my visit to the shop and could only stare at this music which nobody had told me about," he said years afterward. "Sometimes even now, when I look at the covers of that old music, I see again the interior of that old and musty shop with its faint smell of the sea. I took the suites home and read and reread them. For twelve years after that I studied and worked every day at them. I was nearly twenty-five before I had the courage to play one of them in public." When he did play them, the suites were disclosed as a transcendent musical experience, not the abstract exercises they had previously been believed to be.

"For me, Bach is like Shakespeare. He has known all and felt all," he told Bernard Taper in a profile published in *The New Yorker* in 1961. "He is everything. Everything except a professor. Professor Bach I do not know. When people ask me how I play Bach, I say, 'I play him as the pianist plays Chopin.' There is such fantasy in Bach—but fantasy with order."

Casals was of medium stature—not much taller than his Groffriller cello—and not heavily built. The top of his head had been bald since his early twenties. In repose, his face and his blue-gray eyes (behind round glasses) tended to be somber, but a smile imparted radiance and geniality to his face. He was direct in his speech, exceedingly polite, a careful dresser (photographs taken in his youth show him to have been a dandy in a romantic sort of way), and quietly dignified. He relaxed by reading, playing tennis, chatting with friends, smoking a pipe (he was rarely without one) and, in his late years, by watching westerns on television. To hear him play was a moving and memorable experience. He sat with his eyes closed, his head turned sidewise and a little lifted, as though he were communing with some secret muse. His fingering and his bowing were so flawless that they seemed automatic, yet it was evident that they resulted from concentration. He had superb savoir faire. Once when a loose cuff bothered him, he stopped playing, slowly took off the cuff, put it on the floor and resumed playing where he had left off. When a string broke, he would retire from the stage, replace it and, returning to his chair, start the solo from the beginning—such was his drive for perfection.

When Casals played a chamber music program at Perpignan, France, in July 1951, Howard Taubman, then music critic of *The New York Times,* wrote: "As a musician, Casals is all of a piece. Whether he conducts as he did in the second orchestral program of the Bach-Mozart-Beethoven festival ... or plays the cello, there is a fine-grained consistency running through all his musical labors. ... His work at the cello ... was remarkable for its modesty and restraint, and if one listened closely one could hear innumerable felicities of technical mastery. As an admiring violinist observed, 'Do you note the four shades of color he got in one bow?' "

Casals was an ardent supporter of the Spanish Republican government. He never reconciled himself to the Franco regime, which he considered tyrannical; with its victory in 1939 he went into self-imposed exile, living until 1956 in Prades, France, some forty miles from the Spanish frontier. Until 1958 he refused to visit the United States because it recognized Franco. "I have great affection for the United States," he said when he moved to Puerto Rico, "but as a refugee from Franco Spain I cannot condone America's support of a dictator who sided with America's enemies, Hitler and Mussolini. Franco's power would surely collapse without American help." But he bent his attitude sufficiently to play at the United Nations in 1958 because of "the great and perhaps mortal danger [of nuclear war] threatening all humanity." Then in 1961 he relented further and played at the White House. In subsequent years he came to this country for regular yearly visits.

Pablo Carlos Salvador Defiló de Casals was born in the Catalan town of Vendrell, forty miles from Barcelona, on December 29, 1876, the second of eleven children of Charles and Pilar Defiló de Casals. His father was the town organist. "From my earliest days," he recalled, "music was for me a natural element, an activity as natural as breathing." He could sing in tune before he could talk clearly, and at the age of five he was a soprano in the church choir. His father taught him piano, violin, and organ, and when he was eight he began substituting for his father as church organist. Shortly after Pablo's tenth birthday he heard a cello for the first time when José Garcia performed in Vendrell. After some coaxing, the elder Casals bought one for his son and gave him a few lessons. Pablo was fascinated by the instrument and proved so adept at it that he quickly exhausted his father's pedagogical abilities.

With his mother's backing and against the wishes of his father (who wanted the boy to become a carpenter), Pablo—not quite twelve—went with his mother to Barcelona, where he enrolled in the Barcelona Municipal School of Music. To earn his living he played evenings for dances with a trio at the Café Tost; later he persuaded the owner to devote one evening a week to classical music. This attracted serious musicians to the bistro, including Isaac Albéniz, the composer and pianist. When Casals was graduated from music school at the age of seventeen with first prizes for cello, piano, and composition, Albéniz gave him a letter of introduction to Count Guillermo de Morphy, a music patron who was an adviser to Queen Mother Maria Christina in Madrid. The count, taken with the young cellist, introduced him to Maria Christina, who was also charmed and who granted him a monthly stipend of 250 pesetas (about $50) for his studies. He lived in Madrid from 1894 to 1897, attending the Royal Conservatory of Music, playing duets with the queen mother (she was a fair pianist), chatting with the child who was to become Alfonso XIII, and being guided in his general education by the Count de Morphy.

From Madrid, Casals and his mother went to Brussels, but, miffed by an unfriendly reception at an audition there, he went to Paris, where he played at the Folies-Marigny at a wage barely sufficient to keep him and his mother from starvation. After a short time they returned to Barcelona, where Casals got a job teaching at the music school. For two years he taught cello, played it in the Barcelona Opera orchestra, gave concerts in churches, and formed a string quartet, all the while saving money for a return to Paris. In the fall of 1899, just before his twenty-third birthday, he arrived in that city again, carrying a letter of introduction to Charles Lamoureux, the eminent conductor, from de Morphy. When he presented himself for an audition, the conductor was annoyed by the intrusion. Nonetheless, the young man sat down and began to play parts of the Lalo cello concerto. With the first notes, Lamoureux hoisted himself up from his desk and stood facing Casals until he finished playing, whereupon he embraced the young man and said, "My boy, you are one of the elect!" Lamoureux immediately engaged him to play the Lalo concerto with his orchestra, and he made his Paris debut November 12, 1899. He created a sensation there, as he did in London shortly afterward. From then on his career was made, and he never lacked for engagements or for an audience. He commanded top fees, but lived frugally.

For the next twenty years, until 1919, Casals, using Paris as his base, played in the principal cities of Europe and the Americas. He made his New York debut in 1904, playing the Saint-Saëns cello concerto with the orchestra of the Metropolitan Opera and winning a chorus of bravos from critics. Later that season he was the cello soloist in New York in Richard Strauss's *Don Quixote*, with the composer conducting his own tone poem. Many of his performances in those years were of chamber music, which he played with Jacques Thibaud, the violinist, and Alfred Cortot, the pianist. In the United States he also gave chamber music recitals with Harold Bauer, the pianist, and Fritz Kreisler, the violinist, and with Kreisler and Ignace Paderewski, the pianist. In that period he formed intimate friendships with such musicians as Georges Enesco, Maurice Ravel, Camille Saint-Saëns, Sergei Rachmaninoff, Gregor Piatigorsky, Emanuel Feuermann, Artur Schnabel, Eugène Ysaye, and Paul Hindemith. In 1914 Casals married Susan Metcalfe, the American lieder singer. It was his second marriage; the first, to Guilhermina Suggia, a Portuguese cellist in 1906, had ended in divorce six years later. For several years he was the piano accompanist for Miss Metcalfe, a soprano, and at one point he considered dropping his career to further hers. However, the couple parted in 1920.

After World War I and with the breakup of his marriage, the cellist turned his energies to Barcelona, where, in 1920, he founded the Orquesta Pau (Catalan for Pablo) Casals and subsidized it for seven years at a total cost of $320,000 until it became self-supporting. In these years (and afterward) he was its principal conductor. Early in the 1920's he also founded the Workingmen's Concert Association, which gave its members, in return for nominal dues, an opportunity to attend Sunday morning concerts of his orchestra and to set up their own musical groups. As busy as he was in Barcelona, he also found time to give concerts in the United States and in Europe and to appear in what seemed increasingly to be his favorite role, that of a conductor. He led the London Symphony, the New York Symphony, and the Vienna Philharmonic.

When the Spanish republic was proclaimed in 1931, he became one of its eager and hardworking supporters, all the more because the republic restored many of his native Catalonia's ancient rights. He was president of Catalonia's music council, the Junta de Musica, and, during the Civil War, he gave hundreds of benefit concerts abroad for the republic and put a large part of his personal savings at its disposal. The government, in turn, named streets and squares for him and encouraged his exertions to bring great music to the common people. He was in Barcelona in January 1939, when the Franco forces burst into the city, but he made good an escape to France, vowing never to return to Spain while the generalissimo was in power. (Apart from a fleeting trip to Spain in 1955 to attend the funeral of his longtime close friend and housekeeper, Francesca Vidal de Capdevila, he never did.)

After several demoralizing weeks in Paris, during which he grieved for his country, he went to live in Prades among the thousands of Spanish exiles. There he helped to organize the care of the Catalans held in French camps and solicited funds for them from his friends all over the world. He continued to live in Prades in World War II. Toward the end of the war he went on tour again. In the autumn of 1945, however, he cut short a concert trip in Britain and retired to Prades. In explanation, he said he had assumed that an Allied victory would doom not only Hitler and Mussolini but also Franco. The democracies, he went on, had disillusioned him by not acting to topple the dictator; he was therefore suspending his concert career until Spain was freed. He had, he pointed out, ceased playing in Germany with the rise of Hitler, had not played in Italy in the thirties, nor had he appeared in Russia after the Bolshevik Revolution. He said he could not separate his beliefs as a human being from his conduct as an artist.

Casals lived quietly and simply in Prades for close to twelve years. In 1950, however, he was prevailed upon to soften somewhat his vow of public musical silence and take part in a Bach bicentenary festival. The event, which attracted hundreds of music lovers from many parts of the world, was held in the Church of St. Pierre in Prades. The critics found that his bow had lost none of its magic. In that and subsequent Prades festivals he appeared in a triple role—as soloist, as chamber music ensemble player, and as conductor. He was joined in the concerts by many internationally renowned musicians, including Dame Myra Hess, Rudolf Serkin, Joseph Szigeti, and Isaac Stern.

Some indication of a further shift in Casals's thinking came in 1951 in a colloquy with Albert Schweitzer, the humanitarian and philosopher. "It is better to create than to protest," Dr. Schweitzer said in urging the cellist to return to the concert stage. "Why not do both—why not create and protest both?" Casals replied. And he seemed to follow that course in his last years. After a period of self-examination, he went to Mexico in 1956 for his first concert outside the Prades area. It was there, in 1960, that *El Pesebre* had its premiere. The oratorio became the banner of his peace mission, which he carried to many major cities in the Western world. Discussing this crusade, he said in 1962: "As a man, my first obligation is toward the welfare of my fellow men. I will endeavor to meet that obligation through music, the means which God has given me, since it transcends language, politics, and national boundaries."

In August 1957, when he was eighty, he married Marta Montañez, one of his students, who was then twenty-one. They lived in a cheerful modern house on the beach at Santurce, Puerto Rico, where Casals liked to take an early morning stroll before beginning his day by playing a Bach work on the piano. "It is like a benediction on the house," he said. He maintained the unstinted admiration of his fellow artists. One of them, Isaac Stern, put their feelings this way: "He has enabled us to realize that a musician can play in a way that is honest, beautiful, masculine, gentle, fierce and tender—all these together, and all with unequivocal respect for the music being played and faith in it."

Appearing in New York in the summer of 1972 for a free Central Park concert with Stern he pronounced what could stand as his epitaph:

"What can I say to you?" he asked the assemblage. "I am perhaps the oldest musician in the world. I am an old man, but in many senses a very young man. And this is what I want you to be, young, young all your life, and to say things to the world that are true."

———————————✤———————————

SOL HUROK

If Sol Hurok, one of the world's foremost impresarios, had thought to stage his death at the age of eighty-five, he could scarcely have made it more characteristic of the extravagance of one of his own productions. He had lunched elegantly with Andrés Segovia, the classical guitarist and close friend, who was among the many distinguished artists whose appearances in the United States he had sponsored. As customary, Hurok was in an expansive mood, for he rarely permitted himself to be publicly in despair. Luncheon over, he went off to see David Rockefeller, another of his famous friends, at the Chase Manhattan Bank at 1 Chase Manhattan Plaza. By mistake, he was driven to 1 New York Plaza, where Rockefeller also kept an office, and when he got off the elevator at the seventeenth floor, he suffered a massive heart attack.

Hurok was the last of the personal impresarios. Even in his final years, talent management had become a faceless corporate industry, operated more for profit than for art. Hurok's singularity was that however much he liked profit, he cared for art the more. The marquee headline "S. Hurok Presents" had usually been followed by the name of a great musical artist, a ballet group, an opera company, a folklore ensemble, a symphony orchestra, or a theater troupe. Their common denominator was their uncommon talent. Many of them, moreover, were the fruit of Hurok's persistent efforts to bring distinguished virtuosos and ensembles, notably from the Soviet Union, to American audiences, and his pioneer campaign to promote the dance, especially ballet, in the United States.

Singly and together, these artists were what Solomon Isaievich Hurok liked to call "S. Hurok Attractions," with the last word capitalized even when he spoke about his offerings without a proper name. Using the word "Attractions" for his glittering performers connoted that Hurok was no ordinary purveyor of artistic talent but an impresario, one of the few who could legitimately claim that majestic Old World appellation. Defining the word as it applied to him, Hurok explained a few years before his death that an impresario "is a man who discovers talent, who promotes it, who presents it, and who puts up the money and takes the risk."

"That's my main work," he went on, "which is a lot different from a mere agent, a booker, a fellow who works strictly on percentage."

This description was not unduly immodest, for Hurok had a remarkable ability to discern what American audiences would like. "He was absolutely illiterate musically," one observer said, "but he had a fantastic sense of what was excellent." He looked for projection, that indefinable something that comes over the footlights and strikes an audience in its solar plexus. Hearing Marian Anderson, then an unknown contralto in Paris, for the first time in 1935, Hurok recalled that he felt chills dance up and down his spine, and his palms got damp. He knew immediately that she would project, and he signed her to a contract with a handshake. The contralto was one of his biggest discoveries.

Over the years virtually every big name in music and the performing arts was presented by Hurok. In addition to Miss Anderson and Segovia, these included Artur Rubinstein, Isaac Stern, Mischa Elman, Sviatoslav Richter, Emil Gilels, the Oistrakhs, Feodor Chaliapin, Anna Pavlova, Isadora Duncan, Victoria de los Angeles, Roberta Peters, and Jan Peerce. Among the dance groups there were the Sadler's Wells Ballet, the Royal Ballet with Margot Fonteyn, the Bolshoi Ballet with Galina Ulanova, the Kirov Ballet of Leningrad, and the Moiseyev Dance Company. Among theatrical troupes were the Old Vic and the Comédie Française. There were Kabuki players from Tokyo and parading Guards regiments from Britain.

The short, rotund Sol Hurok, who liked to say that what he did "was not a business, but a disease," often treated his artists with opulent grandeur. When Miss Ulanova arrived in New York with the Bolshoi in 1959, the impresario ushered her into a three-room hotel suite that held a refrigerator stocked with caviar and champagne and other necessaries of a ballerina's life. On a table were an electric percolator and an unopened tin of the finest coffee. (Miss Ulanova liked coffee.) There were flowers all over, and in one room there was a specially constructed ballet barre, with full-length mirrors. "So, my dear, you can practice here if you wish," Hurok said with an expansive wave of his gold-headed walking stick. (He had a silver-headed one for less stately moments.)

After the premiere at the Metropolitan Opera House, he gave the Bolshoi company a party at the St. Regis Roof with two hundred notables as guests. He served champagne, piroshki, caviar, beef Stroganoff, chicken Hurok (sliced chicken with white sauce over a bed of rice and noodles), plus dancing to an eleven-piece orchestra. The party cost at least $15,000.

In all, Hurok invested $100,000 of his own money and committed himself to expenses of $350,000 to bring the Bolshoi here.

It was part of his panache to gamble on an "Attraction," but in this case he had a sure winner, and the hotel suite for Miss Ulanova and the party were in keeping with his view of himself as a great impresario. To be great, he once said, means "first of all you have to love the things you do," adding: "How much do you love this Attraction or that personality? How much do you owe the American public? Those are the important things. The money you think about later."

Hurok's bravura behavior might have had another side, though, according to a man who knew him for a generation. "Sol has a great need to justify himself," his friend remarked. "The way he fulfills himself is in doing things big and getting his name in print. He needs a feeling of recognition. That's why he overtips and throws his money around, though in some respects he can be a penny pincher. He unconsciously remembers the old days when things were precarious. But always he wanted to be the grand seigneur and, in a curious way, he has succeeded."

A man of impressive ego, Hurok liked to socialize with his eminent stars, and among the photographs he displayed on his office walls were pictures of him waltzing with Moira Shearer and Miss Fonteyn, the British ballerinas, and doing the conga with Katharine Dunham, the American dancer. He once fox-trotted with Miss Pavlova at the Palisades Amusement Park in New Jersey, but there was no photographer to record the event. On another occasion, he played in *Petrushka,* dancing with the bear.

Often before the curtain rose on his stars, Hurok visited them in the dressing rooms to assure them that they would be great. Afterward, he ranged the back of the house, applauding louder than anyone else and shouting well-placed "bravos." To concert-hall habitués Hurok was an immediately recognizable figure with his black horn-rimmed glasses and his round, expressive face—and, of course, his stick.

Even when he was not on parade, Hurok attended concerts and the opera—especially the opera. The ushers knew him and they always managed to find him a seat in the back of the house. I saw him frequently at the Metropolitan in Lincoln Center in the sixties and early seventies. On chilly evenings he had an immaculate fur-collared coat and a black homburg that made him seem like a figure from la belle époque, at the very least a baron or a magnate. In conversation, it was evident that he listened to music with a keen and appreciative, if romantic, ear. He felt, he said, that music was ennobling to the human condition.

Hurok's much-publicized fractured English and Russian accent were something of a put-on. When he was on stage, so to speak, as an impresario, his accent thickened and he searched for memorable mots; but in private his accent was less distinctive and his phrasings were fairly straightforward. In whatever setting, he liked to convey the impression that he stood to lose his shirt in every Attraction he presented; but, pinned down, he would concede that he considered himself too shrewd to take needless risks. The public Hurok was always a participant in his own Attractions; the private person was more reticent, less conspicuous.

In keeping with his station and his palate, Hurok liked to eat in New York at Le Pavillon, and its closing a few years before his death sorrowed him. He was fond not only of the food but also of the deference he was accorded there and at other costly and elegant restaurants. He talked over a meal in his persona as an impresario. The word "ballet" came out as "bolly" or "bollay," and the Old Vic was always "Uld Wick." He sometimes, too, spoke in Goldwynisms, one of which—"When people don't want to come, nothing will stop them"—has become a concert-business classic.

At the pinnacle of his profession Hurok could say "I'm not bragging when I say I am responsible" for the great growth of American interest in the ballet and full houses for classical music, for his success was hard-earned. "When other managers are out playing golf or something," a man in the business observed, "Mr. Hurok is on Fifty-seventh Street (his office then was on the corner of Fifty-seventh and Fifth Avenue) making plans."

His regal office, in which he was very much the patriarchal monarch ("I play a one hundred percent role"), was far removed from the lower middle class circumstances of his boyhood and youth in czarist Russia. Born in Pogar, a small town not far from Kharkov, on April 9, 1888, he was the son of a hardware merchant and his wife, Israel and Naomi Hurok. When he was seventeen, the boy was sent to Kharkov with one thousand rubles to learn the hardware business.

But his sights were set on the United States, where there were relatives, and he arrived here in May 1906, with $1.50. There was a brief period in Philadelphia and then a job as a stock boy in a New York hardware concern. Out of his wages of $7 a week he managed to hear Chaliapin at the Metropolitan Opera House, then downtown, and told a friend: "Someday I am going to manage artists like Chaliapin, maybe even Chaliapin."

Living in the Brownsville section of Brooklyn, Hurok became engaged in activities of the Socialist party, in whose behalf he took his initial managerial step in 1911. With chutzpah in hand, he persuaded Efrem Zimbalist to play at a party fund-raising concert at a bargain rate. The violinist was a great success in Brownsville, and Hurok was off and running.

His next venture was to form, with a partner, the Van Hugo Musical Society, which sponsored Zimbalist in a Carnegie Hall concert. By 1916 Hurok was prepared to work full-time at his career. Among his first successes were Sunday concerts at the Hippodrome, at Forty-third Street and what was then Sixth Avenue, where, at a $2 top, the public thronged to hear such musical stars as Eugène Ysaye and Ernestine Schumann-Heink.

These triumphs led Hurok to present Pavlova, from whose performances he made $25,000, and Chaliapin, on whose opera tour he lost $150,000. He also presented the irrepressible Isadora Duncan, who bared one of her breasts in Symphony Hall, Boston, and was, as a result, almost banned in that city. Hurok was momentarily nonplussed, but he managed to surmount the crisis and, in time, became accustomed to artistic temperament.

"If they're not temperamental, I don't want them," he later remarked of his clients. "It's in the nature of a great artist to be that way. There's something in them—some warmth, some fire—that projects into an audience and makes it respond. Give me the temperamental artist every time."

From virtually the outset of his business, Hurok was fascinated by the ballet. The Ballet Russe de Monte Carlo was among his early triumphs. But not all his ballet experiences were happy, and he once contemplated a book to be called "To Hell with Ballet." Hurok persevered sufficiently, however, to become "the King of Ballet," and manager of the Ballet Theater from 1942 to 1946 and again for the 1955–56 season. In the 1950's he imported the Sadler's Wells, later the Royal Ballet, for a succession of cross-country tours. And at last, in 1959, he brought in the Bolshoi Ballet, perhaps the high point of his role as a dance impresario. The run was sold out in advance.

Before and since, Hurok dealt with the Soviet government as a leading American agent for its artists. Long before there was an official cultural exchange, he was the agency through whom such Soviet groups as the Moiseyev and such instrumentalists as the Oistrakhs appeared in American halls. For his efforts he was decorated by New York City in 1961, and a number of his distinguished artists—Rubinstein, Stern, and Miss Anderson—attended a dinner for him at the Waldorf-Astoria, for which William Steinberg conducted the Pittsburgh Symphony.

With the help of Ruth Goode, once his press agent, Hurok wrote *Impresario* in 1946, which later became a movie called *Tonight We Sing*. He continued his story of his life in *S. Hurok Presents: A Memoir of the Dance World*, published in 1953. In early 1969, when he was eighty, the impresario sold S. Hurok Concerts, Incorporated, then grossing between $8 million and $10 million a year, to the Transcontinental Investing Corporation. "Hurok will be bigger than ever—tell the people that," he said then, adding that the acquisition would permit him to reach the youth audience, which "was not following concert music the way they used to." At the time Hurok was offering sixty attractions a season that were playing more than two thousand concert dates to five million American patrons.

Many of those Attractions had been under his auspices for a

long time—the Russian troupes since the 1930's, Rubinstein since 1937, Stern since the late 1930's, and Segovia since 1943. These and other friends gave him a dinner in 1967. "I didn't ask for it," he said. "The friends who will come to this dinner to pay respects—this is my balance in the books."

After Hurok sold his business, he seemed to many to have gone into a decline. Martin Feinstein, long in charge of public relations, left the staff amid reports of a falling out, and Hurok's presentations appeared to limp a bit. He himself maintained his cheery disposition in public and insisted that he was doing better than ever.

Hurok moved his offices from Fifth Avenue and Fifty-seventh Street to the Avenue of the Americas and Fifty-sixth Street. This office was fire-bombed January 26, 1972. A young woman employee was killed and thirteen persons were injured, including Hurok, who was borne from the scene cloaked in his fur coat. He suffered from smoke inhalation, but quickly recovered. Because of Hurok's prominent role in bringing Soviet artists to this country, the attack was attributed to the Jewish Defense League, a militant organization, but a case against two members of the league was dismissed in federal court in 1973.

The fire bombing was the subject of a poem by Yevgeny Yevtushenko in *Izvestia,* the Soviet government newspaper. The Soviet poet referred to Hurok by his first name and patronymic and paid tribute to Miss Iris Kones, who died in the fire. The poem was titled "With Bombs Against the Arts."

To mark Hurok's eighty-fifth birthday (it had been privately celebrated in April) and his sixty years as an impresario, a crowd of fifteen hundred persons assembled in the Metropolitan Opera House for a gala in May 1973. The audience included diplomats, royalty, aristocrats, social registerites, and famous musicians and dancers. The program, steeped in nostalgia, included Van Cliburn at the piano, Isaac Stern playing a violin, a solo by Margot Fonteyn in a *Swan Lake* excerpt, Shirley Verrett singing Donizetti, and Mikhail Lavrovsky and Natalia Bessmertnova of the Bolshoi Ballet.

Hurok had hoped to cap his career by presenting both the Bolshoi Ballet and the Bolshoi Opera in the United States, but his plans were set back when Soviet authorities declined to schedule the troupes' appearance here in 1975.

One of the impresario's last bookings here was Maria Callas, who came out of retirement for a concert tour. Her first concert was canceled—she said she was indisposed—but she sang the night of Mr. Hurok's death at Carnegie Hall. Miss Callas and Giuseppe di Stefano, the tenor who was her partner on tour, said that their performance was "a tribute to him." A moment of silence was also observed at the performance of *L'Elisir d'Amore* at the Metropolitan Opera House.

Of the various medals and awards bestowed on him, Hurok was most proud of New York's Handel Medallion and the Diamond Jubilee Medal of New York City. When former Mayor John V. Lindsay presented them in 1973, Hurok said with elegant simplicity, "New York is where I started, and I hope to finish the job in another fifty years."

THOMAS HART BENTON

Thomas Hart Benton, an artist whose specialty was the homespun American scene painted with immediately recognizable realism, died in Kansas City at the age of eighty-five. Boldly colored, stylized, direct, his paintings were, like the man, to be savored rather than criticized on esthetic grounds. He captured on canvas or in murals such elements of American life and folklore as farmers scything hay, Jesse James pulling off a holdup, gaunt Ozark hillbillies and their mournful sweethearts, black sharecroppers, soldiers in honkytonks, riverboats plying the Mississippi, Cartier discovering the St. Lawrence, miners hunched from years in the pits, folks at home. There was little subtlety in these works, and that was the essence of their appeal. Nor was there much guile to

244

their creator, a cocksure, crusty, craggy, tobacco-chewing, whis-key-drinking, profane, pugnacious product of the Middle West. He was Harry S Truman's favorite ("the best damn painter in America"), as he was the first choice of thousands of others who so voted him in art-show polls. They liked him not only because he painted in a people's idiom, without affectation, but also because he told off esthetes, museum curators, art dealers, and abstraction-ists. He personified (and celebrated) what some might disdain as low culture but what others esteemed as the essence of the Ameri-can democratic spirit.

Sometimes, though, Benton, in defending his straightforward realism, indulged in a bit of philistinism. "It is patently absurd to stick a Cézanne watercolor in the face of an average intelligent American citizen and expect him to find much in it," he once said. "The same goes for a Braque or Kandinsky pattern. Most Ameri-cans on seeing them would say: 'If that's art, to hell with it.' " Benton knew better, but he couldn't resist being argumentative when the mood was upon him.

The artist spent his formative years in Neosho, Missouri, an Ozark town of two thousand persons, where he was born April 15, 1889. It was a place with a courthouse square, church suppers, a swimming hole, farmers in jeans, and an occasional band concert. His father was Maecenas Eaton Benton, a congressman and awe-some spellbinder known as "The Little Giant of the Ozarks." His great-uncle, for whom he was named, was Missouri's legendary first senator. Young Thomas was a restless schoolboy. Shortly after he was fifteen, he once recalled, he purchased "a derby hat, learned to waltz, and went to dances." "I gave up all pretense of school," he said, "spending the hours when I should have been learning Latin in the pool halls." He quit high school when he was seventeen, and by luck got his first job as an artist that summer on *The Joplin American.*

For $14 a week the youth sketched prominent Joplin residents every day, likenesses that were crude but recognizable, a tribute to his ability to learn by doing. Most of his pay went over the bar, to the alarm of his family, who packed him off to the Western Military Academy in Alton, Illinois, which promised to keep its students out of saloons. Bored, he broke away to Chicago in 1907 to study at the Art Institute for a year.

"From the moment I first stuck my brush in a fat gob of color, I gave up the idea of newspaper cartooning," he said. "I made up my mind I was going to be a painter." And, of course, he wanted to look the part. "I bought a black shirt, a red tie, and a pair of peg-top corduroy pants," he said. "I wore the outfit with a derby hat which, when I let my hair grow, sat high on my head."

This ensemble, however, did not last for long—yielding to the derision of the neighborhood girls on the South Side; but its replacement by more seemly garb did not diminish Mr. Benton's attachment to art.

"I still held to the idea that I was a genius," he said. When he was nineteen he set out for Paris. "It did not take me very long after I arrived to realize that my gifts were of an extremely limited nature and that my 'genius' was purely an imaginary affair," he recalled. Nonetheless, he remained for three years. "The story of my life in Paris is the story of all who went there before the Great War—a lady friend to look after you and run you, a studio, some work, and a lot of talk," he said. Actually, in this period Benton became strongly influenced by advanced artistic movements, including cubism, as his early paintings attest. He returned to the United States in 1912 and set up in a studio in New York, where he painted without much success. But he did cut a dapper figure in his French clothes and walking stick, an outfit that stood him in splendid stead when, as hack work, he painted portraits of Theda Bara and other silent-movie queens for $7 a day. Benton later regretted that he missed an important artistic experience. "While I was working in the movies, I never once regarded the material offered there as fit for serious painting," he said. "I missed the real human dramas that existed side by side with the acted ones and in my studio I painted lifeless symbolist and cubist pictures, changing my ways with every whiff from Paris."

World War I, with service at the naval base at Norfolk, Virginia, was a turning point in the artist's evolution. While he was making drawings of the base for the architects, his interests became "in a flash" of an objective nature. "The mechanical contrivances of building the new airplanes, the blimps, the dredges, the ships of the base, because they were interesting in themselves, tore me away from all my grooved habits, from my play with colored cubes and attenuations, from my esthetic drivelings and self-conceits," he said.

At the same time Benton discovered his potential audience, "boys from the hinterlands of the Carolinas, from the Tennessee country, from all over the South"—people who "had never been subjected to any esthetic virus." Back in New York after the war, the painter was ready to venture into Americana—the theme he clung to for the rest of his life. His particular friends at that time were Alfred Stieglitz, the photographer; Horace Traubel, biographer of Walt Whitman; Thomas Craven, the art historian; Max Eastman, the radical writer; and the painters Stanton Wright, Boardman Robinson, Leon Kroll, Jackson Pollock, John Steuart Curry, and Grant Wood. Benton, Curry, and Wood were the chief exponents of American regionalism. All three were natives of the Midwest, and their most famous pictures reflect life in that general area.

In the 1920's and early 1930's, Benton, to eke out a living, taught at the Chelsea Neighborhood Association, in the public schools, and at the Art Students League. He married Rita Piacenza, one of his students, on February 19, 1922. For the first several years, the couple lived a hand-to-mouth existence, until Albert Barnes, the eccentric Philadelphia collector, purchased some of Benton's paintings. After that, he began to achieve a measure of public success.

The artist acquired a summer home on Martha's Vineyard, where he lived part of every year for most of the rest of his life. "Martha's Vineyard had a profound effect on me," he said. "The relaxing air, the hot sand on the beaches where we loafed naked, the great and continuous drone of the surf, broke down the tenseness which life in the cities had given me." Of equal, if not greater, significance for his artistic development, he began to roam the nation. These trips took him to camp meetings, to backwoods farms, to the oil fields of Texas, to coal mines, to ranches, to Holy Roller assemblies, to cornfields and rice fields and wheat fields and hayfields. Everywhere he went he talked with people, prayed with them, sang, played the harmonica, and caroused.

Out of these sights and sounds came his regional paintings: "Cotton Loading on the Mississippi," "The Jealous Lover of Lone Green Valley," "Roasting Ears," "Louisiana Rice Fields," "Threshing Wheat," "Old Man Reading," "July Hay," "Cotton Pickers," and scores of others. These pictures, although not representational or postcard art, were simple and direct compositions. Critics in general regarded them as skillful but not great. There was a certain monotony to them, it was said, and a touch of jingoism. Untutored art lovers, however, liked Benton works for their undeniable immediacy. They sold well in the original and in reproduction, and many went into museum collections.

From his nomadic ventures came the most memorable chapters in Benton's autobiography, *An Artist in America*, which was published in 1937 and revised in 1951. In these recollections, the artist reproduced the unaffectedness of life beyond the paved roads, the physical reality of lust and crime and poverty. The most important artistic consequence of Benton's wanderings was "America Today," his mural at the New School in New York, painted in 1930. Alvin Johnson, the school's director, gave the artist the wall space but no money. "Itching to get a crack at a real mural, I set out," Benton said. "I worked six months preparing my scheme and three months in actually painting it." Of the work, he said, "I have tried to show that man is the master, not the servant, of his job." In vigorous strokes and vivid colors the mural portrays cowboys, small farmers, roustabouts, miners, subway riders, prizefighters, engineers—workers and wage earners. The large painting not only made Benton's national reputation, but it also contributed to a revival of mural painting.

In later years he did a mural for the Whitney Museum of American Art in New York, which is now at the New Britain

(Connecticut) Institute of Art; a mural for the State of Indiana and one for the Missouri capitol at Jefferson City; two works for the New York State Power Authority; and a mural in the rotunda of the Harry S Truman Library in Independence, Missouri, that depicts that area's role in the opening of the West. In 1973 he completed "Joplin at the Turn of the Century" for that city. In 1974 the artist began a work for the Country Music Foundation in Nashville. Explaining why he worked in old age, he said, "You can't retire from art. You can't retire like a man would retire from business or a job. It is life to me. What the hell would I do?"

With the rise of his reputation, Benton became financially secure. His pictures began to sell, and toward the end of his life a representative painting could fetch up to $90,000. In 1935 Benton decided that he was fed up with the effete East. He moved for good to a rambling stone mansion in Kansas City, where he taught for several years at the Kansas City Art Institute. But he visited New York often. On these trips, to see old friends or to attend exhibitions of his works at the Associated American Artists gallery, Benton delighted in giving New York and cities in general the back of his tongue. "Humane living is no longer possible within them," he asserted, adding that "New York is a highly provincial place."

Combative by temperament, the artist liked to kick at the esthetes in art work. He started a to-do in 1941 by declaring that "if it was left to me I wouldn't have any museums. I'd have people buy the paintings and hang them anywhere anybody had time to look at them," he continued. "I'd like to sell mine to saloons, Kiwanis and Rotary clubs and chambers of commerce—even women's clubs." Billy Rose, the showman and art patron, was then operating a nightclub, Billy Rose's Diamond Horseshoe, a red-plush place at 235 West Forty-sixth Street in New York. He promptly hung Benton's "Persephone," a fleshy nude in a Missouri landscape, in the club lounge. The artist later lent the painting to the Metropolitan Museum of Art, where it attracted throngs of the curious. It was good publicity all around.

Continuing his attack on museums, the artist charged that "the average museum is a graveyard run by a pretty boy with a curving wrist and a swing in his gait" and that "art is being ruined by museums and the third sex." These views reportedly affronted the Kansas City Art Institute, and Benton quit his post there. In that same period, the artist succeeded in stirring up a controversy in St. Louis when he exhibited his "Susanna and the Elders" there. The nude, with red fingernails and short hair, is shown about to take a dip as two appreciative oldsters look on. This airy treatment of the Old Testament Apocrypha story shocked the clergy and gave Benton headlines.

When the United States entered World War II, Benton did a series of paintings, "The Year of Peril," in which he sought to state the meaning of the war. The pictures were purchased by Abbott Laboratories, a drug manufacturer, and presented to the government. Later, the artist did pictures for several other corporations, including the American Tobacco Company and the King Korn Stamp Company, which offered an oil for 1,975 trading-stamp books in 1965. The artist was extremely proud of "The Year of Peril" series and just as scornful of their critical reception. The critics, he said, "performed as usual for my doings." The ten poster-size executions were deliberate propaganda pictures, designed to stir a realization of the grimness of war; and in truth they were not very good. But Benton used them to even a few scores with his enemies.

There were some who believed that Benton had mellowed with age, but they were disabused, for he was as tart-tongued in his eighties as he had been in his fifties. Of intellectuals he said a couple of years before his death, "They don't like art. They like to talk about it, they don't look at it." Of critics: "I furnish the stuff for them—the stuff for them to damn me." A friend once asked him what made him so mean. "Another friend asked me the same thing once," he replied. "She wanted to know what made me so damned mean." "You're not mean, Tom," Mrs. Benton interjected. "You're vulgar, but you're not mean."

As to his rank as an artist, Benton had this to say: "I don't know, of course, the ultimate value of what I do. But I have an inner conviction that I have come to something that is in the image of America and the American people of my time. My American image is made up of what I have come across, of what was 'there' in the time of my experience."

❖

CHIANG KAI-SHEK

Twenty-two years after rising to the leadership of China in a bloody coup against the Communists in 1927, Chiang Kai-shek lost the mantle he had so dearly gained and so precariously maintained to a triumphant Communist revolution. Thrust aside at the age of sixty-two by the convulsion that shook half a billion people and an ancient culture, he spun out his long life on the island of Taiwan in the East China Sea 110 miles from the mainland.

There he presided sternly over a martial group of two million Nationalist refugees and about eleven million Taiwanese. At first he talked aggressively of returning to the mainland; but as that possibility faded he waited hopefully for the Communist regime to collapse of its inner tensions and for the Chinese to welcome back a faithful statesman. That did not take place either. On the contrary, the People's Republic of China grew in internal strength and international might, displacing Chiang's regime in the United Nations in 1971 and winning diplomatic recognition by 1972 from all the major powers except the United States. Even this country, as a result of President Richard M. Nixon's visit to Peking in 1972, all but dropped Chiang diplomatically. His bitterness in his last years was enormous.

During his years as China's leader, Chiang ruled a country beset by intractable domestic strife as well as by armed conflict with Japanese invaders. Although China had a national government for these two decades, there was so much political, social, and economic turmoil, so much Japanese aggression to cope with—it started in 1931 in Manchuria and intensified in 1937—that national unity was more fiction than reality. Nonetheless, he was the visible symbol of China; a member, with Franklin D. Roosevelt, Winston Churchill, and Josef Stalin, of the Big Four; his nation's supreme commander in World War II; and the principal architect of a domestic policy that aimed, however unsuccessfully, at internal stability. To the world, his lean, trim, erect figure bespoke resoluteness and determination. His asceticism and personal austerity seemed to befit a man of dedication to the idea of a China resurgent against insuperable odds.

As the head of a country that had suffered a quarter-century and more of political decay, Chiang faced Herculean tasks once his Nationalist government at Nanking was recognized by the Western powers in November 1928. With the nation in fragments, he chose to seek political unification by force of arms before attacking fundamental social and economic problems, especially those centering on agriculture, in which the great bulk of the population was engaged. Only later, and under enormous pressure, did he turn his attention to rebuffing the Japanese. The choice proved unwise, for his campaigns and his battles with local satraps permitted the Communists to befriend the peasantry, harness the forces of social revolution that had been gathering since 1911, and, ultimately, to align themselves with a nascent nationalism in the anti-Japanese war.

Had China been more than a geographical expression in the 1920's, Chiang might have imposed a functioning government on it. But the weaknesses of the social system were such that his regime was quickly enmeshed in corruption and guile. Compounding this state of affairs, the Chinese family system, once a force for stability, proved unsuited to modern nationalism. Many officials thought more of bettering their families than they did of furthering the national interest, a concept difficult in any case for many Buddhist and Confucian-oriented Chinese to grasp and apply. One result was the widespread nepotism, from which Chiang himself was not entirely immune; it enfeebled the government and its bureaucracy.

To many Americans Chiang was a heroic and embattled figure, the embodiment of a "new" China struggling to adapt politically and culturally to the twentieth century. He was widely pictured as indomitable and as a bulwark against communism in Asia. From the 1940's onward, his chief promoters and partisans were collectively known as the China Lobby. According to W. A. Swanberg, the historian and biographer, "the China Lobby was an amorphous group, preponderantly Republican, boosting Chiang for reasons of anticommunism and also as an issue against the Democrats." It included such persons as Alfred Kohlberg, an importer of Chinese lace; Representative Walter H. Judd, Republican of Minnesota; Senator William F. Knowland, Republican of California; Anna Chennault, widow of the Flying Tiger leader; Thomas Corcoran, the Washington lawyer; Senator Styles Bridges, Republican of New Hampshire; William Loeb, the New Hampshire publisher; and Henry R. Luce, the publisher of *Time, Life,* and *Fortune.* Because of an emotional and ideological commitment to Chiang, Luce was among the lobby's most powerful members. His periodicals published eulogistic articles about Chiang and optimistic assessments of the situation in China.

From 1945 to 1949, the lobby tirelessly pressured Congress

and the administration for military and economic aid to Chiang. At least $30 million of the aid was reported to have been pocketed by his generals. In all, about $3 billion in arms and aid was given him, Seymour Topping estimated in his book *Journey Between Two Chinas.* Much of the military equipment, he added, wound up in the hands of the Communists. At the same time General David Barr, chief of the American military advisers to Chiang, reported that there was "complete ineptness of military leaders and widespread corruption and dishonesty throughout the armed forces." Such was the influence of the China Lobby, however, that this somber evaluation of Chiang's leadership was submerged. The notion was advanced that abandonment of the generalissimo would be an act of surrender to communism.

After the Nationalist debacle, which had been foreseen by General Barr and many other Americans on the scene, the China Lobby helped to savage a number of Foreign Service officers in China who had long warned of Chiang's fatal shortcomings. In the McCarthyite atmosphere of the early fifties, such diplomats as John Paton Davies and John Carter Vincent were accused of having "lost" China to the Communists. Even Dean Acheson, Truman's secretary of state, and General George C. Marshall, who had headed a fruitless mission to China just after the war, were not immune from attacks, although both were staunch anticommunists. Indeed, in the early fifties, the myth was widely propagated that Chiang was more the victim of State Department "subversives" than of his own weaknesses.

Even in exile in Taiwan, Chiang retained a remarkable image in the United States. The China Lobby and Luce continued to praise him and to urge American financial and military support; but he also fitted into the Communist-containment policy of the Eisenhower administration, a circumstance that helped to fortify his position militarily and diplomatically. A pro-Chiang policy carried over into the 1960's and early 1970's.

Another aspect of Chiang that appealed to many in this country was his conversion to Protestantism—he joined the Methodist

Church in 1931—and his professed devotion to New Testament ideals. Missionaries portrayed the generalissimo in a favorable light, citing his protection of their activities and his comprehension of Christian ethics. Chiang, however, was not a missionary ruler, despite his creation of the New Life Movement, a politicospiritual program containing elements of Christianity. Deeply imbued with Confucian thought, he believed with the pre-Christian philosopher, "If the ruler is virtuous, the people will also be virtuous." He also believed in rigorous self-examination of his moral actions and he kept a diary in which he set down every week the results of his introspection. This gave him both an inner certainty and an impermeability to criticism. Scolding his subordinates, he seemed like a Savonarola, an impression reinforced by his drawn, monk-like face with its severe cropped mustache and his shaven pate. Like a monk, he set aside a time for daily meditation and Bible reading, and he regularly attended Sunday religious services.

Unlike some of his associates, Chiang Kai-shek, whose given name can be rendered in English as "Firm Rock," led an austere and frugal life, albeit in surroundings of imperial opulence. He made a point of eating simply and sparingly, drinking powdered milk or weak green tea. He did not smoke, gamble, or indulge in recreations more frivolous than walking. He dressed customarily in a neat but undistinguished brown high-necked tunic and matching trousers. Relaxing at home he would wear a traditional long gown and skull cap. He spoke a rough Mandarin for state occasions, although his conversational tongue was the Ningpo dialect.

Another aspect of Chiang's traditionalism was his belief in a system of personal loyalty, in which the subject was loyal to the ruler, the son to the father, the younger to older. This led to situations in which he imputed disloyalty to his critics; it also led to his reliance on a very small circle of advisers, only a few of whom felt they could speak up with impunity. Added to this was a shortness of temper that exhibited itself in bizarre ways. Once, for example, Chiang was witnessing a movie at home that contained a scene displeasing to him. He stalked out and ordered the hapless projectionist thrashed soundly. On a more consequential level, he was capable of jailing or otherwise punishing those who crossed him.

Chiang was very much a product of the breakup of the Manchu dynasty and the conditions of near-anarchy that ensued. He was born in the waning years of the dynasty—on October 31, 1887 at Fenghua, Chekiang Province, one hundred miles south of Shanghai. The son of a petty salt merchant and his "second wife," or concubine, he had a grim boyhood. On his fiftieth birthday he recalled: "My father died when I was nine years old. The miserable condition of my family at that time is beyond description. My family, solitary and without influence, became at once the target of much insult and abuse. It was entirely due to my mother [a devout Buddhist] and her kindness and perseverance that the family was saved from utter ruin. For a period of seventeen years—from the age of nine until I was twenty-five—my mother never spent a day free from domestic difficulties."

The events of his youth are obscure, but somehow he was able in 1906 to enter the Paoting Military Academy, where he did well enough to be sent to Japan in 1907 for two years of advanced instruction. There he became acquainted with a number of Chinese revolutionaries, including, it is said, Dr. Sun Yat-sen, one of the principal founders of modern China. He joined the Tung Meng Hui, a secret society that was the forerunner of the Kuomintang, the Nationalist party, which he dominated after Dr. Sun's death in March 1925. When revolts broke out in China in October 1911, Chiang resigned from the Japanese Army (he had signed up as an officer), returned to the mainland, and took the field against the Manchu forces. A capable commander, he led a successful attack on Hangchow and later held military positions in the Shanghai area.

In the next ten years, however, his fortunes were mixed. It is believed that at one point he quarreled with Dr. Sun. According to O. Edmund Clubb's *Twentieth Century China*, Chiang "made his [temporary] exit from the political scene in 1913 and engaged in brokerage in Shanghai for nearly a decade. . . . It was during that period that he established connections with the powerful political and financial figures in Shanghai that were to have so important an influence on his later orientation."

By 1921–22 Chiang returned to military-political life as chief of staff of Dr. Sun's Canton-based regime. Rickety and in constant clash with warlords and with the shadowy official government in Peking, this regime sought and received military and political help from the newly established Soviet Union. Chiang was sent to Moscow to help organize this assistance, meeting many of the top Soviet revolutionaries in the process. One result of his mission was that scores of Soviet advisers went to China and became influential in the Kuomintang, attempting to give it a left-wing orientation. Indeed, members of the new Chinese Communist party were encouraged to join it. Chiang, as another consequence of the mission, organized the Whampoa Military Academy, which trained officers for the Kuomintang army.

With Dr. Sun's death the bond between the Communists and Chiang's more conservative group in the Kuomintang dissolved; and in a tragedy of plot and counterplot he slaughtered thousands of Communists and workers in Canton and Shanghai and, in 1927–28, organized his own Nationalist government at Nanking. According to some China specialists, Chiang was materially helped by Shanghai financial interests and wealthy landowners. "The bankers and industrialists of Shanghai, led by the brilliant Soong Kung Family group, had now come to terms with Chiang," George H. Kerr wrote in *Formosa Betrayed.* "Apparently, Chiang made a bargain. In return for financial support on a large scale he agreed to exclude left-wing elements and Communists from the new 'National Revolutionary Government.' The bargain was cemented by a marriage between Chiang and an 'unclaimed jewel' of the Soong family, the beautiful Soong Mei-ling, aged twenty-six, the youngest sister of T. V. Soong [the powerful banker]."

The marriage with the American-educated and Christianized Miss Soong was clouded at the outset by disputes over Chiang's divorce from a previous wife. His subsequent baptism, however, mollified his missionary critics, who became his most persistent and influential advocates among Americans. Over the years Madame Chiang was not only a close confidante of her husband but also his best link with the economic power structure. Members of her family held key government and party posts and dealt also in diplomacy.

With the coup that brought Chiang to power, the Chinese Communist party was shattered. Its leaders and some members found refuge in the mountains of Kiangsi. Over the next few years Chiang, with the advice of imported German generals, sought to eliminate the Communists, who after breaking free of an attempt to trap them in Kiangsi conducted the epic Long March through the wilderness of western China, reaching Yenan in the northwest in 1934–35. Meanwhile Chiang's regime failed to achieve unification of China. True, there was a national currency and a national legislative apparatus; but what passed for a national administration at Nanking was in fact only one of many regional factions of limited authority and influence. Instead of subduing the more powerful northern warlords, Chiang preferred to make deals; if they would accept him as titular head of state, he in return would respect their local sovereignty. Thus the Nationalist regime became a loose coalition of military chieftains bound to Chiang by pledges of personal loyalty.

To students and patriots of virtually every political stripe, Chiang's policies seemed irrelevant in the face of Japanese aggression. The Japanese threat was unmistakable from 1931 onward, but his "pacification" projects postponed a confrontation while permitting the Japanese to gobble up Manchuria and convert it into a puppet state. Alarmed by the possibility that the Japanese would strike southward, the northern warlords rebelled in 1936. Chiang arrived in Sian, Marshal Chang Hsueh-liang's capital, in December 1936, to investigate, and was promptly arrested. The generalissimo, attempting to flee in his nightgown, was easily captured.

Chang, known as the Young Marshal, presented his superior

with a series of demands that included immediate cessation of the civil war against the Communists in favor of a general policy of armed resistance to Japan in cooperation with the Communists. Some insurgents wanted to execute Chiang, but he was saved by the timely intervention of the Communist leader Chou En-lai. In weird negotiations involving the Communists, the Chang dissidents, and high officials from Nanking, Chiang capitulated and was released. The shotgun alliance also had one notable side effect—a decision by the Soviet Union to bolster Chiang with air power and military advisers. The Japanese, perturbed at the prospect of a unified China, struck south from Peking in 1937–38. The ferocity of the onslaught, while it held the united front together for a time, drove Chinese troops out of key coastal cities and obliged the government to shift its capital from Nanking to the smaller interior city of Chungking. However, when the Japanese armies stalled and the war entered a seven-year period of attrition, the Chiang-Communist alliance disintegrated.

With United States entry into World War II in late 1941, American strategists saw China as a potentially effective front against Japan, and military and economic aid was dispatched there. However, Chiang's relations with Americans sent to help him were less than cordial, especially those with General Joseph W. (Vinegar Joe) Stilwell, who was sent to Chungking in 1942 as Chiang's chief of staff. Meanwhile, to overcome Chiang's pronounced reluctance to take the field against Japan, the generalissimo was invited, toward the close of 1943, to confer with President Roosevelt and Prime Minister Churchill at Cairo. There he obtained a promise for the postwar return to China of Manchuria and of Formosa (Taiwan), which had been under Japanese rule since 1895. A plan for joint Allied action in Burma was also agreed upon. Stilwell, who loved the Chinese and spoke their language, was Roosevelt's choice to be Commander in Chief of Chinese and American forces in China. But Chiang and the outspoken general fell out. In his report to the War Department, Stilwell said that Chiang sought to "dominate rather than unify and lead" China against Japan.

Confiding to his diary, the general was even more blunt. He wrote: "I never have heard Chiang Kai-shek say a single thing that indicated gratitude to the President or to our country for the help we were extending to him. Invariably, when anything was promised, he would want more. He would make comparisons between the huge amounts of Lend-Lease supplies going to Great Britain and Russia with the meager trickle going to China. He would complain that the Chinese had been fighting for six or seven years and yet we gave them practically nothing. It would have of course been undiplomatic to go into the nature of the military effort Chiang Kai-shek had made since 1938. It was practically zero."

By 1944, with the military situation in China in disarray save in the Communist-controlled areas, the United States proposed that Stilwell be given command of the Nationalist troops. However, according to *Stilwell and the American Experience in China* by Barbara Tuchman, Chiang "thoroughly intended in his own mind to stay out of the war . . . no matter how much of east China was lost, until the Allies should defeat Japan and he could emerge on the winning side." Mrs. Tuchman said the generalissimo proved devious, giving Stilwell the impression in an interview in September 1944 that he was indeed commander of the Chinese Army. At the same time, he interposed conditions, among them control of millions in American lend-lease supplies lest any arms get into the hands of the Communists, whose efficient troops Stilwell wanted to use against the Japanese.

Chiang's backing and filling infuriated Stilwell. He often referred to the generalissimo in private as "the Peanut," and in his diary he began to use such phrases as "that hickory nut he uses for a head." "He is impossible," the general wrote at one point. In addition to lend-lease control, Chiang wanted effective authority over the general in the matter of strategy and tactics. In attempting to reach an understanding through the wily T. V. Soong, the general remarked that what Chiang really wanted in a commander was "an over-all stooge." In the face of his calculated reluctance to place Stilwell in full command, President Roosevelt sent the generalissimo a strong, almost peremptory cable, saying, in part: "It appears plainly evident to all of us here that all your and our efforts to save China are to be lost by further delays."

Stilwell himself handed the message to Chiang, writing afterward that the "harpoon" hit the generalissimo "in the solar plexus and went right through him." Shocked though he was by the president's bluntness, Chiang almost immediately rose to heights of wrath. According to Mrs. Tuchman, "He knew he could not accept the American demand . . . without opening the way to his own discard. If the Americans succeeded in imposing Stilwell on him against his will, they might do likewise in the matter of the Communists." The result was a formal demand for Stilwell's recall, an action to which a weary President Roosevelt acceded. He was not prepared "to impose an American commander against the express wishes of a chief of state," Mrs. Tuchman said. The general's reaction was succinct and prescient: "If Old Softy gives in on this as he apparently has, the Peanut will be out of control from now on."

The general's leavetaking had overtones of comic opera. Chiang offered him the Special Grand Cordon of the Blue Sky and White Sun, a decoration that was refused. There was, though, a final tea. Describing it, Mrs. Tuchman said: "Chiang Kai-shek, with T. V. Soong at his elbow, was gracious. He regretted all this very much, it was only due to differences of personality, he hoped Stilwell would continue to be China's friend. . . . The guest was laconic."

Chiang's hold on the Nationalist leadership was prolonged, at least temporarily, by mounting American successes against Japan in the Pacific in 1945 that culminated in that country's unconditional surrender in August. In December 1945, after the close of the war, President Truman sent General George C. Marshall to China with orders to unify and pacify the country. He exerted enormous pressure on Chiang and the Communists to end the civil strife that had erupted afresh with the defeat of Japan. On January 10, 1946, a cease-fire accord was signed; but the truce was quickly breached and before long civil war raged openly through the nation. With three million troops to Mao Tse-tung's one million,

Chiang gained the upper hand in the first few months of the war; but once the Communists felt strong enough to mount an offensive in the spring of 1947, it was clear where the initiative lay.

As Maoist forces were overrunning the country, the United States issued a 1,054-page white paper, writing off Nationalist China and attributing Communist successes to Chiang's military and political errors. Published in the summer of 1949, the State Department document dourly recounted Chiang's dissipation of more than $3 billion in American aid between August 1945 and the middle of 1948. In asserting the futility of additional help, Secretary of State Acheson said: "A large proportion of the military supplies furnished the Chinese armies by the United States since V-J Day has fallen into the hands of the Chinese Communists through the military ineptitude of the Nationalist leaders, their defections and surrenders, and the absence among their forces of the will to fight. It has been urged that relatively small amounts of additional aid—military and economic—to the National Government would have enabled it to destroy Communism in China. The most trustworthy military, economic and political information available to our Government does not bear out this view. A realistic appraisal of conditions in China, past and present, leads to the conclusion that the only alternative open to the United States was full-scale intervention in behalf of a Government which had lost the confidence of its own troops and its own people."

Earlier, as Nationalist defeats turned into a rout, air and naval units were transferred to Taiwan along with gold and silver bullion. "The generalissimo also clamped tighter military and police control over the restive Taiwanese," according to Seymour Topping in *Journey Between Two Chinas.* "The Nationalist troops . . . looted and stripped the island, which had been developed with Japanese capital [since 1895]. Many Kuomintang officials expropriated land from the Taiwanese for themselves. In February and March, 1947, the Taiwanese demonstrated against the sacking of their island, demanding that the Nationalist governor, Chen Yi, reform his corrupt, dictatorial administration.

"Chen Yi's response was to bring in additional troops from the mainland and put down the demonstration in an orgy of killing in which between 10,000 and 20,000 Taiwanese were massacred, including several thousand of the island's political and economic leaders and intellectual elite. On the generalissimo's orders, Chen Yi eventually was shot for his excesses but the population of the island . . . remained hostile to the mainlanders."

In December 1949, Chiang flew to Taiwan, declaring Taipei the temporary capital of China. In the next two decades he received hundreds of millions in American military aid that permitted him to build a smartly turned-out armed force. Over the same period private American capital flowed into the island and built up a network of light industry, chiefly in textiles and electronics. Sweatshop labor costs—Chiang was not tolerant of trade unions—contributed to creation of an economic boom. Thriving industry, however, was accompanied by repressive military rule. Simultaneously, the Nationalists introduced land reforms and scientific agricultural practices that permitted the island abundant crops, some of them for export.

With the Korean conflict in June 1950, the United States assigned its Seventh Fleet to the Strait of Taiwan and began to bolster Chiang as a counterweight to communism in Asia. Political, economic, and military assistance was poured into the island. In May 1951 an American mission began to equip and train a new Nationalist army, which eventually totaled 600,000 men and ate up the bulk of the island's budget. In 1954 the United States and the Chinese regime concluded a mutual defense treaty.

Chiang, for his part, began to think of returning in triumph to the mainland. Inaugurated for a fourth term as president in 1966, he called himself an "undiscouraged old soldier," and vowed that he "would exterminate Mao Tse-tung and his cohorts, liberate our mainland compatriots and establish on the ruins a new country of unity and freedom." In private, however, he was less sanguine about his chances. He hoped for a return, of course, but he expected that it would follow a political collapse on the mainland. Meanwhile he engaged himself in keeping his army on the ready and in improving the economy of Taiwan. Paradoxically, as the island became more prosperous, many among his followers grew more concerned with benefiting from Taiwan's wealth and less eager to embark on uncertain military ventures.

Toward the close of his life Chiang was more of a presence than a reality. He rarely left his palatial residence on the outskirts of Taipei except to visit a favorite resort in the southern part of the island. After being sworn in for his fifth six-year term as head of state in 1972, he quietly permitted his elder son, Chiang Ching-kuo, the child of his first marriage, to assume day-to-day control of the government and the party. Never far out of influence, though, was his wife, who, like her husband, was a true bitter-ender.

AUGUST 27, 1975

❖

HAILE SELASSIE

The last emperor in the three-thousand-year-old Ethiopian monarchy, Haile Selassie died in a small apartment in his former palace. He was eighty-three years old, and had been deposed in a military-led popular uprising the previous September. Although he was looked upon from abroad, especially from the United States, as a paternal figure, His Imperial Majesty the Conquering Lion of the Tribe of Judah and Elect of God ruled his ancient realm as a medieval autocrat.

Seized in an army-led coup after almost a year of roiling discontent in his country, Haile Selassie, who was accustomed to ride in Rolls-Royces, was hustled from his spacious and opulent palace in the back seat of a blue Volkswagen. The final confrontation between the aged emperor and the robust army men resembled an improbable opera scene. Haile Selassie scolded and insulted the officers as insolent, and they, with mounting ire, decided to take him to a military camp. On the way, he was jeered by Addis Ababa crowds yelling "Thief! Thief!"

The emperor's troubles were noticeable in 1973 with rumblings in the countryside and mutterings in the peasant-based army over government attempts to hush up a drought that took a hundred thousand lives in two northern provinces. This unrest was compounded in 1974 by military mutinies over low pay and by a secessionist guerrilla war in Eritrea. In the spring and summer, there were popular outbursts in Addis Ababa that forced Haile Selassie to make a show of trimming his absolute power, but his regime was too permeated with dry rot to respond to the needs of the people.

Ironically, Haile Selassie initiated the changes that led to his downfall—the military training program that exposed Ethiopian officers to representative institutions in the United States and the establishment of Haile Selassie I University, where students learned to think about political economy. The emperor, however, could not seem to adapt to new concepts, and he lost touch with his subjects in his later years, showing more affection for his pet cheetahs and dogs, diplomats said, than for his human entourage.

In the working out of Haile Selassie's cautious reforms, a thin layer of technocrats and intellectuals was created, a group that perceived the country far differently from the tradition-bound emperor. The reform process created a dependency on the United States, which equipped the army and which drew Ethiopia into the periphery of superpower politics. The United States supported Ethiopia because of the country's strategic position on the Red Sea. The Soviet Union responded by equipping the military forces of Somalia, which also lies on the Red Sea and abuts Ethiopia on the southeast. For years the two countries quarreled over their border, adding to tensions inside both nations.

The combination of circumstances that led to Haile Selassie's downfall tended to obscure his accomplishments in leading a largely illiterate, rural, and feudal country with two thousand languages and dialects into the nineteenth, if not the twentieth, century. It also shadowed his contributions to African unity. An African who met the emperor at the United Nations Security Council session in Addis Ababa in 1972 summed up a widespread feeling when he said: "Haile Selassie is one of the world's great men. He did a lot for his country and early became a respected voice for Africa and for the third world."

If the pace of change was snailish under the emperor, it was deliberately so. "We must make progress slowly so as to preserve the progress we have already made," he said frequently of his reign, in which slavery was legally abolished and a very limited democratic structure was instituted. But he was also regarded as one who ruled too strictly by prerogative for the benefit of his family and friends. At his ouster he was popularly accused as an exploiter who had secretly sent billions of dollars to private bank accounts abroad.

The drama of his departure from power and the intrigues that preceded it were kin to the events of his long life. Coming to power in a palace coup, and later discomfiting his enemies in battle, Haile Selassie was driven into exile by the troops of Fascist Italy after the civilized world had spurned his eloquent and poignant appeal for help. Restored to his capital in World War II, he obtained for Ethiopia a coastline on the Red Sea, skillfully courted foreign economic aid, strove to improve education, squashed one attempted coup, and, despite the anachronisms of his person and the archaicisms of his country, emerged as an elder statesman of African anticolonialism.

The prestige and power of Haile Selassie, waxing over more than a half century, made him a personage larger than life. With a splendid sense of theater, he lived up to, and even surpassed, the role in which he was cast. Once the emperor was distributing gifts to men who served the Ethiopian cause in World War II. After he had finished, one man approached him and complained that he had been overlooked. "You lie," Haile Selassie replied, calling the petitioner by name and citing the exact place, day, and hour that he had been rewarded for obtaining a string of mules for the army. The man flushed and trembled, for he had never suspected that the emperor would remember, since scores of others had been honored at the same time. He started to inch away. The emperor summoned him back and tossed him a bundle of banknotes.

Such magnificent and munificent gestures tended to obscure the fact that the emperor looked emaciated, and was only five feet four inches tall. But he had an imposing presence and an air of command whether he was seated at his desk in military uniform with a blazing array of decorations across his chest, or standing, caped, on the rostrum of the League of Nations, or motoring, bolt upright in his green or maroon Rolls-Royce, through the dusty streets of Addis Ababa while his subjects lay prostrate in his path.

What helped to make Haile Selassie so physically imposing was his bearded and dark-complexioned face, his aquiline nose over full lips, and his steady, penetrating black eyes. It was a mien both melancholy and fearsome, the visage of one who ruled by the precepts of John Stuart Mill as well as by those of Niccolo Machiavelli, by compassion as well as cruelty; for he was generous to loyal subordinates, he hanged the rebellious, and he once kept a rival imprisoned in golden chains. The limit of his emotional expression was a sad smile, so enigmatic that his true feelings seemed deeply mysterious.

To many in the West, especially in the United States, Haile Selassie was a storied figure. He was the 225th emperor of Ethiopia in a line that he traced to Menelik I, who was credited with being the child of King Solomon and the Queen of Sheba, identified in Ethiopia as Queen Makeda. (The constitution of 1955 specified Haile Selassie's direct descent from Menelik I.)

Unbending on protocol and punctilio, the emperor in his public appearances recalled the splendor and opulence of Suleiman the Magnificent or Louis XIV, with the difference that he lived and worked in a modern atmosphere and journeyed abroad in a commandeered Ethiopian Airlines plane. He once had three palaces; but after he transformed the Gueneteleul Palace into the Haile Selassie I University in 1960, he was reduced to a palace to live in—the Jubilee—and one to work in—the Ghibi.

Around the clock, he was guarded by lions and cheetahs, protected by imperial bodyguards, trailed by his pet papillon dogs, flanked by a multitude of chamberlains and flunkies, and sustained by a tradition of reverence for his person. He took seriously the doctrine of the divine right of kings, and he never allowed his subjects to forget that he considered himself the elect of God. He combined in his person the temporal sovereignty of the state and the leadership of the Ethiopian Orthodox Church, the country's established church.

In moments of relaxation—and these were few, for he was an extraordinarily hardworking monarch—Haile Selassie displayed considerable charm. He spoke softly (in halting English, if necessary), and he had a mind well furnished with small talk derived from his daily scrutiny of the world press and from viewing films and newsreels. He also absorbed information from his extensive travels about the world. His talk, though light, was not likely to be gay or mirth-provoking or quotable. He referred to himself always by the imperial "we." In his later years he was a lonely man beneath the panoply of office. He had outlived his wife of fifty years, who died in 1962, and four of his six children. He had, though, more than a dozen grandchildren and some great-grandchildren, with whom he liked to surround himself at dinner.

In African affairs, Haile Selassie's courage and his tenacity as a nationalist gave him a position of leadership among such anticolonialist statesmen as Jomo Kenyatta of Kenya, Sekou Touré of Guinea, and Kenneth Kaunda of Zambia. Despite his autocratic rule, the emperor represented independence from overt foreign domination as well as the artful acquisition of foreign economic aid. It was Haile Selassie who convoked the first meeting of the Organization of African Unity in 1963 and devised the charter for the thirty-eight-nation bloc. Its headquarters are in Addis Ababa.

At his suggestion a United Nations economic commission for Africa was set up. Its secretariat is also in Addis Ababa in a lavish $1.75-million building erected at the emperor's bidding.

In Ethiopia, he was an object of veneration to the masses of people until his overthrow, but to the new urban elite the centralization of authority in his person and the tepidity of reform had been unpalatable for some time. The two constitutions the emperor granted, one in 1931 and the other in 1955, were both criticized because the cabinet was responsible to Haile Selassie and because there was no provision for political parties.

Economic reform, especially changes in the age-old system of land tenure, was far too slow, critics said, with the result that the country's agriculture and animal husbandry—the mainstays of its economy—were operated on a primitive level. Coffee, cereals, and beans were the main cash crops; meat and animal products also contributed heavily to the gross national product. Manufacturing and power, on the other hand, accounted for only three percent of the G.N.P.

Haile Selassie's kingdom was a wild and sprawling country of 455,000 square miles (about the size of Texas, Louisiana, Arkansas, and Oklahoma combined) and 26 million people (an accepted guess in the absence of any census). There were a score of tribes, at least one so primitive that its men castrated their enemies to win favor with intended brides. There were many languages, but Amharic, the official tongue, was spoken in some degree by only fifty percent of the people. Although the state religion was a Monophysite Christianity, a substantial portion of the population, perhaps forty percent, was Moslem. In addition, there were Animists and Judaists. The multiplicity of religions and customs accented Ethiopia's lack of homogeneity and its general backwardness, for it was a country without a developed highway or rail system, and without organized health and social services. The bulk of the people lived in mud and straw huts, even in Addis Ababa.

In the capital, the contrast between the old and the new was especially striking, for its few modern buildings cast their shadow on the far more numerous ancient structures that included, until a few years ago, the imperial brothel and the square in which public hangings were carried out.

Of the dominant Amhara tribe, Haile Selassie was born on July 23, 1892. He was named Lij Tafari Makonnen and he was the only legitimate son of Ras Makonnen, governor of Harar, to survive infancy. The boy's father was a cousin and close ally of Emperor Menelik II, who was without a legitimate direct male heir. When Ras Makonnen died in 1906, his son, who already had a rudimentary education and spoke French, was summoned to the court of Addis Ababa, where he was further schooled both in book learning and in the devious intrigues of Menelik's household. Tafari was passed over on the death of Menelik II in 1913 in favor of the emperor's grandson Lij Yasu, a handsome, dissolute, and athletic young man. Tafari, meanwhile, had married Lij Yasu's niece, Waizero Menen, after her divorce, and had attained practical experience in government as governor of a province.

Lij Yasu, who was never formally crowned, was converted to Islam and excommunicated by the Ethiopian church. In the palace coup that followed, Tafari made himself the heir presumptive to the throne and regent for Zauditu, a daughter of Menelik, who was proclaimed empress.

Emerging as the strong man, Tafari got rid of the husband of the empress, putting her under his control, and, capturing Lij Yasu, imprisoned him for the rest of his life. The golden chains in which he was held were not so confining, however, as to prevent him from enjoying the variety of women Tafari supplied to him.

Tafari was less indulgent with his other warlord enemies among the nobles. "He creeps like a mouse, but he has the jaws of a lion," one of them said. By force of arms and executions, he brought an end to the chaos that threatened to envelop Ethiopia and turned his country's eyes ever so slightly toward the outside world.

In 1923 Tafari had the kingdom accepted as a member of the League of Nations. He acted in the hope that league membership would exempt Ethiopia from the colonial ambitions of other countries. In the following year Tafari, having bulwarked his power at home, undertook an extensive foreign tour. "We need European progress," he explained, "only because we are surrounded by it." Everywhere he went in Europe, Tafari, with his six lions, four zebras, and thirty attendants, created a lasting impression. His modern outlook won him friends; so did his assertions that Ethiopia required innovation and development.

One fruit of his trip was the Tafari Makonnen School, which he founded and staffed with European teachers. (Education was one of the chief interests of Tafari when he became emperor, and he established primary and secondary schools throughout the country as well as the Haile Selassie I University. Even so, at the end of his reign, only 500,000 school-age children of a potential 3.2 million were enrolled.)

Friction between the empress and her regent grew in the late 1920's. Believing in 1928 that she had the upper hand, the empress attempted a coup, but she was thwarted by the cunning and alertness of Tafari, who forced her to crown him king of Ethiopia. Two years later, after her mysterious death, Tafari was crowned emperor and took the name of Haile Selassie, which means "Power of the Holy Trinity." The coronation on November 2, 1930, was an event of unparalleled sumptuousness in a city that one observer said, "resembled a shantytown with wedding-cake trimmings." There were only one or two buildings of more than one story; the rest was a tumbled mass of mud huts. Distinguished foreign delegations mingled with the city's twenty thousand prostitutes. Describing the coronation, Leonard Mosley wrote in his book, *Haile Selassie: The Conquering Lion:*

"Shortly before dawn on the morning of November 2, before the world press, the foreign guests and a great concourse of rases [nobles] in their lion's manes and most resplendent robes, Abuna Kyril [the archbishop] anointed the head of Haile Selassie and placed on it the triple crown of Ethiopia.

"Simultaneously, the rases put on their coronets, then made

their obeisances to him, after which the celebratory shooting, shouting, loolooing, feasting, dancing and drinking broke out all over the city."

The emperor's initial ventures into reform, in which he changed the status of his people from chattels of the nobles into subjects of the state, culminated in a constitution in 1931. Although its limits on the royal prerogative were negligible, it was a small step away from feudalism. At the same time, administrative changes improved the civil service and a tax system was introduced. Road-building and other public works were undertaken. Several edicts against slavery were promulgated, if not enforced.

In 1934 Benito Mussolini, the dictator of Fascist Italy, moved against Ethiopia in a border incident. His pretense, that of bringing civilization to a backward country, concealed Italian imperial ambitions for an African colony to supplement Italian Somaliland and Eritrea. In the diplomatic footwork that followed the border clash, the emperor referred the dispute to the League of Nations for mediation; but Britain and France gave Mussolini to understand that he could expect a free hand in Ethiopia. "Could we not have called Musso's bluff and at least postponed this war?" Winston Churchill asked later. "The answer I'm sure is yes. We built Musso into a great power."

Deserted by Britain and France, Ethiopia fell to Italian arms shortly after the Fascist invasion began on October 2, 1935. By April 1936 the conflict ("This isn't a war, it isn't even a slaughter," a British eyewitness said. "It's the torture of tens of thousands of men, women and children with bombs and poison gas") was over. On May 2 Haile Selassie went into exile.

The emperor went first to Jerusalem to pray and then to Britain as a private guest. Still convinced that the League could be rallied to his cause, he appealed to it and its members not to recognize the Italian conquest. Shamed, the League permitted him to state his case, and his appearance before the delegates assembled in Geneva on June 30, 1936, was a moment in history that few witnesses ever forgot.

Aloof, dignified, gazing in contempt at the Fascist journalists who shouted at him, and looking directly at the uneasy, shuffling delegates, he began his speech in Amharic by saying: "I, Haile Selassie I, emperor of Ethiopia, am here today to claim that justice that is due to my people and the assistance promised to it eight months ago by fifty-two nations who asserted that an act of aggression had been committed in violation of international treaties."

After reciting the principal events of the war and his betrayal by the big powers, he continued:

"I assert that the issue before the assembly today is not merely a question of the settlement in the matter of Italian aggression. It is a question of collective security; of the very existence of the League; of the trust placed by states in international treaties; of the value of promises made to small states that their integrity and independence shall be respected and assured. . . .

"In a word, it is international morality that is at stake. . . .

"Outside of the Kingdom of God, there is not on this earth any nation that is higher than any other. If a strong government finds that it can, with impunity, destroy a weak people, then the hour has struck for that weak people to appeal to the League of Nations to give its judgment in all freedom. God and history will remember your judgment.

"Placed by the aggressor face to face with the accomplished fact, are states going to set up the terrible precedent of bowing before force?

"I ask the great powers, who have promised the guarantee of collective security to small states—those small states over whom hangs the threat that they may one day suffer the fate of Ethiopia: What measures do they intend to take? . . . What answer am I to take back to my people?"

As Haile Selassie concluded what was certainly his saddest (and greatest) hour and moved from the tribunal to a scatter of embarrassed applause, he murmured:

"It is us today. It will be you tomorrow."

In practical terms, the emperor's speech was a magnificent but futile gesture, for one by one the powers recognized the Italian regime in East Africa. Haile Selassie went to live as an unwanted guest in Bath, England; he was so impoverished that the local bookshop stopped his credit.

The emperor was rescued from this seedy oblivion on May 10, 1940, when Italy entered World War II as an enemy of Britain. Churchill, long a friend, had him flown incognito, as Mr. Strong, to Africa. Landing at Alexandria, he spent the night in the men's room of the Italian Yacht Club before going on to Khartoum in the Sudan. There he helped to organize an army of liberation with the aid of Orde Wingate, one of the most picturesque British officers in the war. The result of these exertions was that Haile Selassie returned to his country on January 20, 1941, and made his state entry into Addis Ababa on May 5 in the back of an Alfa Romeo motor car. It was five years to the day since the Italians had entered the city. The country remained under British administration until January 1942, when London recognized Ethiopia as a sovereign state.

In the years that followed the restoration Haile Selassie enhanced his personal power while slowly beginning to solve the country's grave economic and social problems. Some advance in education was also made, for two hundred school buildings were put up between 1942 and 1952. In this period, too, a new force was reaching adulthood in the kingdom—the educated elite whose travels and schooling abroad made them restive over their nation's introversions. Partly as the result of pressure from this group and partly because of the rising tide of anticolonialism in Africa, Haile Selassie granted a new constitution in 1955. It promised his subjects equal rights under the law, plus a vote; but it also retained his traditional prerogatives. One clause read:

"By virtue of His Imperial Blood as well as by the anointing which He has received, the person of the Emperor is sacred. His dignity is inviolable and His Power indisputable. He is, consequently, entitled to all the honors due Him in accordance with tradition and the present Constitution. Anyone so bold as to seek to injure the Emperor will be punished."

The surface placidity of Ethiopia was shattered in 1960 when Haile Selassie was absent on a state trip to Brazil. The imperial bodyguard mutinied and some members of the royal family, including Crown Prince Asfa Wossen, joined an attempt to dethrone the emperor and promote faster social and economic progress. The emperor returned to Addis Ababa, crushed the revolt, and had the commander of the bodyguard publicly hanged for treason. The crown prince was put out of favor, from which he finally emerged, but slowly.

The attempted coup led the emperor to try to communicate more directly with his subjects in radio talks and to indicate, in his paternal fashion, what he was doing for them. One such advance was foreign aid. In the final years of his reign Haile Selassie contrived to obtain help from diverse sources without creating crosscurrents among the donors. Italy and Yugoslavia built dams for him; the Addis Ababa airport was constructed by the United States; the Soviet Union put up a polytechnic institute on the shores of Lake Tana, source of the Blue Nile.

The emperor much enjoyed state visits—to Marshal Tito of Yugoslavia, to Queen Elizabeth II of Britain, and to the United States, where he was the guest of the last five presidents before Gerald R. Ford. In all, he traveled to more than sixty countries, including China. Yet neither royal progresses nor infusions of foreign aid could save him, since neither was directed to bettering the economic and social inequities of the country; and when these were expressed in revolution, the emperor could not contain the demand for rapid change. In disgrace, he lost all.

ST.-JOHN PERSE

St.-John Perse, the romantic poet who won the Nobel Prize for Literature in 1960, was eighty-eight years old when he died in the seclusion of his villa at Giens, on the French Riviera. Marie-Réné-Auguste-Alexis Saint-Leger Leger, to give him his baptismal name, was a triple image. As Alexis Leger he was a professional French diplomat of impressive suavity and limited accomplishment. As himself he was a gracious aristocrat who preferred his own company to the glitter of society and the clatter of the salon. As St.-John (pronounced SIN-jin) Perse, he was a major poet of candescent belief in the indestructibility of humanity.

The derivation of his pen name was a mystery that he declined to solve and toward the spelling of which he was indifferent. It appeared in several forms—St.-J. Perse, Saint-John Perse, and, most often in the United States, as St.-John Perse. He did explain, however, that he chose the pseudonym to keep his identity as a poet separate from his personality as a diplomat. Even after he had retired from the diplomatic service he considered himself as one who would rather look at panoramas of woods and sea than be chairbound with pen in hand. "I am not a career man of letters," he said simply, "because I don't want to be a slave to my métier."

Nonetheless, the Nobel Prize confirmed the rapturous regard Perse's peers expressed for him as one of the most original of contemporary poets. His audacious use of pungent imagery and arcane symbolism set him apart, as did his celebration of the inexhaustible power of life to triumph over disaster. His language was ambagious, lyric, and cadenced, studded with subtle metaphors and sprinkled with delicate melodies more evident to the ear than the eye. Among poets writing in English, Archibald MacLeish, T. S. Eliot, and Louise Varèse were drawn to Perse and influenced by him. Despite formidable problems of nuance, his poetry was translated into English, Russian, German, Spanish, Dutch, Finnish, Romanian, Italian, Swedish, Greek, Danish, Serbian, Hindi, Japanese, Bengali, and Oriya.

As poets go, Perse was not productive; he published only seven volumes, all slender. They were *Eloges* (1911), *Anabase* (1924), *Exil* (1942), *Vents* (1945), *Amers* (1957), *Chronique* (1959), and *Oiseaux* (1962). Nevertheless, Gallimard, his French publisher, had no difficulty in 1965 in assembling *Honneur à Saint-John Perse,* a book of 817 closely printed pages devoted to appraisals of his life and work.

For all the homage that the literary world paid him, Perse was not a poet to comprehend at a glance. His early reputation rested mainly on *Anabase,* described as "a series of images of migration, of conquest of vast spaces in Asiatic wastes, of destruction and foundation of cities and civilizations." It presents the poet as a conqueror who marches, pauses briefly, and departs for unknown places.

Even T. S. Eliot, who translated *Anabase* into English and whose praise of Perse drew English readers' attention to him, believed that Perse's opacities were considerable. "The reader," Eliot wrote in his preface, "has to allow the images to fall into his memory successively without questioning the reasonableness of each at the moment; so that, at the end, a total effect is produced." Eliot judged that reading the poem six times would provide a fair start on understanding its meanings. For those less perceptive or less self-reliant, Eliot offered a "tentative synopsis" of the poem's ten divisions and explained that the word "anabase" (anabasis) was to be taken as Xenophon had used it—a journey or migration upward.

Although Perse's poems are not easy on the eye, there is a musical quality to them, as there is to parts of James Joyce, which can best be appreciated by reading them aloud (in French) or by hearing them read. Most of the poetry is written in what looks like prose. Technically, Perse used the *verset,* a meterless blank verse halfway between prose and poetry; but the absence of meter is scarcely noticeable, so skillful is the arrangement of language.

Perse's images are often drawn from the sea, beside which he passed his childhood and on which he liked to roam, from the Gobi and China, where he was posted for several years as a diplomat, and from the solitude of nature. He could present the most majestic aspect of nature in an earthy figure of speech. What makes him difficult reading is that his images lack a superficially logical order, that they are expressed in a syntax that is the poet's own and in a recondite vocabulary. One of his poems, taken from *Chronique* (published by Pantheon Press), illustrates his mature style and suggests his view of life. As translated by Robert Fitzgerald, part of the poem reads:

> Great age, you lied; a road of glowing embers, not of ash . . .
>> With face alight and spirit high,
>>> to what extreme are we still running? Time measured
>>> by the year is no measure of our days. We hold no

---

traffic with the least nor with the worst. Divine turbulence
be ours to its last eddy. . . .
Great age, behold us on our limitless ways. Cracking
of whips on all the passes! And a loud cry on the
height! And this great wind from elsewhere meeting
us, a wind that bends man over the rock like the
ploughman over the glebe.
O Death adorned with ivory gauntlet, you cross in vain
our paths cobbled with stones, for our way lies
beyond. The squire-at-arms accoutred in bones whom we
house and who serves for a wage, will desert this evening
at the bend in the road.

Perse's poetry tended to be impersonal, without political or social
allusions. He was not unattentive, however, to the poet's role in
the world. "In these days of nuclear energy, can the earthenware
lamp of the poet still suffice?" he asked in his speech accepting the
Nobel Prize. "Yes," he replied, "if its clay reminds us of our own.
And it is sufficient for the poet to be the guilty conscience of his
time."

In conversation, Perse or his alter ego, Alexis Leger, talked
with ease and brilliance on subjects ranging from ocean currents to
whistling swans, French poetry, the Library of Congress, and
American politics. In a dinner jacket he stood aristocratically
erect, with a graceful control of his carriage, manners, and language. His swarthy complexion, black mustache, and piercing
black eyes were his hallmarks in society, as they were when he
dressed in rough clothes and a beret to tramp the countryside near
his home in Washington or his villa on the Riviera, near Toulon.

Perse was born on a family-owned coral island, Saint-Leger-les-
Feuilles, near Guadeloupe, on May 31, 1887. His father was a
lawyer and his mother's family were plantation owners. He spent
much of his childhood on Guadeloupe, where he was informally
educated by the island's Roman Catholic bishop and by his nurse,
a Hindu priestess.

.His formal education, eventually covering law, medicine, and the humanities, began in France when he was eleven. After taking his degree, he joined the French Foreign Service in 1914. Two years later he was assigned secretary of the French embassy in Peking. It was during vacations there that he traveled across the Gobi on horseback and sailed the South Seas between Fiji and the New Hebrides. He also became friends with Chinese sages and spent many hours in retreat in a former temple in the hills near Peking.

In 1921 Perse returned to Paris at the request of Aristide Briand, the foreign minister, whose collaborator he became in an attempt to limit armaments and to bring about Franco-German reconciliation. He was promoted through successive posts at the Quai d'Orsay until he became secretary-general of the Ministry of Foreign Affairs in 1932—the highest permanent official in the ministry. At the same time he was named ambassador of France. In his new post Perse helped give continuity to French foreign policy in the years preceding World War II. Because he opposed appeasement of Germany, he was removed from his ministerial post in 1940. Following the capitulation of France in June 1940, he went to Britain and Canada and then to the United States, where Archibald MacLeish obtained for him a consultantship in French poetry at the Library of Congress. The Vichy government of France stripped him of his honors and his income.

After the war, Perse's French citizenship, his titular rank as ambassador, and his honors were restored. At his death he was a grand officer of the Legion of Honor, a commander of the Order of the Bath, and a recipient of the Grand Cross of the British Empire. He held the Charles Eliot Norton Chair of Poetry at Harvard in 1947 and received an honorary doctorate from Yale in 1959. In 1958 Perse married Dorothy Milburn Russell of Washington. The couple, who were childless, lived in the Georgetown section of the capital and at their villa in Giens.

✛

THORNTON WILDER

Thornton Wilder, who died while taking an afternoon nap at his home in Hamden, Connecticut, was seventy-eight years old and the holder of three Pulitzer Prizes as a playwright and novelist. Although he partook of the twentieth century, his literary creations were singularly aloof from its preoccupations with politics, psychiatry, and explicit sex, concentrating instead on what he perceived as the universal—and timeless—verities of human nature. His plays and novels seemed to examine mankind from a distant Olympian platform, from which the overall features were more evident than any fine geographical detail.

His was a consciously chosen perspective. "I am interested in the drives that operate in society and in every man," the stocky, owlish-appearing writer remarked in a moment of self-disclosure a few years before his death. "Pride, avarice, and envy are in every home. I am not interested in the ephemeral—such subjects as the adulteries of dentists. I am interested in those things that repeat and repeat and repeat in the lives of the millions."

These quintessences were probed for, summarized, and recounted in seven novels and two major serious plays published over fifty years, an output hardly prolific by the standards of most writers. Nonetheless, these works, written in an elegant yet simple style, lifted Wilder to the front ranks of American men of letters. Of his three Pulitzers, the first in 1928 was for the novel *The Bridge of San Luis Rey,* the second in 1938 for the play *Our Town,* and the third in 1943 for the drama *The Skin of Our Teeth.* For *The Eighth Day,* his penultimate novel, he received the National Book Award in 1968. For the whole body of his work, he received the National Medal for Literature of the National Book Committee. This honor, along with $5,000, was conferred at a White House ceremony in 1965. Articulating the attitudes of thousands of readers, Mrs. Lyndon B. Johnson told the shy, quiet writer that he had succeeded in making "the commonplaces of living yield the gaiety, the wonder, and the vault of the human adventure."

"Unlike some modern writers," the First Lady went on, "you respect your fellow man and you respect the American language. You have never confused being modern in language with a dreary reliance on four-letter words. You have never assumed that realism in writing means a cloying self-pity or a snappish disdain for others. You have written with an understanding, affectionate rapport with your subjects which to me is the hallmark of genuine literature."

Although this view was by no means unanimously endorsed by literary and theater critics (Wilder was acclaimed by Edmund Wilson and drubbed by Dwight Macdonald), he held the sustained attention of middlebrows. Not only did his fiction continue to sell years after publication, but his serious plays were revived hundreds of times. Even the insubstantial *The Matchmaker,* transmuted into the musical *Hello, Dolly!,* was a perennial favorite. The qualities that accounted for Wilder's enormous popular appeal were his evident talent as a storyteller and his singular knack of dressing up his parables as realistic fiction. At the same time, he posed cosmic questions, "those old teasers Heredity and Environment, about gifts and talents, and destiny and chance." He phrased his question in *The Eighth Day* this way:

"This John Ashley—what was there in him (as in some hero in those old plays of the Greeks) that brought down upon him so mixed a portion of fate: unmerited punishment, a 'miraculous' rescue, exile, and an illustrious progeny?"

As in his other books, Wilder explored the questions, but did not give unequivocal answers. In *The Bridge of San Luis Rey*, for example, the question was: Why did the collapsing bridge plunge five particular persons to death? The conclusion left uncertain whether the disaster was the work of God or the result of chance. Equally ambiguous was Wilder's answer, in *The Ides of March*, to the question: What is greatness? If his novels offered the reader no certitudes, they did affirm a sense of human possibilities, an optimism that life can be satisfying. Although he was essentially a metaphysician, his novels (and his plays) were infused with humor and wit. "Because we live in the twentieth century, overhung by very real anxiety, we have to use the comic spirit," he once explained. "No statement of gravity can be adequate to the gravity of the age in which we live."

In contrast to his fiction, which was notable for its adherence to form, his major plays broke with the usual rules of the theater. When Wilder showed *Our Town* to Edward Sheldon, a knowledgeable friend and playwright, Sheldon said, "Of course, you have broken every law of playwriting. You've aroused no anticipation. You've prepared no suspense. You've resolved no tensions." The play also lacked elaborate scenery and its plot was sketchy. Yet it did succeed, as did the more rambunctious *The Skin of Our Teeth*. This play, in which the action was out of orthodox sequence, was the story of Everyman spread over five thousand years, from the Flood to Armageddon.

"*Our Town* is the life of the family seen from a telescope five miles away," Wilder explained. *"The Skin of Our Teeth* is the destiny of the whole human group seen from a telescope eleven thousand miles away." The themes of these plays, as well as those of the books, were not intended to be innovative. Indeed, he believed that "literature is the orchestration of platitudes," and that its function is not to reveal new truths so much as to trigger those that lie within everyone.

Until he was sixty-five and began what he called his retirement, Wilder indulged an uninhibited appetite for life. Full of bounce and bubble, entirely without airs and immensely interested in people, he fueled himself on travel and conversation. His friendships ranged from truck drivers to waitresses ("I don't pinch. I just relish human beings"), from Sigmund Freud to a Chicago hoodlum named Golfbag, from Robert M. Hutchins to Gene Tunney, and from Gertrude Stein to Texas Guinan, the nightclub entertainer.

Indeed, when Wilder was teaching in Chicago, he took to visiting Miss Guinan's club and she would sometimes call on him to take a bow. "Come on up here, Thornton," she would cry out. "Folks, give Thornton a nice hand. He's the best little writer in these United States." His genius for finding rapport with virtually every person he met was especially striking in his relationships with students. "Teaching is a natural expression of mine," he once remarked, and he was very good at it with teenagers (at Lawrenceville) and college youth (at the University of Chicago and at Harvard). Lecturing on creative writing or the classics, he was a showman. Describing his platform performance, *Time* said in 1953:

"He would fling his arms about, jump from the platform and leap back again. Talking at trip-hammer speed, he was sometimes in front of the class, sometimes at the back, sometimes at the window waving to friends. Wilder could play the blind Homer, a Greek chorus, or the entire siege of Troy. Even his pauses were planned, with an actor's timing, to keep his audience in suspense."

Wherever he went he was trailed by students ("my Kinder") as if he were the Pied Piper; and he was never too busy ("On my grave they will write: 'Here lies a man who tried to be obliging' ") to engage them in talk, spinning off ideas in English, French, German, Italian, or Spanish. He also liked to lecture his friends, filling gaps he discerned in their knowledge. Garson Kanin, the director, once observed, "Whenever I'm asked what college I attended, I'm tempted to reply 'Thornton Wilder.' "

Wilder's propensity for instructing others was a trait he acquired from his father, Amos Parker Wilder, a Maine-born newspaper publisher and editor in Madison, Wisconsin, who counted the day lost when he did not add to his children's fund of information. Thornton, the second of five children, was born to Amos and Isabella Thornton Niven Wilder in Madison on April 17, 1897. When the boy was nine, the family moved to Hong Kong, where the elder Wilder was stationed as United States consul general. He attended a German school there and later, a school for missionaries' sons at Chefoo. Afterward, his parents sent him to California to prepare for Oberlin College in Ohio, which he entered in 1915. Two years later he transferred to Yale, served for a year in the Coast Artillery during World War I, and took his degree in 1920. At Yale, the youth continued his omnivorous reading in world literature, wrote for *The Lit,* turned out plays and came under the influence of William Lyon Phelps, the distinguished teacher. Said the professor of his student, "I believe he is a genius." "Oh, tut-tut-tut, Billy," Thornton's father replied, "you're puffing my boy up way beyond his parts."

Preparing to become a teacher, Wilder spent a postgraduate year at the American Academy in Rome and returned to the United States in the fall of 1921 to teach French at Lawrenceville, a boys' preparatory school near Trenton. He passed eight years there ("I am the only American of my generation who did not 'go to Paris' ") drilling teenagers in French irregular verbs, getting a postgraduate degree at Princeton, and working on *The Cabala,* his first novel. A mannered story of a group of Roman aristocrats, ancient gods in modern dress, the novel was a critical success. He also scored a small triumph with *The Trumpet Shall Sound,* which was produced by the American Laboratory Theater.

Meantime, from a Prosper Mérimée play he conceived the idea

for *The Bridge of San Luis Rey,* which was published in 1927 and brought Wilder instant national and international fame. The novel's opening sentence set its tone: "On Friday noon, July the twentieth, 1714, the finest bridge in all Peru broke and precipitated five travelers into the gulf below." The book was, according to the critics, "a little masterpiece," a work of "genius," an expression of "pure grace." These were estimates with which the public agreed, for the book sold 300,000 copies in a year—an astronomical figure for that time—and was translated abroad. Peru even found a bridge to fit Wilder's fictive one.

The writer used his royalties to buy a house in Hamden, Connecticut, on the outskirts of New Haven, and to travel with his sister Isabel to Europe. There he was the lion of the day, dining with Arnold Bennett and George Bernard Shaw and touring Germany; he showed up on the Riviera with F. Scott Fitzgerald and Glenway Wescott. He also found time to write *The Woman of Andros,* which was inspired by a Terence play. This novel earned Wilder more critical applause, especially for its "harmonious limpidity of style." About this time, Edmund Wilson, one of the country's most influential critics, began to rank Wilder with Ernest Hemingway, Fitzgerald, and William Faulkner; on the other hand, in the Depression of the early thirties, when novels of social significance seemed important, he came under attack. The most fervent assault was written by Michael Gold, a Marxist critic, for *The New Republic* under the title "Wilder: Prophet of the Genteel Christ."

Gold said that Wilder ignored the social injustices of America while writing for a "small sophisticated class." "Is Mr. Wilder a Swede or a Greek, or is he an American? No stranger would know from the books he has written," Gold said. He went on to argue: "[Wilder] has all the virtues Veblen said this leisure class would demand, glossy high finish, caste feeling, love of the archaic . . . This Emily Post of culture will never reproach them; or remind them of Pittsburgh or the breadlines."

Wilder was disquieted by this and similar criticism. In 1931 he published his first works about contemporary America, *The Long Christmas Dinner and Other Plays in One Act.* And in 1935 he wrote *Heaven's My Destination,* a novelistic attempt at social realism. It was witty and satiric; but it failed to please either the realists or the esthetes. Amid these controversies he was teaching at the University of Chicago at the invitation of his friend, Robert Hutchins. The job permitted the author to teach for a half-year and to travel the rest of the time. It also gave him an introduction to Gertrude Stein that was the start of a close friendship. When he left Chicago in 1936 he paid a long visit to the expatriate American writer's villa in France.

Our Town, which was staged in 1938, portrayed life in fictive Grover's Corners, New Hampshire, as representative of all small-town life. Frank Craven played the Stage Manager when the play opened at Henry Miller's Theater in New York, after a shaky try-out in Boston. It was a hit on Broadway from the start; it moved Alexander Woollcott, the critic, to tears and the mot, "I'd rather comment on the Twenty-third Psalm than *Our Town."*

Wilder himself took the role of the Stage Manager for two weeks during the play's Broadway run and later played it in several summer stock productions. He also appeared in revivals of *The Skin of Our Teeth,* enjoying himself hugely.

The reputation of *Our Town* fluctuated with the years, and by 1968 the Pulitzer Prize drama's relevance was questioned. Reviewing a revival then, Clive Barnes, *The Times*'s drama critic, said: "Mr. Wilder has described his play as 'an attempt to find a value above all price for the smallest events in our daily life.' To do this, however, he has produced a pretty Andrew Wyeth-like landscape, almost doomed by its superficial attractiveness. There is no malice in Grover's Corners and no death; the citizens' rites of passage proceed tidily from the cradle to the grave, and everyone lives, massaged by good thoughts and compliant to God's will. It would be a great life if anyone lived it. No, I fear that Grover's Corners is merely ye olde American township, Anglo-Saxon to the core, lovable, supremely marketable and supremely phony."

Shortly after *Our Town* made its bow, Wilder staged *The Merchant of Yonkers,* which did not do well at the box office. He rewrote it as *The Matchmaker* in 1955, and it did better, but not nearly so well as *Hello, Dolly!,* the saucy musical adapted from it. After *Our Town* Wilder scored again on Broadway with *The Skin of Our Teeth.* The story of man's constant struggle for survival and his astonishment over why he struggles was praised in *The Times* as being presented "with pathos and broad comedy, with gentle irony, and sometimes a sly self-rallying."

"All I ask," said Mr. Antrobus, the play's everyman, as the curtain fell, "is a chance to build new worlds and God has always given us that. And given us [opening a book] voices to guide us and the memory of our mistakes to warn us." Coming at a low point in World War II, *The Skin of Our Teeth* touched audiences with its message of courage and hope. Tallulah Bankhead played Sabrina, the eternal temptress; Fredric March was Mr. Antrobus; and Florence Eldridge was his ever-faithful wife. In a 1955 revival the cast included Mary Martin, Helen Hayes, George Abbott, and Florence Reed.

During the war years Wilder served in the Army as a lieutenant colonel in air intelligence, posted in North Africa and Italy. On his return to Connecticut he worked on *The Ides of March,* a novel of Rome in Julius Caesar's time. He was also invited by Harvard to occupy the Charles Eliot Norton chair for the academic year 1950–51. In 1957 he restricted his correspondence, cut off most interviews, and virtually dropped out of the active world. The step was not retirement, for Wilder began patiently to write *The Eighth Day.* Always a careful writer ("The incinerator is the writer's best friend"), he worked patiently over the four-hundred-page novel that was designed to demonstrate that man is not an end but a beginning.

The title had Biblical overtones. As one of the characters explains: "The Bible says that God created man on the sixth day and rested, but each of those days was many millions of years long. That day of rest must have been a short one. Man is not an end

---

but a beginning. We are the beginning of the second week. We are children of the eighth day." The book, issued in 1967, received mixed notices. Praising it, Eliot Fremont-Smith wrote in *The Times:*

"*The Eighth Day,* a novel in what might be called the old tradition, is a very fine performance—honest, intelligent, suspenseful, profoundly moving and all done quietly, with dignity, without trick or need for entreaty.

"If a touch of patronizing is finally felt (not during the reading but afterwards in reflection), this, like the sense of affirmation, may be endemic in all grand designs, God's or Mr. Wilder's. But few will feel it, and fewer still will mind. What matters is that one of the country's recognized master artists has produced his best and most absorbing novel."

From this view there was strong dissent, typified by Stanley Kauffmann's review in *The New Republic,* which said: "There is no question here of whether Wilder has sustained claim to serious consideration; seriousness does not even enter into it. Although the Wilder views are recognizable, this new book almost seems to have been written by another man, an imitator inferior to the feeblest Wilder we have previously seen. The writing—by a man distinguished in his youth for style—is without grace, though he strains for it constantly; the characters are stagey, hollow, unrealized; the plot, full of arthritic twists, is attenuated and undramatic although the author himself seems generally breathless with excitement; the theme, as apprehended here, is sophomoric."

Although officially retired in his latter years, Wilder produced *Theophilus North,* his last novel, between his seventy-fifth and seventy-sixth birthdays, working in his Hamden home. Shortly before it was published, he told *Publishers' Weekly* that the idea for the book had come to him quite suddenly. It was based in part on some of his own experiences from what he called his "schoolmastering" days. He worked methodically, pinning notes to himself on a bulletin board in his study to retain details that came to mind for later use.

Set in the Newport, Rhode Island of 1926, the story is told by its central character after whom the book is named. The fictional Mr. North, retired from his prep-school job, supports himself by teaching tennis to boys and girls in the seacoast town, by reading in any of several languages to people who desire such a service, and helping them in other small but imaginative and sometimes humorous ways. Granville Hicks, reviewing it in *The New York Times Book Review,* said: "Wilder's tone remains consistently lively, is often comic, and the book is extraordinarily entertaining. There are those, I have no doubt, who will call it corny, and sometimes it comes close to sentimentality. . . . But in spite of an excess of sweetness now and then and some obvious manipulation for the sake of happy endings, the stories hold the reader in a firm grip."

Malcolm Cowley and other literary critics thought of Wilder as "an optimist by instinct, in the fashion of an older America," and the author was often faulted in his later years for what critics saw as his old-fashioned hopeful Weltanschauung. But Hicks saw in the author's last two novels an underlying somberness best expressed in a passage of *The Eighth Day,* when, already in his sixties, Wilder had written:

"It is the duty of old men to lie to the young. Let these encounter their own disillusions. We strengthen our souls, when young, on hope; the strength we acquire enables us later to endure despair as a Roman should."

PAUL STRAND

Paul Strand, whose still and motion pictures continue to gain in critical esteem, died at the age of eighty-five in Oregeval, a French village west of Paris. An artist of the camera, ranking with Alfred Stieglitz, Edward Steichen, Edward Weston, Walker Evans, Ansel Adams, and Dorothea Lange, Strand achieved fame for such photographs as "Blind Woman Newsdealer" and "The Family," and for such documentary films as *The Plow That Broke the Plains* and *Redes,* whose English title was *The Wave.*

Many specialists endorsed the view of Walter Rosenblum of Brooklyn College, who believed that Strand had exerted "a decisive influence on the development of photography" in this century. "We owe a debt to Strand as we do to Beethoven or

Rembrandt, Mozart or Picasso," Professor Rosenblum said. "It is what we gain from the work of every significant artist, a greater insight into reality, a more secure understanding of who we are and how we relate to the important truths of our being."

Strand's contribution was to break away from the soft-focus romanticism of the early twentieth century and to create an entirely new way of seeing with a camera. The new way was a search for the truth of life in the faces, dress, and movement of people, in such artifacts as machines, houses, and churches, and in unadorned nature.

A thinking man's photographer, he articulated a point of view for his mature social realism, which he sometimes called "organic realism," that he adapted to a wide variety of subjects. He once said, "We conceive of realism as dynamic, a truth which sees and understands a changing world and in turn is capable of changing it in the interests of peace, human progress and the eradication of human misery and cruelty and toward the unity of all people."

Long before the phrase became fashionable, Strand was *un homme engagé*, committed to humanitarian causes and proud of it. He was on this account accused of idealizing his subjects and of being "a proletarian realist." One such accuser was Gene Thornton of *The New York Times,* who remarked a few years ago that Strand's photographs "of humble people show them not as they too often are—ignorant, brutish, frantic and grasping—but as they would be if society were properly organized: noble, calm, possessed of dignity." In depicting peasants and fishermen, Thornton believed, Strand was "idealizing a type that is vanishing everywhere in the world." Like Norman Rockwell and Andrew Wyeth, he went on, the photographer was trying to establish "a contemporary Arcadia."

More representative of prevailing opinion (and more affirmative) was the judgment of Hilton Kramer, who saw Strand as "both a historic figure and a great artist." Reviewing a 1972 retrospective, the critic wrote in *The New York Times:* "There is a strong element in Strand photographs of sympathetic identification with the subject matter, but the overriding impulse is toward esthetic refinement. The result is a formal purity that is breath-taking . . . We feel photography lingering in the shadow of great modern painters."

Strand's artistry lay not only in his superbly keen and sympathetic eye, but also in an obsessive and tireless perfectionism. Dorothea Lange was living in Taos, New Mexico, in 1931, and, according to Milton Meltzer's biography, "used to see a man in a Ford pass by almost every morning, looking very sober, driving with serious purpose down the road. . . . 'I thought he was an artist, but he always went by at the same time and at the same time at night he would come back.' " Later she discovered it was Paul Strand. "It was the first time I had observed a person in my own trade who took his work that way. He had private purposes that he was pursuing, and he was so methodical and so intent on it that he looked neither to the right nor to the left."

He made his own prints in his own darkroom, often putting in three days of solid work before he was able to produce a negative or a print to his satisfaction. Sometimes, he conceded late in life, he retouched negatives and cropped them in the enlarger "when there's a functional reason for doing it." Typically, he employed big, heavy equipment, chiefly an eight-by-ten-inch Deardorff view camera or a five-by-seven-inch Graflex. "I just don't like that little thirty-five-millimeter image," he said. Nor was he wooed by color. "It's a dye; it has no body, or texture or density, as paint does."

Despite the general esteem for Strand among his peers, it was only in the last thirty years of his life that he attained anything like public recognition. This began in 1945 with an exhibition of his work at the Museum of Modern Art in New York that attracted wide attention. Then the Metropolitan Museum of Art and other major museums across the country organized shows that gave the photographer a large measure of public appreciation. With it came material rewards: by 1975 prints of his work on platinum paper were fetching $32,000 each, while prints on silver paper sold for $3,000. Even so, Strand, who had moved to France in 1950, paid little heed to pecuniary matters.

The start of his career was marked by a strong element of serendipity—and a Brownie fixed-focus box camera. Born in New York on October 16, 1890, he was the only child of Jacob and Matilda Stransky, who changed their name shortly before their son's birth. The family was Bohemian in origin. Jacob Strand was a low-income salesman for French and German cookery wares. The Strands gave their son a Brownie on his twelfth birthday, with which he took random snapshots that seemed magical to him.

Two years later, the boy was enrolled, at great financial hardship to his parents, in New York's Ethical Culture School. There, in 1907, he met Lewis W. Hine, a young biology teacher, who gave a hobby class in photography, an offshoot of his own free-lance efforts to photograph immigrants at Ellis Island and children at work in Southern textile mills. An inspirational teacher, Hine communicated his sense of social values to young Strand and introduced him to Stieglitz and to the work of photographers who exhibited at the Little Galleries of Photo-Secession at 291 Fifth Avenue. This experience convinced him that a camera could be a powerful instrument for discovering reality and that what he himself wanted in life—he was then seventeen—was to become "an artist in photography."

For two years after graduation in 1909 he worked at odd jobs and made pictures in his spare time; then, on impulse, he sank all his savings into a two-month European tour. Back in New York, he set up shop as a commercial photographer—portraits, mostly—while experimenting on his own account with enlarged negatives, gum prints, and soft-focus lenses. His critic-appraiser was Stieglitz, with whom he formed a close friendship and who eased his way into "291," as the Photo-Secession group was known. "In 1915 I really became a photographer," Strand said later. "Suddenly there came that strange leap into greater knowledge and sureness."

The results of that "strange leap" were evident in his first one-man show, given him by Stieglitz and "291" in 1916. Mostly cityscapes and pictures of New Yorkers unposed and in motion, the photographs cumulatively emphasized both the energy and the anxiety of people and the fixity of the city's architectural forms. To make his unposed pictures of people, Strand attached a decoy lens to his camera, so that he did not seem to be focusing on the persons whose pictures he was taking. His photographs were the first candid-camera pictures in the history of the art, and the idea was quickly picked up by other photographers here and abroad.

Although the candids were in strong contrast to Stieglitz's poetic lyricism, Stieglitz recognized his protégé's talents. He devoted an entire issue of the magazine *Camera Work* to Strand photographs. Introducing the 1917 collection, Stieglitz wrote, "His work is rooted in the best tradition of photography. His vision is potential. His work is pure. It is direct. It does not rely upon tricks of the process."

From city scenes Strand turned to experiment with abstractionism, with close-ups of machine forms, rocks, and landscapes. However impressive these photographs were, they did not sell briskly; so, in an effort to make money, he ventured into cinematography in 1921. With some help from Charles Sheeler, a painter, he made *Manhatta*, a Whitmanesque view of New York City that employed lines from *Leaves of Grass* for captions and bold camera angles to capture metropolitan throngs, buildings, and scenes. The movie, also entitled *New York the Magnificent*, was a pioneer documentary film and one of the first to express a poetic feeling for a city by accenting its abstract and polygot forms. Today the film seems self-conscious, yet its innovations and conception are obviously those of an audacious experimentalist seeking out new possibilities for camera art.

Impressed by the versatility of motion pictures, Strand invested in an Akeley camera—then the best of its kind—and trained himself to be a free-lance newsreel man. He sold his products to Fox and Pathé and made background shots for MGM and Famous Players. At the same time in the twenties he was among those photographers who supported experimental painting and "pure" photography over pictorialism. Meanwhile he was developing a professional credo, by which he was guided the rest of his life.

Summing it up, he once wrote that a photographer must evolve and maintain "a real respect for the thing in front of him, expressed in terms of chiaroscuro through a range of almost infinite tonal values which lie beyond the skill of the human hand."

"The fullest realization of this," he continued, "is accomplished without tricks of process or manipulation, through the use of straight photographic methods. It is in the organization of their objectivity that the photographer's point of view toward life enters in and where a formal conception born of the emotions, the intellect, or of both is as inevitably necessary for him before an exposure is made as for the painter before he puts brush to canvas.

"Photography is only a new road from a direction, but moving toward the common goal, which is life."

From the mid-twenties to the early thirties, Strand exemplified his credo in photographs of natural forms—blasted trees in the American West, driftwood, rocks and plant life along the Maine coast, landscapes on the then-isolated Gaspé Peninsula of Quebec. To these he began to add, in the early thirties, photographs of ghost towns and adobe villages, which seemed to Strand to make a statement on popular culture and the passage of time. There was a shift of emphasis to people, especially to the disinherited, which became pronounced in his Mexican photographs of 1932–33, exhibited in Mexico City to enormous Mexican acclaim. Among those who were impressed was Carlos Chaves, the composer, then minister of fine arts, who appointed Strand chief of photography and cinematography in the Secretariat of Education.

Strand took the gesture seriously. The result was the 1935–36 film *The Wave,* which told the story of a successful fishermen's strike in the Bay of Vera Cruz. Photographed and supervised by Strand, the movie, which employed no professional actors, was a popular and artistic success in Latin America, Europe, and the United States. "Every close-up, every foot of the film pushes home the emotional content of the film," wrote Professor Rosenblum in an analysis for *American Photography Annual,* 1952.

To a Mexican artist, Míguel Covarubbias, the movie was "the

deepest, most descriptive record ever made of Mexican life." A print is now one of the jewels of the Museum of Modern Art's film archive. Viewed some forty years after its production, *The Wave* seems to have retained its pristine vitality and human dimension. According to stories at the time of the filming, Strand, a man of medium build and enviable bustle, shot and reshot the movie's scenes in an attempt to achieve emotional and historical realism. This may be apocryphal, for the movie appears to flow as a seamless whole, with nothing forced or creaky.

Now deeply committed to cinematography, Strand joined Ralph Steiner and Leo Hurwitz to film the famous Depression documentary, *The Plow That Broke the Plains,* for which Virgil Thomson wrote the score. Produced for the federal Resettlement Administration (later the Farm Security Administration), the film, which dealt with the consequences of drought in the Midwest, was directed by Pare Lorenz. It was praised in 1936 (as it has been since) as a photographically powerful movie, one of the finest of American documentaries. Its filming brought out the less pleasant aspects of Strand's temperament in quarrels with Lorenz, for the photographer could be testy when he was challenged on some artistic point.

While applause for *The Plow* was still ringing, Strand and Hurwitz set up a movie-producing company, Frontier Films, which lasted from 1937 to 1942 and which put together documentaries that are still regarded as classics of the genre. They were *Heart of Spain, Return to Life, White Flood, United Action,* and *Native Land;* of these only *Native Land,* a two-hour movie that took two years to shoot and edit, was photographed and co-directed by Strand. To make it, Strand went to public documents, particularly those gathered by the Senate Civil Liberties Committee, also known as the LaFollette Committee, that implicated corporations in antiunion activities as they sought to stem the growth of the CIO in the New Deal years. At its release in 1942, *Native Land* was not widely exhibited, but its reputation as a vitally American documentary has grown with the years. In today's climate its indictment of business mentality and industrial morality seems mild.

After a decade as a cinematographer, Strand returned at the age of fifty-three to still photography, which occupied the remainder of his professional career. One of his first "new" pictures, among his very best, was a haunting portrait of a Vermont farmer, titled "Mr. Bennett," which was featured in the Museum of Modern Art's retrospective of 1945, its first exhibition for a photographer. For the next five years Strand lived in New England as he compiled material for *Time in New England,* his first book, a collection of painstaking images of nature and architecture and, above all, of the faces of people. One of the most praised of these was a photograph of Susan Thompson, the wife of a Maine lobsterman.

After working in the New England milieu, he decided that he wanted to do a study of a village "to find out and show many of the elements that make this village a particular place where particular people live and work." He considered trying an American village, but then developed reservations about the United States. "The intellectual and moral climate of the United States was so abused, and in some cases poisoned, by McCarthyism that I didn't want to work in an American village at that time," he explained to Calvin Tompkins a couple of years before his death. "It was not in any way a rejection of America; it was a rejection of what was in America just then." Thus, in 1950, he transplanted himself to France. His first loving photographic impressions of his second country appeared in his book *La France de Profil* in 1952.

There were subsequent journeys in Europe and books to celebrate them—*Un Paese* about Italy; *Tir A M'hurain* about the Outer Hebrides; and fleeting impressions of Egypt, Morocco, Ghana, and Romania. Edward Steichen tried to lure him back to the United States in 1956 for an exhibition of his photographs at the Museum of Modern Art; and President Lyndon B. Johnson made an effort in 1965 with an invitation to a White House festival. Neither had any luck, for Strand regarded his self-exile as a form of protest against United States foreign policy, which he believed was malign in 1956 and malevolent in 1965.

Strand felt congenial in France, where Hazel Kingsbury, his third wife, also a photographer, helped him in his work by notating his pictures. He received old friends and his house was sort of a shrine for younger photographers. Shortly before he died, a group of them asked him to explain what he was all about. He replied:

"I don't have esthetic objectives. I have esthetic means at my disposal, which are necessary for me to be able to say what I want to say about the things I see. And the thing I see is something outside myself—always. I'm not trying to describe an inner state of being.

"The only great issue is the necessity for the artist to find his way in the world, and to begin to understand what the world is all about."

SAMUEL ELIOT MORISON

The undisputed grand old man of American historians, Samuel Eliot Morison was both long-lived—he died at the age of eighty-eight—and immensely productive into his old age—he published *The European Discovery of America* when he was eighty and a lively book on Samuel de Champlain when he was eighty-two. A masterly narrative historian who could make events march with exciting pace, he was also a pleasure to read for his polished phrases and for the enthusiasm with which he communicated the past. The year before his death he was described by Archibald MacLeish in a bicentennial poem as "our Yankee Admiral of the Ocean Sea . . . You know better, none better how the Bay wind blows fierce in the soul." It was an apt depiction, for Professor

Morison was the author of a biography of Christopher Columbus under the title *Admiral of the Ocean Sea;* he himself, moreover, was often addressed as Admiral not only because he was a retired rear admiral in the Naval Reserve, but also because he had the commanding presence of an old-fashioned admiral, and perhaps because the honorific seemed suited to one whose major books dealt with the sea.

Like Francis Parkman, the great nineteenth-century American historian, and Thucydides of ancient Greece, Professor Morison combined impeccable scholarship with adventure in chronicling voyages that he himself reenacted. This gave his books a special vividness and depth, which won for them not only academic laurels, but also such popular accolades as the Pulitzer Prize. "My constant aim has been to write history and historical biography in a manner that would be authentic and interesting," the tall, spare, salt-water-beaten professor once told me. "I have always endeavored to live and feel the history I write," he went on in his Boston voice. "For example, *The Maritime History of Massachusetts* was a product both of research and of my hobby of sailing along the New England coast. In preparation for *Admiral of the Ocean Sea: A Life of Christopher Columbus,* I made voyages to the West Indies and across the Atlantic in sailing vessels, checking Columbus's routes, methods, and landfalls. And for *The History of U.S. Naval Operations in World War II,* [it came to fifteen volumes] I obtained a commission in the United States Navy, took part in many operations [he won seven combat stars and a Legion of Merit with a combat clasp] and learned at first hand how the Navy fights."

The naval narrative with its crackling prose was unofficial—some called it "Sam Morison's history"—and won the Swiss-Italian Balzan Foundation Prize of $51,000 in 1963. His Columbus biography had taken the Pulitzer Prize in 1943; and a second Pulitzer was awarded him in 1960 for *John Paul Jones,* a life of the Revolutionary War figure who is often considered the father of the American Navy. *The European Discovery of America: The*

Southern Voyages A.D. 1492–1616 was an extension of Professor Morison's earlier interest in Columbus, but, more than that, it was a synoptic account of the voyages of discovery and exploration undertaken by Columbus, Magellan, and Sir Francis Drake. Two of these crowning achievements—those of Columbus and Magellan—were made in the service of the king of Spain, while the third was under British patronage.

The greatest voyage of all, Professor Morison concluded, was the one led by Ferdinand Magellan through its most difficult stages and completed by Sebastian de Elcano. Magellan sailed from the Plata River in South America with nearly half the earth's circumference stretching unknown before him. He brought his fleet (less one ship that deserted) through the three-hundred-mile strait that modern sailing manuals describe as impossible for sailing ships and dangerous for steam, and took off westward with nothing to guide him but an idea of the latitude of some of the places on the farther side of the Pacific and his own erroneous notions about the ocean's width and shape. His first contact with civilized life after leaving the Canary Islands in October 1519 was in the Philippines, in March 1521.

Professor Morison's biography of Champlain, a less majestic work than *The European Discovery of America,* is an attractive, lively portrait of a person whom the author clearly considered to be one of the eminent men of the seventeenth-century Age of Exploration. Like its forerunners, the book is full of sea lore, and it bears traces of the fact that its author had followed Champlain's footsteps through Canada and along the New England coast. His magisterial volume on the Southern voyages was preceded, in 1971, by his book on the Northern explorations. His chronicle covered the period from A.D. 500 to 1600, and, as was his wont, he undertook many of the trips himself before describing them. The book contains the customary Morison bursts of gusto. His final paragraphs convey the flavor. They read:

"In closing let us not forget the gallant ships and the brave mariners who lost their lives pursuing these voyages for a century after Cabot, or men like Raleigh who financed them; Cabot himself and both Corte Reals lost with all hands no one knows where; Gilbert, lost with all hands off the Azores; Frobisher, mortally wounded in the war with Spain; John Davis slain by Japanese pirates; Verazzano, killed and eaten by cannibals; Raleigh, beastly executed by James I as part of his cringing policy toward Spain.

"These men, and the thousands of mariners whose remains lie under the seamless shroud of the sea, deserve to be perpetually remembered as precursors of two great empires in North America."

Professor Morison's favorite book, the one of which he was proudest, was *The Oxford History of the American People*, published in 1965. "It's my legacy to my country," he told me in a conversation in 1969 at his Boston home. "It represents my cumulative knowledge over almost fifty years and my mature thinking about American history." The 1,176-page volume (its title derived from its publication by the Oxford University Press) traces the major strands in the nation's history from prehistoric man to the assassination of President John F. Kennedy in 1963. Intended for the general reader, the book, without neglecting political history, treats popular sports and pastimes, eating and drinking customs, developments in fine arts, music and medicine, sexual mores, and Indian culture and history. And, of course, there are paragraphs in praise of great ships and their builders, such as David McKay and his Flying Cloud. Typical of Professor Morison's feeling for these ships, and typical also of his general prose style, is this description of nineteenth-century American sailing vessels:

"These clipper ships of the early 1850s were built of wood in shipyards from Rockland in Maine to Baltimore. Their architects, like poets who transmute nature's message into song, obeyed what wind and wave had taught them, to create the noblest of all sailing vessels, and the most beautiful creations of man in America. With no extraneous ornaments except a figurehead, a bit of carving and a few lines of gold leaf, their one purpose of speed over the great ocean routes was achieved by perfect balance of spars and sails to the curving lines of the smooth black hull; and this harmony of mass, form and color was practiced to the music of dancing waves and brave winds whistling in the rigging. These were our Gothic cathedral, our Parthenon; but monuments carved from snow. For a few brief years they flashed their splendor around the world, then disappeared with the finality of the wild pigeon."

Primarily a storyteller in the nineteenth-century mold, Morison concentrated on history as stirring drama. He was much less concerned with the dynamic processes of economic and social change, and he was virtually blind to the contributions of blacks and women, ethnic groups and workers to the making of the United States. A Brahmin to his fingertips, he was the prisoner of an elitist attitude about the common people, nor did he venture into the intellectual life of history; he had many biases and few concepts. Give him, though, a scene to describe, a story to relate, and there was none better.

New England was this patrician's earliest and most profound influence. He was born July 9, 1887, in Boston at 44 Brimmer Street, in a mansard-roofed house in the Beacon Hill area that his grandfather had built in 1869 and in which Professor Morison lived most of his life. His parents were John and Emily Eliot Morison, who raised their son, he recalled, in "an atmosphere in which scholarship, religion, and the social graces were happily blended." After preparation at St. Paul's School, the young man entered Harvard in 1904, hoping to major in mathematics. He was detoured to history, he said later, by Professor Albert Bushnell Hart, who suggested that the Harvard junior write a theme on an American figure who meant something to him personally. The choice was his great-great-grandfather, Harrison Gray Otis, the Federalist leader, whose papers were filed in the student's wine cellar. The theme led to a doctoral thesis and to Professor Morison's first book, *The Life and Letters of Harrison Gray Otis, Federalist,* which was published in 1913. "It was a succès d'estime, selling only seven hundred copies," he recalled more than a half-century later when he revised it as *Harrison Gray Otis, 1765–*

1848: the Urbane Federalist. The book, though, was the foundation for his early reputation and his first teaching appointments at the University of California and at Harvard. His interest in mathematics was not entirely wasted, for he used his knowledge of it in navigation. "The proudest moment of my life was making a landfall in the West Indies on the first Columbus expedition in the face of doubts from my shipmates," he told me.

After serving in the Army in World War I, Professor Morison was an attaché to the Russian division of the American Commission to Negotiate Peace, and he was also a delegate on the Baltic commission of the Paris Peace Conference. Displeased by the Versailles Treaty, he resigned in 1919 and resumed teaching at Harvard. His courses included one on the history of Massachusetts, from which sprang *The Maritime History of Massachusetts,* one of his most successful books, as well as *Builders of the Bay Colony.* As a teacher, he was among Harvard's most popular, for he took his students out of the classroom on field trips to historic sites, and he lectured to them with grace and wit. He went to Oxford for three years in 1922 as the first incumbent of that university's new chair of American history. There he worked on a textbook for British students of United States history, parts of which were enlarged into *The Growth of the American Republic,* a textbook for American students that was written in collaboration with Professor Henry Steele Commager of Columbia. It became a classic, going through a number of editions from 1930 to 1970.

Appointed a professor at Harvard in 1925, he devoted the next ten years largely to studies about that school, culminating in a multivolume *Tercentennial History of Harvard College and University,* which appeared in 1936 and which won for him the Jusserand Medal and the Loubat Prize, both academic distinctions. After that, he embarked on his study of Columbus for the 450th anniversary of the discovery of the New World. Between 1937 and 1940 he made four trips in sailing vessels in the waters that Columbus had explored, crossing and recrossing the Atlantic in 1939–40 as commodore of the Harvard Columbus Expedition.

"No biographer of Columbus [before me] appears to have gone to sea in quest of light and truth," Professor Morison said rather tartly in the preface to his *Admiral of the Ocean Sea*. "And you cannot write a story out of these fifteenth and sixteenth century narratives (the usual sources of Columbus biographies) that means anything to a modern reader merely by studying them in a library with the aid of maps. It may be compared with those ancient books on natural science that were compiled without field work or experimentation."

The book, hailed for its erudition and its good writing, commended its author to President Franklin D. Roosevelt, himself a sailor, in 1942, when the historian proposed to write "a full, accurate, and early record" of the Navy's role in World War II. For the purpose, he was commissioned a lieutenant commander in the Naval Reserve (he was retired with the rank of rear admiral in 1951), and between 1942 and 1945 he covered almost all the battle areas and naval operations of the war. He was an eyewitness to the North Africa landings in 1942 and participated in the Central Solomons campaign the following summer and in the Gilbert Islands assault. He was at Salerno in 1944, and he saw the battle for Okinawa from the bridge of the *Tennessee*. In all, he served on a dozen ships, jotting down his notes in pencil on yellow pads. These, with official reports and enemy records, became the basis for his narrative, the first volume of which came out in 1947. The complete work took fifteen years.

During those years Professor Morison also wrote eight other books, including *The Story of the Old Colony of New Plymouth, Intellectual Life of Colonial New England,* and *John Paul Jones: A Sailor's Biography*. This, too, was the fruit of on-the-scene research into Jones's principal battles. Almost ten years later, in 1967, he produced another biography of an American naval figure, *Old Bruin—The Life of Commodore Matthew C. Perry*. It, too, was adjudged a minor masterpiece of research and writing.

Professor Morison was often crusty and witty in his judgments of American personalities. For example, in *The Oxford History* he gave these assessments of some presidents:

"Thomas Jefferson was no social democrat but a slaveholding country gentleman of exquisite taste, lively curiosity and a belief in the perfectibility of man. His kind really belonged to the eighteenth rather than the nineteenth century."

"President Jackson had so many limitations that it is doubtful whether he should be included in the ranks of the really great Presidents. His approach to problems was too personal and instinctive, his choice of men, at times, lamentably mistaken; and, unlike the Roosevelts, he had little perception of underlying popular movements, or of the ferment that was going on in the United States."

"Lincoln wielded a greater power throughout the war than any other President of the United States prior to Franklin D. Roosevelt; a wider authority than any British ruler between Cromwell and Churchill. Contemporary accusations against him of tyranny and despotism read strangely to those who know his character, but not to students of his Administration. Lincoln came near to being the ideal tyrant of whom Plato dreamed, yet, nonetheless, he was a dictator from the standpoint of American constitutional law."

"A mean, thin-lipped little man, a respectable mediocrity, [Calvin Coolidge] lived parsimoniously but admired men of wealth and his political principles were those current in 1901. People thought Coolidge brighter than he was because he seldom said anything; but, as he admitted, he was 'usually able to make enough noise' to get what he wanted."

"Franklin D. Roosevelt was one of the most remarkable characters who ever occupied that high office. A patrician by birth and education, endowed with an independent fortune, he was a Democrat not only by conviction; he really loved people as no other President has except Lincoln, and as no other American statesman had since Franklin. Appreciation he prized in return but opposition did not sour him. He combined audacity with caution; stubborn as to ultimate ends, he was an opportunist as to means, and knew when to compromise."

"Eisenhower was one of the best men ever elected President of the United States. Yet he failed in the historic role cast for him.

What went wrong? To put it simply, [John Foster] Dulles on the international scene, and the President's want of experience on the domestic scene."

"With the death of John Fitzgerald Kennedy something died in each of us; yet the memory of that bright, vivid personality, that great gentleman whose every act and appearance appealed to our pride and gave us fresh confidence in ourselves and our country, will live in us for a long, long time."

Professor Morison's first wife was Elizabeth Shaw Greene, a painter, whom he married in 1910. In 1949, four years after her death, he married Priscilla Barton, some years his junior. She accompanied him on his travels to the Far East to revisit scenes of World War II and on his trips to collect material for his biographies of Jones and Perry. She also shared her husband's hobby of sailing his yawl out of Northeast Harbor on Maine's Mount Desert Island, his favorite vacation resort. Professor Morison considered that life had dealt well with him. "I've had a very happy career," he told me in 1969. "I have been very fortunate in combining a hobby of sailing with a profession of history. I have no complaints against life at all."

✠

JAMES A. FARLEY

As returns from the 1930 New York gubernatorial race filtered in to the Biltmore Hotel headquarters of the state Democratic Committee that November 4 night, its freshman chairman issued a statement: "I do not see," the tall, bald, bluff James A. Farley said, "how Mr. Roosevelt can escape becoming the next presidential nominee of his party, even if no one should raise a finger to bring it about."

The next day, when the tally showed that Franklin D. Roosevelt's plurality was 725,000 (Farley's prediction had been only 350,000), the chairman announced: "We have elected as governor the man who will be the next president of the United States."

That display of prescience—discounted at the time as the mere boastful rhetoric of elation—was typical of the master political organizer and salesman of the 1930's. His foresight in those years was grounded in a patient accumulation of facts and remarkable acuity in interpreting them. At the same time he contributed to the realization of his forecasts by his own dedicated diligence as a political worker, his dazzling attention to detail, and his imperturbable geniality. In 1930 Farley was just another Democratic chairman, scarcely known outside his state; but over the next ten years he was a figure of national importance—chairman of the Democratic National Committee, postmaster general of the United States, the man who effectively provided the New Deal's muscle. As the dynamo of the Democratic party, he dispensed patronage and energized state and county leaders to get out the vote.

Although his influence declined markedly after 1940, he kept up his reflexive interest in party matters and prided himself on having attended every national convention since 1924. He might have been less reduced politically if he had not split with President Roosevelt in 1940 over the convulsive third-term issue; but he did raise a fuss, resigned his cabinet and national party posts, and entered the world of business. When he died at the age of eighty-eight, his consequential era was forty years behind him.

Farley was probably the last of the national professional politicians with a distinctive personal style. He was Jim to thousands of party workers, to whom he sent chummy letters signed in Irish green ink. "The secret of Jim Farley's success is not one possessed by the ordinary politician," Roger Baldwin, the civil libertarian, wrote in 1934. "He is not given to moving men in masses. With Jim it's one man at a time. The effect is like one of those endless chains which appear every so often—the recipient tells ten others. When Jim Farley leaves a man, that man is not only a loyal and devoted friend of Farley's, but he does not stop until he has lined up his own friends likewise."

An admitted "political drummer," Farley possessed a truly encyclopedic memory for faces and names, a total recall that visibly impressed the man who was remembered. In the campaign of

1932 he was aboard the Roosevelt campaign train when it stopped
at a small Western town. "Hello, Jim," a man in the shadow of the
depot sang out. Farley couldn't see the man, but he glanced at the
name of the railroad station and shouted, "How are you, Frank?
Glad to see you." He explained that some months previously a
man named Frank had written him a number of letters and that he
had remembered the name by associating it with the town. He was
meticulous in such matters, even extending his recollection to
members of the family. "Don't forget what kind of a tree it was
that little Johnny fell out of and which arm he broke," he advised.

Not a boss in the malodorous sense of the word, Farley ran the
Democratic party with considerable sophistication and benignity.
He put a high premium on party loyalty and he was quite unhypo-
critical in using patronage to cement that loyalty. Attacked as "the
master spoilsman of all time," he conceded that he did all he could
to fill every available job with a deserving Democrat, provided the
applicant was qualified.

For much of the decade of his national importance Farley
worked in harmony with Roosevelt, whom he called "Governor"
or "the boss," but never Frank or Franklin. The two broke publicly on the third-term issue in 1940, although Farley's party loyalty was strong enough to lead him to support the president for
reelection. In a series of articles called "Why I Broke With Roosevelt" in *Collier's* magazine (later expanded into a book, *Jim Farley's Story*), he wrote that there was "no sharp, clean fracture of
friendship" with the president, but rather a "slow, imperceptible
drifting apart of political principles." There were differences over
such things as, in 1938, an attempted "purge" by Roosevelt of
Democratic officeholders who opposed his New Deal policies. At
heart Farley was a conservative (but not a reactionary) Democrat,
whereas Roosevelt was an innovator; one was a professional politician, the other a politician by acquired taste. One of Farley's
grievances against Roosevelt, for example, was that in the latter's
second term the president's confidence went to "a small band of
zealots who mocked at party loyalty and knew no devotion except

to their leader." Another grievance was the social difference between the two, one an Elk and an Eagle, the other a Hudson Valley squire and a Harvard Club member. With undisguised feeling, Farley recalled that he had never been invited to pass the night in the White House and only twice had made a cruise on the presidential yacht."Mrs. Roosevelt once said, 'Franklin finds it hard to relax with people who aren't his social equals,' " he related. "I took this remark to explain my being out of the infield."

But in an earlier book, *Behind the Ballots,* issued in 1938, Farley wrote, "I think there's another quality about the President that most people overlook, and that is the fact that there isn't a snobbish bone in his body." *Behind the Ballots* praised Roosevelt unreservedly for his sincerity and for an absence of any feelings of social superiority.

After 1940 Farley's leverage in national affairs diminished. He resigned as New York State Democratic chairman in 1944 and gave most of his time to his business as head of the Coca-Cola Export Corporation. He did not, however, lose his hankering for high elective office, for as late as 1962 he considered seeking the Democratic nomination for governor of New York. It was a forlorn ambition, as forlorn as his hope to run on a presidential ticket in 1940 with his friend Cordell Hull. Farley closed out his political career as campaign chairman for Abraham D. Beame, the losing Democratic candidate for mayor of New York in 1965 against John V. Lindsay, the Republican.

Affable and expansive in his best years, Farley accumulated an impressive number and variety of friends in high places. They admired him for his probity and his fellowship and his storytelling; but his conservative cast of mind put him out of joint with the masses of voters, to whom he could not seem to communicate warmth and appeal and concern for their welfare. It was a curious lack, underscored by the relatively few friendships he had with the important labor leaders who were a vital element in the New Deal coalition.

Standing six feet two and a half inches and weighing 215 pounds, he was an impressive figure. His head was bald, with just a fringe of hair. His face was open. His manner invited confidence. He attributed his robust health to regular exercise, good diet, a weekly Turkish bath, and complete avoidance of liquor and tobacco (but not gum, which he habitually chewed). "When I was confirmed in the Roman Catholic Church at twelve," he explained, "I took a pledge not to drink or smoke until I was twenty-one. When I reached that age I was in politics and my mother suggested that I shouldn't drink or smoke. I've never done either. I don't think I could have carried on when the pace was hard if I had."

From childhood James Aloysius Farley developed an aptitude for unremitting toil. He was born May 30, 1888, at Grassy Point in Rockland County, on the west bank of the Hudson, the son of James and Ellen Goldrick Farley. The elder Farley was a brick manufacturer and one of the few Democrats in the county. "I was born a Democrat," his son delighted to say. At the age of eight, James was a torchbearer in a local parade for William Jennings Bryan, the Democratic candidate for president in 1896. When the boy was not quite ten his father was killed by a horse and his mother was left with a half-interest in a brick-cargo schooner, a small insurance policy, and five sons, of whom he was the second. He sold newspapers and ran errands and later helped his mother when she bought a small grocery shop and saloon. Summers he worked as a machine boy in a brickyard for $1 a day. Between times he played baseball and learned to waltz. His formal schooling ended with graduation from Stony Point High School in 1905, although he studied bookkeeping for nine months in New York at the Packard Commercial School. He worked briefly for a paper company as a bookkeeper and then joined the Universal Gypsum Company, for which he worked fifteen years as a bookkeeper, company correspondent, and salesman. In 1926 he formed his own company to deal in building supplies and three years later merged it with five other concerns to form the General Building Supply Corporation, of which he was president until he became postmaster general in 1933.

Farley entered politics in 1912 by announcing his candidacy for town clerk of Stony Point, a Republican stronghold. While selling on the road, he wrote postal cards to all the voters of Stony Point, who responded to this unusual campaign technique by electing him to the unpaid office. Afterward, he sent thank-you notes to every voter. Thus he remained in that post until 1918, making himself useful and agreeable by such devices as selling hunting permits from door to door and delivering marriage licenses personally. Meanwhile, he was organizing the Democrats in Rockland—they elected him county chairman in 1918—and was becoming favorably known to party leaders throughout the state. The first reward for his exertions was conferred on him by Governor Alfred E. Smith—he was appointed port warden of New York City for 1918–19. Then he returned to Stony Point for two years as town supervisor. He attained his highest elective public office in 1922—one term as a state assemblyman. He made the mistake of voting "wet" on Prohibition enforcement, and his politically "dry" constituents rejected him in 1924.

Governor Smith was fond of Farley, who had helped materially in his 1922 renomination fight against William Randolph Hearst, the publisher, and appointed him to the State Athletic Commission, of which he was chairman from 1925 to 1933. As, in effect, supervisor of wrestling and boxing in New York, Farley banned the practice of ending boxing matches on fouls and of permitting bouts between boxers of mixed weights. He also barred the staging of wrestling matches, almost all of which were fixed, as anything more than exhibitions.

His most controversial ruling kept Jack Dempsey from fighting Gene Tunney in New York for the world's heavyweight championship. He held that Dempsey had a preexisting obligation to meet Harry Wills, which should be fulfilled before the Tunney bout. The result was that the Dempsey-Tunney fight, with its million-dollar gate, was staged in Philadelphia. "Farley was a fair and honest commissioner, always on the level," John Kiernan, a *Times* sports writer of that time, recalled. "He was a pleasure to deal with." As commission chairman, he was a conspicuous figure at prizefights, where he sat at ringside with his friends, mostly politicians to whom he had distributed free tickets. He was also a baseball fan and a patron of the racetrack.

Meanwhile he was unsparingly active in the Democratic party, of which he was elected state secretary in 1928. That year he helped to manage Roosevelt's first campaign for governor, winning his admiration in the process. Two years later, as chairman of the Democratic state committee, Farley ran the Roosevelt campaign, which was notable for its success in the traditional Republican upstate strongholds. It was also memorable as an example of Farley's personal style, his extraordinary capacity for suffering fools gladly. At his office in the Biltmore he listened to all comers. "They're all Democrats, and I never turn any of them away without a hearing," he remarked at the time. "I had a fellow in here this morning who said he wanted to help the party. Said he couldn't make a speech but would go any place and sing a song for us. He meant it. All kinds of people come in here, I see them all, make them feel at home and never turn them away without hearing suggestions."

A few days after the election Roosevelt called in Edward J. Flynn of the Bronx, a trusted political adviser, and Louis McHenry Howe, his gnomish aide-de-camp, and told them privately, "I believe I can be nominated for the presidency in 1932." It was decided to organize for the campaign and to send Farley to sound out party leaders across the nation. Happily there was a grand lodge convention of the Elks scheduled for Seattle in July 1931, and Farley, a devoted Elk, planned to attend. In one afternoon at Hyde Park, New York, Roosevelt and Farley devised a nineteen-day itinerary that would take Farley to Seattle by way of eighteen states and 1,100 Democratic leaders.

Describing the tour in *The Crisis of the Old Order,* Arthur M. Schlesinger Jr. wrote: "The three weeks were a whirl of handshakes, luncheons, dinners, conferences in hotel rooms, sleeper jumps through the sweltering heat, names and faces meticulously registered in memory, reports sent back to New York by special delivery, sweat mopped off the big man's streaming face. . . . Farley's method was adroit and tactful. There were three potential candidates from New York, he might first suggest—Roosevelt, Smith, and Owen D. Young. Then he would lead the conversation along designed lines, until he could see whether it was appropriate to get down to business." When the talk got down to cases, he flashed his carefully prepared election charts that showed how popular Roosevelt was not only in the cities but also in New York's hinterlands. It was his sales clincher. Of course, each of the 1,100 leaders received a personal letter from "Jim."

As news of Farley's enthusiastic reports seeped through the national Democratic organization, John J. Raskob, the party's national chairman, and Al Smith, its titular leader, became concerned. Neither favored Roosevelt. Smith, who had brought Farley along, was especially bitter, even though he had, after his 1928 defeat, decided not to seek another nomination. He had changed his mind by 1931, and had expected that Farley would help him. "Farley betrayed me," he complained. "Wait and see him betray Roosevelt."

Scenting a winner, Farley pressed on with Roosevelt, and at the opening of the Democratic convention in Chicago in June 1932, a total of 566 delegate votes was pledged or instructed for the New York governor—200 votes short of the two-thirds then required to nominate. After an initial setback, Farley set about to rally the convention to Roosevelt. "Unhurried and tireless, his pink bald head gleaming, his hand forever outstretched, the correct name always on his lips," Schlesinger wrote, "he greeted men and women he had met on his trip a year earlier, cheered the pessimistic, soothed the angry and exuded an atmosphere of smiling confidence." Then, in the fierce haggling with Hearst over the delegate bloc pledged to John Nance Garner, he was instrumental in persuading the publisher to swing to Roosevelt lest a weary and deadlocked convention pick a Hearst bogeyman. "It's in the bag!" exclaimed Farley after the tortuous dealings had been concluded. And when Roosevelt arrived at the Chicago airport, on his way to deliver his acceptance speech, he singled out Farley. Seizing his hand, the governor said, "Jim, old pal—put it right there—great work!"

In the campaign, his green ink flowed ceaselessly as his splendid organizing talents coalesced a fractious party into a winning one. He predicted a popular plurality of 7.5 million for Roosevelt over President Herbert Hoover, and he was less than a half million too generous. As postmaster general and chairman of the Democratic National Committee in 1933, Farley had more than 100,000 Civil Service-exempt jobs to dispense. He delayed awarding these for a couple of months while he prepared a card index to show how every member of Congress voted on every Roosevelt proposal. Less than enthusiastic Rooseveltians were penalized until they mended their ways. This rough-and-ready patronage system earned its author much resentment, but it also drew praise from unexpected quarters. Harold L. Ickes, the curmudgeon secretary of the interior, conceded that Farley had played the game honestly. Of himself Farley said, "While many criticize the spoils system, I have always felt that it is just as easy to find a good Democrat as a good Republican or vice versa, and that the party in power should reward its own."

In his first four years as postmaster general, Farley was subject to unjust criticism when ten Army pilots were killed following cancellations of commercial airmail contracts. He was also attacked for the sale of unperforated postage stamps and gifts of special issues to friends, but he countered by establishing a philatelic bureau.

"The 1936 election was one of the high-water marks of American politics," Farley wrote in *Jim Farley's Story*. "Some have been kind enough to call it 'the campaign without a mistake.' I wouldn't go so far, nor do I consider it the peak of my career. Personally, I prefer the campaign of four years later, when I suffered defeat, but went down fighting for a principle."

Despite his disclaimer, the 1936 Roosevelt race against Governor Alf M. Landon of Kansas, was run virtually without hitches. Again Farley's letter-writing—80,000 "Jim" notes were mailed out—and his skills as an organizer played a powerful role. He was acutely aware of the magnitude of the victory in the making; and while *The Literary Digest* was forecasting a Landon triumph, he put this accurate prediction in a Democratic headquarters pool: "Landon will only carry Maine and Vermont. Seven electoral votes." He continued as postmaster general and party chairman for four more years, but his intimacy with the president was ended. He received a fairly routine letter of thanks for his campaign efforts ("Dear Jim: You were right—so right that I thought you were more of an optimist than a prophet"), but the letter, predated to November 4, 1936, was not delivered until the following January. "I hadn't received any previous letter, thanking me for my services, since 1930," Farley complained in 1948.

However, until the third-term issue arose, the two were on distant but affable terms. "Outwardly we were as friendly as ever," he wrote. "It was just that I found myself outside the White House door."

The third-term question was, for Farley, both a matter of principle and one of personal ambition. He was against it on principle and against it, too, "because I might have been Vice President or even President," but for Roosevelt. In *Jim Farley's Story*, he quoted the president as saying, "Go ahead, Jim" in approval of his plan to seek the nomination. That Roosevelt ultimately turned to himself was a move that he never forgave. As a last gasp, the conservative Senator Carter Glass of Virginia put Farley's name in nomination at the 1940 convention, and he got seventy-two votes on the roll-call. It was his final national hurrah, for he resigned almost immediately from the cabinet and the party chairmanship to become board chairman of the Coca-Cola Export Corporation.

Farley, however, held on to the New York chairmanship, which he used in 1942 to block James M. Mead, Roosevelt's choice for the gubernatorial nomination. John J. Bennett Jr., Farley's man, won the nomination but lost handily to Thomas E. Dewey, the Republican. Two years later Farley stepped down as state chairman. That year he was a pro forma supporter of Roosevelt for a fourth term. Mrs. Farley, however, frankly avowed her support for Dewey.

Far from profiting from public office, Farley was in debt after his years in Washington. He received $65,000 for his memoirs and that, with his business income, which mounted over the years, permitted him to live in comfort at the Waldorf Towers in New York. As a world salesman and gladhander for Coca-Cola, he spent much of his time traveling for the company and exuding goodwill. During the war, when sugar was in short supply, he had used his Washington connections to good advantage so that the company always received its allotment. Roosevelt was said to have been informed of the dealings and to have let them pass. He did not harbor a grudge; in any case, Farley was a genuinely likable person to whom business was more a matter of friendship than of cold contracts.

He was a compulsive joiner. The Knights of Columbus, the Order of Red Men, the Elks, the Eagles, the Hibernians, the Friendly Sons of St. Patrick, the Lotos Club, and scores of others all claimed him. He enjoyed them all, as he did the honors that flowed to him—at least thirty-five honorary doctorates, scores of crosses and gold medals, and hundreds of scrolls. He was also a compulsive diner-out, either for business or pleasure. For his company, in the year that he marked his seventy-fourth birthday, he attended 176 dinners and luncheons, by no means an exceptionally high number for him. It was in keeping that he died dressed for dinner, having put on his tuxedo before lying down for his usual preprandial catnap.

Jim Farley's genius was personal politics, getting to know the men and women who constituted "the machine," and binding them to a winning candidate. He worked for two enormously popular leaders—Al Smith and Franklin Roosevelt—and they brought him to the pinnacle of his abilities. He never regretted his vocation. "Would I do it all over again?" he asked rhetorically. "The answer is yes—without a moment's hesitation or a single shade of doubt. Politics is the noblest of careers."

❖

LOTTE LEHMANN

Among the most illustrious and regal operatic sopranos and lieder singers of the first half of the twentieth century, Lotte Lehmann was eighty-eight when she died in Santa Barbara, California. Mme. Lehmann—she was of that era when prima donnas were always deferentially addressed as "Madame"—performed in every major opera house in Europe and the United States and under every celebrated conductor in a flower-filled career that extended from 1910 to 1945.

Beautiful and well proportioned, she was a lovely Eva in *Die Meistersinger,* a dramatic Sieglinde in *Die Walküre,* a radiant Elsa of Brabant in *Lohengrin,* an awesome Elisabeth in *Tannhäuser,* and a matchless Marschallin in *Der Rosenkavalier,* a role to which her name was especially attached. In her lieder singing, which continued until 1951, she excelled in works by Schubert, Schumann, Brahms, Wolf, and Strauss. Her accompanists included such virtuosos as Bruno Walter and Paul Ulanowsky.

Although she had long been famous in Europe and had made her American debut with the Chicago Civic Opera in 1930, Mme. Lehmann did not make her Metropolitan Opera bow in New York until 1934, when she was almost forty-six years old. Vexed, she then scolded the Met's management, accusing it of being "passive" and of "taking no interest in me." The management cowered and denied it all.

Despite her successes in New York, and the raptures she excited among critics and opera-goers, she said after she left the company that "I never really felt at home on this longed-for stage." The Metropolitan, she insisted, "came as a sort of anticlimax." Nevertheless, she returned in 1962 to direct a production of *Der Rosenkavalier,* and her relationship with the management then was serene.

In her opera prime Mme. Lehmann was statuesque, with thick, short, walnut-colored hair, dark brown eyes and a plump and childlike face. She made an indelible impression as she moved about the stage, for she was an actress of uncommon talent, passion, and communicativeness, as well as a singer of great emotional range and limpidity. "I give myself to my part with all my soul," Mme. Lehmann explained. "I cannot think of technical matters while I sing, because I live what I sing so completely that there is no room left for anything else."

She had a voice that for a Wagnerian soprano was not large in volume. Her pianissimo, however, was of exquisite quality and her fortissimo pierced the climaxes of the orchestra without difficulty. Her enunciation, even in moments of tense dramatic activity, was remarkably clear. Her voice was much esteemed by her peers. Hearing her for the first time, Enrico Caruso embraced her and exclaimed, *"Ah, brava, brava! Che bella magnifica voce! Una voce Italiana!"*

Other singers were equally generous in their praise. Among composers, Richard Strauss preferred Mme. Lehmann in his operas above all other sopranos. Conductors, even including the mercurial Arturo Toscanini, admired her abilities.

Although Mme. Lehmann sang Sophie and Octavian in *Der Rosenkavalier,* a third soprano role, that of the Marschallin—a woman with much experience in affairs of love—was her most famous. Discussing it, Harold C. Schonberg, music critic of *The New York Times,* wrote:

"Talking about it, strong men snuffle and break into tears. They discuss her with the reverence of a legal mind talking about Justice Holmes, or a baseball connoisseur analyzing Hornsby's form at the plate, or the old-timer who remembers Toscanini's Wagner at the Metropolitan Opera. In short, she was The One: unique, irreplaceable, the standard to which all must aspire.

"She generated love," Mr. Schonberg continued, in explanation of her extraordinary rapport with audiences. "Lehmann in her concert and opera days had only to walk on stage to reduce the audience to a melting blob. She was the most aristocratic of artists, and also the most intelligent. Whether or not her interpretations were worked over, they always sounded spontaneous and instinctive."

Vincent Sheean, the writer, who heard Mme. Lehmann many times, was haunted by her. "The peculiar melancholy expressiveness of her voice," he wrote, "the beauty of her style in the theater, the general sense that her every performance was a work of art, lovingly elaborated in the secret places and brought forth with matchless authority before our eyes, made her a delight that never staled.

"She was like that Chinese empress of ancient days who commanded the flowers to bloom—except for Lotte they did."

Mme. Lehmann had an immense repertory, perhaps one hundred roles, for her early career was fashioned in German opera houses where she had to sing virtually everything. In addition to Wagner and Strauss, in all of whose major operas she appeared, her principal roles were Leonora in *Fidelio,* Floria Tosca in *Tosca,*

Donna Elvira in *Don Giovanni,* Tatiana in *Eugen Onegin,* Manon in *Manon Lescaut,* Mimi in *La Boheme,* Marguerite in *Faust,* and Turandot in *Turandot.*

Her New York debut on January 11, 1934, was made as Sieglinde in *Die Walküre,* with Arthur Bodansky conducting. Hubbard Hutchinson, covering the event for *The Times,* wrote: "She had not been on the stage ten minutes when it was apparent beyond doubt that she was a Wagnerian soprano of first rank. To those familiar with her lieder singing, her finished phrasing, precise in definition yet always plastic, and her cystalline diction were no surprise. Yet even her admirers in the recital field were not altogether prepared for the other qualities she brought to her superb impersonation; her telling restraint and sureness as an actress. At the end of the first act a cheering audience recalled her seven times.

"But if her first act was of a sort to startle the critical faculty into sharp attention and admiration, her performance in the second had an electrifying quality that swept that faculty away for once and made even the guarded listener a breathless participant in the emotions of the anguished Sieglinde."

She was still an impressive artist when she appeared in *Der Rosenkavalier* for almost the last time toward the close of her career in 1945. "Although Mme. Lehmann's voice possessed less volume than formerly and was used with caution on top notes," *The Times*'s Noel Straus wrote, "her every phrase was so replete with meaning and so deeply communicative that never has her artistry in the role worked with greater conviction of impressiveness."

Mme. Lehmann appeared with virtually all the great singers of her era, including Ganna Walska, Maria Jeritza, Lauritz Melchior, Lily Pons, Ezio Pinza, Feodor Chaliapin, Frieda Hempel, Richard Tauber, and Lawrence Tibbett. In addition to Toscanini and Bodansky, her principal conductors were Sir Thomas Beecham, Otto Klemperer, Franz Schalk, and Bruno Walter.

As a lieder singer Mme. Lehmann ranked at the top. "Lehmann brought to the concert stage an alliance of words and song, an intensity and an understanding, that gave audiences a new insight into artist and music," Schonberg recalled in a *Times* article on the singer's seventy-fifth birthday. "Lehmann's voice was a large one of rather dark coloration. She may not have been one of the great vocal technicians, and she admits as much. Her singing could have moments of effort, moments when her vocal unease was characterized by breathiness.

"In a curious way, those moments were part of her charm. They suggested to the audience that she was not an inhumanly perfect singing machine; that she, too, was human, with human limitations. Nobody cares about those occasional lapses, as they would have cared with a lesser artist, for at all times the flame of Lehmann's inspiration burned so strongly that it burned away the imperfections."

It was at a lieder recital in New York's Town Hall in 1951 that Mme. Lehmann announced her retirement as a singer. Stepping to the footlights at intermission, she said, "This is my farewell recital."

"No! No!" the audience cried.

"I had hoped you would protest," the soprano continued when the shouting had abated, "but please don't argue with me. After forty-one years of anxiety, nerves, strain, and hard work, I think I deserve to take it easy."

Then, referring to the aging Marschallin, who gives up her young lover in *Der Rosenkavalier,* Mme. Lehmann said, "The Marschallin looks into her mirror and says, 'It is time.' I look into my mirror and say, 'It is time.' "

Many in the throng wept.

Later, backstage, she remarked, "It is good that I do not wait for the people to say: 'My God, when will that Lotte Lehmann shut up!' "

A true diva, Mme. Lehmann lived on a royal scale and thought in royal terms. Opera audiences were "my audiences"; the public was always "my public"; the conductor was "my conductor." Those were not expressions of egotism so much as they were those of a queen accepting her due.

The singer's home outside Vienna, where she lived until World War II, was sumptuously furnished. Her Park Avenue apartment in New York was equally lavishly got up, in what one visitor called a "fussily Victorian" manner.

She traveled with two Viennese maids and a housekeeper, two Pomeranians, a make-believe white Persian cat, and four huge leather folders of pictures: one of her mother, another of her father, a third of her brother, Fritz, and a fourth of her husband. All these photographs were set up not only in Mme. Lehmann's home or hotel room, but also in her dressing room at the opera house or concert hall. In the dressing room they were joined by two miniature Indian totem poles, the root of a Christmas tree, three rosaries, an ancient doll named Poupee, a lace handkerchief embroidered with the opening phrases of the principal arias in a dozen of her operatic roles, a ring that once belonged to Sarah Bernhardt, a small wooden elephant, a fan presented by Geraldine Farrar, and an ivory squirrel.

Before each performance Mme. Lehmann was wont to kiss the pictures of her mother, her father, her brother, and her husband and to kiss the doll. She also said the beads of one of her rosaries.

Although Mme. Lehmann was Prussian by birth, she adopted Austria as her country, Vienna in particular. She liked its gemütlichkeit and its cuisine, whose rich pastries she was seldom able to pass up.

Lotte Lehmann was born in Perleberg, Germany, on February 27, 1888. Her singing lessons began when she was twelve years old, with Erna Tiedke in Berlin. She studied there later with Helene Jordan and Eva Reinhold. After further study with Mathilde Mallinger, a Wagnerian star, she made her debut in a bit part with the Hamburg Opera. Her first major role was in Hamburg in 1910, when she sang Freia in *Das Rheingold.* It was at Hamburg that she met Otto Klemperer, who encouraged her artistic development, and one of her early triumphs was as Elsa of Brabant in *Lohengrin,* with Klemperer conducting.

In 1914 she scored heavily in London as Sophie in *Der Rosen-*

kavalier, with Sir Thomas Beecham in the pit. She was shortly engaged for the Vienna Court Opera. There she perfected her Wagnerian roles and met Giacomo Puccini and Strauss. She was the Young Composer in the Vienna premiere of Strauss's *Ariadne auf Naxos* and she sang the title role of Puccini's *Suor Angelica* at its Vienna premiere.

Triumph followed triumph in the 1920's. She toured South America in 1922 and in the same year sang the Marschallin at Covent Garden, London. Three years later she was Christine in the Vienna premiere of Strauss's *Intermezzo*. Her first *Fidelio,* sung that year, was such a success that it was repeated in Paris, London, and Stockholm. In 1928 she was at the Salzburg Festival in *Der Rosenkavalier* and *Fidelio*. Musical Europe was at her feet. She was called to LaScala to sing under Toscanini, who was as charmed by her as she was by him.

Mme. Lehmann's American debut occurred on October 28, 1930, when she sang Sieglinde at the Chicago Civic Opera House. Afterward she toured the country in lieder recitals. During World War II Mme. Lehmann, who had become an Austrian citizen, was naturalized as an American. After her retirement from the Metropolitan she made her home in Santa Barbara. In California she became a patron of the theatrical arts, gave master classes in lieder singing and operatic performance, taught at the Music Academy of the West in Santa Barbara, and painted in oils.

Mme. Lehmann published four books—*Eternal Flight,* a novel issued in 1937; *Midway in My Song,* an autobiography that came out in 1938; *My Many Lives,* a second autobiography that appeared in 1948; and *Five Operas and Richard Strauss,* which was issued in 1964.

The singer was married in 1926 to Otto Krause, a one-time Austro-Hungarian cavalry officer, who died in 1939. The couple had no children. Krause, as was fitting, stood in the background of his wife's career.

—————————————— ✤ ——————————————

ANDRÉ MALRAUX

Intellectual and man of action, chameleon and adventurer, writer of two of the century's lavishly praised novels, André Malraux died of lung cancer in France at the age of seventy-five. His life, the stuff of which legends are spun, was filled with contradictions and garnished with question marks. Friends and critics alike were disquieted by him: Was he a modern man of ideas who wanted to be defined by his actions? Was he a brilliant impostor? Were his ideas profound or were they airy apothegms uttered for theatrical effect? These and other questions were raised about him not only because his career embraced both a liaison with communism and a marriage to conservative Gaullism, but also because his life was carried on in an atmosphere of almost unrelieved flamboyance. As

329

a young man he had said, "I love to displease"; and as an adult he created displeasure in virtually all his undertakings.

At various times and for various causes, Malraux was an archeological adventurer, a novelist, a daredevil aviator, a polemicist, an orator, a member of the French Resistance, a politician, and the official guardian of French culture. Searching out romance (and money as well) he tried to smuggle Khmer statuary out of the jungles of Indochina; helped to organize a foreign air brigade for the Spanish republic in 1936; and he sat in the inner councils of Charles de Gaulle's Fifth Republic. Whatever he undertook, he did with incomparable flair.

Malraux's credentials as an intellectual were established by two books written early in his life, novels that, independent of the circumstances surrounding their composition, are triumphs of the creative imagination. One was *La Condition Humaine (Man's Fate),* which explores the concept of self-sacrifice as a sometimes necessary step to winning a happier future for an oppressed society; the other was *L'Espoir (Man's Hope),* which asserted a belief in a life-affirming humanism of fraternity. In both books, the writer exhibited an uncanny ability to create a sense of scene and character through vivid action; their breakneck pace almost made them thrillers, but they were more than that because of the significance of their themes. Their author was as compelling a talker as he was a writer. A taut, saturnine, glossy-haired man with hot eyes sunk in hollows of darkness and a pronounced facial twitch, he was a nonstop monologist on virtually any topic. A chain-smoker of cheap cigarettes, he brought forth his words in a haze of smoke; and his lighted cigarette jabbed the air, performing what one observer described as "a kind of aerial dogfight." His French contemporaries found him dazzling but elusive; André Gide put him down as "an adventurer"; to others he was "the Byron of his age"; or much less flatteringly "a Chateaubriand," an inventor of stories about himself.

On many details of his life he was either silent or evasive. It is known, however, that Georges André Malraux was born in the

Montmartre quarter of Paris on November 3, 1901, the only child of Fernand Malraux and Berthe Lamy. His father, who was a minor stock-exchange dabbler, separated from his mother shortly after the boy's birth, and he was brought up by his mother in the dismal Parisian suburb of Bondy. "I didn't like my youth," he once remarked, an understandable reaction to the poverty in which he was reared. His schooling was haphazard; much of his learning came from the shelves of the local libraries, but it was not enough to gain him admission to the Lycée Condorcet. By the time he was in his teens, he had decided that he wanted to be a writer. His beginning was modest, an article on cubist poetry in a magazine started by a bookseller for whom he worked; but it led to other articles in a magazine called *Action* and to introductions to the intellectual community of Paris, including Max Jacob, the evasive poet, and Daniel-Henry Kahnweiler, the canny art dealer. In 1920–21, the young Malraux was almost as well known as a dandy as a writer, for he went about, cane in hand, in silk-lined cloaks, wore a rose in his buttonhole and sported a tiepin. He met and married Clara Goldschmidt; the couple spent about two years bobbing around Europe until their money ran out in 1923. (Miss Goldschmidt recalled their life in a surprisingly unrancorous book, *Memoirs,* published some years after their divorce in the forties.)

Casting about for ways to get money, Malraux found that his imagination was fired by the prospect of traveling to Indochina, an area that had fascinated him from his reading, and by the possibility of looting Khmer stone statuary for sale to art buyers in Europe or America. The Malrauxs and their companion, Louis Chevasson, set sail for the Far East. They journeyed to a small temple not far from Angkor Wat and sawed out some good bas-reliefs, which they attempted to smuggle out of Cambodia. Their efforts were maladroit, for the French colonial authorities quickly arrested Malraux and Chevasson. After several months, which Malraux spent getting acquainted with ordinary Indochinese, he was sentenced to three years in jail, while Chevasson got eighteen months. In the interval of appeal, Mrs. Malraux returned to Paris, where she rallied the intellectual community by lurid descriptions of her husband's plight. A public declaration of his "literary worth" was signed by, among others, André Gide, Louis Aragon, François Mauriac, and André Maurois.

On appeal, the writer received a suspended sentence, as did his associate. After a brief return to France, the Malrauxs were drawn back to Saigon in 1925; there, with the help of Paul Monin, another anticolonial Frenchman, they published two gadfly newspapers devoted to attacking the French administration of the colony and calling for an end to the exploitation of the indigenous population. This pass at journalism lasted until 1926, and it included Malraux's only visit to a Chinese city—Hong Kong—until a brief trip to Shanghai in 1931. Out of his year in Indochina there arose the legend of André Malraux as a participant in the Chinese Revolution, as a hero of the Canton revolt of 1925, and as a specialist on Chinese communism, a legend he did nothing to discourage, although he was honest enough not to supply details, as Chateaubriand had in relating his fake conversation with George Washington. He did, however, lie to Edmund Wilson, telling him in 1933 that he had been a "Kuomintang commissar first in Indochina and then in Canton."

Returning to Paris, Malraux believed himself a revolutionary, because of his anger with the bourgeois society he had seen in Saigon, its corruption, its suppression of the rights of the Indochinese population; and he expressed his feelings in four books that owe their force to his Indochina experiences as well as to his infatuation with the irrationalism of Nietzsche and Dostoevsky. *The Temptation of the West* is cast as an exchange of correspondence between a young Frenchman, fascinated by the Orient, and a Chinese, astonished by the efficiency of the West. *The Conquerors* is a semi-historical novel centering on a strike in Hong Kong and Canton, in which the central character is a Swiss-born revolutionary adventurer and the secondary is Michael Borodin, the Comintern representative in China. The third book was *The Royal Way,* the story, highly colored, of the author's troubles with the colonial regime over the Khmer statuary. The fourth was the celebrated *Man's Fate*, the anchor of his fame as a novelist.

A narrative of a group of revolutionaries involved in the Shanghai rising of 1927, which was put down by Chiang Kai-shek, the book introduced several dominant characters—Kyo, the half-caste son of a French intellectual and a Japanese mother; Katow, a Russian revolutionary; Chen, the Chinese terrorist; Ferral, a French imperialist banker; an ironic and beautiful Valerie; and Clappique, whose role is that of the fool. A story of torture and violence, the book reaches its peak in the memorable scene of Kyo and Katow waiting to be thrown into the steaming boiler of a railroad locomotive on orders from Chiang's political police. Both are equipped with cyanide pills; Kyo takes his and dies while Katow, the perfect comrade, gives his to two other prisoners so that they may escape suffering and goes unquakingly to his death. The title of the book—and to some extent its major theme—is taken from Pascal, for whom man's condition is like that of a prisoner in chains. The theme is submerged, however, in a dazzling recreation of what seems like a heroic revolutionary moment; the scene appears authentic, the conversation profound, the cause ennobling. The novel was a huge success, winning for Malraux the important Prix Goncourt in 1933, a triumph for which he had shamelessly intrigued.

Amid general huzzahs for *Man's Fate*, it remained for one fellow novelist, Ilya Ehrenburg, to speak of it with critical detachment. "Malraux's . . . characters are alive and we suffer with them, we suffer because they suffer, but there is nothing that makes us feel the need for such a life and such suffering," he wrote. "Isolated in the world in which they live, these heroes seem like hotheaded romantics. The revolution experienced by a great country becomes the story of a group of conspirators. These conspirators know how to die heroically, but from the first pages of the novel, it is clear that they must die. They reason to an enormous extent . . . Certainly, they spend a lot of time distributing guns, but it is hard to say what the guns are to be used for. . . .

When the revolution is defeated, it is not the defeat of a class, or even the defeat of a party, it is the effect of a fatality that hangs over the half-caste Kyo or the Russian Katow."

Malraux had a somewhat different version of his novel's theme. "No one can endure his own solitude," he said. "Whether it is through love, fantasy, gambling, power, revolt, heroism, comradeship, opium, contemplation, or sex, it is against the fundamental angst that, consciously or not, the characters of this novel—Communists, Fascists, terrorists, adventurers, police chiefs, junkies, artists, and the women with whom they are involved—are defending themselves, engaged as they are to the point of torture and suicide in the Chinese revolution, upon which for some years the destiny of the Asian world and perhaps the West depended."

With the renown that accompanied *Man's Fate,* Malraux was projected as a spokesman for anti-Fascist writers. In this capacity he attended the Writers' Congress in Moscow in 1934 and the Congress of Writers for the Defense of Culture in Paris the next year. He defended Ernst Thälmann, the German Communist leader, and protested the show-trial of Georgi Dimitrov, the Bulgarian Communist who was framed by the Nazis with three companions for allegedly setting fire to the Reichstag in Berlin. He wrote *Days of Wrath,* a widely read novella about a jailed German Communist who is freed when a comrade assumes his identity. He protested the Italian invasion of Ethiopia. As a fellow traveler (but not a Communist), the writer played an exemplary, if highly individual, role in opposing the growth of fascism.

In the summer of 1936, Malraux went to Spain to join the battle against the Fascists. "The Byron of the age," in Hugh Thomas's apt phrase, performed prodigies of scrounging in France to round up perhaps fifty aircraft, enough at the time for the government's only squadron, and mercenaries to fly some of them. Given the rank of *coronel,* the writer was an unlikely aviator, but every testimony is that he displayed incredible physical courage and exerted genuine moral authority in his command of the brigade, which operated from August 1936 to March 1937.

With his second- and third-hand planes, Malraux and his fliers were superb; carrying twenty-pound bombs that had to be heaved out of the craft by hand, members of the squadron sometimes scored important hits. Their leader was credited with some sixty-five flights over the Fascist lines and with once, at least, raking the enemy with pistol fire. From his experiences and observations came *Man's Hope,* a sprawling novel centering on the theme of fraternity. The book's individual scenes contain some of Malraux's best writing; tension, drama, evocation of the Spanish war, its desperation, its binding spirit are all displayed. It is a virtuoso book.

By February 1937, the Spanish republic was acquiring an air force of its own, not a very big one, to be sure, and Malraux came to the United States to enlist public support for the Loyalist cause. Even without his airman's braided uniform and rakish hat, he was an electrifying presence. "He spoke with such fire that his body itself seemed to be speaking glorious French," Alfred Kazin observed. "His rhythms were so compelling that the audience swayed to them."

After the defeat of France in 1940, Malraux lived in the so-called free zone, where he was occupied with literary and family problems until 1944, when he joined the Resistance under the name of Colonel Berger. He was captured by the Nazis within a few weeks, imprisoned in Toulouse, and very shortly liberated when the city fell to the Free French. This episode, much magnified in the retelling, gave the writer the reputation of having been an important figure in the Resistance. Actually, his more active military duties came after the liberation of Paris, when he was given command of a brigade that operated in the Alsatian sector from September 1944 to February 1945.

During the war, for reasons that are still obscure, the writer became progressively disenchanted with communism and more and more receptive to the French nationalism epitomized by Charles de Gaulle. It was to the general that he turned in the summer of 1945, joining his staff and accepting the post of minister of information in the first de Gaulle government. The admiration of the writer for the general was mutual and long-lasting. Malraux remained attached to de Gaulle as the embodiment of a new France to the very end. When the general's cabinet fell in early 1946, his minister retired to a more private life. Nominally the propaganda chief for the Gaullist party, he spent most of the next decade working on the three-volume *Psychology of Art, The Walnut Trees of Altenburg,* a novel, and *The Metamorphoses of the Gods,* another volume attesting his preoccupation with art.

Malraux returned to public life with the birth of the Fifth Republic in 1958 and was minister of culture for more than ten years under a succession of premiers, all of whom were ranked by de Gaulle as president. "On my right, then as always, was André Malraux," the general later wrote. "The presence at my side of this inspired friend, this devotee of lofty destinies, gave me a sense of being insured against the commonplace. The conception which this incomparable witness of our age had formed of me did much to fortify me. I knew that in debate, when the subject was grave, his flashing judgments would help to dispel the shadows."

Malraux's long-term accomplishments as minister of culture were debatable. He undertook a number of propaganda tours; he promoted regional culture centers in France; he encouraged large exhibitions of art and cultural exchanges with other countries; he scrubbed the grime of centuries from a number of Paris's historic buildings; he inventoried the nation's monuments and artistic riches; and he agitated in general for culture. Nonetheless, the culture centers aside, he never got around to elaborating or carrying out a culture policy for France. He was a whirlwind of motion, of panache, but he left little evidence of substance. Shortly after the student explosions of May 1968 and de Gaulle's retirement, Malraux, in 1969, departed the cabinet for private life. After the death of de Gaulle in 1970, he spent his time traveling and writing. He wrote about the general in one small and moving book and about himself in two volumes of *Antimemoirs.* His personal life was not happy. After separation from his first wife in the thirties, he had lived with Josette Clotis, a writer who was killed in a train accident in the forties. Their two sons died in automobile crashes. His second wife, who had been married to his younger half-brother, a victim of the Nazis, left him in the sixties. He often speculated on death, and he was often in ill health in his final years.

When he died toward the close of 1976, his legend had so merged with reality that it had become to all intents and purposes the truth. *"Malraux est mort,"* proclaimed *Le Monde*, the unsensational Paris daily in one of its rare big headlines. The president of the republic paid homage as did France's reigning literary figures. He possessed an enormous storehouse of imagination, and not the least of its fruits was himself. In this respect André Malraux molded the twentieth century, with its revolutions and its cultural thirst, to his own image.

ANTHONY EDEN

Anthony Eden, who won renown as Britain's foreign secretary for his stubborn opposition to the Fascist powers in the 1930's, but whose career as prime minister was wrecked by intransigence in the Suez bungle of 1956, died at the age of seventy-nine. In the twenty years between the blight of his political ambitions and his death, he lived in that comfortable twilight in which the British often shroud wayward, once-popular figures. He was named earl of Avon in 1961; he sat in the House of Lords when he fancied; he tended his roses; he visited with such old American friends as W. Averell Harriman; and he wrote a polished but unrevealing memoir.

When he died after a long bout with a liver ailment, the encomiums were proper and tepid. Alec Douglas-Home, a fellow Conservative and also a former prime minister, spoke for many when he remarked, "It was particularly distressing that Suez virtually brought an end to his political career and he was particularly unhappy at the breach in relations with the United States, for he had always worked hard to keep intimate contact with our main ally." The Suez fiasco had irked both President Dwight D. Eisenhower and his cannonading secretary of state, John Foster Dulles, who at the time were trying to fry some anti-Soviet fish in Hungary. They regarded Suez as a nasty and unwelcome sideshow.

For Robert Anthony Eden, Suez was bitter indeed, for he had spent more than thirty years in public life as preparation for the prime ministership before attaining it in 1955. His tenure lasted but twenty-one months. It was cut short by a failed attempt to invade Egypt over control of the waterway in October 1956, which also involved some odoriferous backstairs diplomacy. The ignominy of the moment tended to obscure the brilliance of his successes as a political leader who had sat in the House of Commons since 1923 and who had led his Conservative party to a notable electoral victory in 1955. It also cast a shadow on his unquestioned gifts as an international negotiator and his achievements as foreign secretary, a post he occupied with great diligence and éclat for more than ten years between 1935 and 1955.

Apart from the first three years, when he was Stanley Baldwin's and Neville Chamberlain's foreign secretary, Eden served under Winston Churchill, whose forceful omnipresence served to conceal his protégé's strengths and weaknesses. As a staunch advocate of rearmament and firmness against the menace of fascism in the thirties, he personified his generation's striving for European peace in the face of constant threats by Hitler and Mussolini; and, in World War II, he typified his country's popular ideal of Allied unity against Hitlerism. In the toing and froing of diplomacy, moreover, he cut a dash in the manner of romantic heroes of fiction; his black homburg ("the Anthony Eden hat") was his trademark. That and his guardsman's mustache, his suave and polished self-assurance, and his fixity of purpose made him an emblem of Britain standing up to Continental bullies.

A man with an inherited sense of noblesse oblige, Eden was born in County Durham on June 12, 1897, in the glowing afternoon of the British empire, in the morning of which his ancestors had played a part. One was royal governor of colonial Maryland; another was Earl Grey, whose Reform Bill of 1832 brought the middle class into electoral politics. The family baronetcy had been established in 1672 by Charles II. Sir William Eden, Anthony's father, was an eccentric country squire who, besides his interests in fox-hunting and gardening, was a better than average amateur painter and a first-rate boxer. He fancied uttering advice, admonishing his son frequently: "There is one thing in life, and that is to run straight. Don't, for God's sake, play a double game." Anthony's mother, Sybil Frances Grey, was a gentle, retiring, cultivated woman of great beauty, whose portrait was painted by James McNeill Whistler.

Young Anthony entered Eton in 1911, where he enjoyed a mild success as an athlete and won a prize for excellence in divinity subjects. Photographs of the time show a tall, slim, slightly rabbit-toothed youth staring gravely from under an Eton topper. In 1915, at the age of eighteen, he went to France to fight as a member of the King's Royal Rifle Corps. Years later, when he was dining with Adolf Hitler, a lance corporal in the war, they discovered that they had been opposite each other on the Somme front. Hitler drew a diagram of the position from memory on the back of a menu, which Eden kept as a souvenir.

Eden, who concealed his youthfulness behind a very bushy mustache, won the Military Cross for saving a soldier's life and emerged from service as a brigade-major. In the war, his eldest brother, John, had been killed, as was a younger brother, William. Timothy, Eden's surviving elder brother, inherited the baronetcy.

"War I hated for all I had seen of it among my family and friends," Eden said afterward, "for the death, muck and misery, the pounding shell-fire and the casualty clearing stations."

At Oxford, which Eden entered after the war, he took a first in Oriental languages (Persian was his specialty) and dabbled in painting. He got his start in politics in 1922 by being beaten for the House of Commons. "A year later," he reminisced, "a by-election at Warwick and Leamington gave me an unexpected opportunity to defeat my sister's mother-in-law, the countess of Warwick, who had taken up the cause of socialism. I represented this constituency, or rather it remained faithful to me, for more than thirty-three years."

A fortnight before the by-election, Eden married Beatrice Helen Beckett, daughter of Sir Gervase Beckett, a banker and owner of the politically influential *Yorkshire Post*. It was a fashionable marriage that promoted his career not only among the peers and squires of Yorkshire, but also among their kind who were running the Conservative party. Through these associations Eden learned to respect the party's hierarchy, an attitude that was later said to have kept him from fracturing his relations with the leadership over points of principle.

Eden's wife was not so devoted to politics as he. In June 1950 he won a divorce on the ground of desertion. She had been in the United States for some time. Two sons, Simon and Nicholas, were born to the couple. Simon was killed in World War II, and Nicholas inherited the earldom.

In the House of Commons or as a campaigner, Eden was a determined but not a brilliant speaker. His manner controlled even under sharp attack in the House, he rarely made a fighting comeback or a telling rebuttal. Patient repetition was his rhetorical device.

Despite this handicap, Eden's rise was spectacular. After only three years in Parliament he was designated parliamentary private secretary to Sir Austen Chamberlain, the foreign secretary and a half-brother of Neville Chamberlain. Between 1926 and 1929 Eden acquired his basic training in foreign affairs at a time when Sir Austen was among the strongest champions of the League of Nations.

In 1931 Eden was named undersecretary of state for foreign affairs, and in 1934 he was put in charge of League of Nations affairs with full ministerial rank, first as lord privy seal and then as minister without portfolio. As a minister, Eden was frequently Britain's spokesman at League sessions and conferences in Geneva, and he met Hitler for the first time in 1934, about a year after he had become the German chancellor. "Hitler was an oddly sympathetic character," Eden told me in an interview in 1967. "He took pains to be reasonable and was extremely well-informed, but intractable in negotiations." Acutely aware of the Nazi menace from the outset, Eden began to counsel British firmness and rearmament. His private views failed, for some time, to evoke a wide response in a smug British society that was certain Hitler could be contained or should be appeased.

Shortly after his visit to Berlin, Eden journeyed to Rome for the first of many meetings with Mussolini. The Italian-Ethiopian War was brewing, and Eden tried in vain to persuade the Italian dictator to submit the dispute to the League of Nations. "Mussolini, contrary to myth, never shouted at me," Eden recalled in 1967. "He was very sober, quiet, and depressing. He had a journalist's mind, active and playing with different subjects, with a good deal of knowledge."

Mussolini, for his part, scoffed at Eden publicly as "the best dressed fool in Europe."

In December 1935, in the middle of the short and brutal war, Sir Samuel Hoare was obliged to resign as foreign secretary amid public outcries over a proposal to appease Mussolini. Prime Minister Baldwin picked Eden to replace him. Then only thirty-eight, he was the youngest foreign secretary in almost a hundred years. He was a strict taskmaster, an industrious reader of dispatches and telegrams, an endless negotiator, and a tireless conciliator; but he was more the instrument than the arbiter of foreign policy.

Thus, in the spring of 1936, when Hitler marched into the demilitarized zone of the Rhineland and when France, Belgium, and Czechoslovakia urged united action on Britain, Eden could do no more than warn Germany of the consequences of its actions. Similarly, in the Spanish Civil War, he supported a policy of nonintervention, which deprived the Republican government of its right to buy guns for its defense while permitting Hitler and Mussolini openly to arm Franco. His private attitudes, however, were far more anti-Fascist than his public actions, a circumstance that eventually caused him to resign in 1938.

The break with Neville Chamberlain came in early 1938, when the prime minister wanted to begin talks with Mussolini on an overall settlement with Italy that would recognize her conquest of Ethiopia. Eden, who favored a policy of obduracy, resigned. At the time Eden's critics charged that he quit over protocol, not principle; that he was miffed because Chamberlain was dealing with Mussolini behind his back. "I had resigned because I could not agree with the foreign policy which Mr. Neville Chamberlain and his colleagues wished to pursue," he wrote in his memoirs.

Expanding on this in his 1967 interview, Eden said in a tart voice: "It was not over protocol, Chamberlain's communicating with Mussolini without telling me. I never cared a goddamn, a tuppence about protocol. The reason for my resignation was that we had an agreement with Mussolini about the Mediterranean and Spain which he was violating by sending troops to Spain, and Chamberlain wanted to have another agreement. I thought Mussolini should honor the first one before we negotiated for the second. I was trying to fight a delaying action for Britain, and I could not go along with Chamberlain's policy."

Eden remained out of the government for eighteen months, but he was not inactive in privately promoting opposition to fascism. For this his popularity was enormous.

Despite sharp differences, Eden was recalled to the cabinet as secretary for the dominions at the outbreak of World War II in September 1939. He regarded it as a war assignment, but his position became far more congenial when Churchill stepped in as prime minister in May 1940. Eden was back as foreign secretary in December of that year. In this situation his contributions to forging the Grand Alliance against Hitlerism were tremendous. Not only did he deal with the Allied envoys in London, but also he traveled to Washington to confer with President Franklin D. Roosevelt and to Moscow to negotiate with Marshal Josef Stalin. He was at all the Big Three conferences.

Of the statesmen with whom he dealt in the war, Eden liked Roosevelt for his "true charm," but he admired Stalin as "the ablest negotiator I have ever seen in action." "He had a very clear sense of purpose," Eden remarked in 1967. "He was never violent in speech, nor brash, but quiet and [he] insisted on the things that mattered to him. Stalin was ruthless and cruel, no doubt, but remarkable."

In his memoirs Eden was less enthusiastic about Roosevelt. "Roosevelt was familiar with the history and geography of Europe," he wrote. "Perhaps his hobby of stamp collecting had helped him to this knowledge, but the academic yet sweeping opinions which he built upon it were alarming in their cheerful fecklessness. He seemed to see himself disposing of the fate of many lands, Allied no less than enemy. He did all this with so much grace that it was not easy to dissent. Yet it was too like a conjuror, skillfully juggling with balls of dynamite, whose nature he failed to understand."

Eden left the Foreign Office when the Churchill government was defeated by Labor in July 1945, but he retained the post of Conservative party leader in the House of Commons. In the interval between 1945 and his return as foreign secretary in 1951, he had the job of explaining to Conservatives in Parliament and to his party at large the merits of membership in the United Nations and of cooperation with the United States.

Eden's private life in the early 1950's was a mixture of great happiness and severe illness. One occasion for happiness was his marriage in 1952 at the age of fifty-five to Clarissa Spencer-Churchill, thirty-two-year-old niece of his good friend and mentor. Another was the bestowal on him of the Order of the Garter in 1954, which made him Sir Anthony Eden. His illness—a gastric and gallbladder disorder—occurred a year earlier and obliged him to undergo surgery at the Lahey Clinic in Boston.

On Churchill's resignation as prime minister in April 1955, Eden, who had been his deputy as well as foreign secretary, succeeded to the post for which his experience and his temperament seemed to have especially prepared him. But an auspicious beginning rapidly gave way to an inglorious end; a year after attending a much-publicized meeting that created "the spirit of Geneva," Eden was embroiled in the Middle East.

His troubles began in July 1956, when Egypt's president, Gamal Abdel Nasser, nationalized the Suez Canal Company, in which Britain and France held a controlling stake. In Commons Eden announced that he could not accept any scheme for the future of the canal that would leave it "in the unfettered control of a single power, which would exploit it purely for the purposes of national policy." A Suez Canal users' association was confected, which Nasser immediately denounced as designed to "rob Egypt of the canal." Then, on October 29, Israeli forces invaded Sinai, avowedly to eliminate Egyptian commando bases from which incursions into Israel had assertedly been made. Actually the move aimed to pressure Nasser to yield back the canal, then a lifeline to colonial Asia.

Later research demonstrated that the Israelis served as a cat's paw in a case of secret collusion with France, in which Eden joined. "Although Eden doubtless did his best to avoid direct commitment," Hugh Thomas wrote in *The Suez Affair,* "there now seems little doubt that he did indeed nail Britain's colors to the unfamiliar mast of Franco-Israeli collaboration." Thomas concluded that Eden's statement to Commons that there was "not foreknowledge that Israel would attack Egypt [was a] straightforward lie." Talking to me for his obituary in 1967, Eden acknowledged that there had been secret dealing with the French and that he had indeed had "intimations" of the Israeli assault. "I have no apologies to offer," he insisted, asserting that "the joint enterprise and the preparations for it were justified in the light of the wrongs [the invasion] was designed to prevent."

In any event, hard upon the Israeli incursion, Britain and France opened their offensive, which shook world opinion. It was all over by November 6, when a cease-fire was ordered. By then the United Nations General Assembly, by a vote of sixty-four to five, had adopted a United States resolution calling for a halt to the operation.

Eden's popularity in Britain dropped, and even Churchill remarked, "I'm not sure I should have dared to begin; but I am sure I should not have dared to stop." Under the strain of failure, Eden resigned in January 1957, to be replaced by the vapid Harold Macmillan.

Reflecting on the canal incident in his talk with me, Eden took the high ground. The abortive invasion, he contended in his reedy baritone, was aimed at maintaining the sanctity of international agreements such as that under which the Suez Canal had been operating. "I am still unrepentant about Suez," he said. "People never look at what would have happened if we had done nothing. There is a parallel with the thirties. If you allow people to break agreements with impunity, the appetite grows to feed on such things."

Eden's historical blunder was evident: he misidentified the Egyptian nationalist strongman with the prewar Fascists; he was prepared to behave toward Nasser as he would have reacted to Mussolini and Hitler. Complicating his misconception of the strength and claims of postwar nationalism was an unwillingness to face the waning of Britain as a world power now obliged to heel at an American whistle. Once upon a time, Britain could install khedives in Cairo, but no longer.

Amid bouts of illness and the writing of his political memoirs after 1957, Eden and his wife vacationed in Barbados and led a retired country life. The memoirs, in three unremarkable volumes, were drawn largely from his official diaries; they were titled *Facing the Dictators, The Reckoning,* and *Full Circle.*

In 1961 he was elevated to the peerage as the earl of Avon. He was made a viscount at the same time. His full title was Viscount Eden of Royal Leamington Spa in the County of Warwick, and Earl of Avon.

After he took his seat in the House of Lords, Eden continued to comment on foreign affairs. In a television interview in 1966, he called on the United States to halt its bombing of North Vietnam and to concentrate on developing a peace plan "that might conceivably be acceptable to Hanoi." The bombing of North Vietnam, he argued, would never settle the conflict in South Vietnam. "On the contrary," he declared, "bombing creates a sort of David and Goliath complex in any country that has to suffer—as we had to and as I suspect the Germans had to, in the last war."

In his retirement, Eden turned to paintings and gardening for relaxation. "Painting is one of my great interests," he said in his 1967 interview. "Unlike most politicians, I stopped painting when I became a politician, so I take my pleasure in enjoying art, not in creating it. Although I have never been rich, I have tried to buy pictures that please me. Paintings have been a very pleasant escape for me. When I didn't want to listen to other politicians speaking, I would always think of my paintings. It is essential to have some diversion like that, otherwise you will go mad.

"The Foreign Office was a terribly stern taskmaster. The amount of detail and the number of telegrams I was obliged to read left very little time for reading other things, so I have not found it relaxing to read. Of course, if my wife says, 'You must read this', I try to."

Eden smiled. It was the smile of a man who seemed happy to be removed from the world of immediate affairs.

---❖---

CHARLES CHAPLIN

No motion picture actor so enthralled the world as did Charles Spencer Chaplin, a London ragamuffin who became an immortal artist for his deft and effective humanization of unprivileged man's tragicomic conflicts with fate. In his long life—he died at the age of eighty-eight—he made a comparatively modest number of movies, a few more than eighty between 1914 and 1967, yet he elucidated with stunning accuracy the theme of the little fellow capriciously knocked about by life, but not so utterly battered that he did not pick himself up in the hope that the next encounter would turn out better. His harassed yet gallant everyman was the Little Tramp, part clown, part social outcast, part philosopher. He was "forever seeking romance, but his feet won't let him," Chaplin once explained, suggesting that romance connoted not so much courtship as the fulfillment of fancy. Stumble Chaplin's everyman might, but he always managed to maintain his dignity and self-respect; he sometimes, moreover, felled a Goliath through superb agility, a little bit of luck, and a touch of pluck. There was pathos to the Little Tramp, yet he did not want to be pitied. The essence of Chaplin's humor was social satire, sometimes subtle as in *The Kid* and *The Gold Rush*, sometimes caustic as in *The Great Dictator* and *Monsieur Verdoux*. "The human race I prefer to think of as the underworld of the gods," he said. "When the gods go slumming they visit the earth." What they saw mostly was uncelestial folly.

In ridiculing that folly Chaplin displayed affection for the dauntless common man. He was serious and funny at the same time, and it was this blend of attitudes that elevated his comedy beyond film slapstick into the realm of artistry. A serious theme in *The Gold Rush*, for example, is man's inhumanity to man. The comedy arises from the hero's adversity, illustrated by his boiling and eating of his shoe with the éclat of an epicure. The element of contrast exemplified by that scene was at the root of Chaplin's comedy, which tickled the fancy of millions despite some notoriety that came to him through marital and political misadventures. The Little Tramp, the comedy character that lifted its creator to enduring fame, was neatly accoutered in baggy trousers, outsize shoes, an undersize derby redolent of decayed gentility, a frayed short cutaway, and a sporty bamboo cane. A jet-black mustache completed the costume. What made it all fit together was that it complemented Chaplin's slight stature—he was five feet four inches tall—and his slimness—he weighed about 130 in his prime years.

Although he often suggested that the costume was a studied contrivance, the fact seems to be that it was arrived at by accident in 1914 when he was breaking into films with Mack Sennett. Sennett, famous for his Keystone Kops and other comic shorts, sent Chaplin to Venice, California, to make a bit of film eventually called *Kid Auto Races at Venice.* He was told to wear something funny, and he assembled, on a grab bag basis from other members of the company, pants belonging to Roscoe (Fatty) Arbuckle, size fourteen shoes each placed on the wrong foot, a tight coat, a colleague's derby, a prop cane, and a false mustache that he cut down to fit his face. The splayed shuffle was a touch made up on the spur of the moment.

With a few exceptions Chaplin used the costume for about twenty-five years, and it was his symbol for a lifetime. The artistry with which it was employed evolved, of course, so that the Little Tramp of *Modern Times* was a far more complex character than that in *Kid Auto Races at Venice.* The explanation for this was Chaplin's study of the structure of comedy. Desiring to make audiences laugh, he analyzed the ingredients of his approach to comedy and each scene that went into the whole. "All my pictures are built around the idea of getting me into trouble and so giving me the chance to be desperately serious in my attempt to appear as a normal little gentleman," he wrote early in his Hollywood career. "That is why, no matter how desperate the predicament is, I am always very much in earnest about clutching my cane, straightening my derby hat and fixing my tie, even though I have just landed on my head."

One of his basic routines had to do with dignity. "Even funnier than the man who had been made ridiculous is the man who, having had something funny happen to him, refuses to admit that anything out of the way has happened, and attempts to maintain his dignity," he wrote in 1918. He continued, "I am so sure of this point that I not only try to get myself into embarrassing situations, but I also incriminate the other characters in the picture. When I do this, I always aim for economy of means. By that I mean that when one incident can get two big, separate laughs, it is much better than two individual incidents. In *The Adventurer* I accomplished this by first placing myself on a balcony, eating ice cream with a girl. On the floor directly underneath the balcony I put a stout, dignified, well-dressed woman at a table. Then, while eating the ice cream, I let a piece drop off my spoon, slip through my baggy trousers and drop from the balcony onto this woman's neck. The first laugh came at my embarrassment over my own predicament. The second, and the much greater one, came when the ice cream landed on the woman's neck and she shrieked and started to dance around. Only one incident had been used, but it had got two people into trouble, and had also got two big laughs. Simple as this trick seems, there were two real points of human nature involved in it. One was the delight the average person takes in seeing wealth and luxury in trouble. The other was the tendency of the human being to experience within himself the emotions he sees on the stage or screen."

In his early days in Hollywood, Chaplin had little to say about how his movies were constructed or filmed. Later, though, he achieved artistic control, and he took infinite pains in perfecting each scene, often shooting hundreds of feet of film for a few minutes of final screen action. "With only a rudimentary idea in his head he concocted the story as he went along," Theodore Huff wrote in *The Literature of Cinema.* "Some pictures changed completely in the course of production. He improvised a scene or a series of gags, then discussed the results the next day in the projection room. A bit might be used or all of it might be reshot; or the whole project might be scrapped and some other idea substituted. . . . In *City Lights* the meeting of the blind flower girl and the tramp took months before the variation that satisfied Chaplin was reached."

Some of his best comic situations resulted from his keen-eyed observation of life around him. "I watch people inside a theater to see when they laugh. I watch them everywhere to get material which they can laugh at," he explained. "I was passing a firehouse one day and heard a fire alarm ring. I watched the men sliding down a pole, climbing onto the engine and rushing off to the fire. At once a train of comic possibilities occurred to me. I saw myself sleeping in bed, oblivious to the clanging of the fire bell. This point would have universal appeal, because everyone likes to sleep.

I saw myself sliding down the pole, playing tricks with the fire horses, rescuing my heroine, falling off the fire engine as it turned a corner, and many other points along the same lines. I stored these points away in my mind and some time later, when I made *The Fireman,* I used every one of them."

Added to Chaplin's talent for perceiving the comic potential in everyday occurrences was his skill at using contrast. "Contrast spells interest," he once remarked. "If I am being chased by a policeman, I always make the policeman seem heavy and clumsy while, by crawling through his legs, I appear light and acrobatic. If I am being treated harshly, it is always a big man who is doing it; so that, by the contrast between the big and the little, I get the sympathy of the audience, and always I try to contrast my seriousness of manner with the ridiculousness of the incident."

Entering motion pictures in what was virtually the medium's infancy—before the advent of feature-length films and, of course, color and sound—Chaplin was obliged to rely on situational comedy and on pantomime, the use of mute gestures and facial expressions to convey emotion. Transcending linguistic barriers, this form of body language permitted the actor to be readily understood by peoples everywhere. "I am known in parts of the world by people who have never heard of Jesus Christ," Chaplin said matter-of-factly early in his career. Indeed, after only two years on the screen, "he was unquestionably the top figure in the motion-picture industry," according to Huff. Audience demand for his pictures was phenomenal. One New York theater, for example, played his films continuously from 1914 to 1923, stopping only because the building burned down. By 1917 world-renowned performers had visited his studios—Ignace Paderewski, Leopold Godowsky, Nellie Melba, Harry Lauder. When the Nijinsky ballet played Los Angeles, its dancers spotted Chaplin in the audience and halted the show for a half-hour while they embraced him. His popularity at the box office won him a million-dollar contract—a stupendous sum in 1917—for eight pictures over eighteen months. Some notion of the adulation of the actor may be gathered from the response to his bond-selling tours during World War I—crowds of 30,000 in New York, 65,000 in Washington, 40,000 in New Orleans. Going to Europe in 1921—*The Tramp, Shoulder Arms* and other of his classics had preceded him—Chaplin was mobbed in London and Paris. The latter city declared a public holiday for the premier of *The Kid.* "Charlie," "Charlot,"—his first name in any language bespoke affection amounting to idolatry.

At the same time he widened his intellectual and social world, meeting and becoming friendly with Max Eastman, the radical writer; Upton Sinclair, the Socialist novelist; James M. Barrie, the British playwright; H. G. Wells, the British writer; Waldo Frank, the American novelist and social critic; St. John Irvine, the British dramatist; and Georges Carpentier, the lithe heavyweight boxer. Throughout his life he enjoyed the shuttlecock of wits with bright and learned men and women. He read omnivorously, if not systematically, in world literature, but outside his own field he was not an organized thinker. His reaction to injustice was from the heart: he was against it and he responded forthrightly.

When success came, he was inevitably taken up by society figures—Mrs. William K. Vanderbilt, Elsie de Wolfe, Princess Xenia of Greece, and hundreds of others who cooed over him. Although Chaplin was not vain, certainly not in his early years, he was impressed by the lavish world of great wealth and assured social position. The latter portion of *My Autobiography,* written after his forced absence from the United States and in perhaps an understandable mood of irritation, is mostly a catalogue of the socially prominent Europeans who paid attention to him. The social lion was one of Chaplin's least attractive roles.

His moment was the silent and early sound-era of the movies, when comic invention was at a premium. Other comic actors of that time—Buster Keaton, Harry Langdon, Harold Lloyd, the Marx Brothers, and W. C. Fields among them—also passed through that moment, but none with the possible exception of Keaton rivaled Chaplin in exploiting it to create a genre. The creativity of his mind and the fertility of his imagination were nurtured by the medium, and the medium, in turn, nurtured him. One explanation was that after 1917 his command over his pictures was total. He was the author, producer, star, director, and chief cutter. Moreover, as Huff's book noted, "He himself played every character in every one of his pictures, to show the actors, men and women, exactly how he wanted them to do a character or a scene. And he accompanied each actor's miming with a running commentary of suggestions, criticism or encouragement." In one film, *The Great Dictator,* he served as hairdresser in the belief that he could do a better job than a professional coiffeur of arranging Paulette Goddard's hair to resemble a scrubwoman's. This impulse to perfectionism, costly in terms of time and film exposed, caused Chaplin many moments of anxiety and self-doubt. His usual solution was to spend a couple of days in bed working through his problem.

Chaplin's egotism did not let him admit defeat. "You have to believe in yourself—that's the secret," he once advised his son Charles Jr. "I had that exuberance that comes from utter confidence in yourself." Even as a London waif "I thought of myself as the greatest actor in the world," he recalled.

Born April 16, 1889, in south London, Charles Spencer Chaplin was the son of a vaudevillian and a music-hall soubrette whose stage name was Lily Harley. By an earlier union, Chaplin's mother, Hannah, had a son, Sydney, four years the actor's senior. Sydney was to become his half-brother's business manager. The elder Chaplin was a heavy drinker. "I was hardly aware of a father, and do not remember him living with us," his son wrote. The couple separated shortly after he was born, and for a time Mrs. Chaplin was able to support herself. But her voice lost its quality, and "it was owing to her vocal condition that at the age of five I made my first appearance on the stage. I remember standing in the wings when mother's voice cracked and went into a whisper. The audience began to laugh and sing falsetto and to make catcalls. It was all vague and I did not quite understand what was going on. But the noise increased until mother was obliged to walk off the stage. When she came into the wings she was very upset and argued with the stage manager who, having seen me perform before mother's friends, said something about letting me go on in her place. And in the turmoil I remember him leading me by the hand and, after a few explanatory words to the audience, leaving me on the stage alone. And before a glare of footlights and faces in the smoke, I started to sing, accompanied by the orchestra, which fiddled about until it found my key." The lad captivated his audience, especially when "in all innocence I imitated mother's voice cracking," and he was greeted by laughter and cheers and applause.

Very shortly, however, Mrs. Chaplin's fortunes dwindled, and she and the two children were obliged to enter the Lambeth workhouse. Then the boys were dispatched to an orphanage outside London. "Although we were well looked after, it was a forlorn existence," Chaplin wrote of those years. The institution practiced flogging, and at the age of seven he received a severe caning. Moreover, for suspected ringworm, his head was shaved and iodined and he was put in an isolation ward. Sydney went off to sea for a while and young Charles passed through a succession of workhouses. Mrs. Chaplin was committed briefly as insane. When she was released, the small family again lived in penury, relieved slightly when Charles joined a troupe of clog dancers. He never forgot his days of poverty and the struggle for the necessities of life. Nor, when he was wealthy and famous, did he neglect his mother, seeing to it that she was well cared for in her eventual emotional breakdown. Finally, he took her to California, where she died.

Clog dancing lasted only briefly, followed by weeks and months of catch-as-catch-can existence. "I [was] newsvendor, printer, toymaker, doctor's boy, etc., but during these occupational digressions, I never lost sight of my ultimate aim to become an actor," Chaplin recalled. "So, between jobs I would polish my shoes, brush my clothes, put on a clean collar and make periodic calls at a theatrical agency."

At twelve and a half his persistence was rewarded, and he received a small stage part, then toured the provinces as Billy in William Gillette's *Sherlock Holmes.* Later he played the part with Gillette in London, receiving favorable notices. An awkward age followed, however, in which he received several burlesque bookings. Then came a substantial run in *Casey's Court Circus,* in which he impersonated a patent-medicine faker. In this engagement, according to the Huff biography, Chaplin decided to become a comedian. He also learned the unimportance of the spoken word. "Once, while playing in the Channel Islands," Huff wrote, "he found that his jokes were not getting over because the natives knew little English. He resorted to pantomime and got the desired laughs."

His success landed him a job with the Fred Karno Company. "With Karno he learned the hard way, traveling all over Britain and going twice to America," according to John Montgomery, a writer on films. "The repertory was varied: there were sketches about drunks, thieves, family relations, billiards champions, boxers, Turkish baths, policemen, singers who prepared to sing but somehow never started, conjurers who spoiled their own tricks and pianists who lost the music . . . a wide variety of subjects, mixed with a little honest vulgarity." The Karno troupe was Chaplin's polishing school, for it taught him the rich lessons of his trade by which the actor makes an audience laugh. In 1913, Mack Sennett, then the producer of short film comedies for an insatiable public, signed the actor for $150 a week. "I hated to leave the troupe," he recalled. "How did I know that pictures were going to be a successful medium for pantomime? Suppose I didn't make good?"

Nevertheless, he joined the Sennett group in Los Angeles, and made his debut in *Making a Living,* a one-reeler that appeared in 1914. In those early Sennett comedies, there was no scenario. "We get an idea, then follow the natural sequence of events until it leads up to a chase, which is the essence of our comedy," Sennett explained. Chaplin changed that by adopting an identifiable character—the Little Tramp—which allowed the public to single him out from other comedians. In his year with Sennett, Chaplin played in thirty-five films, including *Tillie's Punctured Romance*, a six-reeler that also starred Marie Dressler and Mabel Normand. It was the screen's first feature-length comedy, and it is occasionally shown today in various cut-up versions. Others of the Keystone or Sennett films have been mutilated or rearranged, according to the Huff book, which notes, "Rarely does one come across an unmutilated Keystone original." The originals of these films were shown around the world and they inspired such songs as "When the Moon Shines Bright on Charlie Chaplin." The renown they brought enabled him to shift to the Essanay Company for the then grand sum of $1,250 a week. For Essanay he made fourteen films in 1915, including *The Tramp*, his first generally recognized classic and the first in which he introduced a note of pathos. In the picture, Chaplin, a tramp, saves a farmer's daughter, played by Edna Purviance, from a robber gang, for which he is rewarded with a job on the farm. Routing the gang again, he is shot in the leg and nursed by the daughter. The tramp's happiness is unbounded until the girl's sweetheart arrives. Realizing his fate, the tramp scribbles a farewell and departs. In the fade-out, Chaplin's back is to the camera. He walks dejectedly down a long road. Then he pauses, shrugs his shoulders, flips his heels and continues jauntily toward the horizon. Several variations on this theme were used in later Chaplin films, notably in *Limelight*.

After his Essanay period Chaplin went to the Mutual Company for $670,000 a year. He was twenty-six, three years out of vaudeville and perhaps the world's highest-paid performer. The sudden advent of wealth had little immediate effect on his life-style. When he signed his Mutual contract he remarked, "Well, I've got this much if they never give me another cent—guess I'll go and buy a whole dozen ties." He was living at the time in a small hotel room and he kept away from Hollywood parties, preferring to roam at night through Los Angeles's poorer districts. Shortly, however, he moved to larger quarters, hired a secretary, bought an automobile, and acquired Toraichi Kono as combination valet, bodyguard, and chauffeur. Kono, as he was generally called, remained with the actor for about twenty years, serving as the keeper of his privacy. In time Chaplin grew passionately attached to money. Although he was not a tightwad, neither was he a conspicuous spender, save on his own comfort. In the end, his fortune was in the millions. He insisted toward the close of his life that he had been actuated all along by money. "I went into the business for money, and the art grew out of it," he said. "If people are disillusioned by that remark, I can't help it. It's the truth."

However, those who were close to Chaplin in his early film years were impressed by his painstaking search for artistry. In doing the two-reel *The Immigrant* in 1917, for instance, he shot 90,000 feet of film to obtain the 1,809 feet of the finished picture. His dozen Mutual films were all two-reelers. They included some ranked among his best—*The Floorwalker, The Fireman, The Vagabond,* and *Easy Street.* The negatives were not preserved, and the worn and duplicated prints that are sometimes shown at "Chaplin festivals" bear only slight relationship to the quality of the original films.

When the Mutual contract was up, Chaplin went to First National for $1 million for eight pictures over eighteen months. For the first time he was his own producer in his own studio. Actually, he made nine pictures over five years, and these included some of his greatest achievements—*A Dog's Life, Shoulder Arms,* and *The Kid.* Sparing of caricature, *A Dog's Life* derives its humor from the parallels between a dog's existence and that of a vagabond. *Shoulder Arms* is everyman at war, and, according to Jean Cocteau, "It moves like a drumroll." For *The Kid,* he employed Jackie Coogan, a five-year-old with mischievous brown eyes. Hailed as "a picture with a smile—perhaps a tear," the movie was a chapter out of Chaplin's own slum life. It contains little horseplay and much emotional intensity. Coogan's tears were real, induced by the sad stories Chaplin spun for him at necessary moments.

While preparing *The Kid* for release, Chaplin was embroiled in the first of several marital and extramarital episodes that were to plague him. Good-looking and attractive to women, he was involved in a score or more of alliances, many with glamorous actresses, but these were usually discreetly handled. Not so with his first two marriages. In 1918, when the actor was twenty-nine, he abruptly married sixteen-year-old Mildred Harris. They were divorced two years later in a fanfare of publicity. Four years afterward he married Lolita McMurry, also sixteen, whose stage name was Lita Grey. She was ensconced in her husband's forty-room mansion, from which Chaplin soon fled. Two children, Charles Jr. and Sydney, were born of the union, which ended in 1927 after a sensational divorce case, in the course of which Chaplin pictures were barred in some states at the urging of women's clubs.

The actor's third wife was Pauline Levy, a chorus girl whose film name was Paulette Goddard. The two met in 1931, when Miss Goddard was twenty, and were married in 1936. They were divorced in 1942 without public fuss. Meanwhile, in 1941, the actor met Joan Berry, a twenty-one-year-old aspiring actress known as Joan Barry. She later charged that he was the father of her daughter, and Chaplin was once again the subject of lurid headlines. He was indicted for allegedly taking Miss Barry across state lines for immoral purposes, but this charge was dropped and he was acquitted of three related accusations. Miss Barry, however, filed a paternity suit, in which blood tests demonstrated that Chaplin was not her child's father. Nonetheless, a jury found against him and he was ordered to support the infant. In the midst of these troubles, in 1943, Chaplin, then fifty-four, married eighteen-year-old Oona O'Neill, the playwright's daughter, over her father's vigorous objections. Their marriage proved happy and lasting, and it produced eight children.

Chaplin's later films were made for United Artists, a company he founded in 1919 with three Hollywood friends, Mary Pickford, Douglas Fairbanks Sr., and David Wark Griffith. His initial picture for this company was *A Woman of Paris,* a comedy of manners that he produced and directed without starring in it. Considered a milestone in screen history for its influence on movie style, it was based in part on the life of Peggy Hopkins Joyce, briefly Chaplin's mistress, and it stressed social sophistication. In it Adolphe Menjou made his debut as a suave philanderer. *The Gold Rush*—"the picture I want to be remembered by," Chaplin said—came out in 1925 and it once again confirmed his hold on the public. It has been frequently revived and much analyzed. Less successful with the critics was *The Circus,* which opened in 1928. It seemed to lack the feeling of *The Gold Rush,* and its comedy twists were short on flair. Its defects, however, appeared less evident in revivals. Starting work on *City Lights* in 1928, the actor faced a crisis in the advent of talkies. He was fearful that spoken dialogue would impair the character of The Tramp, cause difficulties in his reliance on pantomime, and cut into foreign sales. Moreover, many of his effects had been achieved by undercranking the camera, a feat impossible at the set speed of a motor-driven sound camera. After some thought, he decided to defy the new technology, and *City Lights* was produced as a silent picture with a musical score. The story of the blind flower girl, played by Virginia Cherrill, used more than 800,000 feet of film over two years. The tragicomedy was an enormous triumph when it opened in 1931, and has outgrossed many slick sound films in revivals over the last forty years. Many critics rank *City Lights* as among Chaplin's greatest creations. The picture's appeal was one factor in Chaplin's conquering tour of Europe and the Orient—a whirl of meetings with statesmen, writers, artists, and celebrities. Returning to Hollywood, he embarked upon *Modern Times,* a satire on mass production, which at the time gave the actor a reputation as a radical. "It [the picture] started from an abstract idea, an impulse to say something about the way life is being standardized and channelized, men turned into machines—and the way I felt about it," he said of his social parable. The Little Tramp disappeared with *Modern Times,* and with *The Great Dictator* Chaplin joined the sound-picture ranks. A ferocious ridicule of Hitler and Mussolini, the film has grown in stature over the years as its political implications have been more fully realized. "I want to see the return of decency and kindness," he said at the time. "I'm just a human being who wants to see this country a real democracy."

Despite *The Great Dictator,* the 1940's were difficult years for Chaplin. His private life provided a headline festival for the tabloid press; he was vexed by income-tax trouble; his wartime speeches calling for a Western second front to crush Hitler irked many conservatives; and *Monsieur Verdoux* did poorly at the box office. This fugue of troubles was intensified by the advent of the Cold War. The actor came under fire for introducing Henry A. Wallace at a political rally and for protesting the deportation of Hanns Eisler, the composer, a onetime Communist. Westbrook Pegler, the columnist, denounced him, and Representative John E. Rankin, a right-wing legislator from Mississippi, demanded his deportation. Chaplin's life "is detrimental to the moral fabric of America," Rankin asserted, urging that he be kept "off the American screen and his loathsome pictures be kept from the eyes of American youth."

Finally, in 1952, the actor, who had remained a British subject, was virtually exiled by the United States. While he was sailing to Britain on holiday, President Harry S Truman's attorney general, in what must surely rank as among the most vapid of the Cold War's actions, announced that he could not reenter the country unless he would prove his "moral worth." Understandably outraged, Chaplin spent the remainder of his life in Europe, settling on a thirty-eight acre estate at Vevey, Switzerland. In the first years of his "new" life, he was active in motion pictures, making *A Countess From Hong Kong* and *The King in New York,* the latter a thumb-at-the-nose against the baser aspects of American life. He developed into a devoted family man, shepherding his growing family with what his sons and daughters sometimes thought was too much authority. He also proved a vivacious host. Close friends saw him as a shy and vulnerable man who excelled at a small dinner or garden party, which gave him a chance to act some of his routines. At such affairs, he was almost always on stage.

I spent a brief time with Chaplin in 1971, visiting him in Vevey.

By then, his effervescence had largely disappeared and he was verging on senility. The twinkle was still in his clear blue eyes; the smile was that of a beamish child. As the United States emerged from the irrationality of the Cold War, amends of a sort were made to the great actor. He was invited to this country in 1972 to receive a special Oscar from the Motion Picture Academy and to accept homage in New York. He could do little more than bow and smile in response. A belated knighthood followed. More important than these baubles of recognition of his genius was a swing in critical opinion, which vindicated his earlier belief that *Monsieur Verdoux* was a brilliant movie. Its satire of a business- and war-minded world was more appreciated in the context of the sixties and seventies than it had been in the late forties. Some good words, in addition, were managed for his final films. Lesser works in the canon they might be, but still worthy.

In his final years Chaplin looked back dimly but with happiness on his early days at Keystone and Essanay. When I asked what was special to him in that time, he replied, "I was able to try anything in those days. I was free."

———————————————❖———————————————

MARY PICKFORD

For the two decades spanning World War I and the 1920's, Mary Pickford reigned supreme as "Queen of the Movies," "America's Sweetheart," and "the Girl with the Golden Curls." Beloved in her heyday as the woman with the face so fresh and so innocent and with the smile so beguiling, she became the first movie star to have her name emblazoned in marquee lights, the first to be paid in the thousands of dollars a week, and one of the first to achieve an international reputation. Audiences believed in her utterly, for her miming—necessary in silent films—exuded invincible sweetness of character. She embodied the American Dream, having risen by her own talents from rags to riches, indeed to very great wealth.

Miss Pickford entered films in 1909, when she was a fifteen-year-old stage actress, and came into her own in 1917 with *The Poor Little Rich Girl* and *Rebecca of Sunnybrook Farm.* For the next dozen years, virtually everything she touched was transmuted into success and fame, culminating in an Oscar for her role in *Coquette,* her first sound picture, in 1929. She outshone her contemporary female stars. Great and polished as were the Gish sisters, Lillian and Dorothy, Greta Garbo, Gloria Swanson, Louise Brooks, Pola Negri, and Constance and Norma Talmadge, Miss Pickford excelled them all in box-office appeal.

In the years of her triumphs, she captured public adulation in *Daddy Long-Legs, Pollyanna, Little Lord Fauntleroy,* and *My Best Girl.* And, of course, there was *Little Annie Rooney* and *Amarilly of Clothesline Alley.* Unlike many present-day films, these were unabashed photoplays, or narratives. *Little Annie Rooney,* for example, is the story of a waif, an alley-cat roughneck, first the daughter and then the orphan of a widowed Irish policeman, who matches wits with a gang of boys and emerges triumphant. In 1925, when the film was made, it rarely played to an empty seat—or to a dry eye. From 1917 on, Miss Pickford ranked with Charlie Chaplin and Douglas Fairbanks Sr., her husband, as the most conscientious of actors. She was perceptive enough to select the best technicians, directors, and supporting actors, and generous in giving them credit; and she herself was a dedicated actress who left little to chance.

The advent of sound and the breakup of her marriage to Fairbanks ended her career. Her last picture, *Secrets,* made in 1932 and released the following year, was undistinguished, and she retired. "I knew it was time to retire," she remarked in 1965. "I wanted to stop before I was asked to stop." Expanding on this theme, she said with characteristic candor, "I left the screen because I didn't want what happened to Chaplin to happen to me. When he discarded the Little Tramp, the Little Tramp turned around and killed him. The little girl made me. I wasn't waiting for the little girl to kill me."

For the rest of her life Miss Pickford was the chatelaine of Pickfair, her bizarre Beverly Hills mansion, which she shared with her third husband, Charles (Buddy) Rogers. After a trip abroad in 1965, she took to her capacious bed, announcing that she had worked hard since she was five years old and now deserved a rest. Except for occasional nocturnal rambles in Pickfair, she remained there, subsisting on light foods and whiskey—a quart a day, according to Robert Windeler, her biographer. A stroke did her in, and she was buried in private.

At the zenith of her career, the five-foot, 110-pound Mary Pickford won the hearts of movie patrons because she possessed a look of unquenchable goodness and innocence. Sinister scoundrels, silent and gesturing, sought her ruin; but she was brave and sweet through it all. When she played a rich girl, she exhibited humility; and when she was in rags, she was patient. By the standards of a later era, these films were saccharine, but this was what audiences seemingly wanted as the country was manipulated into World War I and flimflammed into the "normalcy" of the unsettling twenties. It did not matter that Miss Pickford's curls, which appeared to grow longer as she grew older, took an hour to prepare with curling irons. Nor did it matter that she was almost thirty when *Little Lord Fauntleroy* was released, for she had mastered the illusion of eternal youth.

(*Fauntleroy,* incidentally, is a splendid example of Mary Pickford's versatility. She played both Cedric Errol, the sissy with sausage curls who inherits a British title, and his mother, Dearest. The trick photography was the work of Charles Rosher, who shot all Pickford films from 1918 to 1928. A technical genius, he devised the double-image scene in which Dearest kisses her son, a scene that took sixteen hours to film and that is still regarded as a masterpiece.)

The impression of innocence that Miss Pickford conveyed was such that it was an event of much moment when she was kissed on the silver screen for the first time. That occurred in 1927; the movie was *My Best Girl,* an amiable satire of lower middle class life. Ironically, the man she kissed was Buddy Rogers. A year later, Miss Pickford abandoned her little-girl image altogether by bobbing "the most famous head of hair since Medusa's." A much press-agented event, the shearing took place in New York on June 21, 1928, amid a jostle of cameramen.

Silent films put a premium on good acting, and Mary Pickford, like Louise Brooks, was among the most adept and most innately sure performers. She was also enormously disciplined, a trait notably lacking in the playgirl Miss Brooks. Explaining her capacity to portray others, she said: "I hadn't any 'methods' of acting. It was easy for me to act the part of a child because I adored children. I forgot I was grown up. I would transform myself into a child for the time being and act as she would under similar circumstances." Even after her fame was assured, she was a hard and meticulous worker. She was usually up at five A.M. and at the studio by six. Shooting began at nine and finished by five-thirty, but often, because she had total control of production, she did not get home before eight o'clock; and some nights she and Fairbanks ate dinner in costume. Her social life was reserved for weekends and between pictures, when Pickford-Fairbanks parties tended to be lavish, if not gaudy.

Pickfair visitors in the twenties ate from a solid gold dinner service, with a footman behind every chair. A formal dinner for a dozen might include the duke and duchess of Alba, Charles A. Lindbergh, Babe Ruth, Albert Einstein, and Lord and Lady Mountbatten. Apart from such dinners, Miss Pickford was not a free spender; her business shrewdness did not allow for frittering away money. From 1919 to her retirement, she earned at least a million dollars a year as an actor-producer with United Artists; then there were large sums from real-estate investments and from her holdings in United Artists. Her fortune at her death was estimated at $50 million.

Like most Hollywood stars of her time, Mary Pickford was an illusion. Her name was not her own, nor was she a creature of the cinematic art. The first child of a British father and an Irish mother, she was born in Toronto on April 9, 1893, and christened Gladys Smith. Her father died when she was four, and her mother ran a penny-candy counter and took in sewing to keep the family—there were two other children—afloat. Necessarily, the household atmosphere was pinchpenny, with education a luxury, so that Gladys's entire formal schooling consisted of six or seven months of instruction spread over two years. The child was not much more than five when she made her acting debut with her sister, Lottie, in *The Silver King,* a now happily forgotten melodrama at the Toronto Opera House, which needed extras. The girls were hired at $10 a week because the stage manager boarded with Mrs. Smith.

Almost immediately, Charlotte Smith became a stage mother, who managed her daughter's career until she died in 1927. "To the very last day she lived, her word was law," Miss Pickford once recalled. When the stock company passed to other plays, the child got a temporary vaudeville role, and then worked with other stock companies in such favorites of the time as *Uncle Tom's Cabin,* in which she was Little Eva, and *The Little Red Schoolhouse,* in which all the Smiths played for a total of $20 a week. In the theatrical season of 1901–2, the future Mary Pickford was billed as Baby Gladys Smith in an American touring company of *The Fatal Wedding.* A quick study, even though she could barely read, the child (with her mother and sisters) was almost always on the road until she was eleven and had outgrown Baby Gladys.

Late in the 1904 season, she got to play a title role for the first time, that of Dolly in a melodrama called *The Child Wife.* She earned $25 a week on the road; a year later she went up to $40 in *The Gypsy Girl.* Often hastily carpentered, these plays nonetheless demanded robust acting skills and an ability to establish immediate rapport with audiences. They were invaluable training for Broadway assignments.

Gladys Smith was in a further succession of such dramas until 1906, when she announced, "I'm thirteen and at the crossroads of my life." She determined, she said, "to land on Broadway or give up the theater for good." After several attempts, she managed an interview with David Belasco, the reigning producer, then casting for *The Warrens of Virginia.* After an audition, she was accepted for $30 a week and joined the cast, which included Cecil B. De Mille, later one of her directors. Belasco did not consider Gladys Smith a sufficiently glamorous name, and with a princely wave of her hand, he made his newest acquisition Mary Pickford, the "Pickford" from Charlotte Smith's maiden name. *The Warrens* was a big success, opening in New York late in 1907 and running through May 1908 before going on the road for almost a year.

On tour in Chicago, Miss Pickford saw her first motion picture, something called *Hays Tours.* The flickers, as some dubbed them, had been brought into being the year of the actress's birth by Thomas Alva Edison and William Dickson, a brilliant laboratory assistant. The early films were shown in makeshift theaters—nickelodeons—and acting in them was not considered proper by serious thespians. But, down on her luck in the spring of 1909, Miss Pickford climbed the stone steps of the American Mutoscope and Biograph Company offices and studios at 11 East Fourteenth Street in Manhattan. There she encountered David Wark Griffith, the saturnine genius who was then Biograph's only director. After a screen test, she was signed on for $5 a day and joined the permanent acting company, which included the ineffable Mack Sennett.

The next day she appeared before the camera in *Her First Biscuit,* a split-reel farce filmed in a day; she was among several itinerant actors attempting to eat a simulated batch of leaden biscuits. In those times, movies were made from one-reel synopses, not from scenarios, so scenes owed much to a director's spontaneity; they were produced at the rate of three or four a week to meet an insatiable public demand. The story, or the incident, was the point, not the players, who were anonymous. In these circumstances, it is not surprising that Miss Pickford, in her first two years with Biograph, acted in seventy-four films in a great variety of roles.

"I played scrubwomen and secretaries and women of all nationalities," she remembered. "I got what no one else wanted and I took everything that came my way because I decided that if I could get into as many pictures as possible, I'd become known and there would be a demand for my work." Actually, at Biograph, Miss Pickford quickly developed into a leading lady whose restrained acting style, a legacy of her stage experience, contrasted favorably with the more exaggerated pantomimes of the other players, many of whom were vaudeville graduates. At the same time, the actress (and her mother) pressed for, and received, higher pay until she was making $175 a week, then a very large sum.

From Biograph, Miss Pickford went to Carl Laemmle's Independent Motion Picture Company where she made about thirty films, most of them under the director Thomas H. Ince, a pioneer in the art of movies. In 1912, however, she returned to Biograph and Griffith and his innovative cameraman, Gottlieb Wilhelm Bitzer, fabled for the metronomic steadiness of his cranking. (Many cameras were hand-cranked at the rate of sixteen frames a second until after World War I.) By 1913—her twentieth year—when she was working for Adolph Zucker's Famous Players and Paramount, her films were four and five reels long. Mary Pickford then established herself as America's Sweetheart. The momentous billing came in 1914, and the film was *Tess of the Storm Country*. There followed such successes as *Cinderella, Fanchon, the Cricket, The Foundling, Poor Little Peppina,* and *The Pride of the Clan,* the actress's first seven-reeler, or, by modern measurement, full-length movie, released in 1917. These movies, all for Paramount or Famous Players-Paramount, established Miss Pickford as a national institution. Her name crowded any theater exhibiting her films and she was the subject of seemingly endless illustrated articles in the new Hollywood phenomenon, the fan magazine.

The year 1917 was Mary Pickford's *annus mirabilis,* a time of quantum change. Not only was her first feature-length film released then, but for the first time she played the role of a child in a full movie. In this epic occurrence she was Gwen, wistful, touching, and ten years of age, in *Poor Little Rich Girl.* She was a somewhat older child in *Rebecca of Sunnybrook Farm,* also made in

1917. Thereafter, she was the movies' little girl, typecast forever as "The Face."

Miss Pickford's already enormous popularity was further enhanced in 1920 by her marriage to Douglas Fairbanks, the gymnastic actor and hero of such swashbuckling movies as *A Modern Musketeer*. Dashing, daring, and handsome, he was the symbol of respectable manhood, while Miss Pickford epitomized smiling innocence. They were both married to others when they met, and their romance, conducted under the watchful eyes of Miss Pickford's mother, had its moments of strain. Both were uncertain of public reaction if they were to obtain divorces and to marry; but the legalities were discreetly handled by their lawyers, and gossip was muted. The result was that Doug and Mary, as the couple became known, were immediately hailed as the all-American husband and wife by moviegoers. It was one of the first marriages made in Hollywood and it was a great triumph. When Doug and Mary traveled to New York in 1920, two years after the nuptial ceremonies, their trip was like a royal progress and throngs jammed the streets outside their New York hotel. Later, when they arrived in Britain on a European tour, roses were dropped on their ship at Southampton by a circling aircraft. The couple co-starred only once, in a sound movie in 1929 very liberally adapted from *The Taming of the Shrew*.

The idyll ended in the early thirties, shortly after sound had come to the movies. Miss Pickford closed out her acting career with *Secrets,* her 194th film. Fairbanks fell in love with Sylvia Hawkes, a British musical comedy actress who was married to Lord Ashley. There were well-publicized divorces all around, and Fairbanks married Lady Ashley. In 1937, Miss Pickford was married to Buddy Rogers, a bandleader eleven years her junior. They adopted two children, Ronald and Roxanne. With her marriage, Miss Pickford receded from the limelight until she was only a distant memory to those who had once cheered her, or wept with her, on the screen. And then she became the recluse of Pickfair, a legend.

INDEX

Grateful acknowledgment is made to the following for permission to reprint copyrighted material:

Doubleday & Company, Inc., and Robert Hale Ltd.: An excerpt from *The Cardinal Spellman Story* by Robert I. Gannon. Copyright © 1962 by Fordham University.

E. P. Dutton and J. M. Dent & Sons Ltd.: A selection from *Faust* by Johann Wolfgang von Goethe, translated by Sir Theodore Martin. Revision and annotations Copyright 1954 by W. H. Bruford. An Everyman's Library Edition.

Farrar, Straus and Giroux, Inc.: An excerpt from Edmund Wilson's poem "Dedication," which appears in *The Crack Up* by F. Scott Fitzgerald, edited by Edmund Wilson. Copyright 1942 by Edmund Wilson. Copyright renewed © 1970 by Edmund Wilson.

Holt, Rinehart and Winston: Selections from *Ho Chi Minh on Revolution*, edited by Bernard B. Fall. Copyright © 1967 by Frederick A. Praeger, Inc.

Macmillan Publishing Co., Inc., and Faber and Faber Limited.: A selection from "Nevertheless" from *The Collected Poems* by Marianne Moore. Copyright 1944 by Marianne Moore, renewed Copyright © 1972 by Marianne Moore.

The New York Times: All obituaries by Alden Whitman. Copyright © 1965, 1966, 1967, 1968, 1969, 1970, 1971, 1972, 1973, 1974, 1975, 1976, 1977, 1979 by The New York Times Company.

Princeton University Press: Poem by St. John Perse, from *Chronique*, Vol. 1, as translated by Robert Fitzgerald, Bollingen Series LXIX. Copyright © 1961 by Princeton Unversity Press.

Viking Penguin Inc. and Faber and Faber Limited: "Values in Use" from *O to Be a Dragon* by Marianne Moore. Copyright © 1956, 1959 by Marianne Moore.